ANCIENT MESOAMERICA

Selected Readings

JOHN A. GRAHAM
*Department of Anthropology
University of California
Berkeley*

PEEK PUBLICATIONS
982 El Cajon Way
Palo Alto, California

Copyright 1966
by
John A. Graham

Second Printing 1967
Third Printing 1968
Fourth Printing 1969
Fifth Printing 1970
Sixth Printing 1971
Seventh Printing 1973
Eighth Printing 1974

Manufactured in the United States of America

PREFACE

The constantly expanding enrollments experienced in recent years in college courses previously of more modest dimension have resulted in a variety of problems in teaching. Of these, one of the most important is the increasing difficulty and impracticality of assigning library reserved readings. When enrollments finally swell into the several hundreds, it becomes physically not feasible for the library to administer a long reading list regardless of the efficiency and inspired efforts of the library staff. Unless one chooses the unsatisfying expedient of relying solely upon a handful of course texts, the best solution to this particular teaching problem is the compiling of some of the more important articles into a book of readings. And, such a book of readings has several additional merits. By making the readings available for consultation at any moment it offers a considerable savings in valuable time and the inconvenience of an often futile recourse to overcrowded libraries. Further, when the course readings are made available in an inexpensive paperback edition, the student need make only a modest investment while the compiler can periodically revise the collection with timely new articles.

The present compilation of readings is designed for my junior-senior level course in Mesoamerican archaeology and culture history at the University of California, Berkeley. As is evident from the table of contents, the present book is not intended as a substitute for general course texts nor does it pretend to be a fully comprehensive reader in the subject. It is intended to provide a sampling of readings treating various significant aspects of the reconstruction and interpretation of pre-Columbian Mesoamerican civilization. While a few of the articles are basically factual and represent source readings, most are interpretative essays illustrating a variety of investigative techniques and approaches. Many papers deal with a single cultural tradition, many of the methods, concepts, and theoretical frameworks are equally applicable to other traditions of the Mesoamerican "Oikoumene". Several articles flatly contradict each other, reflecting quite different approaches and attitudes; these help to illustrate the process of scientific advance, communicating the excitement of new research and interpretation. The contrasting interpretations of texts, readings, and lectures awaken students to important interpretative alternatives, sometimes of their own creation.

Obviously there are many fine papers that would be most desirable to include here in addition to the present selection. In order to maintain an inexpensive volume, however, it has been necessary to hold the length to the present size. This has frequently meant a painful selection and has automatically precluded from the beginning the inclusion of many significant but lengthy papers.

Since my very small contribution to this volume has been largely clerical in nature, it is only proper, and is my pleasure, that I express my deep appreciation to the authors and original publishers of the various articles comprising this volume. Through their warm generosity and friendly cooperation, many students will profit much.

John A. Graham

Berkeley, California

MESOAMERICA: Its Geographic Limits, Ethnic Composition and Cultural Characteristics*

by Paul Kirchhoff

IN THE geographic classifications of the native cultures of America which take in the whole Continent or which at least deal with a particular region from a continental point of view, one may easily distinguish two types.

In the first of these, one accepts one or the other of the usual divisions of the American Continent, based on political geography or biogeography. Most Americanists either divide the Continent simply into North and South America, or interpose between the two parts a third, whether it be "Mexico and Central America" or, as some American (U.S.) anthropologists call it, "Middle America." In the first case, as a general rule, one accepts as the boundary between North and South America, the biogeographical dividing line which follows the course of the San Juan River, between Nicaragua and Costa Rica. In the second case, one includes in

* Translated by Dr. Norman McQuown from *Acta Americana*, Vol. I, No. 1, 1943.

Reprinted by permission of the publisher from HERITAGE OF CONQUEST by Sol Tax. Copyright The Free Press 1952.

"Mexico and Central America" all the territory between the northern frontier of the Mexican Republic and the eastern border of Panama; in "Middle America" the same region, excluding at times the north of Mexico, including at times the Antilles.

Both divisions and their variants which we have noted here have serious drawbacks when they are used for anything more than a mere geographic localization of cultural phenomena of the native world, or in order to set the geographic limits for programs of investigation or publication. The biogeographic boundary between North and South America, although it coincides with a local boundary between regions with clearly marked cultural characteristics, nevertheless does not constitute a cultural boundary between North and South America, inasmuch as to the north of it, the culture of the Sumo and the Misquito and even that of the Paya and Jicaque, is just as "South American" as that of the Chibcha of Central America. In reality, this term lacks any precise meaning, since in South America, whatever the extension we wish to give to the term may be, there are cultures as different one from another, as those of the Fuegians, the Caribs and the Inca. On the other hand, the remaining cultures of Central America and Mexico do not give evidence of any "North American" characteristics, but, on the contrary, perhaps have more in common with certain cultures of South America than with any of North America. Actually, their similarities to certain North American cultural areas, such as those of the Southeast and in part of the Southwest of the United States, are evidenced in large measure in traits which both have in common with certain cultural areas of South America.

The drawbacks of the triple division mentioned are perhaps even greater. Neither the aggregate of the republics of Mexico and Central America, nor "Middle America" in any of the senses just mentioned, constitutes for the anthropologist a region which stands out from the other cultures of the Continent, and which therefore merits especial study. In fact, those who accept one or the other of these triple divisions, far from considering "Mexico and Central America" or "Middle America" as a cultural unit—opposed as such to North or to South America—, continue to recognize as basic the division between North and South America, assigning certain cultures of this region to North America and others to South America.

The second type of geographic classification groups the native American cultures in five large areas:

1. The food-gatherers, hunters and fishers of North America.
2. The interior cultivators of North America.
3. The superior cultivators ("High Cultures").
4. The inferior cultivators of South America.
5. The food-gatherers and hunters of South America.

The anthropologists who accept this type of division, which, like the previous one, has many variants which we do not mention, recognize either explicitly or implicitly that within the areas of the so-called superior cultivators are included, by way of exception, individual tribes or even whole cultural areas which cannot be considered superior cultivators, neither with respect to their general cultural level, nor with respect to plants and techniques of cultivation. In the same way, at times food-gatherers and hunters are included in the areas of the inferior cultivators.

Their inclusion within the areas of superior culture is justified by the fact that notwithstanding their lower cultural level, they share with the other tribes of the area in which they are included a considerable number of cultural traits; whether this be due to the fact that these tribes have been left behind by the more advanced tribes, thus preserving a part of the old common culture, or to recent cultural diffusion. This point of view leaves their individuality to the cultural areas (in the sense of a group of tribes with cultures which are not merely superficially similar, but are fundamentally alike) and allows one at the same time to group them in "superareas" and subdivides them into "subareas." Within the area of the inferior cultivators of North America, the "Southeast" and the "Southwest" (in the sense of "The Greater Southwest" or "Arid North America") constitute such superareas; and within the area of the superior cultivators one can mark out a superarea "Mesoamerica" whose geographic limits, ethnic composition and cultural characteristics at the time of the Conquest, we propose to study in this article.

The present work is based on a series of studies of distribution initiated by the International Committee for the Study of Cultural Distribution in America, created by the XXVIIth International Congress of Americanists. Although these studies are still far from being complete, it is already possible to present certain general outlines for the purpose of posing new problems. This aim of our article has made unnecessary the inclusion of notes or bibliography.

Geographic Limits and Ethnic Composition

On the basis of the studies mentioned above, one may postulate that at the time of the Conquest, there were present in Mesoamerica a series of tribes which we may group in the following five divisions:

1. Tribes which speak languages not yet classified, such as the *Tarascan*, the *Cuitlatec*, the *Lenca*, etc.
2. All the tribes of the *Maya, Zoque,* and *Totonac* linguistic families. According to certain investigators, the languages of these three families, to which one should probably add the *Huave*, form a group which we might call *Zoque-Maya* or *Macro-Mayan*.
3. All the tribes—except two—of the *Otomi, Chocho-Popoloca* and *Mixtec* families, which seem to form, together with the *Chorotega-Mangue* family, a group called *Otomangue;* and all the tribes of the *Trique, Zapotec* and *Chinantec* families, which some investigators consider related to the previous group, forming a great group called *Macro-Otomangue*.
4. All the tribes of the *Nahua* family and a series of other tribes of *Uto-Aztecan* affiliation, among them the *Cora* and the *Huichol*, whose grouping in families is still not definitive.
5. All the tribes of *Tlappanec-Subtiaba* and *Tequistlatec* families which belong to Sapir's *Hokan* group.

An analysis of the ethnic composition of Mesoamerica, at the time of the Conquest, shows the following:

a. Of all the linguistic families which form part of Mesoamerica, only one, the *Otomi*, has some members (the *Pame* and the *Jonaz* which are perhaps only subdivisions of a single tribe), which do not belong to the Mesoamerican cultural unit.

b. Two linguistic groups, formed by some of these families, the *Zoque-Maya* and the *Macro-Otomangue*, should their reality be demonstrated, would be found to be entirely within Mesoamerica.

c. Tribes of these two groups, and also of the *Nahua* reach, probably as a result of migrations, to the farthest geographic limits of Mesoamerica, both in the North (of the *Zoque-Maya* group, the *Huastec;* of the *Macro-Otomangue*, the *Otomi;* and of the *Nahua* family, the *Cazcan* and the *Mexicans*) and in the South (of the *Zoque-Maya* group, the *Chol-Chorti*, of the *Macro-Otomangue*, the *Chorotega,* and of the *Nahua* family, the *Nicarao*).

All of this shows the reality of Mesoamerica as a region whose inhabitants, both the very old immigrants and the relatively recent ones, were united by a common history which set them apart as a unit from other tribes of the Continent, their migratory movements being confined as a general rule, once they had entered the area of Mesoamerica, within its geographic limits. In some cases tribes of different families or linguistic groups took part in these migrations together.

In spite of the fact that it had linked its fate firmly to that of Mesoamerica, the *Nahua* family, both because it had many linguistic relatives, more or less close, outside of Mesoamerica, and in view of its traditions concerning one or a number of migrations from the North, shows itself to have played, within our area, a cultural role very different from that of the linguistic families listed under "2." These, like the tribes not yet linguistically classified, seem to lack linguistic relatives within any reasonable distance of Mesoamerica, which leads us to believe that they both, i.e., the *Maya, Zoque, Totonac, Tarascan, Cuitlatec*, etc., not only have lived for a long time within the territory occupied by the cultural aggregate of Mesoamerica, but that they have perhaps played an important part in the very process of its formation.

The *Macro-Otomangue* group, or at least its *Otomangue* subgroup composed of the *Otomi, Chocho-Popoloca, Chorotega* and perhaps the *Mixtec* families, in spite of its dissemination within the territory of Mesoamerica, does not give us the impression that it is equally deep-rooted or that it has played as important a role in the formation of Mesoamerica as the *Zoque-Maya* group, but it seems more probable that it entered the Mesoamerican orbit when the area already existed as a cultural unit. Tribes of these families not only appear curiously associated in their geographic distribution with *Nahua* tribes (almost as in South America, and the Antilles, the Arawak with the Caribs), but in several cases we also have historical traditions concerning common migrations of the Toltecs of *Nahua* speech with *Otomi* peoples (according to Sahagún), or with *Mazatec, Popoluca* and *Otomi* (according to the *Historia Tolteca-chichimeca*), and of the *Nicarao* with the *Chorotega* (according to Torquemada). Furthermore we have on the one hand traditions about a migration of the Otomies from the northwest (according to Ixtlilxochitl) and on the other the fact that the *Pame* and the *Jonaz* live to this day outside the Mesoamerican territory, immediately to the north of it.

The numerical and geographical isolation which we find in the *Tlappanec-Subtiaba* and *Tequistlatec* families at the time of the Conquest, suggests that the role that they played in the history of Mesoamerica either was never very important, or goes back to a very distant past; unless one must consider them as relatively recent immigrants to a Mesoamerica already formed.

The proper estimation of the role of each linguistic family or group in the history of Mesoamerica, together with the solution of the problem of determining since when a cultural superarea has existed and what has been its geographic extension, and what its cultural foci have been in different periods, presupposes, in addition to the completion of the already begun studies of cultural distributions at the time of the Conquest, the carrying out of similar studies for different pre-Columbian periods; the utilization of both of these types of studies for the division of Mesoamerica into subareas which will be different in number and extension for different periods; and more excavations in regions which at the time of the Conquest were outside of Mesoamerica, but which in previous times formed part of it, such as have been carried out in a broad zone in the north of Mexico, occupied at the time of the Conquest by tribes of inferior culture.

What we can already assert at this time is that the northern frontier of Mesoamerica was distinguished from the southern boundary by a much greater degree of mobility and insecurity, with alternating periods along it of expansion northward and retraction toward the south. The periods of retraction are due in part to invasions of groups of lower culture situated to the north of Mesoamerica.

This difference between the frontiers to the north and the south, as well as the differences existing between various sections of each of the boundaries, are due, at least in part, to the fact that Mesoamerica is the last link to the north in the chain of superior cultivators. Actually, only in a short section of the southern frontier did Mesoamerica, at the time of the Conquest, border on another area of superior cultivators (the *Chibcha*), while along the rest of this frontier its neighbors were inferior cultivators (the *Jicaque* and *Paya* and the *Sumo* and *Misquito*). In the northern frontier the situation was even more unfavorable, since with the exception of two quite short sections, one in Sinaloa and another insignificant one on the coast of the Gulf, where its neighbors were inferior cultivators, Mesoamerica bordered directly on food-gatherers and hunters.

At the time of the Conquest, the last tribes of Mesoamerican culture on the southern boundary (which runs, more or less, from the mouth of the Motagua River to the Gulf of Nicoya, passing through Lake Nicaragua) were the *Chol-Chorti*, the *Lenca* (and perhaps the *Matagalpa*), the *Subtiaba*, the *Nicarao* and the *Chorotega-Mangue*; on the northern boundary (which runs more or less from the Rio Panuco to the Sinaloa, passing along the Lerma), the *Huastec*, the *Mexicans* of Meztitlan, the *Otomi* and *Mazahua*, the *Tarascan*, the *Coca*, the *Tecuexe*, the *Cazcan*, part of the *Zacatec* (there were *Zacatec* who were food-gatherers and hunters), the *Tepehuan*, the *Acaxé* and the *Mocorito*. Although the southernmost tribes, the *Subtiaba*, *Nicarao* and *Chorotega-Mangue* are so unmistakably Mesoamerican in their culture that there can be no doubt as to their inclusion in this superarea, such doubts can arise with respect to the *Lenca* on the one hand and with respect to many tribes situated along Lake Chapala and the Rio Sinaloa on the other, since in both cases we find a cultural level quite inferior to that characteristic of tribes most representative of Mesoamerica. Notwithstanding this lower cultural level (which is also found among some tribes and even in some cultural areas in the interior of the territory of Mesoamerica), we include these tribes in Mesoamerica, because of the very considerable number of markedly Mesoamerican cultural traits, which in most cases go precisely to the frontiers which we have indicated. Thus for example, up to the northwestern boundary we find such cultural elements as the cultivation of chile, sweet potato, and fruit trees, the domestication of ducks and "voiceless dogs," metallurgy, the game played with rubber balls, etc. (see below), i.e., elements which Mesoamerica has in common with more southern cultures and which here reach their northern limit.

Culture Traits

In the distribution studies undertaken by the International Committee for the Study of Cultural Distributions in America to clarify the problem of Mesoamerica, studies which in turn profit from all the investigations carried out previously by other scholars, we have found three large distribution groups:

I. Traits exclusively or at least typically Mesoamerican.

II. Traits common to Mesoamerica and to other American cultural superareas.

III. Traits significant for their absence in Mesoamerica.

I

For the purpose of this first exposition of the problems in Mesoamerica, we prefer to combine in a single list, both those traits which are found exclusively in Mesoamerica, and also those, which, although they are sometimes found outside, seem, nevertheless, to be characteristically Mesoamerican. With respect to the latter, we do not refer only to cases in which Mesoamerican traits are found in some tribes outside of Mesoamerica but bordering on it (such as the game with rubber balls among some food-gatherers and hunters of the north of Mexico), where the diffusion is undeniable, but also to cases such as that of the Pawnee of North America or that of the coast of Ecuador or northern Peru, where there is a grouping of traits so typically Mesoamerican that it allows of no other interpretation but that of cultural diffusion.

On the other hand, we include in this list, only a few of the traits exclusively Mesoamerican but rare there, since most of these suppose for their existence that of others more widely found.

We consider as Mesoamerican traits the following:

A certain type of digging-stick (*coa*); the construction of gardens by reclaiming land from lakes (*chinampas*); the cultivation of lime-leaved sage (*chía*) and its use for a beverage and for oil to give luster to paints; the cultivation of the century plant (*maguey*) for its juice (*aguamiel*), fiber for clothing and paper, and maguey beer (*pulque*); the cultivation of cacao; the grinding of corn softened with ashes or lime.

Clay bullets for blow-guns; lip-plugs and other trinkets of clay; the polishing of obsidian; pyrite mirrors; copper tubes to drill stones; the use of rabbit hair to adorn textiles; wooden swords with flint or obsidian chips along their edges (*macuahuitl*); corselets padded with cotton (*ichcahuipilli*); shields with two hand-grips.

Turbans; sandals with heels; one-piece suits for warriors.

Step pyramids; stucco floors; ball courts with rings.

Hieroglyphic writing; signs for numerals and relative value of these according to position; books folded screen-style; historical annals and maps.

Year of 18 months of 20 days, plus 5 additional days; combination of 20 signs and 13 numerals to form a period of 260 days; combination of the two previous periods to form a cycle of 52 years; festivals at the end of certain periods; good and bad omen days; persons named according to the day of their birth.

Ritual use of paper and rubber; sacrifice of quail; certain forms of human sacrifice (burning people alive, dancing dressed in the skin of the victim); certain forms of self-sacrifice (extraction of one's blood from the tongue, ears, legs, sexual organs); the flying game or ritual (*juego del volador*); 13 as a ritual number; a series of divinities. Tlaloc, for example; concept of several other worlds and of a difficult journey to them; drinking the water in which the deceased relative has been bathed.

Specialized markets or markets subdivided according to specialities; merchants who are at the same time spies; military orders (eagle knights and tiger knights); wars for the purpose of securing sacrificial victims.

II

The group of traits common to Mesoamerica and to other American cultural superareas* is divided into various sub-groups for which we give representative examples, with the caution that mentioning a trait for a particular superarea does not imply that it is found in all the component areas:

a. Southeast, Southwest, *Mesoamerica, Chibcha, Andes,* Amazonia: cultivation, ceramics.

b. Southeast, Southwest, *Mesoamerica, Chibcha, Andes,* Northwest Amazonia: cultivation of corn, beans, and squash.

---

* For this first orientation we recognize, in an entirely provisional form, the following superareas (the names of the superareas of superior cultivators are italicized):

Southwest (of North America, in the sense of "The Greater Southwest" or "Arid North America," i.e., including both inferior cultivators and food-gatherers and hunters).

Southeast (of North America).

Chibcha (excluding those who have cultural affinities with the Andes, such as, for example, the *Muisca*).

Andes (including the arid coast of South America).

Amazonia (including all the tropical forest of South America and the Antilles, but excluding the *Chibcha* of the tropical forest).

c. Southeast, *Mesoamerica, Chibcha, Andes:* human sacrifice.

d. Southeast, *Mesoamerica, Chibcha, Andes,* Northwest Amazonia: cultivation of the sweet potato; blowguns, head trophies.

e. Southeast, *Mesoamerica, Chibcha,* Amazonia: cannibalism.

f. Southeast, *Mesoamerica, Andes,* Northwest Amazon: confession.

g. Southwest, Mesoamerica, Chibcha, Andes: cultivation in the hands of the men; constructions of stone or mud; sandals.

h. Southwest, *Mesoamerica, Chibcha, Andes,* Northwest Amazonia: cultivation of cotton.

i. *Mesoamerica, Chibcha, Andes:* terracing for cultivation; hanging bridges; gourd rafts. Some of the traits of this group, perhaps the majority of them, are known within Mesoamerica only in the southern part.

j. *Mesoamerica, Chibcha, Andes,* Northwest Amazonia: cultivation of sweet cassava, chile (*ají*), pineapple, avocado, papaya, zapote, various kinds of "plums" or spondias (*jobos*); fattened voiceless dog; duck; woven shields, lances; metallurgy; roads paved with stones; markets.

These traits, contrasting with the preceding group, with the exception of woven shields and lances, go as far as the northern boundary of Mesoamerica.

k. *Mesoamerica, Andes:* clans of the *calpulli-ayllu* type; taking out the heart of living human beings; sprinkling sanctuaries with the blood of sacrificial victims.

In addition, there is a considerable group of traits common to the superior cultivators of Mesoamerica and the inferior cultivators of Amazonia:

l. *Mesoamerica,* Amazonia: basket-work blowing fan; flat clay plates on which to cook bread (*comal*); game with rubber balls which cannot be touched with the hands; wooden drum with languettes.

It is worthy of note that the traits of this group which reach the northern and southern boundaries of Mesoamerica are not known among the Jicaque, Paya, Sumo and Misquito tribes which border directly on Mesoamerica and are inferior cultivators like the Amazonian tribes.

Finally, an even more striking group of traits which Mesoamerica has in common with people who are not even cultivators:

m. *Mesoamerica,* food-gatherers and hunters: underground ovens; steam bath.

The traits which Mesoamerica, superarea of superior cultivators, has in common with other areas of superior cultivators or of inferior cultivators, or with both of these at the same time, pose a series of very important problems concerning both the formation of Mesoamerican culture within the aggregate of American cultures based on cultivation, and the relations existing between the superior and inferior cultivators. The division which we have made of these traits into various groups is designed to pose most effectively these problems. It does not seem possible to arrive at definitive conclusions before the distribution studies initiated by the aforementioned Committee have been completed.

One is struck by the fact that Mesoamerica, an area of superior cultivators within which no non-cultivating tribe survives, shares certain traits, lacking among the superior and inferior cultivators of South America, *with the American food-gatherers and hunters,* on whose North American area it borders directly along a part of its northern boundary, whereas it finds itself separated from the South American food-gatherers and hunters by other cultivators both superior and inferior. The fact that these traits go as far as the southern boundary of Mesoamerica, and no farther, tends to separate Mesoamerica from the other great areas of superior cultivators, as well as from the areas of inferior cultivators of South America (with which, on the other hand, it shares such significant traits). But one must remember that these traits characteristic of hunters and food-gatherers are not and cannot be basic to or constitutory of Mesoamerican culture, although undoubtedly they lend it a "flavor" distinct from that of the other areas of superior cultivators, especially those traits which like the steam bath have come to be linked so intimately with Mesoamerican culture. But even though it is true that these traits come to the end of their North American distributional area at the southern boundary of Mesoamerica, they can't be called "North American" because they are also found among the food-gatherers and hunters of South America, unless we want to call these latter likewise "North American."

In order to have been able to reach the extreme south of South America, through all the region recently occupied by superior and inferior cultivators, these traits must have spread before the formation not only of Mesoamerica and the other areas of superior cultivators, but before the beginning of cultivation itself, disappearing later in certain regions.* Their presence in Mesoamerica and absence in the other areas of cultivators in South America, allows of one of two explanations: either they disappeared only in the areas of (superior and inferior) cultivators situated to the south of Mesoamerica, but not in the latter, or they first disappeared in both regions, to be later reintroduced into Mesoamerica from the north by new invasions of food-gatherers and hunters. In any case, the extension of these elements up to the southern boundary of Mesoamerica, even though it does not give to Mesoamerica a "North American" character and does not allow us to draw an ethnographic boundary between North and South America which would coincide with our southern boundary of Mesoamerica, does demonstrate what we have asserted in previous paragraphs and with different arguments: the fact that Mesoamerica is undoubtedly a cultural unit which has had its own history for a long time, common to all its inhabitants, even with respect to those traits which are *not* basic to it.

III

The traits of the third group whose distribution is related to the problem of Mesoamerica are those whose absence in Mesoamerica is characteristic. This group is divided into various sub-groups:

a. Southeast, *Chibcha*: adornment of the edge of the ear.

b. Southeast, Southwest, *Chibcha*, Northwest Amazonia: matrilineal clans.

c. Southeast, Southwest (food-gatherers and hunters of Nuevo Leon), *Chibcha*, Northwest Amazonia: drinking the ground-up bones of deceased relatives.

d. Southwest (Sinaloa-Sonora), *Chibcha*, Amazonia: poisoned arms.

These types of distribution, to which one should probably add others, lead one to suspect that we are dealing with elements once present in Mesoamerica, either merely in the *territory* later to become Mesoamerican or within the Mesoamerican cultural aggregate

* We know only one case of the use of the steam bath among the food-gatherers and hunters of South America. The second South American case, not cited up till now in the comparative literature and one which must be the result of a different and much later diffusion from a Mesoamerica already existing as a cultural unit, is found among the superior cultivators of the coast of Ecuador. Unfortunately there are no details of the steam bath found there, so that we do not know whether it had the structural details which distinguished the Mesoamerican steam bath from that of more northerly tribes.

itself. Especially suggestive is the case of the custom of drinking the ground-up bones of one's deceased relatives, corresponding to which within Mesoamerica we find a custom which may perhaps be interpreted as a more evolved phase which has taken its place, the custom of drinking the water in which the deceased relative has been bathed.

With the preceding we might contrast certain cultural traits of the cultivators of South America which go as far as the southern frontier of Mesoamerica, but do not pass it:

e. *Chibcha, Andes:* cultivation of coca.

f. *Chibcha, Andes,* Amazonia: cultivation of palm trees.

The distribution of these two groups of traits leads us to believe that they never were a part of Mesoamerican culture.

Notwithstanding its entirely provisional character, we felt that it was time to present to the readers of this new journal the preliminary results of the investigations of Mesoamerica initiated by the International Committee for the Study of Cultural Distributions in America, not only in order to report on the present state of these investigations, but also in order to stimulate a thorough critical discussion of the method followed and the results obtained to date. The author of the present article, in his capacity as secretary of the Committee, would like very much to receive suggestions as to the best way to continue this work, together with data on other investigations which bear directly or indirectly on the problem of the cultural individuality and the history of Mesoamerica, whether from investigations already completed or from those in process of being carried out.

TRAITS COMMON TO MESOAMERICA AND TO OTHER CULTURAL SUPERAREAS OF AMERICA: AND TRAITS SIGNIFICANT FOR THEIR ABSENCE IN MESOAMERICA

Presence of traits—X Absence of traits—O	South-east	South-west	Meso-america	Chibcha	Andes	Ama-zonia
Cultivation	X	X	X	X	X	X
Ceramics	X	X	X	X	X	X
Corn	X	X	X	X	X	X*
Beans	X	X	X	X	X	X*
Squash	X	X	X	X	X	X*
Human sacrifice	X	O	X	X	X	O
Potato	X	O	X	X	X	X*
Blowgun	X	O	X	X	X	X*
Head trophies	X	O	X	X	X	X*

* In the Northwest.

Presence of traits—X Absence of traits—O	South-east	South-west	Meso-america	Chibcha	Andes	Ama-zonia
Cannibalism	X	O	X	X	O	X
Confession	X	O	X	O	X	X*
Cultivation done by men	O	X	X	X	X	O
Construction of stone or clay	O	X	X	X	X	O
Sandals	O	X	X	X	X	O
Cotton	O	X	X	X	X	X*
Terracing for cultivation	O	O	X	X	X	O
Hanging bridges	O	O	X	X	X	O
Gourd rafts	O	O	X	X	X	O
Sweet Cassava	O	O	X	X	X	X*
Chile (ají)	O	O	X	X	X	X*
Pineapple	O	O	X	X	X	X*
Avocado	O	O	X	X	X	X*
Papaya	O	O	X	X	X	X*
Zapote	O	O	X	X	X	X*
Spondia	O	O	X	X	X	X*
Fattened voiceless dog	O	O	X	X	X	X*
Duck	O	O	X	X	X	X*
Woven shields	O	O	X	X	X	X*
Lances	O	O	X	X	X	X*
Metallurgy	O	O	X	X	X	X*
Roads paved with stone	O	O	X	X	X	X*
Markets	O	O	X	X	X	X*
Clans of the *calpulli-ayllu* type	O	O	X	O	X	O
Removing heart from living persons	O	O	X	O	X	O
Sprinkling sanctuaries with blood	O	O	X	O	X	O
Basketwork blowing fan	O	O	X	O	O	X
Plates for cooking bread	O	O	X	O	O	X
Game with rubber ball	O	O	X	O	O	X
Wooden drum with languettes	O	O	X	O	O	X
Adornment of edge of ear	X	O	O	X	O	O
Matrilineal clans	X	X	O	X	O	X*
Drinking ground-up bones of deceased relatives	X	X	O	X	O	X*
Poisoned weapons	O	X	O	X	O	X
Coca	O	O	O	X	X	O
Palm trees	O	O	O	X	X	X

* In the Northwest.

THE SECOND MAMMOTH AND ASSOCIATED ARTIFACTS AT SANTA ISABEL IZTAPAN, MEXICO*

Luis Aveleyra A. de Anda

AMONG THE numerous problems still to be resolved in the archaeology of Mexico, one could not find a more captivating, more fundamental, and at the same time, less known one, than the early genesis of the native civilizations of Mesoamerica. Lack of knowledge of preceramic developments, which are the truly *formative* ones of the high prehispanic cultures, leaves the whole complicated sequence of better-studied civilizations without a real foundation. The investigation of this field requires collaborative research in the geological and paleontological sciences.

Curiously enough, these initial phases of prehistory in Mexico, in which a great scarcity of data is to be expected, already reveal a cultural picture of a definite form. The existence of a level of nomadic hunters of paleolithic type, at the end of the Pleistocene and within a natural environment different from the present in landscape, flora, and fauna, has been established definitely in the Valley of Mexico, and furnishes a point of departure for the study of human activity in the center of the country.

The present work reports a new discovery related to this phase of prehistory in the Valley of Mexico. The results obtained are not new, but rather, complimentary to previous investigations. The coexistence of man and fauna now extinct in this region was already indicated in the recent work of Mexican and foreign geologists (Arellano 1946a; Bryan 1946, 1948; de Terra 1946, 1949), and confirmed later by investigations and findings of the Dirección de Prehistoria of the Instituto Nacional de Antropología e Historia (Maldonado-Koerdell and Aveleyra 1949; Aveleyra and Maldonado-Koerdell 1952, 1953; Martínez del Río 1952).

Antecedents. The extraordinary prehistoric riches in the vicinity of Tepexpan in the northeast part of the Valley of Mexico, and the associations obtained there of man and fauna in the Pleistocene, render this zone one of the most important on the continent for the study of "paleo-Indian" cultures. Since more than a century and a half ago discoveries of fossil skeletal remains exposed in the plain of Tepexpan and adjacent sites have been made, but have been reported mainly in popular style in newspapers and magazines. Scientific information is, unfortunately, very scarce (Reyes 1923, 1927; Díaz Lozano 1927; Arellano 1946b). The findings of Reyes and Díaz Lozano are not very illustrative of human prehistory in the region, due perhaps to the exploratory techniques directed, from the paleontological point of view, at recovering fossils purely for their taxonomic and museum value. In the case of the mammoth skeleton excavated by Arellano (1946b) a possible association with an obsidian flake is mentioned.

In 1947 the discovery of Tepexpan Man, the first fossil human remains found in Mexico and one of the most remarkable discoveries in America, crowned the patient labor of Arellano and Bryan in the sediments of the Valley, and the integration of these problems achieved by Helmut de Terra.

The finding of Tepexpan Man aroused doubts about its authenticity in certain foreign circles, based principally on faults of observation on the part of the discoverers, and on some methodological dogmas in details of the exploration. This rigorous criticism, it must be warned, although well justified, was the product of a "tele-appreciation" of the facts, and without the appropriate knowledge of the series of previous investigations done by de Terra which were forming a perfectly clear picture of the geological, glacial, and lacustrine landscape of the region. Discoveries achieved a few years later bore out de Terra's belief in the existence of man as the hunter of mammoths in the Valley of Mexico at the end of the Pleistocene.

In 1952, only a few days after the Dirección de Prehistoria initiated its first field work, it was rewarded with the lucky finding of the first fossil mammoth at Santa Isabel Iztapan, scarcely 2 km. from the site of Tepexpan Man (Aveleyra and Maldonado-Koerdell 1952, 1953) and about 20 km. northeast of Mexico City. In

---

* Based upon Aveleyra's *El Segundo Mamut Fósil de Santa Isabel Iztapan, México, y Artefactos Asociados* (Publicaciones de la Dirección de Prehistoria, No. 1, Instituto Nacional de Antropología e Historia, Mexico, 1955). Translated and abridged by Alex D. Krieger. For more extended explanations, and especially for numerous fine photographs of the different stages of excavation, see the original.

direct association were 6 implements of stone, adding in a remarkable way to the picture of prehistoric man as a hunter of mammoths in this vicinity. The presence, in the plain of Tepexpan and nearby sites, of not less than a dozen skeletal remains of mammoth (including the findings of Reyes, Díaz Lozano, Arellano, and others), together with the new discoveries of Tepexpan Man and the first mammoth at Iztapan, all of them in a limited area, was a sure indication that toward the end of the Pleistocene, the zone of Tepexpan-Iztapan must have been the scene of systematic mammoth hunting on the edge of ancient Lake Texcoco.

The discovery of the second mammoth at Santa Isabel Iztapan also resulted from the plans for exploration of the Dirección de Prehistoria in this region. At the beginning of excavation of the first mammoth in March, 1952, a special effort was made to encourage local people and authorities to inform the Dirección about all "giant bones" they would find when excavating ditches and wells. At the end of May, 1954, notice was received of large bones found in digging an irrigation ditch in the village of Santa Isabel Iztapan. On inspecting the place it was proved that the bones in view were in situ and consisted of a portion of the base of the cranium and the proximal sectors of both tusks of a mammoth. Fortunately in this case, unlike the case of the first mammoth in which the cranium was destroyed by the local people when trying to extract it, the parts originally discovered were left in place and protected until the arrival of the Dirección de Prehistoria. The only pieces removed from

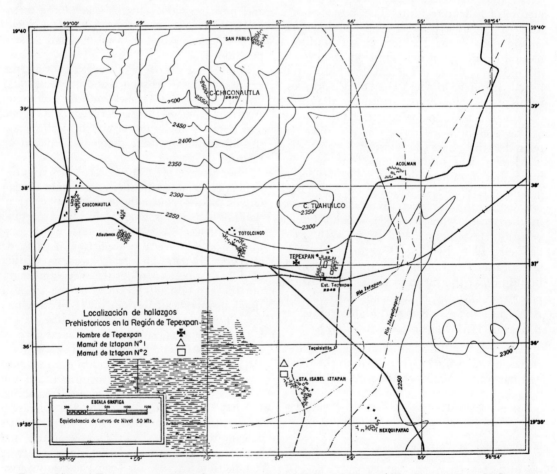

Fig. 1. Map of Tepexpan area in northwestern portion of Valley of Mexico. The Pan-American Highway runs north from the village of Chiconautla (at the left); the road to San Juan Teotihuacán runs eastward through Tepexpan and Acolman, then north to the pyramids of Teotihuacán (off map to upper right). The marginal marshes of present Lake Texcoco appear at the lower left. Mexico City lies about 20 miles southwest of Tepexpan.

their original place were both upper molars (the first part of the skeleton which the picks encountered on deepening the ditch) which were kept in a safe place and later given to the author.

The exploration began on June 1, 1954, and ended on the 12th. It was in charge of the author and Arturo Romano Pacheco, physical anthropologist of the Dirección, to whom should be credited the unsurpassed excavation technique employed. Manuel Maldonado-Koerdell was in charge of the geological study (see Appendix) and collaborated actively in the excavation, as did a student of the Escuela Nacional de Antropología e Historia, Francisco Gonzáles Rul. In some phases of the exploration we also had the help of Pablo Martínez del Río, Joaquín Cortina Goríbar, and the students Lilia Trejo de la Rosa, Mónica Bopp, and Carmen Block.

We must acknowledge the invaluable financial help received from several persons: the important annual subsidy received from Petróleos Mexicanos through its director Antonio J. Bermúdez, has been indispensable to almost all the investigations achieved by the Dirección since the date of its foundation; the sum annually donated by Bruno Pagliai beginning in 1955 will permit the Dirección to devote full time to the works related to the prehistory of Mexico; and to Gilberto Loyo, Secretario de Economía Nacional, are due the legal procedures which culminated in the acquisition of additional mobile equipment. José Kimball took the photographs of the artifacts. Most of the other photographs were taken by the anthropologist Arturo Romano. Miguel Ricardez, cartographer of the Secretaría de la Defensa Nacional, kindly prepared the map of the region which is included here (Fig. 1). Finally, it is necessary to mention the decisive collaboration of the local authorities of Santa Isabel Iztapan, especially the enthusiastic help of the brothers José and Rosendo Cortés, who originally reported the finding and made possible the exploration on their property.

Location of the Discovery and Local Topography. The second mammoth at Iztapan was found approximately 350 m. south of the first one (Aveleyra and Maldonado-Koerdell 1952), and some 2600 m. south (and slightly west) of the site of Tepexpan Man (Fig. 1). The locality, together with the plain of Tepexpan toward the north and the surrounding terrain, forms part of the great sloping plain resulting from the retreat of the waters of the present Lake Texcoco in its northeast portion. The plain shows all the distinctive characteristics of the ancient lacustrine deposits except where modern cultivation has modified the surface of the terrain. In the surroundings of Santa Isabel Iztapan and the neighboring town of Tequisistlán there are plots of maize and vegetables, and some isolated *ahuejote* trees which may indicate the presence of prehispanic chinampas in the region. The noncultivated zones, such as the plain of Tepexpan, are covered by thin, coarse pasture, dotted with alkali spots bare of vegetation.

The most important nearby elevations are located to the north and northeast of the site. These are the hills of Chiconautla and Tlahuilco, formed by volcanic breccia, ashes, and lava flows. Precisely on the slopes of these hills were located the prehistoric shores which correspond to the Pleistocene levels of Lake Texcoco. The hill of Chiconautla with an elevation of 2630 m. forms the eastern margin of the "bottle-neck" which still connected the lakes of Texcoco and Xaltocan in colonial times.

The courses of the present streams in this zone empty into the lake toward the west and southwest of Santa Isabel Iztapan and are not of permanent character. Most of them are branches of the delta of the Río San Juan, and they are known by the names of Río Iztapan, Río Nexquipayac, and Río Nuevo from north to south, respectively. None of these channels, however, pass sufficiently near the site of the mammoths at Iztapan to alter, or to have altered in any form, the stratigraphy resulting from the slow deposition of mud in the lacustrine depths. This circumstance, as will be seen later, is important in connection with the position of the mammoth remains.

The remains of both Iztapan mammoths were located considerably farther into the lake basin than the site of Tepexpan Man. Toward the end of the Pleistocene, in the times when the pachyderms were hunted, the lake margins must have been more than 3 km. beyond the present town of Santa Isabel Iztapan, toward the north and northeast, on the skirts of the Chiconautla and Tlahuilco hills. In spite of this, the difference in elevation between these shores and the zone of Santa Isabel Iztapan is so slight that the depth of the waters of the lake at the location of both mammoths must not have been greater than 60 to 70 cm. Near the present town of Tequisistlán and Santa Isabel Iztapan there is a slight elevation of the terrain above the general level of the sloping plain. It is possible, therefore, that during the Pleistocene era there might have existed here a kind of peninsula or tongue of land, more or less firm, from which the hunters could operate with greater ease.

The lake which existed at the time of these hunts must have been that which de Terra (1947: 20) referred to as El Risco Lake III (elevation 2240 m.), and which he considered the one associated with Tepexpan Man as well (de Terra 1949, Table I). This shore of El Risco Lake III has been totally destroyed by erosion in the region of Tepexpan, but its remnants are observed in localities nearby such as at El Risco. On the slopes of the Chiconautla and Tlahuilco hills there remain today only vestiges of the higher, and consequently more ancient shores of the Upper Pleistocene era: El Risco Lake I (2263 m.) and El Risco Lake II (2257 m.), both too elevated to have been contemporaneous with that of Tepexpan Man and the elephants of Iztapan.

Techniques of Excavation. The first fossils were found by José Cortés when deepening a drainage ditch which serves as a boundary for his farm land. This operation revealed, without harming in the least degree, part of the base of the skull and the inferior portion of the alveoli, as well as a small sector of the proximal third of both tusks. From the curve of these tusks, it was known from the beginning that the skull was inverted.

The exploration followed a minutely cautious technique, adapted to the special conditions of the terrain and taking advantage of experience acquired in excavating the first mammoth of Iztapan and other similar works of the Dirección. The procedure is fundamentally the same as that followed with a delicate human burial, giving special attention to control over the geological strata overlying the bones, and to the

Fig. 2. Excavation of mammoth skeleton in progress.

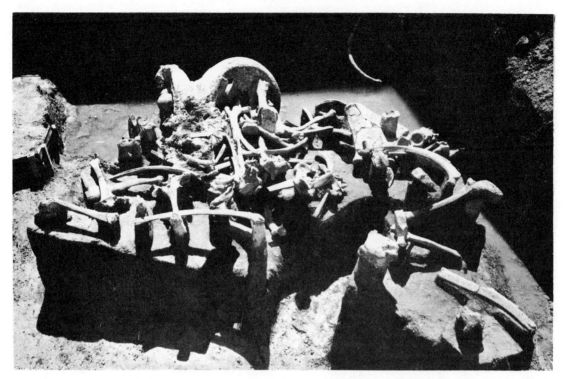

Fig. 3. Excavation of mammoth skeleton completed. Hose for pumping seep water appears at upper right.

search for associated implements which, because of their small size, require very laborious dissection of the deposit surrounding every one of the bones.

The first phase of this work was to discover the maximum area of dispersion of the bones by means of little test trenches. It was soon seen that the greater part of the remains lay to the east* of the skull, so that it was necessary to widen considerably this side of the pit and to cut down a tree in this sector. Without yet deepening the excavation over the area which covered the bones, the 4 walls were made even wider for the double purpose of providing comfortable free space for working around the skeletal remains, and of locating possible additional bones which could be isolated from the principal group (as at Iztapan No. 1). In its final dimensions the pit was 7.05 m. east to west by 5.30 m. north to south.

The next step was to deepen the free area around the skeletal remains up to the 4 walls, which at all times were kept perfectly smooth and vertical, with 90° corners. The pit around

---

* This was mistakenly referred to as "west" in the original report, page 12. A.D.K.

the skeleton was deepened to a level much below the bones, so as to leave the whole mass on a bank of clay, a circumstance which permitted greater comfort during the exploration and which made possible the excavation of many little tunnels and bridges around the bones, leaving them in place on pedestals of clay (Fig. 2). These operations were executed with gardening tools, spatulas, needles, and brushes. Shovels and picks were used exclusively for cleaning the pit around the skeleton. The problem of seeping water, which began to appear in abundance around the skeleton when the excavation reached approximately 1.60 m. in depth, was solved by means of a pump.

The Mammoth Remains. The skeletal remains were delimited within an area 3.60 m. north to south by 4.75 m. east to west. The highest bones (the inverted tusks) were found at 1.40 m. below the surface. This level is 20 cm. higher than that of the uppermost bone of the first mammoth at Iztapan (Aveleyra and Maldonado-Koerdell 1952: 14). The remains of the second mammoth, however, were totally included within the lowest geological stratum present, which in this vicinity is a greenish

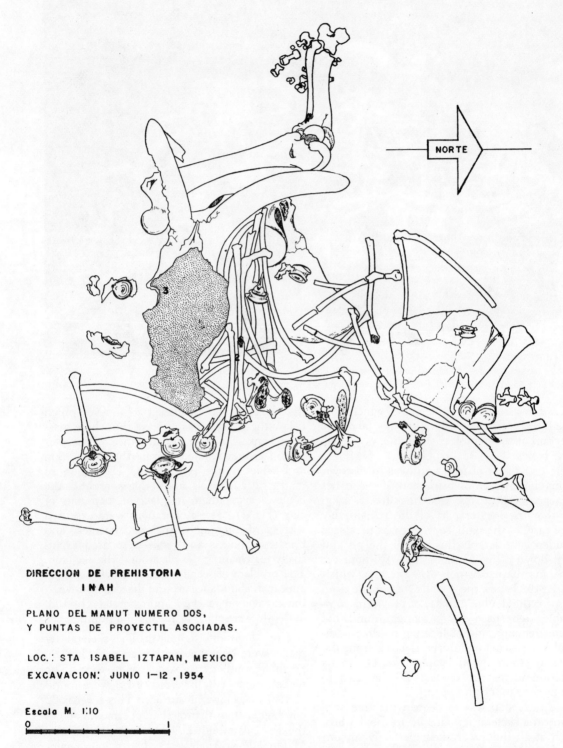

Fig. 4. Ground plan of second mammoth skeleton at Santa Isabel Iztapan. Shaded area represents the broken-off under portions of the skull. The positions of 3 stone artifacts are shown, numbered to correspond to the text.

muck (*limo verde*) belonging to the Becerra formation, the terminal phase of the Upper Pleistocene. The same lacustrine facies of the Becerra formation completely surrounded the skeleton of the first mammoth at Iztapan (Aveleyra and Maldonado-Koerdell 1952: 12-13), as well as the remains of Tepexpan Man when discovered by de Terra and his associates in 1947.

Although the geological deposits at the 2 Iztapan sites are the same, those at Mammoth 2 are less clearly seen than the corresponding ones at Mammoth 1. At Mammoth 2 there is a more gradual transition in coloration and texture of the materials from one stratum to another, which might be due to the fact that this locality is located farther into the ancient lake than the first one, and consequently was subject to more stable conditions of moisture and deposition. Both mammoths, however, lay in exactly the same geological position, completely enclosed within the green muck of the Upper Becerra formation, which lay immediately below a *marshy equivalent* of the Totolzingo formation of the early Postglacial period. In the photograph (Fig. 5 b), this deposit can be clearly seen as a black band overlying the lighter colored Becerra formation.

As for the taxonomic classification of the mammoth, the very bad preservation of the upper molars (the only ones recovered), the crowns of which are completely obliterated, does not permit identification of the species. The great robustness and curvature of the tusks suggests, however, that they may belong to an imperial mammoth, *Mammuthus (Archidiskodon) imperator* Leidy, the largest of the American proboscideans. This suggestion is reinforced on considering that all mammoths discovered up to date in the plain of Tepexpan and nearby places have been identified as imperial mammoths. In an interesting study Maldonado-Koerdell (1955) explains the very probable coexistence of 2 species of mammoth in the Valley of Mexico during the Upper Pleistocene, describing 2 molars of *Mammuthus (Parelephas) columbi* Falconer in the important prehistoric site of Tequixquiac. According to Maldonado-Koerdell the 2 species had different habitats within the Valley of Mexico; the Columbian mammoth lived on the surrounding elevations covered with forest, and the imperial species on the pastures of the lower plains near the lake.

As to the age of the second mammoth of Santa Isabel Iztapan, the large size of the bones and tusks, the pronounced smoothness of the crowns of the molars, and the complete ossification of the epiphyses of the long bones, indicate that it was an adult animal that had reached the period of maximum growth. The first mammoth of Iztapan was a young animal (Aveleyra and Maldonado-Koerdell 1952: 15-16).

The mineralization of the remains is appreciable although not extreme. The bones show a typical dark coloration which characterizes all the fossil remains which are found in this region, and which is due to the impregnation of mineral salts peculiar to the terrain.

The skeleton was incomplete, lacking some large, heavy parts: the mandible (of which there was found only a small fragment corresponding to the symphysis); both humeri; the right ulna; both radii; the left femur and the right scapula. An inventory of the ribs and vertebrae reveals, on the other hand, that the thoracic box and vertebral column were almost complete. As was said above, the skull was also recovered, with its 2 molars and tusks. Besides this, the pelvic girdle and a great number of additional small bones were present (Figs. 3, 4).

All the bones were found totally displaced and out of anatomical relation, with the remarkable exception of the right hind leg (see below). The scattering of these bones, even more than in the case of the first Iztapan mammoth, must unquestionably be referred to human activity. Displacement by natural agents appears impossible to accept. The stratified deposits around the skeleton reveal only very fine sediment, uninterrupted in deposition and horizontal to the slimes of the lacustrine bottom. This type of deposit can only be the result of a slow sedimentation through several millennia without any violent current which could have moved the bones about, even the smaller ones. On the other hand, disturbances due to predatory animals feeding on the carcass of the mammoth must have been at a minimum as the only carnivorous mammal of any size existing in the Valley of Mexico at that time was the dire wolf (*Aenocyon*) and related forms, the powerful sabre-tooth having become extinct earlier. Even admitting the intervention of canidae and other predatory animals, they could have moved only with great difficulty in water more than a half meter deep.

In summary, it appears definite that the position of the skeletal parts when found was practically the same as that in which they were left by the hunters after cutting up their prey. This leads to a very important conclusion: *Given the geology of a site such as that of the mammoths of Santa Isabel Iztapan, the position of skeletal parts alone is evidence of human intervention in its dismemberment; the hydraulic factors rule out other explanations.*

The story of discoveries related to the geological antiquity of man in America has demonstrated that there exist 4* fundamental types of association between extinct fauna and implements of human origin:

(1) Alluvial deposits in which artifacts and fossils have been transported a certain distance from their original place by a force of water,

---

* The original report lists 3 types of association: (1), (2), and (4). I have added (3) with the consent of the author. A.D.K.

---

completely destroying the anatomical relation of the skeletal remains, and where isolated bones of different animals may be mixed in. These associations are usually discovered in the eroded exposures of stream, lake, or aeolian deposits. A typical example is the famous fossil site of Tequixquiac, located just to the north of the Valley of Mexico.

(2) Ancient watering places and other strategic sites at which animals gathered periodically, and where prehistoric man achieved collective hunting (the "butchering grounds" or "kill sites" of North American archaeologists). In these cases there are found masses of fossil bones, many of them broken, in complete disorder and pertaining to dozens of killed mammals. The represented species are usually diverse, and the associated artifacts relatively abundant. Examples of this type of association are some of the more famous sites of primitive man in America such as Lindenmeier, Colorado; Plainview, Texas; Folsom, New Mexico.

Fig. 5. A. View of inverted tusks over articulated right hind leg; the tibia and foot bones at lower left were sunk deeply into the Becerra muck, probably indicating how the mammoth was mired and killed. B. Stratigraphic profile of deposits overlying the mammoth remains (see Fig. 9 for explanation).

(3) Caves to which hunters brought parts of slain animals to be further butchered and consumed. Complete disorder and fragmentary representation of different species are also characteristic. Examples are Sandia and Burnet caves, New Mexico.

(4) Sites in which a single animal was killed and in which, thanks to special geological conditions, the absence of later disturbance has permitted preservation of the remains just as they were abandoned by the hunters. The advantages provided by this last type of association over the 3 preceding ones are obvious, since they can illustrate the hunting customs of prehistoric man in such aspects as the selection of vulnerable points at which to wound the animal, the parts especially selected for food, the techniques of butchering, and so on.

The discoveries at Santa Isabel Iztapan are magnificent examples of this last type of association. The system of exploration used permitted us to keep a detailed record of the exact position of each bone in relation to the others, deriving observations of great interest.

The cranium of the second mammoth, disarticulated and inverted, has special importance. Because of its great weight, this position cannot be attributed to any other factor besides that of human activity. The reason for turning the skull upside down could well have been the extraction of the brain which must have been a favorite delicacy for primitive man. The apparently intentional destruction of the skull base around the occipital foramen seems to confirm this assumption. The skull of one of the mammoths excavated by Arellano (1946b, Figs. 1, 4) in the plain of Tepexpan was found in an analogous position.

The vertebral column and the thoracic box of the mammoth were the parts most minutely dismembered. All the ribs and vertebrae were found dispersed without the least anatomical relationship (Fig. 4). Surely the "loins" and "ribs" of the mammoth were among the parts preferred for food. The limbs were also disarticulated, but in this case many parts were taken away and more widely dispersed. This is especially true of the forelegs, of which only the left ulna was found. The corresponding hind limb was represented by the tibia only. The hind leg, on the other hand, constitutes a remarkable exception from the rest of the skeleton, as it not only was found complete, but also in complete articulation. The proximal end of this limb (head of the femur) rested very near the cotyloid cavity of the corresponding ilium.

Fig. 6. Section of mammoth rib bearing numerous deep cuts made with stone knife.

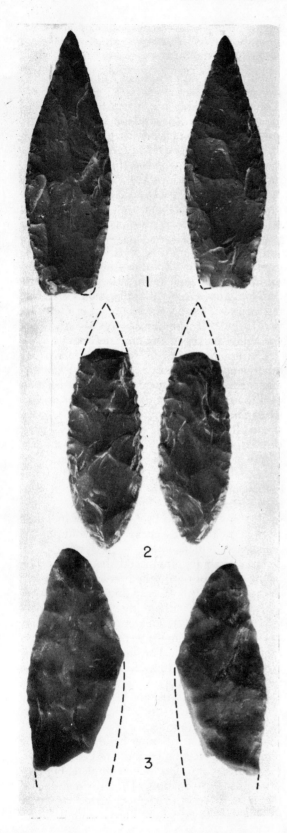

In the photograph (Fig. 5 a), the way in which this articulated leg lay underneath the inverted skull can be appreciated. Its articulation was probably due to the fact that the leg could not be reached during the task of butchering. The foot of this leg was sunk deeply into the mud, immobilizing the animal; this foot was the lowermost point of the skeleton.

The position of the pelvic girdle and the articulated hind leg provides, besides, the only data suggestive of the probable direction which the animal followed immediately before being trapped in the marsh, toward the east, perhaps trying to reach firm land at the east edge of the lake.

Proof of human intervention in the cutting up of the second mammoth at Iztapan, besides the position of the bones, is provided by the marks and scratches found over many of the bones. Some of these scratches could be attributed to the gnawing of predatory animals, after the carcass was abandoned by man. Nevertheless, there are other marks and cuts which must have been made with scrapers and knives to dismember the carcass. In several European Pleistocene localities, by means of statistical studies based on hundreds of bones found in open sites, shelters, or caves with the deposits of primitive man, it has been possible to prove the *constant* presence of certain kinds of marks and cuts at certain key points where the main muscles and ligaments were attached to the bones, and which had to be cut to achieve an effective dismemberment of the animal. A remarkable study of this kind is that accomplished at the Mousterian site of La Quina (Charente), France (Martin 1910). At some localities in the United States similar investigations have been attempted recently (White 1952, 1953, 1954).

In the case of the second mammoth at Iztapan these marks were found on a large number of the epiphyses or articular facets of the long bones, especially on the head of the only femur, around the fossa of insertion of the so-called "round ligament." These marks have been described by Martin quite often in cases of coxofemoral disarticulation (Martin 1910, Pl. 50, 9, 10, 11). There are very frequently also, in cases of intentional skull disarticulation, cuts and transverse grooves over the ridges of the

Fig. 7. Three stone artifacts found in association with second mammoth. Positions are shown in Fig. 4. Dimensions and descriptions are given in the text.

lateral processes of the first cervical vertebra (atlas) of mammals (Martin 1910, Pl. 47, 3, 4, 5). Such marks are clearly observed on the Iztapan mammoth atlas.

Another remarkable object found in the exploration is the rib fragment illustrated in Figure 6. Martin illustrated several cases of incisions on ribs, made, according to him, during the process of defleshing (Martin 1910, Pls. 40-3). However, this fragment of the Iztapan mammoth shows such a quantity of scratches and deep cuts that it is inadmissible that these were simply the result of defleshing a bone. In Figure 6 the front view of this rib shows a series of cuts regular in size and depth, arranged symmetrically on both sides of the ridge. These marks must have an explanation not yet discovered.

Associated Artifacts. During the course of the excavation 3 implements of chipped stone (Fig. 7) were found in irrefutable association with the mammoth remains. Two of them (Nos. 1 and 3) were discovered and photographed in situ. The third artifact (No. 2) was found underneath an aggregate of ribs and vertebrae toward the center of the skeletal remains, while this zone was being explored by means of small tunnels excavated under the bones; therefore, it was not possible to observe its exact location. The position of these implements with respect to the skeleton is recorded in Figure 4.

Artifact 1. This is a lanceolate atlatl (dart) point without shoulders, base slightly concave, and very symmetrically shaped. The edges converge gradually toward the tip and the base from the middle, which is the widest part. Its maximum dimensions are: length 80.2 mm., width 27.4 mm., thickness 8.5 mm. This artifact is skillfully fashioned on both faces from a flake which retains some of the original fracture planes in the middle part of the lower third. It shows pressure flaking, very fine and applied over all of the basal edges, as on most of the early types of projectile points of the Pleistocene and early post-Pleistocene of North America. The tip appears to be somewhat weathered. The material is of igneous origin, probably dacite, of fine texture and dark red color; it is foreign to the Valley of Mexico but abundant in more northern regions, especially the states of Guanajuato and San Luis Potosí. This specimen was found near an isolated rib at the northeastern extreme of the skeletal remains (Fig. 8).

FIG. 8. Artifact 1, a projectile point of Angostura type, in situ.

From the point of view of typology this point is of great importance since it is identified with the recently recognized Angostura type found widely in the Great Plains of the United States. The presence of such points in certain fossil localities of considerable antiquity was pointed out several years ago, but without assigning them a distinctive name (Krieger 1947, Pl. 1 A, C). Even earlier, an example was discovered in Texas in apparent association with mammoth remains (Sellards 1940, Pl. 1, 4). In eastern Wyoming very similar points appeared with bones of fossil bison (Anonymous 1943; Wormington 1949: 65). However, the Angostura type was not recognized formally until the excavations of Hughes in the Long site above Angostura Dam in South Dakota (Hughes 1949), where they were found in deposits belonging to the early Postglacial period and initially described as "Long points." This deposit was later dated at 7073 ± 300 years ago by the radiocarbon method (Libby 1955: 126). Similar points have been described from the Agate Basin in Wyoming (Roberts 1951), and from Bexar and Blanco counties in south-central Texas (Orchard and Campbell 1954).

All archaeological data now available tend to place the Angostura type in a *second lithic level* in the Great Plains, which also includes the Plainview, Scottsbluff, Eden, and probably other types (Krieger 1950: 120 and Fig. 8; Suhm, Krieger, and Jelks 1954: 402). Although this period corresponds to the early Postglacial it is very probable that its beginnings were contemporary with the last Pleistocene glaciers. It succeeds the *first lithic level*, called by Sellards (1952: 17) the horizon of the "Llano Man" of which the Clovis fluted projectile point type is characteristic and which is well within the Pleistocene (Krieger 1950, Fig. 8).

The association of an Angostura point with the second Iztapan mammoth is a firm indication of the presence in Mexico of this second lithic horizon of the paleo-Indian cultures in North America. The Plainview point found in Tamaulipas (Arguedas and Aveleyra 1953), and the projectile point related to the Scottsbluff type found with the first mammoth at Iztapan (Aveleyra and Maldonado-Koerdell 1952, Figs. 8, 9; 1953, Fig. 105, *1*), seem to confirm this.

The association of Scottsbluff and Angostura points with the Iztapan mammoths points to a serious problem. When found in the Great Plains with extinct mammals they are invariably associated with fossil bison, a species which may have survived in that region several thousand years longer than the mammoth. The only exception to this rule is at the Buckner ranch, near the Texas coastal plain, where a peculiar mixture of different types of points was apparently associated with remains of several extinct species, including mammoth (Sellards 1940, Pl. 1, *4, 5, 7, 8*). These may now be identified as an Angostura, a Scottsbluff, a Folsom, and the basal fragment of a Clovis point (Suhm, Krieger, and Jelks 1954: 120-1). Aside from this unique case the projectile points discovered with mammoths in the United States have usually been the fluted Clovis, corresponding to the first lithic level already mentioned (Figgins 1931, 1933; Cotter 1937; Bryan and Ray 1938; Sellards 1938; Haury 1953).

Such a situation in central Mexico can be explained in 2 ways: either the Scottsbluff and Angostura points are more ancient and perhaps originated in Mexico, or the mammoth survived in central Mexico after its extinction in most of the United States. Probably the second alternative is the true one.

Artifact 2. The second artifact was found under a complex of ribs and vertebrae toward the center of the remains. It is a projectile point, leaf shaped, made of brown flint of excellent quality. This material is also foreign to the Valley of Mexico. The specimen lacks the distal extremity, which could not be found in the excavation. Originally, the projectile must have been of a laurel-leaf contour, pointed at both ends. The possibility that the missing end was the original *base* of the projectile must be discarded in view of the general contour of the body and the considerable thickness of the fractured cross section, which does not show a gradual thinning to facilitate hafting. The chipping is bifacial, with scars of irregular flakes over both sides and fine pressure flaking along the edges. A remarkable feature is the intentional serration observed on both edges except on the proximal third; this detail confirms that the true base of the projectile is the lower part as shown in the photographs. The dimensions are: maximum length 61.3 mm., maximum width 24.4 mm., maximum thickness 8.1 mm.

There are no reports to date of the discovery of such double-pointed laurel-leaf projectiles associated with extinct fauna in any site in America.* The form is elementary enough and is found in abundance in diverse cultures of the European continent, in very different chronological horizons. The similarity of this point to the famous "laurel leaves" of the Middle Solutrean of Western Europe is remarkable. This relationship is valid strictly from the typological point of view, without implying a *direct* contact between the paleo-Indian culture and the Upper Pleistocene of Europe. The possibility of extension of the Old World Paleolithic into America is not entirely remote and, at any rate, it must not be discarded a priori. The Solutrean, for instance, has very important foci in eastern Europe and its expansion or influence toward the Asiatic East is possible. The Solutrean shape seems to show in the Sandia type points, the most anciently known so far in America, and is indication enough that infiltrations from the Upper Paleolithic of Eurasia into the New World possibly occurred.** Needless to say, this digression does not pretend to prove a Solutrean affiliation for the second point found with the Iztapan mammoth.

Artifact 3. The third artifact was found in situ approximately underneath the right supraorbital ridge of the inverted skull of the mammoth. In this case the artifact is a biface knife,

---

* This statement is true for association with extinct fauna. However, in Suhm, Krieger, and Jelks 1954, p. 440 and Pl. 99, we described and illustrated the bipointed *Lerma* type first recognized by R. S. MacNeish in southern Tamaulipas. Its distribution was given as western, coastal, and southern Texas in addition to Tamaulipas, and its age estimated as "several thousand years before the Christian era." A.D.K.

** The idea that *Sandia* points can be derived from the Upper Paleolithic of the Old World has already been noted by Bosch Gimpera (1948: 6-8), who relates them with the Gravettian "notched points" which also persisted in the Swiderian stage in Poland. The *Gravettian* and *Swiderian* points, however, are unifacial and very distinct from the bifacial *Sandia* points, which are much more nearly parallel to the "notched points" of the Upper Solutrean. A.D.K.

fashioned from impure flint (chert) of very light color with whitish bands. The shaping was done by percussion completely over both faces, with scars of wide irregular flakes, conditioned perhaps by the poor quality of the material. There is secondary retouching by pressure on some small sectors of the edges. The broken edge coincides with an increase in thickness of the artifact near the middle, and as the breakage is very ancient, it might have happened during the original shaping process. It is probable that the knife originally was of laurel-leaf form with both ends pointed. In its present state the artifact measures 67.2 mm. in length, 34.9 mm. in maximum width, and 9.3 mm. in thickness.

It is evident that this object could never have been destined to be a projectile point, considering its general size, thickness, and irregularity of flaking. Typologically, it is a simple knife which, even after breakage, could still have been used effectively for cutting up the mammoth. The place in which it was found, underneath the skull and near the atlas, could indicate that it was one of the implements used in the complicated task of disarticulating the cranium of the animal. The presence of scrapers, knives, and other cutting implements was also abundantly proved in the exploration of Iztapan Mammoth 1.

Summary. The little "industry" of Santa Isabel Iztapan, found with the 2 mammoths in identical stratigraphic position, scarcely 400 m. apart, provides no less than 10 artifacts. Of these, 3 are projectile points, each of a distinctly different type (Scottsbluff, Angostura, and "laurel-leaf"). This mixture of types in association with isolated remains of extinct animals is almost unique in North America. The great majority of such finds have demonstrated strict uniformity in associated points, as in the recent discovery at Naco, Arizona, of a mammoth with 8 Clovis points (Haury 1953). The only exception known to me besides that of Iztapan is the Buckner site in Texas already mentioned.

The typology of the more ancient lithic industries of Central Mexico is still extremely confused and full of all those unknowns typical of the regions in which prehistoric investigation is barely being started.

Estratigrafía del sitio del Mamut Nº 2

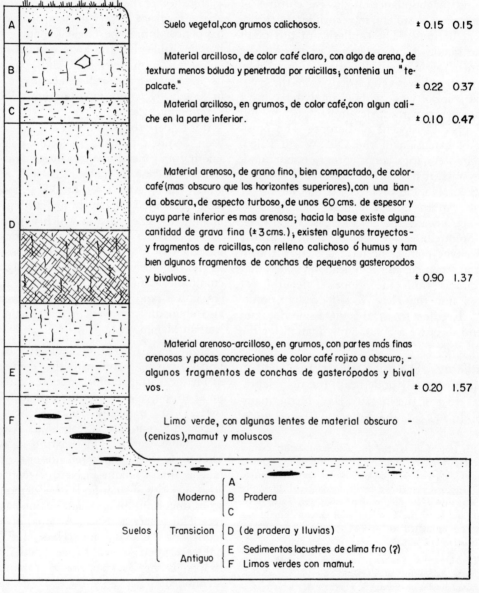

FIG. 9. Stratigraphic column at the site of the second mammoth of Santa Isabel Iztapan. The mammoth was associated with Stratum F, the green muck (*limo verde*).

APPENDIX ON STRATIGRAPHY

Manuel Maldonado-Koerdell

The site of the second Iztapan mammoth is located on the plain left by Lake Texcoco, in its northeast portion, when it retreated westward. The geographical position of this site is more western than the first Iztapan mammoth and, consequently, when the ancient lake covered it this site was deeper under the water. This is an important detail, which contributes toward explaining some little differences in stratigraphy and supports certain paleo-ecological deductions. At the present time, the terrain is used for milpa agriculture, but it is interesting that around the second mammoth there is an abundance of *huejotes* trees (*Salix bonplandiana*) in rows, a sure indication of native chinampa gardens in not very ancient times.

The stratigraphic column at the excavation of the second mammoth is shown in Figure 9. Comparing this column with that at the site of the first mammoth, one notices a greater thickness of the Postglacial sedimentary materials, which measure 1.37 m. as against 0.95 m. at the site of Iztapan Mammoth 1. Also, the different strata are better defined, showing with greater precision the 2 edaphic developments which have taken place during the last 10,000 or 12,000 years. In fact, Horizons A, B, and C correspond to modern soil, of dry to subhumid climate and pasture vegetation (when agriculture is not practiced). Horizon D corresponds to a marshy bottom in which a transition soil originated, in a rainy (or more humid) climate with prairie vegetation, conditioned in its development by the oscillations of the retreating lake; however, the band of peat indicates a period of certain permanency in the waters.

Possibly, Horizon C corresponds to the lower part of the "zona Iluvial" of Bryan (1948), with accumulation of a certain amount of calcium carbonate (represented by the fine basal deposit of caliche), originating in a hot climate. In this case Horizon D would correspond to the "zona vadosa" of Bryan, always saturated with water which maintained continuous vertical oscillations, due to the presence of a mantle of surface water under much more humid climatic conditions. Such conditions would have created this transitional soil, essentially immature, or even perpetually "young," which Bryan describes as typical in the lower Recent of marshes which occasionally dried.

At their contact, there is no well-marked distinction (as in the case of Mammoth 1) between Horizon D and the Becerra formation (Horizon E). Farther down in the Becerra lithological characteristics separate these horizons more clearly, since Pleistocene material acquires a certain lumpy texture with concretions which contrasts with the granular texture and brown color of the younger Horizon D. Besides, the little root channels found higher do not reach the Becerra formation, although at both

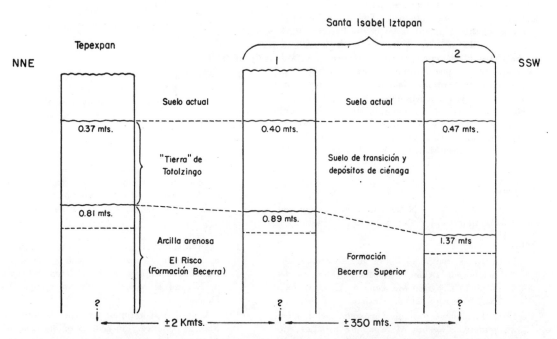

Fig. 10. Stratigraphic correlation chart for the site of the human skeleton at Tepexpan and the 2 mammoths at Santa Isabel Iztapan.

levels there are fragments of gastropod shells and lacustrine bivalves. The lower part of the Becerra formation (Horizon F) has a strong proportion of bentonitic material which gave rise in places to lenticular inclusions of black color. This deposit contained the mammoth remains and corresponds to the level of "green slimes," as in the case of the first mammoth at Santa Isabel Iztapan.

This stratigraphic column, as well as others studied in the Valley of Mexico, reveals fluctuations in the course of the last 15,000 years. It may be estimated that, from bottom to top, Horizons E to A indicate, with some fluctuations, a general tendency toward greater dryness and higher temperature from the beginning of the Recent up to the present, accompanied by retreat of the lake. Horizon D, alternatively under water or dried, reflects these variations in its composition, and toward the end comes to be more altered because of being in the zone of maximum saturation, for through it all the dissolved salts from the upper zones pass, with much oxygen and carbon dioxide. It is possible that the fine caliche deposit of Horizon C corresponds to the Postglacial arid climate, which culminated about 7000 years ago, ending the edaphic process with Horizons B and A.

Horizons E and F correspond to the lacustrine facies of the Becerra formation and were deposited by a complex mechanism of fluvial dragging and aeolian transport, but in a continuous manner and under water of rich organic content. At certain periods of the Upper Pleistocene there was a mixing of abundant ashy materials from the nearby volcanoes (in this case possibly the Tlahuilco, less than 2 km. north, which maintained its activity up to recent times), giving rise to this fine bentonitic deposit with scattered dark lenses where the skeletal remains were contained. The bentonitic characteristics of this lacustrine facies of the Becerra formation is one of the most typical features of the late phases of the Upper Pleistocene in Central Mexico. This volcanic activity took place within a climatic framework of greater humidity (with high lake levels) and lower temperature (with typical vegetation).

Figure 10 presents a correlation of stratigraphy in the 3 localities which thus far have rendered the most important prehistoric materials in the Valley of Mexico: the site of Tepexpan Man, and the 2 Iztapan mammoth sites.

ANONYMOUS
    1943 A New Site. "Notes and News," *American Antiquity*, Vol. 8, No. 3, p. 300. Menasha.

ARELLANO, A. R. V.
    1946a Datos geológicos sobre la antigüedad del hombre en la Cuenca de México. *Memoria del Segundo Congreso Mexicano de Ciencias Sociales*, Vol. 5, pp. 213-9. Mexico.
    1946b El elefante fósil de Tepexpan y el hombre primitivo. *Revista Mexicana de Estudios Antropológicos*, Vol. 8, Nos. 1, 2, 3; pp. 89-94. Mexico.

ARGUEDAS R. DE LA BORBOLLA, SOL., AND LUIS AVELEYRA A. DE ANDA
    1953 A Plainview Point from Northern Tamaulipas. *American Antiquity*, Vol. 18, No. 4; pp. 392-3. Salt Lake City.

AVELEYRA A. DE ANDA, LUIS AND MANUEL MALDONADO-KOERDELL
    1952 Asociación de artefactos con mamut en el Pleistoceno superior de la Cuenca de México. *Revista Mexicana de Estudios Antropológicos*, Vol. 8, No. 1, pp. 3-29. Mexico.
    1953 Association of Artifacts with Mammoth in the Valley of Mexico. *American Antiquity*, Vol. 18, No. 4, pp. 332-40. Salt Lake City.

BOSCH GIMPERA, PEDRO
    1948 Sobre problemas de prehistoria americana. *Acta Americana*, Vol. 6, No. 1-2, pp. 1-16. Mexico.

BRYAN, KIRK
    1946 Comentario e intento de correlación con la cronología glacial. *Memoria del Segundo Congreso Mexicano de Ciencias Sociales*, Vol. 5, pp. 220-5. Mexico.
    1948 Los suelos complejos y fósiles de la altiplanicie de México, en relación a los cambios climáticos. *Boletín de la Sociedad Geológica Mexicana*, Vol. 13, 1st Series, pp. 1-20. Mexico.

BRYAN, KIRK AND C. N. RAY
    1938 Long Channeled Point Found in Aluvium beside Bones of Elephas Columbi. *Bulletin of the Texas Archeological and Paleontological Society*, Vol. 10, pp. 263-8. Abilene.

COTTER, J. L.
    1937 The Occurrence of Flints and Extinct Animals in Pluvial Deposits near Clovis, New Mexico. Part 4: Report on Excavation at the Gravel Pit, 1936. *Proceedings of the Academy of Natural Sciences*, Vol. 89, pp. 1-16. Philadelphia.

DÍAZ LOZANO, ENRIQUE
    1927 Los restos fósiles de elephas encontrados en terrenos de la hacienda de Tepexpan, estado de México. *Anales del Instituto de Geología de México*, Vol. 2, Nos. 6-10, pp. 201-2. Mexico.

FIGGINS, J. D.
    1931 An Additional Discovery of the Association of a Folsom Artifact and Fossil Mammal Remains. *Proceedings of the Colorado Museum of Natural History*, Vol. 10, No. 4, pp. 23-4. Denver.
    1933 A Further Contribution to the Antiquity of Man in America. *Proceedings of the Colorado Museum of Natural History*, Vol. 12, No. 2, pp. 4-8. Denver.

HAURY, E. W., ERNST ANTEVS, AND J. F. LANCE
    1953 Artifacts with Mammoth Remains, Naco, Arizona. *American Antiquity*, Vol. 19, No. 1, pp. 1-24. Salt Lake City.

HUGHES, J. T.
    1949 Investigations in Western South Dakota and Northeastern Wyoming. *American Antiquity*, Vol. 14, No. 4, pp. 270-7. Salt Lake City.

KRIEGER, A. D.
    1947 Certain Projectile Points of the Early American Hunters. *Bulletin of the Texas Archeological and Paleontological Society*, Vol. 18, pp. 7-27. Lubbock.

    1950 A Suggested General Sequence in North American Projectile Points. In "Proceedings of the Sixth Plains Archaeological Conference, 1948," edited by J. D. Jennings. *Anthropological Papers, University of Utah*, No. 11, pp. 117-24. Salt Lake City.

LIBBY, W. F.
    1955 Radiocarbon Dating. 2nd Edition. The University of Chicago Press.

MALDONADO-KOERDELL, MANUEL
    1955 Sobre dos molares de Paraelephas columbi (Falconer) del pleistoceno superior de Tequixquiac, México. *Anales del Instituto Nacional de Antropología e Historia*, Vol. 7. Mexico.

MALDONADO-KOERDELL, MANUEL AND LUIS AVELEYRA A. DE ANDA
    1949 Nota preliminar sobre dos artefactos del pleistoceno superior hallados en la región de Tequixquiac, México. *El México Antiguo*, Vol. 7, pp. 154-63. Mexico.

MARTIN, HENRI
    1910 Recherches sur l'evolution du Moustérien dans le gisement de La Quina (Charente). *Troisième Fascicule, Industrie Osseuse*. Paris.

MARTINEZ DEL RIO, PABLO
    1952 El mamut de Santa Isabel Iztapan. *Cuadernos Americanos*, Vol. 9, No. 4, pp. 149-70. Mexico.

ORCHARD, C. D. AND T. N. CAMPBELL
    1954 Evidences of Early Man from the Vicinity of San Antonio, Texas. *The Texas Journal of Science*, Vol. 6, No. 4, pp. 454-65. Austin.

REYES, A. E.
    1923 Los elefantes de la Cuenca de México. *Revista Mexicana de Biología*, Vol. 3, No. 6, pp. 227-44. Mexico.

    1927 Ejemplar no. 213 del Museo Paleontológico del Instituto Geológico de México. *Anales del Instituto de Geología de México*, Vol. 2, Nos. 6-10, pp. 203-4. Mexico.

ROBERTS, F. H. H., JR.
    1951 The Early Americans. *Scientific American*, Vol. 184, No. 2, pp. 15-19. New York.

SELLARDS, E. H.
    1938 Artifacts Associated with Fossil Elephant. *Bulletin of the Geological Society of America*, Vol. 49, pp. 999-1009. New York.

    1940 Pleistocene Artifacts and Associated Fossils from Bee County, Texas. *Bulletin of the Geological Society of America*, Vol. 51, pp. 1627-58. New York.

    1952 *Early Man in America*. University of Texas Press, Austin.

SUHM, D. A., A. D. KRIEGER, AND E. B. JELKS
    1954 An Introductory Handbook of Texas Archeology. *Bulletin of the Texas Archeological Society*, Vol. 25. Austin.

DE TERRA, HELMUT
    1946 New Evidence for the Antiquity of Early Man in Mexico. *Revista Mexicana de Estudios Antropológicos*, Vol. 8, Nos. 1, 2, 3, pp. 69-88. Mexico.

    1947 Teoría de una cronología geología para el Valle de México. *Revista Mexicana de Estudios Antropológicos*, Vol. 9, Nos. 1, 2, 3, pp. 11-26. Mexico.

    1949 Early Man in Mexico. In "Tepexpan Man," by Helmut de Terra, Javier Romero, and T.D. Stewart. *Viking Fund Publications in Anthropology*, No. 11, pp. 11-86. New York.

WHITE, T. E.
    1952 Observations on the Butchering Techniques of Some Aboriginal Peoples: 1. *American Antiquity*, Vol. 17, No. 4, pp. 337-8. Salt Lake City.

    1953 Observations on the Butchering Techniques of Some Aboriginal Peoples: 2. *American Antiquity*, Vol. 19, No. 2, pp. 160-4. Salt Lake City.

    1954 Observations on the Butchering Techniques of Some Aboriginal Peoples: 3, 4, 5, and 6. *American Antiquity*, Vol. 19, No. 3, pp. 254-6. Salt Lake City.

WORMINGTON, H. M.
    1949 Ancient Man in North America. *Denver Museum of Natural History, Popular Series*, No. 4. Denver.

INSTITUTO NACIONAL DE ANTROPOLOGÍA
E HISTORIA
Mexico, D.F.

NEW EVIDENCE OF ANTIQUITY OF TEPEXPAN AND OTHER HUMAN REMAINS FROM THE VALLEY OF MEXICO

ROBERT F. HEIZER AND SHERBURNE F. COOK

IN JANUARY, 1957 Dr Luis Aveleyra Arroyo de Anda, Director of the Museo Nacional de Antropología in Mexico, and Dr Arturo Romano, Director of the Department of Prehistory of the Instituto Nacional de Antropología e Historia, Mexico, provided us with a series of bone samples of humans and extinct animals which have been recovered under conditions strongly suggestive of contemporaneity and high antiquity. In each case some obscurity and uncertainty over contemporaneity, and therefore antiquity, exists, and it was the hope that tests for nitrogen content and fluoride level of the bones would indicate some solution to the problem of whether the human remains were younger (presumably by reason of intrusion into older deposits) than the animals, or whether the human and animal remains were deposited at approximately the same time and are therefore coeval.[1]

As one control we determined the nitrogen and fluorine content of the femur from a human skeleton excavated by us at Tlatilco, a Preclassic site near Los Remedios on the outskirts of Mexico City.[2] This burial was accompanied by a number of stone and ceramic offerings which indicate that the grave refers to the final stage of the Middle Preclassic with an estimated dating of 700 to 500 BC. Wood charcoal collected from soil surrounding the burial has been radiocarbon dated[3] at 2525 ± 250 years old (568 BC).

The much discussed human skeleton from Tepexpan was represented in our tests by a rib fragment. No animal remains are associated directly with the Tepexpan skeleton,[4] but at a distance of about 2.6 km have been recovered two skeletons of mammoths, each of which was associated with flaked projectile points and other

---

[1] A grant from the Wenner-Gren Foundation for Anthropological Research supported this investigation. The bone samples were secured incidental to a research trip financed by the National Geographic Society. A list of published papers dealing with the chronological significance of bone constituents is contained in an article by the present authors in this journal, Vol. 12, pp. 229-248, 1956.

[2] On the Tlatilco site see Porter, 1953; Piña Chan, 1958.

[3] Sample M-660 (reported in Science, vol. 128, p. 1120, 1958).

[4] On the discovery, geology, and physical anthropology of the Tepexpan skeleton see De Terra, 1947; De Terra, Romero and Stewart, 1949; De Terra, 1957, pp. 160-171; Aveleyra, 1950, chap. 3.

Reprinted from SOUTHWESTERN JOURNAL OF ANTHROPOLOGY, Vol. 15, 1959. pp. 32-42.

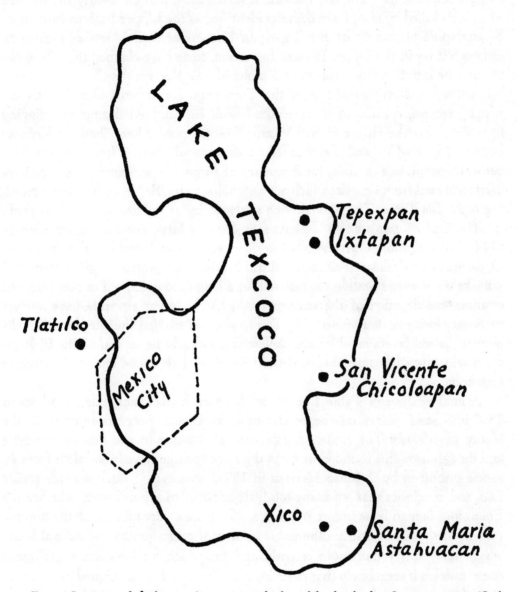

Fig. 1. Location of find-sites. Approximate highest lake level after Lorenzo, 1956. (Scale approx. 1/100,000.)

chipped implements.[5] The two mammoth skeletons, which are clearly the remains of animals killed by man, lie in deposits identified as the Upper Becerra formation. Stratigraphic placement of the Tepexpan human skeleton is less certain since, although it lay in the Upper Becerra formation, some have claimed that the skeleton may be intrusive from overlying deposits of post-Becerra date.[6]

A third find, apparently from the Totolzingo formation which follows the Upper Becerra, consists of a mineralized skull encountered during well-digging operations near the village of San Vicente Chicoloapan at Km 29 on the highway between Mexico City and Texcoco.[7] At a distance of about 2 km from the find-site of the skull, in a sandpit, fossil remains of *Bison, Elephas,* and *Camelops* have been recovered from deposits which are assignable to the Becerra formation according to H. De Terra. The animal bone analyzed by us is from a *Camelops* skull.

The find of two human skeletons at Santa Maria Astahuacan by George O'Neill of Columbia University led to their recovery and study of the site by the Department of Prehistory of the Instituto Nacional de Antropología e Historia.[8] The skeletons were found in the side wall of a long-used open well or pond and the stratigraphic situation of the remains could not be, or at any rate have not yet been, satisfactorily determined. De Terra, who has studied the site recently, tells us that the soil layers in which the skeletons lay clearly lie on top of the El Risco sands which is a lacustrine beach deposit roughly of the same age as the Becerra formation.

A final analysis in Table 1 refers to the Xico human mandible found about 1890 in a sand quarry on the border of Lake Chalco near Astahuacan in the Valley of Mexico. The figures for percent of fluorine in the human mandible and the *Equus* radius found close by in the same stratum have been taken from an article published by Alfonso Herrera in 1893.[9] Aveleyra[10] discusses this earlier find, and concludes that we know too little about it to say definitely whether the *Equus* and human bone are of equal age. The close comparability of the fluorine content of the Xico horse and human with that of other human and animal bones which have been found more recently and for which we have some geological context makes it seem likely that the Xico mandible is in fact, as argued by Herrera, that of an ancient inhabitant of the Valley of Mexico. We would be in a better

---

5 Aveleyra and Maldonado-Koerdell, 1953; Aveleyra, 1956.

6 Black, 1949; Krieger, 1950; Arellano, 1951. For recent reviews of the late Pleistocene and Recent geology of the Valley of Mexico see Mooser, White, and Lorenzo, 1956; Krieger, 1957.

7 A report of this find has not been published. We have been provided information by A. Romano, P. Martinez del Rio, L. Aveleyra A. de Anda, and H. De Terra.

8 Romano, 1955.

9 Herrera, 1893.

position to support this judgment if the find site could be relocated and a geological study made, though this would be difficult and perhaps impossible after a lapse of nearly three-quarters of a century.

Any final evaluation of the significance of the chemical data as these relate to absolute age must await additional bone analyses and radiocarbon check-dates from the Valley of Mexico.[11] At this time we feel justified in making the following assessment.

TABLE 1

Nitrogen and fluorine quantities (shown as percent by weight) of human and animal bones from the Valley of Mexico

Site	Type of bone	Nitrogen	Fluorine	Geological horizon
Tlatilco	Human	0.72	0.046	Recent
Chicoloapan	Human	2.14	1.150	Totolzingo
Tepexpan	Human	0.06	1.540	Becerra
Ixtapan	Mammoth	0.02	1.822	Becerra
Chicoloapan	Camel	0.08	1.860	Becerra
Astahuacan	Human	0.08	1.988	post-Becerra (Totolzingo?)
Xico	Human	–	1.94	?
Xico	Horse	–	1.34	?

The Tlatilco results are roughly comparable to those already on record from the Sacramento Valley of California. In both places one can argue that the general environmental conditions and specific conditions of burial are similar, and it is of interest that the nitrogen and fluorine levels of human bones of about the same age from both areas are similar.[12] The Tlatilco site occupies a position near the foot of the hill of Los Remedios; all other sites considered here lie in the immediate lake basin areas and have been subject to greater influence of ground water.

The Chicoloapan figures for nitrogen we consider to be of doubtful reliability on account of the type of bone (a cancellous or spongy mandible fragment) available for test. It has been shown[12] that great variation of nitrogen level occurs within a single skeleton and that spongy bone tends to run higher in nitrogen than dense bone. The fluorine content does not appear to be subject to such wide varia-

---

11 Other possibly ancient remains are described in Aveleyra, 1950.
12 Cook and Heizer, 1952, p. 20.

tion according to the type of bone and we therefore view the high fluorine content of the Chicoloapan bone as a more reliable indication of its relative age.

The Tepexpan human, Ixtapan mammoth, and Chicoloapan camel bones all have been geologically associated with the Becerra formation and may therefore be considered as a group. The differences in nitrogen content of these three samples are considered as without significance—with such small quantities present differences of this magnitude are not important. The important point is that the nitrogen is essentially gone and in general terms this may be taken as clear indication of a long passage of time since the bones were buried. The rate of disappearance of nitrogen is unknown but the direction of the process (i.e. decrease through time) is clear.[13]

With reference to fluorine, we know that the process involves gradual uptake through time.[14] In this light Tepexpan man looks to be a bit younger than the Ixtapan mammoth and Chicoloapan camel. We are definitely of the opinion that Tepexpan man is ancient, and recent intrusion seems clearly to be ruled out. Whether Tepexpan man might be five hundred, or one thousand, or three thousand years younger than the Ixtapan mammoth we cannot say. The accuracy of the fluorine method is such that it is not possible to invest small percentage differences with precise time intervals. Since the Upper Becerra formation was deposited over a period of time believed to be four to five thousand years, interment of the Ixtapan mammoths and Tepexpan man may have taken place at different times and their remains still lie within the same geological stratum.

With reference to the Astahuacan skeleton, there exists a problem of correlating the post-Becerra deposits, in which De Terra says the bones lie, with low nitrogen and high fluorine levels which make it appear as ancient as, for example, the Ixtapan mammoths which lie in Upper Becerra deposits. Several alternatives may be proposed to account for the apparent discrepancy. Possibly the spring waters at Astahuacan are charged with fluorine, or the geological dating is incorrect. We are simply not in a position to say why the discrepancy exists and trust that further examination may lead to the solution of this problem. We are, however, of the opinion that the Astahuacan human remains are as old as the nitrogen and fluorine levels seem to indicate.

Finally, the Xico human mandible and extinct horse bones, whose fluorine contents were determined nearly three-quarters of a century ago in Mexico, may be taken as roughly equal in age to the Tepexpan-Chicoloapan-Ixtapan finds. Our interest in these finds is largely historical, since the chemical tests are not likely to be precisely comparable to our more recent ones. If, however, they are taken as

---

[13] Cook and Heizer, 1947.

generally accurate, the remains would be assigned to a geological age equivalent to the Upper Becerra formation of the terminal Pleistocene.

Our results, while far from being conclusive, do seem to support the view of high antiquity for the Tepexpan, Chicoloapan, Astahuacan, and Xico human remains from the Valley of Mexico. Fluorine and nitrogen analyses will not provide absolute dates, but may be expected to indicate general magnitude of age if ancillary paleontological and geological data can be referred to.

More determinations of nitrogen and fluorine content of fossil bones from the Valley of Mexico are needed before the method can be said to yield unequivocal results. The fluorine levels seem relatively high for the age of the bones, and this indicates high fluorine content in the local ground water or soils. By combining chemical results with dates derived by the radiocarbon method we may look forward to further progress in this matter. The results presented here are an initial attempt and should be considered as tentative and subject to more precise evaluation in future.

BIBLIOGRAPHY

ARELLANO, A. R.
    1951 *Some New Aspects of the Tepexpan Man Case* (Bulletin, Texas Archaeological and Paleontological Society, vol. 22, p. 217-224).

AVELEYRA A. DE ANDA, L.
    1950 *Prehistoria de Mexico* (Mexico City).
    1956 *The Second Mammoth and Associated Artifacts at Santa Isabel Iztapan, Mexico* (American Antiquity, vol. 22, pp. 12-28).

AVELEYRA A. DE ANDA, L., AND M. MALDONADO-KOERDELL
    1953 *Association of Artifacts with Mammoth in the Valley of Mexico* (American Antiquity, vol. 18, pp. 332-340).

BLACK, G.
    1949 *"Tepexpan Man," a Critique of Method* (American Antiquity, vol. 14, pp. 344-346).

COOK, S. F. AND R. F. HEIZER
    1947 *The Quantitative Investigation of Aboriginal Sites: Analyses of Human Bone* (American Journal of Physical Anthropology, n.s., vol. 5, pp. 201-220).
    1952 *The Fossilization of Bone: Organic Components and Water* (Reports, University of California Archaeological Survey, no. 17).

DE TERRA, H.
    1947 *Preliminary Note on the Discovery of Fossil Man at Tepexpan in the Valley of Mexico* (American Antiquity, vol. 13, pp. 40-44).
    1957 *Man and Mammoth in Mexico* (Hutchinson: London).

DE TERRA, H., J. ROMERO, AND T. D. STEWART
    1949 *Tepexpan Man* (Viking Fund Publications in Anthropology, no. 11).

HERRERA, A. L.
    1893   *El Hombre Prehistórico de México* (Memorias, Sociedad Cientifico "Antonio Alzate" de Mexico, vol. 7, pp. 17-56).

KRIEGER, A. D.
    1950   Review of H. De Terra, J. Romero, and T. D. Stewart, "Tepexpan Man" (American Antiquity, vol. 15, pp. 343-349).
    1957   Review of F. Mooser, S. E. White, and J. L. Lorenzo, "La Cuenca de Mexico: Consideraciones Geológicas y Arqueológicas" (American Antiquity, vol. 23, pp. 191-192).

MOOSER, F., S. E. WHITE, AND J. L. LORENZO
    1956   *La Cuenca de Mexico: Consideraciones Geológicas y Arqueológicas* (Instituto Nacional de Antropología e Historia, Direccion de Prehistoria, Publicaciones no. 2).

OAKLEY, K. P.
    1951   *The Fluorine-Dating Method* (Yearbook of Physical Anthropology, vol. 5 [for 1949], pp. 44-52, New York).

PIÑA CHAN, R.
    1958   *Tlatilco* (Instituto Nacional de Antropología e Historia, Serie Investigaciones 1, 2, Mexico).

PORTER, M. N.
    1953   *Tlatilco and the Pre-Classic Cultures of the New World* (Publications, Viking Fund in Anthropology, no. 19, New York).

ROMANO, A.
    1955   *Nota Preliminar Sobre los Restos Humanos Sub-fósiles de Santa Maria Astahuacan, D. F.* (Anales, Instituto Nacional de Antropología e Historia, vol. 7, pp. 65-74, Mexico).

UNIVERSITY OF CALIFORNIA
BERKELEY, CALIFORNIA

Ancient Mesoamerican Civilization

A long archeological sequence from Tehuacán, Mexico, may give new data about the rise of this civilization.

Richard S. MacNeish

A problem that has long interested the layman, the scientist, and the philosopher has to do with how and why civilizations arose. Any hypothesis or generalization about this social phenomenon must be based on broad comparative historical data. Specifically, one must compare long archeological sequences, from savagery to civilization, which have been uncovered in relatively independent areas. The ancient high cultures of Mexico and Central America (termed Mesoamerica) have always represented an interesting facet of this problem, for here were prehistoric civilizations which apparently arose independently of any of those in the Old World.

It is generally accepted that the development of agriculture is basic to the rise of village and urban life. And so, in our work in Mesoamerica, it was assumed that if we could but find the origins of agriculture—and in the New World this meant maize or corn—then we would be well on the way to finding out where and how civilization evolved in America.

After a number of years of investigation, it became apparent that the desert valley of Tehuacán (about 150 miles south of Mexico City) was the region in which evidence could most likely be uncovered about the beginnings of the domestication of corn (*1*). Precisely why we decided on this area is explained in an article by Mangelsdorf and others in this issue (p. 538), so I confine my discussion to the archeological researches recently undertaken in this southern Puebla valley.

In attacking such an all-inclusive problem, the project was most fortunate in having the cooperation of a number of scientists from a wide variety of fields. Obviously, I am extremely grateful to these various specialists, but I must confess that I say this with a sigh of relief, for at the beginning of the first field season we were far from convinced that the much-vaunted interdisciplinary approach was practicable. We know now that it can and does work, and thanks to our experts' endeavors we have gathered and interrelated specialized studies in botany, corn, beans, squash, human feces, pollen, zoology, geology, geography, physical anthropology, prehistoric textiles, ethnohistory, and ethnography (*2*). These investigations, of course, were in addition to the usual archeological researches carried out so ably by my field staff (*3*).

Before discussing what our diverse group accomplished in the Tehuacán Valley, let me briefly describe the valley itself. It is located in the southern part of the state of Puebla, and in the northernmost section of the state of Oaxaca, in the central highlands of Mexico (see Fig. 1). Efforts were concentrated in a relatively small area, about 70 miles long and 20 miles wide. Although the valley is considerably longer than it is wide, it has a basin-like appearance, for it is ringed by high mountains. The Sierra Madre Oriental is to the south and east, while to the north and west are the Mixteca Hills. Both rise considerably above the Tehuacán Valley floor, which is 1500 meters above sea level. Because of these precipitous mountains the valley is in a rain shadow and extremely dry. Most parts of the valley floor receive less than 600 millimeters of rainfall a year, and some parts receive less than 500 millimeters. Moreover, most of this rain falls during a 2-month period. Needless to say, the resultant vegetation is xerophytic. Thus, the Tehuacán Valley has all the characteristics of a desert.

Intensive archeological investigation in this region has now been under way for 3 consecutive years; in addition, I spent a brief 10 weeks in the area in 1960. Archeological reconnaissance has resulted in the discovery of 392 new sites or prehistoric habitations. These range from small temporary camps to large ruins of cities. At about 30 of these sites test trenches were dug. These were superficial, but even so, one sounding yielded stratified remains with five occupational floors, one above the other. Twelve test trenches in other sites revealed deep stratified remains. Excavations in these particular sites were expanded into major digs and became the basis for establishing a long prehistoric sequence of culture.

In these 12 sites of major excavation (selected from the original 392 sample sites), 140 stratified floors and occupational zones were unearthed. Five of these were open sites or middens, while seven were caves or rock shelters, or both.

Because of the extreme dryness of the area, in over 55 of the floors in the five caves everything had been preserved: foodstuffs, feces, and other normally perishable human remains and artifacts. This type of refuse not only allows one to make an unusually com-

---

The author is the director of the Tehuacán Archaeological-Botanical Project for the Robert S. Peabody Foundation for Archaeology, Andover, Mass.

Reprinted by permission of the publisher; SCIENCE 143; pp. 531–537 (1964); by Richard S. McNeish. Copyright 1964 by the American Association for the Advancement of Science.

Fig. 1. Tehuacán area of Mexico.

plete reconstruction of the way of life of the ancient inhabitants, but gives considerable information about subsistence, food habits, diet, climatic changes, and, in many cases, even indicates which months of the year the floors were occupied.

Although our studies are a long way from completion (it has taken much time to even count and catalog the 750,000 specimens so far uncovered), preliminary results have been most encouraging. Some of these I summarize briefly in the following paragraphs.

Ajuereado Phase

The earliest assemblage of artifacts is called the Ajuereado phase (4). In the caves, we uncovered evidence of seven different occupations, while surface collections have yielded four more sites of this cultural complex. As yet we have only three dates, obtained by the carbon-14 technique, on the final stages of this phase, but another five are being processed. The phase seems to have ended by at least 7200 B.C., and it may have come into being 3 or 4 millennia earlier. Examination of these floors indicates that in this period the inhabitants were grouped together into small, nomadic families or microbands who changed their camps three or four times a year with the seasons (see Fig. 2). As means of subsistence they collected wild plants and they hunted and trapped. Although they hunted such animals as horses and antelope of now-extinct species during the earliest part of the phase, even then most of their meat came from smaller game, such as jack rabbits, gophers, rats, turtles, birds, and other small mammals. In the later part of the phase they trapped only species that exist today. These people, in the so-called "big game hunting stage" (5) or "mammoth-hunting period" (6), were far from being the great hunters they are supposed to have been. As one of my colleagues said: "They probably found one mammoth in a lifetime and never got over talking about it."

Preliminary studies of the pollen and animal bones seem to show that, in this region, the climate of the terminal Pleistocene was only very slightly cooler and wetter than the climate today. The vegetation was probably xerophytic, but not like the present-day desert vegetation in the Tehuacán Valley—it probably was more like the mesquite grasslands of western Texas.

The manufactured tools of this group were not numerous, and all were made by chipping flint. They include a series of bifacially leaf-shaped knives and projectile points, keeled and ovoid end scrapers, flake and bifacial choppers, side scrapers, gravers, and crude prismatic blades struck from even cruder polyhedral cores. No ground stone was utilized, and the floors held few perishable remains, hence we know nothing about the weaving industry or the traps and perishable tools of these peoples. No burials have been found, though there is one fragment of a charred human bone.

This complex (represented by many more artifacts than have been previously found for this time period) seems to be related to the earliest remains found elsewhere in Central America. It must be noted, however, that even at the earliest stage these peoples were not primarily dependent upon hunting and should be called plant and animal collectors rather than hunters. Further, the material culture of the Ajuereado phase continued unchanged even though the Pleistocene fauna became extinct and gave way to modern fauna.

El Riego Phase

Gradually the Ajuereado phase developed into one which we call the El Riego cultural phase. This is extremely well known, for we have dug up 24 floors and have found 14 open camp sites. Ten dates, obtained by the carbon-14 method, allow us to estimate the time of this cultural phase fairly accurately. It seems to fall between 7200 and 5200 B.C. These peoples were seasonally nomadic like their predecessors, but there had been a definite increase in population and some changes in the settlement pattern seem to have taken place. The sites are almost equally divided between very small camps, which obviously represent the family groups or microbands of the dry seasons, and much larger sites, representing camps of related families or macrobands which gathered together in the spring and wet seasons. The means of subsistence was basically plant and animal collecting, supplemented by some hunting—not very different from the previous period, although these peoples seem to have hunted deer in-

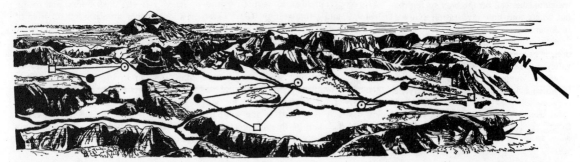

Fig. 2 (hypothetical stage 1). Ajuereado and early El Riego phases. *Community pattern:* Wandering microbands that changed residence seasonally, that is, groups that went from wet-season camps (●) to fall camps (□) to dry-season camps (☉) in an annual cycle. *Population estimate:* Three microbands of four to eight people (the original population). *Estimated age:* Before 6800 B.C. *Subsistence:* Food collectors who hunted and trapped and gathered wild plants. *Occupations found:* About 11.

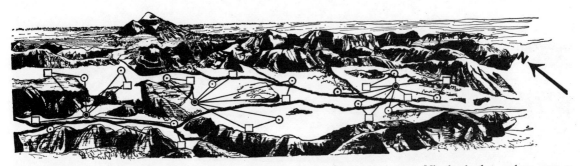

Fig. 3 (hypothetical stage 2). El Riego and early Coxcatlan phases. *Community pattern:* Microbands that coalesce once a year to form seasonal macrobands, that is, microbands that went from fall camps (□) to dry season camps (○) to join others at spring macroband camps (◉). *Population estimate:* Four times the original population. *Estimated age:* 6800 to 5000 B.C. *Subsistence:* Plant collectors who occasionally hunted and trapped, and used squash and chili. *Occupations found:* About 40.

stead of horse and antelope, and the cottontail rabbit instead of the jackrabbit.

As for their hunting and trapping activities, there were no fundamental changes; nor do they seem to have been "forced by the changing climatic conditions that followed the end of the Wisconsin Glaciation to make readjustments" (5). The preserved plant remains, however, seem to show that plant collecting was even more important than it had been in the previous culture. Nevertheless, it was only a seasonal affair. During the dry season, apparently, people still hunted and trapped in small groups and probably nearly starved, but when the spring came, and later the rains, a number of microbands seem to have gathered together in larger groups to live off the lusher vegetation. There is evidence that they were collecting a large variety of plants, and I would guess that this was the period when they finally conceived the idea that if you drop a seed in the ground a plant comes up. This concept is, of course, basic to any beginnings of agriculture. Further, these people were eating some plants which later became domesticated. These included one variety of squash (*Cucurbita mixta*), chili, and avocados. It is also possible that they were gathering and consuming wild corn as well as utilizing cotton (see Fig. 3).

The development of such a subsistence and settlement pattern undoubtedly caused some changes in their social organization. From comparative ethnological data one might guess that these groups were patrilineal bands with some sort of weak temporary leadership in the hands of a male, and perhaps some sort of concept of territoriality (7). Further, there apparently were shamans, or witch doctors, who had considerable power in both the medicinal and the ceremonial fields. These, of course, would not have been full-time specialists.

The tools we dug up gave considerable evidence about the industrial activities of these peoples. For example, they manufactured a number of varieties of contracting-stemmed and concave-based projectile points which were very neatly chipped and were probably used to tip atlatl darts used in the chase. The most prevalent artifacts were, however, the large plano-convex scrapers and choppers chipped from pebbles or nodules of flint. These could have been used for preparing skins, but it seems more probable that they were used for pulping various plant remains. Some blades, burins, and end scrapers of types found in the previous horizon were still made and utilized. The most noticeable change in the material culture was the use of ground-stone and pecked-stone implements. Mortars and pestles were particularly numerous, and there were many milling stones and pebble manos. Tools of both types were probably used to grind up plant and animal remains into some sort of palatable (or unpalatable) stew.

In addition, it is in this period that we found the first evidence of weaving and woodworking—knotted nets, a few small fragments of twined blankets and coiled baskets, fragments of dart shafts, and pieces of traps.

To me, one of the most surprising findings for the El Riego cultural phase was evidence of relatively elaborate burials, which indicate the possibility of complex beliefs and ceremonies. We uncovered two groups of multiple burials. In the first were the skeletons of two children; one child had been ceremonially cremated. The head of the other child had been severed and roasted, the brains had been removed, and the head had been placed in a basket on the child's chest. The other multiple burial included an elderly man, an adolescent woman, and a child of less than 1 year. There was evidence that the elderly man had been intentionally burned, and the heads of both the woman and the child had been smashed, perhaps intentionally. These findings could certainly be interpreted as some sort of human sacrifice, but the correctness of such an interpretation is difficult to prove. In both these burials the bodies were wrapped in blankets and nets and were richly furnished with basketry. Is it not possible that the ceremonialism that is so characteristic of the later Mexican periods began at this time?

In terms of wider implications, the El Riego phase seems to be related to early cultures occurring in Northern Mexico, the U.S. Southwest, and the Great Basin areas which have been classified as being of the "Desert Culture Tradition" (8). The later preceramic phases that follow the El Riego phase in the Tehuacán Valley are difficult to classify in this tradition because they have incipient agriculture and the numerous large choppers, scrapers, and milling stones decrease in importance. In addition, these Mesoamerican cultures developed their own distinctive types of grinding tools, baskets, nets, projectile points, blades, and other implements—all unlike artifacts found in the Desert Cultural manifestations.

Coxcatlan Phase

The phase developing out of the El Riego phase was termed Coxcatlan. About 12 radiocarbon determinations indicate that it existed from 5200 to

Fig. 4 (hypothetical stage 3). Coxcatlan and early Abejas phases. *Community pattern:* Semisedentary macrobands **that had** wet-season fall camps (■) or annual camps (■) but that often separated into **dry-season microband camps** (○). *Population estimate:* Ten times the original population. *Estimated age:* 5000 to 3000 B.C. *Subsistence:* Plant collectors who did increasing amounts of agriculture due to new domesticates (first chili and squash then corn then beans and gourds). *Occupations found:* About 30.

3400 B.C. Twelve components of this phase were uncovered in cave excavations, and four open camps were also found. Although fewer occupations were found than in the El Riego phase, most of them were larger. However, the way of life may have been much the same, with nomadic microbands in the dry season and macrobands in the wet season. The macrobands seem to have been larger than those of the earlier phase, and they seem to have stayed in one place for longer periods. Perhaps this was due to their rather different subsistence pattern (see Fig. 4).

While the Coxcatlan people were still basically plant collectors who did a little animal trapping and hunting, all through this period they acquired more and more domesticated plants. Early in the period they began using wild corn, chili, avocados, and gourds. By the middle of the phase they had acquired amaranth, tepary beans, yellow

Fig. 5 (hypothetical stage 4). Late Abejas, Purron, and possibly early Ajalpan phases. *Community pattern:* Semipermanent villages (✧) composed of a number of microbands living together that occasionally made camps for hunting or planting (△) or collecting (◆). *Population estimate:* Forty times the original population. *Estimated age:* 3000 to 1500 B.C. *Subsistence:* Full-time agriculturists who planted an increasing amount of domesticates. Plant hybridization may have begun. *Occupations found:* About 15.

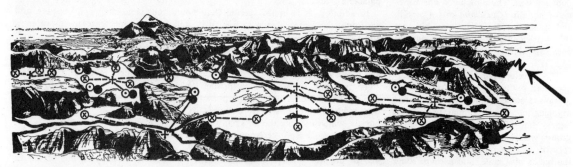

Fig. 6 (hypothetical stage 5). Ajalpan and St. Maria phases. *Community pattern:* Ceremonial centers or villages with temples (✚) with ceremonially affiliated villages (⊗) and seasonal camps (●⊙). *Population estimate:* 150 times the original population. *Estimated age:* 1500 to 200 B.C. *Subsistence:* Full-time agriculturists using many hybrid domesticates. Irrigation may have begun. *Occupations found:* About 60.

zapotes, and squash (*Cucurbita moschata*), and by the end of the phase perhaps they had black and white zapotes. It seems that microbands still came together at some favorite collecting spot in the spring, and it may be that while they were there they planted some of their domesticates. This would have given them food to continue living at that camp after they had consumed their wild foods. As the numbers of domesticates increased, the group could, of course, have stayed together as a macroband for longer and longer periods. But with the onset of the dry season and the depletion of their agricultural "surpluses" they would have broken up again into nomadic microbands.

The changing subsistence and settlement pattern may have been connected with changes in social organization. The bands may still have been patrilineal. But one wonders whether the use of gardens and the more sedentary way of life might not have resulted in bands having definite collecting territories and ideas about property "garden rights." Moreover, a greater dependence upon agriculture (and rainfall) may have made the shaman even more powerful, not only in medicine and in birth and death ceremonies but also in regard to rituals connected with plantings and harvestings. In addition, the more sedentary life involving larger numbers of people may have resulted in some kind of macroband leadership, more stable than just that vested in the oldest or most powerful male in a family.

The industrial activities of the group were not vastly different from those of their predecessors, although different types of tanged projectile points were manufactured. Blades were more delicately made, scrapers and choppers were of new types, and true metates, with manos, were replacing the mortars, pestles, and milling stones. Some minor improvements were also made in the manufacture of nets, coiled baskets, bags, and blankets.

The most distinctive aspect of the Coxcatlan phase is its incipient agriculture. However, I do not want to give the impression that Tehuacán was the only early center of plant domestication or agriculture. In fact, our accruing archeological data having to do with the beginning of New World plant domestication seem to indicate that there was no single center, but, instead, that domesticates had multiple origins (9) over a wide area of Nuclear America and the southern United States. For example, while tepary beans and corn may have been first domesticated near or in the Tehuacán Valley, pumpkins seem to have been domesticated in northeastern Mexico, sunflowers in the southwestern United States, potatoes and lima beans in the highlands of South America, common beans in still another region, and so on (10).

Abejas Phase

The Abejas phase follows the Coxcatlan phase, and we estimate, on the basis of eight carbon-14 determinations, that it existed from 3400 to 2300 B.C. Thirteen occupations have now been uncovered, and eight sites were found in reconnaissance. We are now making plans to excavate what seems to be a pit-house village of the Abejas phase.

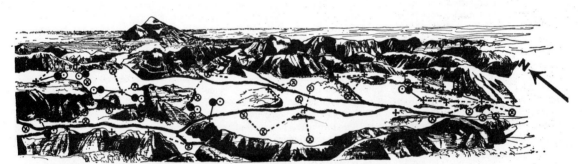

Fig. 7 (hypothetical stage 6). Palo Blanco phase. *Community pattern:* Sacred cities or ceremonial centers (+) with villages (ceremonially and politically) affiliated (⊗) and camps (●○). *Population estimate:* 1000 times the original population. *Estimated age:* 200 B.C. to A.D. 700. *Subsistence:* Full-time agriculturists with irrigation. *Occupations found:* About 160.

Fig. 8 (hypothetical stage 7). Venta Salada phase. *Community pattern:* Secular cities or towns (✪) with (religiously, politically, and economically) affiliated ceremonial centers (+), villages (⊗) and camps (● ○). *Population estimate:* 5000 times the original population. *Estimated age:* A.D. 700 to A.D. 1500. *Subsistence:* Full-time agriculturists and irrigation as well as commerce. *Occupations found:* About 210.

The settlement pattern seems to have changed significantly during this period. Ten of the cave occupations were hunting (dry-season) camps of macrobands, while eight of the macroband settlements were on river terraces in the Valley. The latter appear to have been larger settlements (of five to ten pit houses), and some of them may have been occupied all year round (see Fig. 5). This even more sedentary way of life was made possible by more efficient food production. This was accomplished with plants already known and, in addition, with domesticated canavalia and perhaps pumpkins (pepo) and common beans, as well as some varieties of hybrid corn with teosinte introgression. The people also used cotton and had dogs. However, even with this increase in domesticates, botanical studies and studies of feces reveal that more than 70 percent of their foods still came from wild plants and animals.

Again, many of the older techniques of artifact manufacture continued, though the types are a little different. Some of the types which carry over into much later times originated during this period. These include: split-stitch basketry and the manufacture of stone bowls and ollas, oval metates and large plano-convex manos, obsidian blades made from long cylindrical cores, and other objects.

If this phase provides evidence of a Marxian "Neolithic revolution," the revolution came long after the first plant domestications; the population showed no sudden increase in size, and the artifacts were little better than those of the preceding phase (*11*).

Purron Phase

The next phase, Purron, is dated by six carbon-14 determinations which place it between 2300 and 1500 B.C. It is the least clearly understood phase in the sequence and was represented by only two floors in excavation. The excavated materials include a few plant remains, early tripsacoid corn cobs, manos, metates, scrapers, fine obsidian blades, and a number of very crude, crumbly pieces of broken pottery. The pottery, the earliest so far found in Mesoamerica, has the same vessel forms as the stone bowls and ollas of the previous period. This pottery may not be the first modeled in Mexico but only an imitation of still earlier pottery (as yet unfound) in some other area.

One might surmise that the subsistence and settlement pattern and social organization of the Purron phase was much the same as that of the Abejas phase.

Ajalpan Phase

The following phase, Ajalpan, dated by 18 carbon-14 determinations, is much better understood. It is placed between 1500 and 900 B.C. Seventeen floors were found in the diggings, and two open sites were found during survey. These Ajalpan people were full-time agriculturists; they planted early hybrid corn, mixta, moschata and pepo squashes, gourds, amaranths, beans, chili, avocado, zapotes, and cotton. They seem to have lived in small wattle-and-daub villages of from 100 to 300 inhabitants. Whether they built religious structures is not yet known, but their figurines, mainly female, attest to a complex religious life. Male priests and chiefs certainly must have had considerable power, although the rich female burials and the figurines hint that kinship and property ownership may have had a matrilineal emphasis (see Fig. 6).

Many stone tools of the older types were still made, but one of the more notable industries of this period was pottery making. The pottery, though well made, is usually unpainted, although a few examples of monochrome specular-hemitite red ware are found. A limited number of forms were modeled; the tecomate, or small-mouthed seed jar, is the dominant type of receptacle.

In terms of cultural relationships, the pottery, large figurines, and rocker-dentate stamp decoration are like those found in the earliest cultural manifestations in lowland Mesoamerica—that is, Veracruz, Chiapas, Pacific-lowland Guatemala, and the Pacific coast of Oaxaca (*12, 13*). This does not, however, mean there was a migration, diffusion, or relationship only from the coast to the highlands, for remains from periods of comparable age have not yet been found in highland Mexico. In fact, Ajalpan could well be but a local manifestation of an early widespread horizon in Mesoamerica. Spinden, many years ago, concluded that such a horizon existed, and he called it the Archaic. More and more evidence confirming his original hypothesis is being accumulated (*14*).

Santa Maria Phase

In the subsequent Santa Maria period the pottery still shows resemblances to pottery of the Veracruz coast. But in addition to these resemblances it shows resemblances to the earliest pottery remains in Monte Alban (*15*), the Valley of Mexico (*16*), and other highland regions.

Thus, we have good evidence for correlating a number of sequences from a number of areas, not only with Santa Maria but also with each other. Twenty-three carbon-14 determinations indicated that the Santa Maria period lasted from just before 900 to about 200 B.C. The culture is well known, for we have excavated 38 components and have found about 15 surface sites. The settlement pattern reveals that the people lived in small wattle-and-daub houses in villages which were oriented around a single, larger village having ceremonial structures.

These people were full-time farmers, using all of the plants previously known, although many of these plants had been developed into much more productive hybrids. This may be the period in which irrigation was first used.

Although a few new types of chipped stone tools, woven cotton fabrics, and new kinds of ground-stone tools appear, the great majority of the materials we uncovered consisted of pieces of broken pottery. These vessels were well made. They were mainly monochrome (white or grey), though there were a few bichromes. About half of all the vessels found were flat-bottomed bowls; the rest were ollas, water-bottles, composite silhouette bowls, and other forms. Decoration was usually achieved by incising on the interior bottoms of bowls or on the rims or lips, but a few of the vessels have plain rocker stamping, negative painting, and engraving.

Perhaps it was during this period that Mesoamerica became divided into two units, each with a distinctive cultural development (*12*). One development, in the lowlands, may have been based on milpa (slash-and-burn) agriculture and have culminated in the development of ceremonial centers, run by a priestly hierachy. The other development may have been based on irrigation agriculture and have culminated in the rise of secular cities. The Tehuacán sequence would be an example of this second type.

Palo Blanco Phase

This Santa Maria phase developed into the Palo Blanco period, dated between 200 B.C. and A.D. 700 by eight radiocarbon determinations (see Fig. 7). On the basis of information and materials from 17 excavated components and from about 150 sites found in survey, we are able to make the following reconstruction about the way of life of the people of this phase. They, too, were full-time agriculturalists, and they systematically used irrigation. Besides the previously known domesticates, they had acquired tomatoes, peanuts, lima beans, guavas, and turkeys. They lived in wattle-and-daub villages or hamlets either oriented toward or adjacent to large hilltop ceremonial centers having elaborate stone pyramids, plazas, ball courts, and other structures. Some of these ruins covered whole mountain tops and, in terms of population, might be considered cities, albeit sacred cities. Perhaps these centers were under the authority of priest-kings; if so, the priest-kings certainly must have been assisted by full-time specialists and a hierarchy of bureaucrats, at least to run the irrigation works.

The manufactured products were varied and more elaborate than those of previous phases. The fine grey and orange pottery, the obsidian working, the bark cloth, and the elaborately woven cotton fabrics are particularly distinctive.

In terms of relationships, Palo Blanco seems to be an extension of the Monte Alban III (and IV?) cultures of Central Oaxaca and shows similarities to cultures in the so-called "Classic Period" of Mesoamerica (5). Why this period in the highlands is considered more "classic" than the later periods has never been satisfactorily explained.

Venta Salada Phase

The final period, Venta Salada, is placed, on the basis of five carbon-14 determinations, between A.D. 700 and 1540 (see Fig. 8). Study of the records of early Spanish conquerors of the Tehuacán Valley should shed further light on this phase. Studies made so far reveal that these people were full-time agriculturalists who had irrigation. Further, their economy was greatly supplemented by commerce with other regions. Local salt-making and cotton-processing industries made products for exportation. Politically, the Valley seems to have been divided up into a series of little kingdoms each of which had urban centers with surrounding hamlets. Among the manufactured articles were such distinctive artifacts as polychrome pottery, a wide variety of cotton fabrics, bark cloth, chipped stone tools, and arrow points. Since we have excavated over 15 occupations of this final phase and have found about 200 sites in surface surveys, and also have excellent ethnohistorical records available, it will eventually be possible to reconstruct a fairly clear picture of the culture of the final preconquest phase. So far this has not been done.

Conclusion

Obviously, our studies are far from complete, even though some tentative conclusions have been expressed in this article. As more of our data are analyzed and the results are correlated, the total history of the Tehuacán Valley will become better understood. At present, some 30 authors, including myself, are in the process of getting six volumes about our work in Tehuacán ready for publication. Certainly these final volumes will contain information which will permit more perceptive and specific comparisons to be made with other prehistoric cultural developments in Mexico and South America, as well as with sequences in the Old World. Such analysis should lead to more cogent and better documented generalizations about the how's and why's of the rise of civilization than have been expressed heretofore.

References and Notes

1. R. S. MacNeish, "First Annual Report of the Tehuacán Archaeological-Botanical Project," *Rept. No. 1* (Robert S. Peabody Foundation for Archaeology, Andover, Mass., 1961).
2. Drs. P. C. Mangelsdorf and W. C. Galinat of the Harvard Botanical Museum and E. J. Wellhausen and R. Hathaway of the Rockefeller Foundation studied the corn remains; Drs. T. Whitaker, senior geneticist of the U.S. Department of Agriculture, and H. Cutler, executive director of the Missouri Botanical Gardens, investigated the prehistoric cucurbits, and Dr. L. Kaplan of Roosevelt University studied the prehistoric beans. Dr. C. E. Smith of the U.S. Department of Agriculture made botanical studies in the Tehuacán Valley; Dr. R. Drake, at the University of British Columbia, identified the shells; and Dr. Eric C. Callen, of McDonald College of McGill University, analyzed the human feces found in the caves. Miss Monica Bopp, and later Dr. James Shoenwetter of the University of Southern Illinois, studied various pollen profiles in the valley to determine ancient changes in climate and vegetation. Dr. Carmen Cook De Leonard of the Centro de Investigaciones Antropologicas of Mexico aided us with her knowledge of the ethnohistory and ethnobotany of the Tehuacán Valley, and Mrs. I. Johnson of the National Museum of Mexico examined the textiles we found in the excavations. Kent Flannery, a student at the University of Chicago, identified the 12,000 archeological bones we uncovered; Dr. J. L. Lorenzo, chief of the Prehistoric Section of the Instituto de Antropologia of Mexico, and Dr. J. Moser of the Federal Department of Geology of Mexico surveyed the geology, and Dr. R. Woodbury of the U.S. National Museum, Dr. J. Anderson of the University of Buffalo, and D. Byers of the R. S. Peabody Foundation investigated, respectively, the ancient irrigation systems, the human skeletal remains, and the geography of the Valley. F. Johnson, also of the R. S. Peabody Foundation, carried out a program of dating the archeological remains by the carbon-14 method.
3. The Tehuacán field staff included Mr. Peterson, assistant director; Dr. M. Fowler of the University of Southern Illinois; F. Johnson of the R. S. Peabody Foundation; K. Flannery of the University of Chicago; R. L. Chadwick of Mexico City College; Angel Garcia Cook and A. Arbide of the School of Anthropology of Mexico; and Miss A. Nelken, a student of the Sorbonne in Paris, and her two "Tehuacanero" assistants in the laboratory, N. Tejeda and F. Molina.
4. The names of the various phases were taken from the name of the site or cave where these cultural complexes were first unearthed.
5. G. R. Willey, *Science* **131**, 73 (1960).
6. L. Avelayra Arroyo de Anda, in *Esplendor del Mexico Antiguo* (Mexico, 1959).
7. J. H. Steward, *Bur. Am. Ethnol. Bull.* **120**, (1938).
8. J. D. Jennings, "Danger Cave," *Society of American Archeology Memoir No. 14* (1957).
9. R. S. MacNeish, *Katunob* **1**, No. 2 (1960) (published in Magnolia, Ark.).
10. P. C. Mangelsdorf, R. S. MacNeish, G. R. Willey, "Origins of Middle American agriculture," in *Middle American Handbook* (Bureau of American Ethnology, in press).
11. V. G. Child, *Social Evolution* (Shuman, New York, 1951).
12. R. S. MacNeish, *Trans. Am. Phil. Soc.* **44**, pt. 5 (1954).
13. G. W. Lowe, "The Chiapas Project, 1955–8," *Publications of the New World Archeological Foundation* (Orinda, Calif., 1959); M. D. Coe, "La Victoria, an Early Site on the Pacific Coast of Guatemala," vol. 53 of *Peabody Museum of Archeology and Enthology Publs.* (1961).
14. H. S. Spinden, "Ancient Civilizations of Mexico and Central America," *American Museum of Natural History Handbook Ser. No. 3* (1928); M. Coe, *Mexico* (Thames and Hudson, London, 1962).
15. A. Caso, *Urnas de Oaxaca* (Instituto Nacional de Antropologia e Historia, Mexico, 1952).
16. G. C. Valliant, "Early Cultures of the Valley of Mexico," vol. 35 of *American Museum of Natural History, New York, Anthropological Papers* (1935), pt. 111.
17. The actual investigations were organized under the auspices of the Robert S. Peabody Foundation for Archaeology, Andover, Mass., and were financially supported by generous grants-in-aid from the National Science Foundation and the Rockefeller Foundation. The Tehuacán Project also received support and assistance from the Instituto de Antropologia e Historia of the Government of Mexico.

Microenvironments and Mesoamerican Prehistory

Fine-scale ecological analysis clarifies the transition to settled life in pre-Columbian times.

Michael D. Coe and Kent V. Flannery

A crucial period in the story of the pre-Columbian cultures of the New World is the transition from a hunting-and-collecting way of life to effective village farming. We are now fairly certain that Mesoamerica (*1*) is the area in which this took place, and that the time span involved is from approximately 6500 to 1000 B.C., a period during which a kind of "incipient cultivation" based on a few domesticated plants, mainly maize, gradually supplemented and eventually replaced wild foods (*2*). Beginning probably about 1500 B.C., and definitely by 1000 B.C., villages with all of the signs of the settled arts, such as pottery and loom-weaving, appear throughout Mesoamerica, and the foundations of pre-Columbian civilization may be said to have been established.

Dr. Coe is associate professor of anthropology at Yale University, New Haven, Conn. Kent Flannery is a graduate student in the department of anthropology, University of Chicago, Chicago, Ill.

Much has been written about food-producing "revolutions" in both hemispheres. There is now good evidence both in the Near East and in Mesoamerica that food production was part of a relatively slow *evolution*, but there still remain several problems related to the process of settling down. For the New World, there are three questions which we would like to answer.

1) What factors favored the early development of food production in Mesoamerica as compared with other regions of this hemisphere?

2) What was the mode of life of the earlier hunting-and-collecting peoples in Mesoamerica, and in exactly what ways was it changed by the addition of cultivated plants?

3) When, where, and how did food production make it possible for the first truly sedentary villages to be established in Mesoamerica?

The first of these questions cannot be answered until botanists determine the habits and preferred habitats of the wild ancestors of maize, beans, and the various cucurbits which were domesticated. To answer the other questions, we must reconstruct the human-ecological situations which prevailed.

Some remarkably sophisticated, multidisciplinary projects have been and still are being carried out elsewhere in the world, aimed at reconstructing prehistoric human ecology. However, for the most part they have been concerned with the adaptations of past human communities to large-scale changes in the environment over very long periods—that is, to alterations in the *macroenvironment*, generally caused by climatic fluctuations. Such alterations include the shift from tundra to boreal conditions in northern Europe. Nevertheless, there has been a growing suspicion among prehistorians that macroenvironmental changes are insufficient as an explanation of the possible causes of food production and its effects (*3*), regardless of what has been written to the contrary.

Ethnography and Microenvironments

We have been impressed, in reading anthropologists' accounts of simple societies, with the fact that human communities, while in some senses limited by the macroenvironment—for instance, by deserts or by tropical forests (*4*)—usually exploit several or even a whole series of well-defined *microenvironments* in their quest for food (*5*). These microenvironments might be defined as smaller subdivisions of large ecological zones; examples are the immediate surroundings of the ancient archeological site itself, the bank of a

Reprinted by **permission of the publisher**; SCIENCE 143; pp. 650–654 (1964); by Michael D. Coe and Kent V. Flannery. Copyright 1964 by the American Association for the Advancement of Science.

nearby stream, or a distant patch of forest.

An interesting case is provided by the Shoshonean bands which, until the mid-19th century, occupied territories within the Great Basin of the American West (6). These extremely primitive peoples had a mode of life quite similar to that of the peoples of Mesoamerica of the 5th millennium B.C., who were the first to domesticate maize. The broadly limiting effects of the Great Basin (which, generally speaking, is a desert) and the lack of knowledge of irrigation precluded any effective form of agriculture, even though some bands actually sowed wild grasses and one group tried an ineffective watering of wild crops. Consequently, the Great Basin aborigines remained on a hunting and plant-collecting level, with extremely low population densities and a very simple social organization. However, Steward's study (6) shows that each band was not inhabiting a mere desert but moved on a strictly followed seasonal round among a vertically and horizontally differentiated set of microenvironments, from the lowest salt flats up to piñon forest, which were "niches" in a human-ecological sense.

The Great Basin environment supplied the potential for cultural development or lack of it, but the men who lived there selected this or that microenvironment. Steward clearly shows that *how* and *to what* they adapted influenced many other aspects of their culture, from their technology to their settlement pattern, which was necessarily one of restricted wandering from one seasonally occupied camp to another.

Seasonal wandering would appear to be about the only possible response of a people without animal or plant husbandry to the problem of getting enough food throughout the year. Even the relatively rich salmon-fishing cultures of the Northwest Coast (British Columbia and southern Alaska) were without permanently occupied villages. Contrariwise, it has seemed to us that only a drastic reduction of the number of niches to be exploited, and a concentration of these in space, would have permitted the establishment of full-time village life. The ethnographic data suggest that an analysis of microenvironments or niches would throw much light on the processes by which the Mesoamerican peoples settled down.

Methodology

If the environment in which an ancient people lived was radically different from any known today, and especially if it included animal and plant species which are now extinct and whose behavior is consequently unknown, then any reconstruction of the subsistence activities of the people is going to be difficult. All one could hope for would be a more-or-less sound reconstruction of general ecological conditions, while a breakdown of the environment into smaller ecological niches would be impossible. However, much if not most archeological research concerns periods so recent in comparison with the million or so years of human prehistory that in most instances local conditions have not changed greatly in the interval between the periods investigated and the present.

If we assume that there is a continuity between the ancient and the modern macroenvironment in the area of interest, there are three steps which we must take in tracing the role of microenvironments.

1) Analysis of the present-day microecology (from the human point of view) of the archeological zone. Archeological research is often carried out in remote and little known parts of the earth, which have not been studied from the point of view of natural history. Hence, the active participation of botanists, zoologists, and other natural scientists is highly recommended.

The modern ethnology of the region should never be neglected, for all kinds of highly relevant data on the use of surrounding niches by local people often lie immediately at hand. We have found in Mesoamerica that the workmen on the "dig" are a mine of such information. There may be little need to thumb through weighty reports on the Australian aborigines or South African Bushmen when the analogous custom can be found right under one's nose (7). The end result of the analysis should be a map of the microenvironments defined (here aerial photographs are of great use), with detailed data on the seasonal possibilities each offers human communities on certain technological levels of development.

2) Quantitative analysis of food remains in the archeological sites, and of the technical equipment (arrow or spear points, grinding stones for seeds, baskets and other containers, and so on) related to food-getting. It is a rare site report that treats of bones and plant remains in any but the most perfunctory way. It might seem a simple thing to ship animal bones from a site to a specialist for identification, but most archeologists know that many zoologists consider identification of recent faunal remains a waste of time (8). Because of this, and because many museum collections do not include postcranial skeletons that could be used for identification, the archeologist must arrange to secure his own comparative collection. If this collection is assembled by a zoologist on the project, a by-product of the investigation would be a faunal study of microenvironments. Similarly, identification of floral and other specimens from the site would lead to other specialized studies.

3) Correlation of the archeological with the microenvironmental study in an overall analysis of the ancient human ecology.

The Tehuacán Valley

An archeological project undertaken by R. S. MacNeish, with such a strategy in mind, has been located since 1961 in the dry Tehuacán Valley of southern Puebla, Mexico (2, 9). The valley is fringed with bone-dry caves in which the food remains of early peoples have been preserved to a remarkable degree in stratified deposits. For a number of reasons, including the results of his past archeological work in Mesoamerica, MacNeish believed that he would find here the origins of maize agriculture in the New World, and he has been proved right. It now seems certain that the wild ancestor of maize was domesticated in the Tehuacán area some time around the beginning of the 5th millennium B.C.

While the Tehuacán environment is in general a desert, the natural scientists of the project have defined within it four microenvironments (Fig. 1).

1) *Alluvial valley floor*, a level plain sparsely covered with mesquite, grasses, and cacti, offering fairly good possibilities, especially along the Río Salado, for primitive maize agriculture dependent on rainfall.

2) *Travertine slopes*, on the west side of the valley. This would have been a niche useful for growing maize

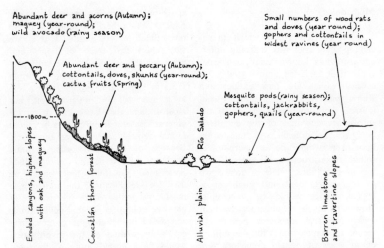

Fig. 1. An idealized east-west transection of the central part of the Tehuacán Valley, Puebla, Mexico, showing microenvironments and the seasons in which the food resources are exploited. East is to the left. The length of the area represented is about 20 kilometers.

and tomatoes and for trapping cottontail rabits.

3) *Coxcatlán thorn forest*, with abundant seasonal crops of wild fruits, such as various species of *Opuntia*, pitahaya, and so on. There is also a seasonal abundance of whitetail deer, cottontail rabbits, and skunks, and there are some peccaries.

4) *Eroded canyons*, unsuitable for exploitation except for limited hunting of deer and as routes up to maguey fields for those peoples who chewed the leaves of that plant.

The correlation of this study with the analysis, by specialists, of the plant and animal remains (these include bones, maize cobs, chewed quids, and even feces) found in cave deposits has shown that the way of life of the New World's first farmers was not very different from that of the Great Basin aborigines in the 19th century. Even the earliest inhabitants of the valley, prior to 6500 B.C., were more collectors of seasonally gathered wild plant foods than they were "big game hunters," and they traveled in microbands in an annual, wet-season-dry-season cycle (*10*). While slightly more sedentary macrobands appeared with the adoption of simple maize cultivation after 5000 B.C., these people nevertheless still followed the old pattern of moving from microenvironment to microenvironment, separating into microbands during the dry season.

The invention and gradual improvement of agriculture seem to have made few profound alterations in the settlement pattern of the valley for many millennia. Significantly, by the Formative period (from about 1500 B.C. to A.D. 200), when agriculture based on a hybridized maize was far more important than it had been in earlier periods as a source of food energy, the pattern was still one of part-time nomadism (*11*). In this part of the dry Mexican highlands, until the Classic period (about A.D. 200 to 900), when irrigation appears to have been introduced into Tehuacán, food production had still to be supplemented with extensive plant collecting and hunting.

Most of the peoples of the Formative period apparently lived in large villages on the alluvial valley floor during the wet season, from May through October of each year, for planting had to be done in May and June, and harvesting, in September and October. In the dry season, from November through February, when the trees and bushes had lost their leaves and the deer were easy to see and track, some of the population must have moved to hunting camps, principally in the Coxcatlán thorn forest. By February, hunting had become less rewarding as the now-wary deer moved as far as possible from human habitation; however, in April and May the thorn forest was still ripe for exploitation, as many kinds of wild fruit matured. In May it was again time to return to the villages on the valley floor for spring planting.

Now, in some other regions of Mesoamerica there were already, during the Formative period, fully sedentary village cultures in existence. It is clear that while the Tehuacán valley was the locus of the first domestication of maize, the origins of full-blown village life lie elsewhere. Because of the constraining effects of the macroenvironment, the Tehuacán people were exploiting, until relatively late in Mesoamerican prehistory, as widely spaced and as large a number of microenvironments as the Great Basin aborigines were exploiting in the 19th century.

Coastal Guatemala

Near the modern fishing port of Ocós, only a few kilometers from the Mexican border on the alluvial plain of the Pacific coast of Guatemala, we have found evidence for some of the

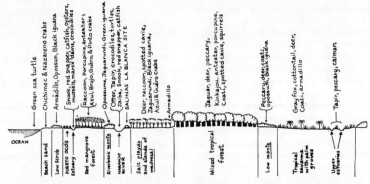

Fig. 2. Northeast-southwest transection of the Ocós area of coastal Guatemala, showing microenvironments in relation to the site of Salinas La Blanca. Northeast is to the right. The length of the area represented is about 15 kilometers.

oldest permanently occupied villages in Mesoamerica (*12*). We have also made an extensive study of the ecology and ethnology of the Ocós area.

From this study (*13*) we have defined no less than eight distinct microenvironments (Fig. 2) within an area of only about 90 square kilometers. These are as follows:

1) *Beach sand and low scrub.* A narrow, infertile strip from which the present-day villagers collect occasional mollusks, a beach crab called *chichimeco* and one known as *nazareño*, and the sea turtle and its eggs.

2) *The marine estuary-and-lagoon system*, in places extending considerably inland and ultimately connecting with streams or rivers coming down from the Sierra Madre. The estuaries, with their mangrove-lined banks, make up the microenvironment richest in wild foods in the entire area. The brackish waters abound in catfish (*Arius* sp. and *Galeichthys* sp.), red snapper (*Lutjanus colorado*), several species of snook (*Centropomus* sp.), and many other kinds of fish. Within living memory, crocodiles (*Crocodylus astutus*) were common, but they have by now been hunted almost to extinction. The muddy banks of the estuaries are the habitat of many kinds of mollusks, including marsh clams (*Polymesoda radiata*), mussels (*Mytella falcata*), and oysters (*Ostrea columbiensis*), and they also support an extensive population of fiddler and mud crabs.

3) *Mangrove forest*, consisting mainly of stilt-rooted red mangrove, which slowly gives way to white mangrove as one moves away from the estuary. We noted high populations of collared anteater (*Tamandua tetradactyla*) and arboreal porcupine (*Coendu mexicanus*). A large number of crabs (we did not determine the species) inhabit this microenvironment; these include, especially, one known locally as the *azul* (blue) crab, on which a large population of raccoons feeds.

4) *Riverine*, comprising the channels and banks of the sluggish Suchiate and Naranjo rivers, which connect with the lagoon-estuary system not far from their mouths. Freshwater turtles, catfish, snook, red snapper, and mojarra (*Cichlasoma* sp.) are found in these waters; the most common animal along the banks is the green iguana (*Iguana iguana*).

5) *Salt playas*, the dried remnants of ancient lagoon-and-estuary systems which are still subject to inundation during the wet season, with localized stands of a tree known as *madresal* ("mother of salt"). Here there is an abundance of game, including whitetail deer and the black iguana (*Ctenosaura similis*), as well as a rich supply of salt.

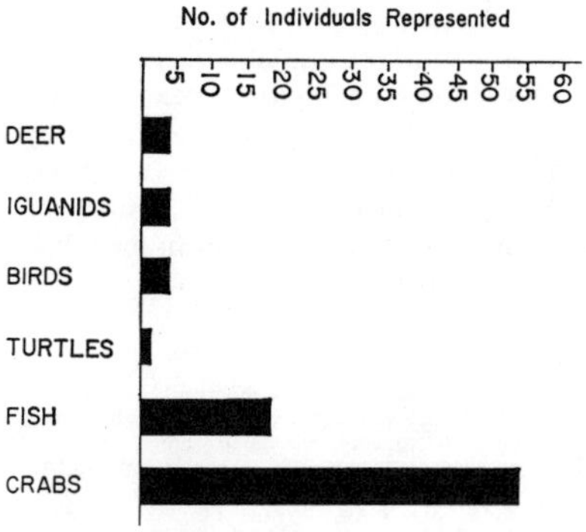

6) *Mixed tropical forest*, found a few kilometers inland, in slightly higher and better drained situations than the salt *playas*. This forest includes mostly tropical evergreens like the ceiba, as well as various zapote and fan palms, on the fruit of which a great variety of mammals thrive—the kinkajou, the spotted cavy, the coatimundi, the raccoon, and even the gray fox. The soils here are highly suitable for maize agriculture.

7) *Tropical savannah*, occupying poorly drained patches along the upper stream and estuary systems of the area. This is the major habitat in the area for cottontail rabbits and gray foxes. Other common mammals are the coatimundi and armadillo.

8) *Cleared fields and second growth*, habitats which have been created by agriculturists, and which are generally confined to areas that were formerly mixed tropical forest.

Among the earliest Formative cultures known thus far for the Ocós area is the Cuadros phase, dated by radiocarbon analysis at about 1000 to 850 B.C. and well represented in the site of Salinas La Blanca, which we excavated in 1962 (*14*). The site is on the banks of the Naranjo River among a variety of microenvironments; it consists of two flattish mounds built up from deeply stratified refuse layers representing house foundations of a succession of hamlets or small villages.

Fig. 3. Animal remains, exclusive of mollusks, found in Cuadros phase levels at Salinas La Blanca.

From our analysis of this refuse we have a good idea of the way in which the Cuadros people lived. Much of the refuse consists of potsherds from large, neckless jars, but very few of the clay figurines that abound in other Formative cultures of Mesoamerica were found. We discovered many plant remains; luckily these had been preserved or "fossilized" through replacement of the tissues by carbonates. From these we know that the people grew and ate a nonhybridized maize considerably more advanced than the maize which was then being grown in Tehuacán (*15*). The many impressions of leaves in clay floors in the site will, we hope, eventually make it possible to reconstruct the flora that immediately surrounded the village.

The identification of animal remains (Fig. 3), together with our ecological study and with the knowledge that the people had a well-developed maize agriculture, gives a great deal of information on the subsistence activities of these early coastal villagers. First of all, we believe they had no interest whatever in hunting, a conclusion reinforced by our failure to find a single projectile point in the site. The few deer bones that have been recovered are all from immature individuals that could have been encountered by chance and clubbed to death. Most of the other remains are of animals that could have been collected in the environs of the village, specifically in the lagoon-estuary system and the flanking mangrove forest, where the people fished, dug for marsh clams, and, above all, caught crabs (primarily the *azul* crab, which is trapped at night). Entirely missing are many edible species found in other microenvironments, such as raccoon, cottontail rabbit, peccary, spotted cavy, and nine-banded armadillo.

There is no evidence at all that occupation of Salinas La Blanca was seasonal. An effective food production carried out on the rich, deep soils of the mixed tropical forest zone, together with the food resources of the lagoon-estuary system, made a permanently settled life possible. Looked at another way, developed maize agriculture had so reduced the number and spacing of the niches which had to be exploited that villages could be occupied the year round (*16*).

Conditions similar to those of the Ocós area are found all along the Pacific Coast of Guatemala and along the

Gulf Coast of southern Veracruz and Tabasco in Mexico, and we suggest that the real transition to village life took place there and not in the dry Mexican highlands, where maize was domesticated initially (*17*).

Conclusion

The interpretation of archeological remains through a fine-scale analysis of small ecological zones throws new light on the move toward sedentary life in Mesoamerican prehistory. In our terms, the basic difference between peoples who subsist on wild foods and those who dwell in permanent villages is that the former must exploit a wide variety of small ecological niches in a seasonal pattern—niches which are usually scattered over a wide range of territory—while the latter may, because of an effective food production, concentrate on one or on only a few microenvironments which lie relatively close at hand.

Fine-scale ecological analysis indicates that there never was any such thing as an "agricultural revolution" in Mesoamerica, suddenly and almost miraculously resulting in village life. The gradual addition of domesticates such as maize, beans, and squash to the diet of wild plant and animal foods hardly changed the way of life of the Tehuacán people for many thousands of years, owing to a general paucity of the environment, and seasonal nomadism persisted until the introduction of irrigation. It probably was not until maize was taken to the alluvial, lowland littoral of Mesoamerica, perhaps around 1500 B.C., that permanently occupied villages became possible, through reduction of the number of microenvironments to which men had to adapt themselves.

References and Notes

1. Mesoamerica is the name given to that part of Mexico and Central America which was civilized in pre-Columbian times. For an excellent summary of its prehistory, see G. R. Willey, *Science* **131**, 73 (1960).
2. R. S. MacNeish, *Science* **143**, 531 (1964).
3. See C. A. Reed and R. J. Braidwood, "Toward the reconstruction of the environmental sequence of Northeastern Iraq," in R. J. Braidwood and B. Howe, "Prehistoric Investigations in Iraqi Kurdistan," *Oriental Institute, University of Chicago, Studies in Ancient Oriental Civilization No. 31* (1960), p. 163. Reed and Braidwood also convincingly reject the technological-deterministic approach of V. G. Childe and his followers.
4. See B. J. Meggers, *Am. Anthropologist* **56**, 801 (1954), for an environmental-deterministic view of the constraining effects of tropical forests on human cultures.
5. See F. Barth, *ibid.* **58**, 1079 (1956), for a microenvironmental approach by an ethnologist to the exceedingly complex interrelationships between sedentary agriculturists, agriculturists practicing transhumant herding, and nomadic herders in the state of Swat, Pakistan.
6. J. H. Steward, "Basin-Plateau Aboriginal Sociopolitical Groups," *Smithsonian Inst. Bur. Am. Ethnol. Bull.* **120** (1938).
7. The pitfalls of searching for ethnological data relevant to archeological problems among cultures far-flung in time and space are stressed by J. G. D. Clark, *Prehistoric Europe, The Economic Basis* (Philosophical Library, New York, 1952), p. 3.
8. See W. W. Taylor, Ed., "The identification of non-artifactual archaeological materials," *Natl. Acad. Sci.–Natl. Res. Council Publ. 565* (1957). For a general article on the analysis of food remains in archeological deposits see R. F. Heizer in "Application of quantitative methods in archaeology," *Viking Fund Publications in Anthropology No. 28* (1960), pp. 93–157.
9. P. C. Mangelsdorf, R. S. MacNeish, W. C. Gallinat, *Science* **143**, 538 (1964). We thank Dr. MacNeish for permission to use unpublished data of the Tehuacán Archaeological-Botanical Project in this article.
10. R. S. MacNeish, *Second Annual Report of the Tehuacán Archaeological-Botanical Project* (Robert S. Peabody Foundation for Archaeology, Andover, Mass., 1962).
11. The research discussed in this and the following paragraph was carried out by Flannery as staff zoologist for the Tehuacán project during the field seasons of 1962 and 1963; see K. V. Flannery, "Vertebrate Fauna and Prehistoric Hunting Patterns in the Tehuacán Valley" (Robert S. Peabody Foundation for Archaeology, Andover, Mass., in press); ———, thesis, Univ. of Chicago, in preparation.
12. M. D. Coe, "La Victoria, an early site on the Pacific Coast of Guatemala," *Peabody Museum, Harvard, Papers No. 53* (1961).
13. The study was carried out largely by Flannery.
14. The final report on Salinas La Blanca by Coe and Flannery is in preparation. The research was supported by the National Science Foundation under a grant to the Institute of Andean Research, as part of the program "Interrelationships of New World Cultures." The oldest culture in the area is the Ocós phase, which has complex ceramics and figurines; the paleoecology of Ocós is less well known than that of Cuadros, which directly follows it in time.
15. P. C. Mangelsdorf, who has very kindly examined these maize specimens, informs us that they are uncontaminated with *Tripsacum*, and that probably all belong to the primitive lowland race, Nal-Tel.
16. To paraphrase the concept of "primary forest efficiency," developed by J. R. Caldwell ["Trend and Tradition in the Eastern United States," *Am. Anthropol. Assoc. Mem. No. 88* (1958)], we might think of the Cuadros phase as leaning to a "primary lagoon-estuary efficiency." We might think the same of the Ocós phase of the same region, which may date back to 1500 B.C.
17. An additional factor which may in part account for the priority of coastal Guatemala over Tehuacán in the achievement of a sedentary mode of life is the presence of an extensive system of waterways in the former region, which might have made it less necessary for local communities to move to productive sources of food. By means of canoes, a few persons could have brought the products of other niches to the village. However, our evidence indicates that the Cuadros people largely ignored the possibilities of exploiting distant niches.

Crops, Soils, and Culture in America

Ralph Linton*

ANTHROPOLOGISTS have long recognized the effect of environment on culture but the interrelations are so complex that it is almost impossible to grasp them in their entirety. The potentialities of any environment for any society are a function of the interaction of the natural environment and the society's techniques for exploiting it. Thus the potential food supply in any region will be determined, for an agricultural people, not only by climate and soil but also by the nature of the crops which they possess and their methods of raising them. To cite a single example, the introduction of wheat and of European methods of cultivation have opened to agricultural settlements thousands of square miles in North America which were not available to Indian groups raising maize by aboriginal methods. It is the purpose of this paper to point out certain of these interrelations which seem to have been overlooked and to suggest their possible influence on the growth of American cultures and on the establishment of particular patterns of settlement in various regions.

It is generally recognized that complex technology and elaborate political organization can only develop or survive in the presence of fairly dense populations. It is also recognized that the possible density of population in any region is normally linked with the local food supply. The exceptions to this rule which occur as a result of modern methods of transport and communication can be ignored in the present discussion. However, it is less generally recognized that the significance of a food supply for population support depends not only on its quantity but also on its qualities. The number of persons who can be fed from a certain area is determined by considerations of a balanced ration and will be only slightly affected by a surplus of any one of the elements necessary for such a ration.

* Swarthmore, A.B., 1915; Pennsylvania, A.M., 1916; Harvard, Ph.D., 1925; now Professor of Anthropology, Columbia.

Reprinted by permission of the publisher from THE MAYA AND THEIR NEIGHBORS; pp. 32-40; by Richard J. Thurman. Copyright 1962 University of Utah Press.

What constitutes a balanced ration is, in itself, an exceedingly complex problem. In spite of the rapid progress of research along this line we are still very much in the dark as to the minimum amount of vitamins and minerals necessary to insure health and it is quite possible that certain as yet unsuspected substances may enter into the picture. The writer is not an expert on nutrition and the present discussion will, therefore, be confined to one of the simplest aspects of the problem, that of a protein and starch balance. There seems to be abundant evidence that although our species can adapt itself to a starchless diet, it cannot survive on one which lacks a certain minimum of proteins and fats. Thus there are human groups who live exclusively on meat and/or fish or on a combination of meat and dairy products but there are no human groups who live on starch foods without the addition of proteins. This means that an agriculture which confines itself to the raising of starch crops cannot form the exclusive basis of a people's food economy.

If we turn to the Old World we find that throughout most of Eurasia and Africa a balanced ration was provided by a combination of starch crops and dairy products. It was the latter, rather than the simple domestication of animals which, in combination with agriculture, made possible large and settled populations. Milking the herd provided many times the proteins and fats which might have been obtained by killing from the herd. In further Asia, where the dairying pattern never penetrated, the need for protein was met in some regions by a local protein crop, the soya bean, and in others by the rearing of pigs and chickens, supplemented by fishing and local small game. Where the people were within reach of the sea sufficient proteins and fats could be obtained by fishing alone. This was the situation which obtained in most of Oceania, where the local crops were almost exclusively starch crops. In Polynesia, where there was no native game, a tribe which was cut off from the sea, was in desperate straits even when it had abundant land for agriculture. In Melanesia, where there is some game in the larger islands, we find that interior populations are usually much sparser than the quantity of land available for agriculture would seem to justify and that there is frequently a trade in fish between the coastal and interior tribes.

In America there were comparatively few domestic animals and those present made only a slight contribution to the aboriginal food supply. Dogs and turkeys were eaten in some places but were luxuries rather than staples, while the South American llama and related species were never milked and were too valuable for wool and transport to be killed except on ceremonial occasions. Proteins and fats had to be obtained by hunting and fishing, by gathering wild plants or by raising special crops. Actually, all the higher American cultures were based on a combination of starch and protein crops just as all the civilizations of the Old World were based on a combination of starch crops and domestic animals.

In his exceedingly stimulating article on American Agricultural Origins [1] Dr. Carl Sauer has stressed the large number of starch crops raised by the American Indians. He concludes on the basis of several sorts of evidence that most of these crops were domesticated independently and in different regions and suggests the probability of the independent invention of agriculture at several points in South and Middle America. He further concludes that these original centers of agriculture were all located in valleys or plateaus of moderate altitude, i. e. in inland regions.[2] This point is of considerable importance to the present discussion, for it means that the earliest American farmers were cut off from sea fishing, one of the surest and most abundant sources of proteins and fats.

In contrast with the multiplicity of American starch crops the number of protein crops was decidedly limited. There were only two of any importance, the peanut and the bean, the latter in numerous varieties. Recent investigations of Russian botanists, summarized by Dr. Sauer,[3] indicate that the peanut was originally a native of Brazil, the bean of Middle America. Whether the domestication of these two plants was contemporaneous with the domestication of starch crops in the same localities cannot be determined at present. However, maize appears in our own Southwest in much older cultural horizons than does the bean and if the two crops appeared in Middle America at the same time it is hard to see why one should have been diffused northward without the other. It seems probable, therefore, that maize culture was established in Middle America before bean culture.

An inland people who had no domestic food animals and who raised only starch crops would have great difficulty in developing or maintaining a dense population. They would have to depend upon hunting and wild foods such as nuts or legumes for their proteins

[1] Sauer, American Agricultural Origins, 1936.
[2] *Op. cit.*, pp. 283–284.
[3] *Op. cit.*, pp. 289–290.

and fats. This would set a fairly low upper limit to the size of population and especially of localized aggregates. To hunt and gather wild foods successfully the people would have to live in small and widely spaced communities. In time such farmers-food gatherers might develop considerable skill in cultivation but a mere increase in the quantity of starch foods raised would not solve their problem. There would be a definite ceiling, set by the supply of wild proteins, beyond which their population could not increase without encountering dietary deficiencies. This, in turn, would set a limit to the level of culture which they could maintain. Large aggregates can afford to support specialists while small aggregates cannot.

Let us assume for the sake of argument that agriculture was invented, and various starch crops domesticated, independently in several places in the New World. If so, there must have been many communities scattered over the two continents who had the habit of crop raising but who were subject to the limitations on population growth imposed by protein deficiency. The domestication of a local protein yielding plant, or the introduction of such a plant through diffusion, would remove this limitation. A new and much higher ceiling for population would be set, depending mainly upon the amount of arable land available, and until this ceiling was reached there would be boom times. The size of local aggregates could be greatly increased and the stage set for rapid cultural advance. If the protein crop was a diffused one, this change might occur with great speed. To a people already familiar with agriculture the acceptance of a new crop is an easy matter as we know from the rapidity with which American food plants spread through the Old World after the discovery of America.

It is interesting to check this hypothesis against the known development of culture in the Southwest. Here we have indisputable evidence of a comparatively brief period of very rapid cultural advance with a strong suggestion that this was correlated with a great increase in population. The period of advance seems to have been preceded by a much longer period, lower limits still unknown, during which the development of culture was slow while it was followed by another long period of comparative culture stabilization. It also seems that the period of rapid advance cannot be accounted for on the basis of sudden contact with and borrowing from some other culture. The Anasazi line of culture development runs uninterruptedly from the Basket Makers to the builders of the great pueblos and unbroken evolutionary series can be traced for most of the elements present. We must conclude that Basket Maker culture received a sudden stimulus of some sort. We know that, although the Basket Makers raised corn and squashes from early times, the bean does not appear in the Southwest until shortly before the period of culture flowering. It seems probable, therefore, that the introduction of this protein crop, with the consequent raising of the population ceiling, was responsible for the sudden release of cultural energy.

There are suggestions for such a period of rapid change and advance in the Southeast also, although the evidence there is much less conclusive and an exact chronology is lacking. The finding of seeds of domesticated and improved rag weed and amaranth in Bluff Dwellers sites and the fact that these crops seem to have been allowed to lapse by the period of first European contact may indicate an independent development of agriculture in this region. Such evidence as we have for the introduction of corn and beans into the Southeast seems to indicate that, if they were not introduced together, the time interval separating the two introductions was short. The sudden advance of Southeastern culture may, therefore, have been due to the introduction of a maize-bean complex into a region where agricultural techniques were already known but where the crops were inadequate. Such an introduction would provide a balanced ration at a single stroke and make possible a rapid population increase.

Even in Middle America there seems to be evidence of a period of rapid cultural advance. Although the Maya civilization did not rise out of darkness as abruptly as once supposed, its sudden flowering in the Old Empire certainly suggests some stimulating factor. May this not have been the addition of beans to a pre-existing agricultural complex? The apparent priority of maize over bean culture in Middle America has already been noted.

Other things being equal, one might expect the period of rapid population advance and cultural flowering to continue in any region until all available new land had been brought under cultivation. After this the population would decline with the diminishing food supply until it stabilized at a level which could be maintained by re-utilization of land. This level would be determined by a combination of the nature of the local soils and of the techniques for exploiting them provided by the particular culture. The latter would, of course, include not only methods of tillage and fertilization or crop rotation but also facilities for land clearance. The importance of weed growth to land re-utilization has been brought out by recent researches of the Carnegie Foundation in Yucatan.[4]

American agriculture, outside two or three centers of high civilization, was comparatively crude. There was only sporadic use of fertilizers or crop rotation, the main method for restoring used soils being simple fallowing. Soils naturally varied with the locality, but there were certain climatic factors which were of importance to both soil exhaustion and rejuvenation. Where rains are light, the substances necessary to crop growth remain in the upper levels of the soil where they are readily available. The fertility of most desert lands when water can be brought to them is proverbial. In tropical regions of heavy rainfall, on the other hand, the warm rains leach out the mineral content of the surface soil and carry it down beyond the reach of ordinary crop roots. In moist temperate regions the conditions are intermediate, depending on quantity and season of precipitation. Thus a soil of given mineral content will grow crops longest under semi-arid conditions, for a shorter time under moist temperate ones and for a still shorter time in a tropical rain belt.

Closely connected with these differences in moisture and temperature is the factor of weed growth. This is of the utmost importance to agriculturalists who lack metal tools. In semi-arid regions weed growth is slow and comparatively scanty, making the annual reconditioning of cleared fields easy. In moist temperate ones the growth is more rapid and abundant, but it reaches its climax in regions of tropical rainfall where the growth is so rapid and dense that almost as much labor is required to reclear a field used even the previous year as to clear long standing jungle.

These factors of soil fertility and weed growth united to impose different patterns of soil utilization in different climatic areas. While the Southwestern tribes could grow corn on the same lands generation after generation, the Indians of the Eastern Woodlands had to change their cultivation every three or four years due to a combination of soil exhaustion and weed seed accumulation. In the wet tropics the same factors, in increased intensity, made it difficult to crop a field more than two years in succession and desirable to clear new fields every year. Recuperation of the land through fallowing followed a similar order. Desert soils recuperated very slowly and areas which had been depleted by long cultivation had to be aban-

[4] Emerson, Milpa System, 1935.

doned for many years. In temperate regions the recuperation was more rapid, due to the heavier plant growth while in jungle areas fifteen to twenty years were required for complete recovery.

Both the total population of an area and the possible size of residential aggregates are intimately related to these factors of soil exhaustion, weed growth and soil recuperation. With Indian techniques of agriculture the long term stabilization point for the population of any area was determined by the possibilities of turnover in fallow and cultivated land. A tribe might actually have bred up to the limits of its assured long term agricultural food supply while much of its territory appeared to be unused. The possible size of the village groups within the tribe was set by the amount of food which could be raised on land exploitable from the village. The extent of this zone of exploitation was roughly determined by the distance to which a man could travel, work in the fields and return on the same day. When it was necessary to guard the fields against raiders, the zone was correspondingly narrowed.

Given the rich soils of semi-arid regions, the scanty weed growth and crops suited to local conditions, large settlements could be established and remain on the same site for several generations. Under such circumstances the population would become so thoroughly rooted that, when soil exhaustion did make itself felt, the people would tend to cling to their settlement until the last possible moment. Perhaps the long dwindling of population which is evident for some of the Southwestern ruined pueblos may have been due to progressive soil exhaustion as well as to the drought period. With the slowness of soil recuperation, fields that had once been exhausted could not be re-utilized for so long a time that the same group would rarely return to them at all.

In tropical rain forests, on the other hand, the soil exhaustion and weed growth were so rapid that villages as large as those of the Southwest would have had to move every two or three years. Actually, the pattern in the American rain forest areas seems to have been that of much smaller local aggregates, but even so a village rarely remained in the same place for as much as a generation. The tribes here had the habit of movement and seem to have drifted long distances with ease. In moist temperate regions, such as the Eastern United States, village movement was also necessary as long as the zone of exploitation was limited by the common residence of the community's members. However, the villagers could remain in one place for a generation or more and moved with corresponding reluctance. Moreover, the rather rapid recuperation of the land under fallowing made it possible for a village to move about within a fairly restricted area, returning to the same territory time after time. This seems to have been the condition which existed among the protohistoric Iroquois and some of the northern agricultural Siouan tribes such as the Winnebago. However, it was most characteristic of the tribes living on the northern margins of the eastern agricultural area, regions in which fortified villages were useful for defense against the neighboring hunting groups. It is interesting to note that whenever this threat was removed, as in the time of Iroquois League dominance, the village populations tended to spread out and the community to remain in the same place for longer intervals.

This fact may provide a clue to the origin of the type of community organization found in the Southeast and in many parts of Middle America. In both these regions we find a development of confederacies or other large political groupings which made large areas comparatively safe from attack. Soils were rich enough here to permit villages to remain in one place long enough to take root. When the soil in the immediate neighborhood of the village began to be exhausted, safety from attack made it possible for the village to expand its zone of exploitation by having its members live at the more distant farms during the agricultural season. In due course of time it might come to be surrounded by isolated families or even hamlets whose inhabitants felt themselves members of the central community although they did not regularly reside there. Since the soil recuperated readily under fallowing, such an extended community might become very large without exceeding the assured year by year food supply. The community would be as firmly rooted in one place as a Southwestern pueblo, but would have quite different characteristics. In particular, the central town from which the scattered population had been derived would tend to become a community center, a place to which the whole group resorted for exchange of goods, councils and ceremonies. This is the pattern which obtains for certain Guatemalan Indian towns today and which probably obtained for most of the Middle American cities of pre-European times. The great temples and squares for assembly found in these cities seem to be quite out of proportion to the apparent size of their constant populations but were adapted to the function of the cities as community centers. Very similar arrangements in town planning are found in our own Southeast where we know that a similar scattering of families on isolated farms existed. These resemblances between the Southeast and Middle America are probably due to a northward diffusion of the pattern, but their acceptance in the Southeast was justified by the similarity of community organization.

In the Southwest this type of community organization never developed. This may have been due in part to the lack of political organizations larger than single villages, with the consequent danger of attack on isolated families. However, soil may also have played a part. With the slowly exhausted, slowly rejuvenated soils of this region there was less stimulus to expanding a village's zone of exploitation while the area required for a really permanent settlement with alternate cultivation and fallowing would have been enormous. The Southwestern village was a highly localized, closely knit community which needed no focal point. Perhaps the failure of the Middle American community center type of town planning to diffuse into the Southwest is due to the fact that the needs to which it was a response did not exist here.

All cultural processes involve a multiplicity of causal factors which, in combination, produce a multiplicity of results. The writer would be the first to admit that the hypotheses which have just been advanced to account for certain observed phenomena of American cultures are much too simple. However, food is the most basic of human needs and the crops and soils from which the American Indians derived it deserve more attention than they have received to date.

THE AGRICULTURAL BASIS
OF URBAN CIVILIZATION IN MESOAMERICA

Angel PALERM

The idea that a relationship exists between irrigation agriculture and the emergence of pre-Columbian urban civilization in Mesoamerica has been advanced by several writers (cf. Armillas, 1951; Palerm, 1952). The introduction of irrigation agriculture creates the possibility of increased population density. This paper will be concerned with the classification of Mesoamerican agricultural systems in their relation to density of population and types of settlement patterns, rural and urban. Likewise the characteristics of Mesoamerican irrigation will be described and the importance of irrigation in Mesoamerica. Out of these considerations the circumstances which made the Valley of Mexico the core of the Central Area of Mesoamerica will be laid bear.

I. The Agricultural Systems and Settlement Patterns in Mesoamerica

The typology proposed here establishes three fundamental agricultural systems: slash-and-burn (roza), fallowing (barbecho) and irrigation (considering the chinampas as a specialized form of irrigation). Our description is based on historical sources and the techniques used today by some native groups. The data on productivity and demographic concomitants and settlement rely mainly on modern fieldwork, but can be checked against information obtained from historical documents.

The slash-and-burn (roza) system

This consists in clearing a section of the forest at a time propitious to the drying of the cut vegetation which is then set on fire. After the fire, the soil is seeded with a digging stick and later weeded periodically. After a varying but generally short time-span, the soil is exhausted and the yield decreases. The field is then abandoned to permit the regeneration of the soil and the return of the forest. A new section is then cut to continue the agricultural cycle. In a very general way, this is the slash-and-burn system typical of the tropical forest of Mesoamerica.

Tajín, a Totonac settlement of Veracruz, Mexico, gave us an opportunity to study the effects of such a system despite the modifications introduced since the Conquest. They are briefly summarized below. (For detailed descriptions, see Kelly and Palerm, 1952, and Palerm, 1952.)

On the average, each Tajín family cultivates a milpa of 1 1/2 hectares, which yields two annual maize harvests. During the initial two or three years the yields are good. After that the milpa is frequently replaced by a vanilla patch which requires the growth of some selected trees. After ten or twelve years the field is abandoned and it enjoys a complete rest for 10 or 12 additional years. We thus have a cycle: milpa -- vanilla patch (with partial return of the forest) -- complete rest. This cycle lasts twenty-four years.

The existence of this cycle implies that 12 hectares of cultivable land are needed for each hectare and a half in actual cultivation. These requirements would be smaller in the absence of the maize-vanilla rotation. On the other hand, the vanilla period also allows for the partial regeneration of the soil and the forest, and vanilla growing, by improving the economic condition of the cultivators, decreases the size of the milpa required per family.

The agricultural pattern functions successfully as long as the cycle is respected and there is sufficient land. If the cycle be contracted, the regeneration of the soil is not adequate. An increase of population is thus only tolerable up to

---

Reprinted from "Irrigation Civilizations: A Comparative Study," PAN AMERICAN UNION, SOCIAL SCIENCE MONOGRAPHS, No. 1, Washington. pp. 28-42.

a certain limit, beyond which land shortages appear. If the cycle is shortened, decreased productivity can be expected. The only solution consists in the emigration of some families in search of new lands.

Naturally, there is a direct relation between population density and the agricultural system, as well as the settlement pattern. The inhabitants can choose between two possibilities: scattered or concentrated settlements. If the latter be picked, the community will tend to cultivate first the land closer to town. In time, the cultivated area is farther and farther away and the distances to the maize fields increasingly inconvenient. Eventually a process of disintegration through small migrations takes place, which may lead to the founding of a new town. Sometimes, again, the migration takes place in a body. Obviously such a system is possible only in the case of small communities. This situation apparently still prevails west of Tajín, in the spurs of the Sierra Madre Oriental.

If a scattered type settlement be selected, the periodic "migration" of the maize fields takes place in a circle around the house, as it does in Tajín. The existence of a small residential nucleus which sometimes functions as a political, commercial and ceremonial center does not modify the dispersion pattern. One hundred sixty-seven families live away from the Tajín residential nucleus and only thirty-five within it.

The "fallowing" (barbecho) system

This method of cultivation also begins with the clearing and burning of existing vegetation. The milpa planted on this field retains its productivity as long as the slash-and-burn maize patch, occasionally longer. The important difference consists in the fact that the fallow periods are incomparably shorter. Frequently it is enough for the rest period to match the number of years under cultivation. The main reason for the disparity is apparently environmental. The "fallowing" system is typically found in cool and temperate parts of Mexico.

We had the opportunity to compare this system with that of Tajín at Eloxochitlán, a Totonac town in the highlands of Puebla, in Mexico. The data are still unpublished. Some of them, dealing with agriculture and some socio-economic aspects can be found in Palerm (1952), and a general summary of the culture in Kelly (1951).

We find two kinds of milpa in Eloxochitlán: The garden or calmil (the milpa of the house) and the milpa proper. Both yield only one crop a year. Productivity per harvest of a fallowed milpa is pretty much the same as that of a slash-and-burn milpa. It is cultivated usually for two or three years and left to rest for about the same period. The calmil is harvested annually; it is fertilized with garbage, the dung of domestic animals and with dry leaves and twigs. The yield per harvest from a calmil is double that of a slash-and-burn or fallowed milpa.

According to our figures (which naturally take into account annual yields as well as productivity-per-harvest), an Eloxochitlán family needs two hectares of milpa and a half-hectare of calmil in order to reach the annual yield of maize which can be harvested in Tajín from 1 1/2 hectares. But while the cultivation cycle in Tajín demands 12 hectares of cultivable land per family, in Eloxochitlán it requires only 6 hectares and a half.

Obviously, the agricultural system of Eloxochitlán allows a greater density of population (almost double) than that of Tajín. In addition, the permanent nature of the calmil (which lives in symbiosis with the house and acts as its pantry) and the almost perennial "fallowed" milpa encourage, if they do not impose, a stability of residence. Almost the whole population of Eloxochitlán lives closely together, within or just outside the political and ceremonial nucleus which contains old, permanent buildings.

The irrigated system

The third element in this comparison is Tecomatepec, a town in the south of the state of Mexico (Palerm, 1952). Here we find, in addition to the fallowing system typical of cool and temperate lands, a recently built irrigation network. Despite such recency, Tecomatepec is located in a zone important for its pre-Hispanic irrigation, which still functions in some places. We found no significant differences between the pre-Hispanic irrigation techniques and those of present-day Tecomatepec.

The water is "bled" from the Calderón river (one of those descending from the Nevado of Toluca), thirty-six kilometers away. A canal (apantle) was dug, forty centimeters wide and thirty deep. This work took eleven years. A small dam was then built to intercept the river and redirect part of the water. Maintenance work on this system is continuous. Each rainy period clogs up or destroys a portion of the canal. In addition, some transversal "mouths" of the canal have to be opened, to facilitate the circulation of natural drainage.

Irrigation does not benefit all the inhabitants of Tecomatepec, but rather those who took part in the work. A group of cultivators from Yerbas Buenas, who cooperated with those of Tecomatepec, take part in the maintenance work and use some of the water. In addition to such cooperation between the two towns, special arrangements had to be made with the settlements whose lands are crossed by the canal and with others who share in using Calderón waters.

The need for firm leadership and authority among the irrigation-cultivators of Tecomatepec is evident. In addition to the slow and lasting excavation, the continuous maintenance, the need for formal agreements with other villages, insurance must be made of the equitable distribution of water between neighbors, who take turns at specified times. A system of sanctions for lack of discipline or abuses extends from deprivation of water for a specified period up to complete prohibition.

Productivity of irrigated agriculture (combined at Tecomatepec with a more consistent use of fertilizers) justifies these efforts. The yield is two and a half times greater than that of fallowed land. Also the same field can yield two crops annually: one with irrigation, the other without. Cultivation proceeds continuously; there is no need to "rest" the soil.

According to our figures, the $1^{1}/2$ cultivated hectares need in Tajin and the two and a half required at Eloxochitlán can be reduced in Tecomatepec to 0.86 hectares. The decrease is even more impressive if we compare the cultivable surfaces need per family: twelve hectares in the slash-and-burn system; six and a half in the fallowing-and-calmil areas; 0.86 hectares in those where it is supplemented by irrigation. According to a communication in 1952 by W. Sanders, in a system relying exclusively on irrigation, like the chinampas, the requirements would fall to only 0.37 hectares for commercial cultivation, and to 0.6-0.7 for mixed subsistence and commercial cultivation.

The opportunities for a dense population are greatly increased through irrigation. The system also requires a settled home and the concentration of the residents in the irrigated zone. Like other towns in the irrigated region, Tecomatepec is "urbanized" and has permanent, well-planned buildings.

Final comparison and conclusion

We have reported on the relations between three traditional agricultural systems, population density and settlement patterns. A community of a hundred families needs 1,200 cultivable hectares in a slash-and-burn system; 650 of fallowed land and calmil gardens; 86 hectares in a mixed system of fallowing and irrigation, and between 37 and 70 in a completely irrigated agriculture (chinampas). The corresponding settlement patterns are:

1) dispersed or small migratory settlements, with frequently changing cornfields in both cases;

2) stable residence, at times in hamlets, at times scattered; almost permanent cornfields;

3) and 4) concentrated and thickly settled communities; permanent cornfields.

II. Irrigation and the Natural Areas of Mesoamerica

The importance of irrigation in Mesoamerica as a fundamental factor in the emergence of an urban civilization can be stated even more emphatically. The earliest urban cultures of the Old World could follow (at least in theory) two alternatives in their agricultural development; either extensive "dry" cultivation or intensive planting with irrigation. Extensive agriculture requires three basic elements unknown in Mesoamerica: the plow, draft animals and adequate means of transport. Maybe one should also add the availability of a metallurgy more advanced than the Mexican. Only a favorable combination of these elements allows the clearance and cultivation of large areas with relatively little labor as well as the necessarily rapid transport of produce in sufficient quantities to feed an urban center.

It seems rather obvious that a rainfall agriculture, never extensive in Mesoamerica, could not accumulate an adequate and constant surplus to maintain the urban centers. It also seems incapable of creating the stimulus required for their development. Both requirements (productive capacity and stimulus) appear with an agriculture based on irrigation, which can develop with a rather primitive metallurgy and in the absence of plows, the wheel or draft animals. Their absence is made up by considerable emphasis on cooperation in work and a measure of political centralization.

Climatic conditions

Our skepticism about the possible relation between rainfall agriculture and the impressively urban character of Mesoamerica increases when we consider the climatic conditions. (See Vivó and Gómez, 1946.) Whetten (1950, pp.13-15) has summarized the main difficulties: 1) two-thirds of the total surface of Mexico is mountainous; only one third can be considered more or less a plain; of this third the greatest part is too dry for cultivation; 2) rainfall is inadequate for a flourishing, non-irrigated agriculture; 52.1% of the country's land cannot be cultivated without irrigation; on 30.6% the harvest is uncertain almost every year; 10.5% suffers from drought one year in four or five; only 6.8% of the land receives sufficient rain. To which we would add that a significant part of the latter is clad with tropical forests (where slash-and-burn agriculture is practiced).

Orographic and hydrographic conditions

Roughly speaking, the central part of Mesoamerica has the shape of a triangle. Its northwestern point rests on the mouth of the Santiago river, the northeastern at the mouth of the Pánuco and the southern in the isthmian part of Chiapas. The greater part of this territory (see Vivó, 1948; Vivó and Gómez, 1946; Tamayo, 1946) is made up of mountainous plateaus in which the major river systems originate. Its western and eastern limits are set by the mountains which descend toward the Pacific and the Gulf of Mexico. While the Gulf shore is lined with coastal plains of low elevation, the Pacific coast is close to the sharply rising mountains. This peculiar formation accentuates the torrential quality of the water courses. While the Gulf rivers eventually quiet down on the coastal plain (with occasional catastrophic floods), those flowing to the Pacific have no opportunity to even out; they flood regularly and reach the sea in turbulent fashion.

If we relate this situation to climatic conditions the conclusion is obvious. The waters which would be best for irrigation (those in the Gulf area) flow mainly through zones of rainy, tropical forests. The rivers on the Pacific side, where irrigation is frequently indispensable, are almost uncontrollable, in terms of pre-Hispanic technology. Sometimes, though, their periodic floods make possible some agriculture along their inundated banks.

Things are more propitious on the plateaus. Although the terrain is rough and craggy, there are also some flat surfaces. Even if the rivers are mostly torrential they could sometimes have been brought under control, even in the pre-Hispanic period. Irrigation is absolutely necessary in some places and highly desirable in others, because of climatic conditions. Two other reasons lead us to think that the plateaus are the most favorable locus in the Mesoamerican area for the development of civilization: 1) the existence of permanent water courses fed by the melting snows of the sierras and the accumulation of subterranean waters; 2) the presence of lakes which play the triple role of ways of communication, a source of food and the basis for the specialized agriculture of the chinampas.

This presentation claims no more than to outline a very general framework within which one can proceed to research and comparison. One could say that the coastal Mexican cultures played a minor role, particularly in the urban period. The key economic, political and military area was on the plateaus.

The natural zones of Totonacapan

Wishing to add something more concrete to this discussion, we thought of commenting on a region well known to us. Totonacapan occupies a large part of the center of the state of Veracruz, the north of Puebla and the eastern part of Hidalgo; the linguistic limits were defined in Kelly and Palerm, 1952, map 1. We can distinguish several natural areas: 1) a coastal zone, hot and dry, with flat grasslands, forming an arid wedge sunk into the rainy tropical forests of Veracruz; 2) a temperate, rainy belt of hills, lying between coast and sierra; 3) a hot and humid zone of tropical rain forests located mostly in the mountains; 4) a rainy, cold area in the highlands of the sierra; 5) another cold and high, but arid and semi-arid zone, sometimes reaching desert proportions, west of the sierra.

Examples of the sites characterizing each zone might be: 1) hot and dry: Cempoala; 2) temperate and rainy: Jalapa; 3) hot and humid: Papantla; 4) cold and rainy: Zacatlán; 5) cold and arid: Tulancingo and Perote, the latter a desert variant.

The demographic and urban conditions of Totonacapan

Our study of population distribution in Totonacapan before 1519 (Kelly and Palerm, 1952, p. 11, table 1) indicates that the greatest density was found in the warm and dry area. We estimate 53-63 inhabitants per square kilometer for the two areas of Cempoala and Jalapa (warm and dry and temperate). Working independently, Sanders (1951) arrived at the figures of 75 per square kilometer for Cempoala and 50 for Jalapa. In the northern part of Totonacapan (Papantla excepted), a hot and rainy zone, our figure was 52-56 inhabitants per square kilometer. Sanders, who includes Papantla, calculates 30.

Even more significant is the distribution of population centers. The sources ascribe 80-120,000 inhabitants to Cempoala; 24,000 to Colipa; 60,000 to Papantla; 120,000 to Jalapa, and lower figures, between 4,000 and 8,000 to Almolonga, Chapultepec, Chila, Jilotepec, Matlatlán, Miahuatlán, Naolinco, Tepetlán and Tlacolulan (Kelly and Palerm, 1952, pp. 8 and 9; see also Table 14 of Appendix A).

To what extent can we consider the four larger settlements to be true urban centers? It is quite probable that not all the population was completely urbanized and that the figures include the outskirts and even some none-too-well integrated hamlets. Yet is evident that the 80-120,000 inhabitants of Cempoala are assigned to the city, not to the province, for which we have other figures (250,000 inhabitants; Kelly and Palerm, 1952, p. 8). Also, the first descriptions of Cempoala portray a completely urbanized pattern: houses, palaces, temples, inner courts, streets, plazas, distribution of running water to private houses and gardens, etc. (Kelly and Palerm, 1952, pp. 8, 62, 176). The evidence for Colipa is weaker as we have no data beyond the population figure: 24,000. This undoubtedly could be verified through excavation.

The case of Papantla is quite different. The source (see Kelly and Palerm, 1952, p. 9; Table 14, Appendix A) is ambiguous and the figure quoted could be attributed to either a town or a province; it is unlikely that a city of 60,000 inhabitants would have received so little notice from the chroniclers. Archaeological evidence is also negative. The pre-Hispanic culture of Papantla is not that of an urban society. The Relación Geográfica of Papantla (Carrión) describes a scattered population. It is almost certain that Papantla was the ceremonial and political center of a scattered people. It is well described by Torquemada (1:248-9). He indicates, first, that not all the ancient inhabitants of New Spain lived in cities; many lived dispersed and scattered, for example the Totonacs... "But one must notice that in some of these provinces the towns which were the capital or the metropolis of the nation or province were somewhat more ordered than the other towns or settlements subjected to them... in this main agglomeration or capital they used to have their temples and worship... The lord and king lived here and their houses were very luxurious: nearby were the houses of the important and noble folk; and although there were no actual streets, the houses were built with some alignment... And such a settlement (somewhat confused and scattered) had one hundred and two hundred houses, sometimes more and sometimes less; the other folk (I mean the rest of the nation or county) who belonged to this capital lived everywhere, over hills and mountains, through valleys and ravines..."

The case of Jalapa presents no greater difficulties. The figure quoted (120,000 inhabitants) must be attributed to both a center, with no more than a tenth of the total population, and a series of dependent rural communities and hamlets. Here again we find a description which is likely to be close to the truth. Written by Hernán Cortés (p. 57), it refers to Jico, a town not far from Jalapa: "A well-fortified town, built in a strong place, because it is on the slope of a steep cliff... and on the plain are many villages and ranches of about five hundred and three hundred and two hundred cultivators, all in all about five to six thousand warriors..."

The remaining places mentioned are more likely villages and towns and not true cities. With Armillas (1951, p. 22), we consider the town, villa, an intermediary form between village and city, a transition between rural and urban life.

To summarize: 1) True cities are found in Totonacapan apparently only in the hot and dry region; along with such urban developments we find considerable concentration of towns and the greatest population density. 2) There is no evidence of urban centers in the hot and humid areas; population density was low and settlements scattered with occasional ceremonial and political centers. 3) While we do not find urban centers in the temperate rainy zone, there is evidence of towns and well-planned ceremonial centers, frequently set up as fortresses. To all this we can also add: 4) the cold and rainy area seems to present a situation similar to the temperate and rainy; 5) the pattern of settlement in the cold and dry zone is similar to that of the hot and dry one.

In conclusion, the greatest density of population and the only true urban development in Totonacapan (with its great variety of natural regions) is located in a warm and dry zone, where we also find the only irrigation system known from the Totonac area. One should also mention that irrigation in this zone benefited from some favorable conditions: 1) level terrain; 2) small rivers, an exceptional condition along the Gulf Coast; 3) permanent water courses, coming in part from snows, very infrequent along the Coast (See Tamayo, 1946, pp. 164-166). Urban development may also have been stimulated through trade with the very distinct natural regions nearby, the proximity of the sea and the availability of water transport. In the cold and arid and semi-arid zones there may have existed another urban center (see, for example, Cortés, p. 59) in which the Totonac had apparently little or no part to play.

To what extent can these conclusions about Totonacapan be extended to include Mesoamerica? Our impression is that a measure of careful generalization is possible. We need a Mesoamerican framework which would combine natural areas with the cultural and which would formulate a systematic relationship between cultivation systems, population and urbanization, utilizing ethnographic, historical and archaeological data.

III. Irrigation in the Central Zone of Mesoamerica

It seemed quite obvious that irrigation agriculture provided optimum conditions for urban development in Mesoamerica. We then decided to study the early sources to determine the distribution of irrigation. The following sources were utilized: 1) Anales de Cuauhtitlán; 2) Relación del origen de los indios...; 3) Ixtlilxochitl; 4) Tezozomoc; 5) Cortés; 6) Sahagún; 7) Epistolario de Nueva España; 8) Gómara; 9) Suma de visitas; 10) Lebrón de Quiñones; 11) Relaciones geográficas, and 12) Ponce.

It is impossible to enumerate here all the villages with irrigation which we have identified. We have done so elsewhere (1954). Here we will indicate only the overall results, grouping the villages within the various states of the modern Mexican republic. In Colima - 10; Federal District - 8; Guanajuato -1; Guerrero - 34; Hidalgo - 19; Jalisco - 50; México - 34; Michoacán - 24; Morelos - 5; Nayarit - 18; Oaxaca - 54; Puebla - 29; Querétaro - 1; Veracruz - 5; Zacatecas - 2; a total of 294.

To this list one should add villages which are reported to have huertas (gardens). We assume that huerta implies some kind of irrigation. Armillas (1949) has argued in the same sense. The evidence is reinforced by the fact that in the majority of cases the garden under discussion was planted with cacao in regions where this plant needs irrigation (see below). In Colima - 14; Federal District 3; Guerrero - 8; Jalisco - 9; Michoacán - 1; Morelos - 1; Nayarit - 1; Oaxaca - 2; Veracruz - 1: a total of 40.

The distribution of cacao cultivation in Mesoamerica will help us to fill in the outline. Can one say with any certainty that a mention of this crop, even if no "garden" is reported, refers to irrigation? Armillas (1949, p. 88) writes: "at least in the western part of Mesoamerica, when the historical sources refer to cacao grown by the natives there is either explicit mention of irrigation or the indirect reference to huertas of cacao ; when we find a reference to cacao in this region which does not specify the techniques of cultivation we can be sure that it is accompanied by irrigation."

One must be careful in using such references to cacao when they refer to areas other than the ones where irrigation was indispensable. Father Ponce (1:295) emphasizes that "the Indians [plant] their cacao orchards where there is water to irrigate them," but he also mentions the province of Yucatán as a place where cacao grew without irrigation "in valleys and in wet and shady spots, though there is little of it and it gives little fruit." We could add to Yucatán practically the whole coast of the Gulf of Mexico, although apparently cacao cultivation of any commercial importance extended only as far north as the Papaloapan river. We know, for example, that in Usila and Chinantla much cacao was grown, taking advantage of the humidity along the riverbanks (Esquivel, pp. 60, 64-67; Quijada, pp. 46, 50). Villages where cacao was grown and irrigation seems certain: In Chiapas - 4;

Colima - 7; Guerrero -11; Jalisco - 9; Michoacán - 1; Nayarit - 7; Oaxaca - 3: a total of 42.

A fourth possible list would include the villages where acequias (canals and ditches) are mentioned, though without any indication of their irrigating use. Actually acequias were used in Mesoamerica for various purposes (communication, defense, drainage, irrigation). Nevertheless, in the cases we have selected the evidence is impressive as they coincide with modern chinampas (which are probably also pre-Hispanic) or show some other indirect association with waterworks. Federal District - 4; México - 2: a total of 6.

The overall total adds up to 382 different villages (duplications have been eliminated) -- an impressive aggregate if we recall the number of sources used. With the exception of some cases culled from the list of acequias the others leave no doubt as to their association with irrigation.

IV. The Antiquity and Importance of Irrigation in Mesoamerica

At least two important questions must be answered before we can definitely relate irrigation to the development of an urban civilization in Mesoamerica: How old is irrigation? What was the level of organization and the importance of these waterworks? We should like to present here some tentative data on this point.

Antiquity

Armillas (1951, p. 24) has suggested that the emergence of urban centers in the Classic Period in Mesoamerica is related to the transformation of agriculture, i.e. irrigation. Two main kinds of evidence seem to support this hypothesis (in addition to the reasons indicated above): 1) the geographic distribution of irrigation; 2) certain archaeological data.

The wide geographic distribution of irrigation may indicate considerable antiquity. Towns practicing irrigation can be found all over the central part of Mesoamerica, with the obvious exception of tropical forests and rainy areas. Outside the central part we find irrigation in the highlands of Guatemala and the Pacific Coast south of the Isthmus of Tehuantepec. Nevertheless, its concentration is greatest in the Valley of Mexico and the headwaters of the Tula, Lerma and Atlixco rivers and in some parts of western Mexico. This clustering and the few irrigated spots in the states of Michoacán and western Guerrero may suggest the possibility of two centers of diffusion: one in western Mexico, the other on the central plateau. This may be due to nothing more than the shortage of data for Michoacán and western Guerrero. According to a personal communication from Sanders in 1952 there may have been another center of diffusion in the highlands of Guatemala.

Other data seem to confirm the suggested relative antiquity of irrigation; Sears' studies of pollen (1951, p. 57) indicate certain fluctuations in the climate of the Valley of Mexico. At the beginning of the Archaic (or Formative) Period the climate was humid, but towards the end of that period it grew progressively drier. This may well be the change which, through its effect on agriculture, stimulated the emergence or extension of irrigation on which the later development of settled centers was based. Another circumstance seems to strengthen the possibility; West and Armillas (1950, pp. 169-170) write that if the tlateles of Chalco and Xochimilco are fossil chinampas as has been thought, the age of this technique must be Late Ticomán-Teotihuacán I, which falls within the dry period outlined by Sears. Unfortunately, no archaeological excavation has yet been undertaken to determine the true nature of the tlateles.

The problem of dating the beginning of irrigation in Mesoamerica can be solved only by archaeological means. The historical sources apparently do not take it any further back than the Toltec era.

The importance of irrigation

The written sources are somewhat more helpful in evaluating the importance of irrigation, not only in so far as its wide geographic distribution is concerned, but also with regard to its significance for particular localities. In writing about the Tacubaya and Coyoacán region, in the Valley of Mexico, López says: "The natives have been seriously injured by being robbed and having been deprived of their estates, lands and water which supported them..... particulary the inhabitants of Tacubaya and the Otomí of Coyoacán..... They had in ancient times taken some water which they brought along the foothills of the sierra..... with which they irrigated their crops in sterile soil and through which they could cultivate many gardens and grow vegetables on which they subsisted, which waters supported more than twenty thousand of your majesty's vassals. These waters the President took away from them or damaged the canals, and near one drainage ditch he built three mills with 6 very powerful stones..." (p.187). In describing Cholula, Cortés says: "This city ....is located on a plain and it has up to twenty thousand houses within the city proper and about as many on the outskirts...It is a city rich in tilled fields as it has much land and most of it is irrigated" (pp.74-75). Cortés also says that the valley of Izúcar is all irrigated with very good canals, well traced and coordinated (p.152; all italics are ours). We do not claim that irrigation was equally important everywhere. It is more likely that the most common variety was the one described by Mota y Escobar (1940, pp.35-36) who say that "they start ditches and small canals for water from the rivers, in some of the towns..."

Once again, archaeology has been of little help so far in the solution of these problems. What do we know of the irrigation system of Cempoala (Gómara, 1:102-103) which García-Payón seems to have identified recently (Kelly and Palerm, 1952, pp.99)? And what of those in southern Hidalgo which made possible flourishing centers and a substantial population contrasting with their present poverty? Sauer (1948, pp.60-61) has shown the importance of irrigation in the valley of Alima, but no archaeologist has followed in his footsteps. The great waterworks (canals, aqueducts, terraces) of the Tetzcutzingo, near Texcoco, Mexico, are still considered by many to have been a resort of King Netzahualcoyotl. Curiously enough when Cook (1949) studied the demographic history of Teotlalpan he did not stop to consider the role of irrigation and its abandonment.

The situation in the Valley of Mexico

If one uses historical sources, at the moment the Valley of Mexico is certainly the best place to study the techniques of irrigation. Despite its alluvial soils, the Valley is not very favorable to agriculture. Its climate has been described as semi-desert, with a relative humidity like that of Pachuca (Hidalgo), and with frequent frosts which add to the difficulties (Gama, 1920, p.31). The florescence of civilization in this arid valley, covered in part by lakes and swamps, was a genuine product of human effort comparable to that of other ancient civilizations.

The Valley was a closed basin, its bottom a series of lakes. Cortés described it:"On the...plain there are two lakes...and one...is of fresh water and the other ...salt water. On one side they are separated by a small chain of very high hills located in the middle of the plain and at one end these lakes meet in a narrow plain found between these hills and the high sierras... And because this salt lake.... has flood and ebb times... at flood time its water flows to the fresh lake as swiftly as an abundant river and at ebb times the sweet runs to the salt" (pp.102-103). Gómara adds that "one has nitrous, bitter and pestilent water and the other is sweet and good and fish breed in it. The salt lake ebbs and floods... The fresh is higher; an thus the sweet flows in the bad..." (1:247-248).

This means that whenever the lakes formed a single system the waters tended to flow toward Texcoco, the lowest point, until the "vessel" was full, when they flooded the rest of the basin (Gama, 1920, p. 21). The peculiar character of this lacustrian system was due to the fact that some of the waters were fresh while others were nitrous, due to the "slow decomposition of sodic and potasic feldspar which abounds in the rocks of the mountains lining the valley" (Gama, 1920, p. 25). If this had been true of the lakes of Chalco and Xochimilco, of Zumpango and Jaltocan, the whole lake country would have been useless for agriculture, and particularly for the chinampas. As the high salinity was confined to the lowest part of the area, the useless section was limited to the eastern side of Lake Texcoco and those areas it reached when in flood, usually western Tenochtitlan.

In addition to topography, the river systems determined which would be the areas most likely to be threatened and damaged by the flood of nitrous waters. While Chalco had good-sized rivers of almost constant flow and Xochimilco used mainly springs, Texcoco was the victim of many strong streams of a torrential nature (Gama, 1920, pp. 25-26). This means that during drought the fresh water (by its altitude and constant supply) flowed toward the nitrous, but in rainy periods (given the torrents and flooding of Lake Texcoco's rivers) the nitrous waters violently flooded the fresh, threatening even the chinampa area of Xochimilco.

The techniques used to conquer the lake

The conclusion seems obvious. The use of chinampas in the fresh section of Lake Texcoco and even the irrigation of the lower reaches were impossible until a system was figured out and built to contain the flood of nitrous waters. Actually, the problem was even more complicated: the fresh waters also had to be kept at a more or less constant level to avoid the drying of the chinampas (which in fact happened after the Conquest) as well as to avoid their being flooded (this was a danger at all times). This applied not only to the sweet section of the central lake, but also to Chalco and Xochimilco and probably Zumpango and Jaltocan. Once the nitrous floods were contained within certain limits, one could start on the gradual conquest of the eastern section of the lake through draining, the rinsing of the nitrous soil, irrigation with fresh water (frequently brought by aqueducts) and the construction of chinampas. The latter were used as house sites, cultivated fields, and, where they crossed the lake, as supports for aqueducts.

An outline of the techniques used can be sketched with the help of the sources. The Tenochca completed these remarkable waterworks but there is little doubt that the foundations had been laid by the chinamperos of Chalco and Xochimilco and by the Texcocans. We are dealing here with techniques whose roots are deep in the origins of civilization in the Valley. The description of chinampa construction has been made by West and Armillas (1950) and need not occupy us here.

The conquest of the lake by the Tenochca

When we first meet them, the Tenochca are established on their island using chinampa techniques to increase the available soil (Torquemada 1:290; Tezozomoc, p. 16). This was also done by the Tlatelolcas (Torquemada 1:291). It is doubtful whether these early "chinampas" were cultivated fields in addition to being house sites. Tenochtitlan, along with the whole western part of the lake, was open to floods of nitrous water. Economic life during the reign of their early kings (Acamapichtli, Huitzilihuitl and Chimalpopoca) does not suggest agriculture (which they had practiced before, away from the lake). Torquemada (1:92-93; 290) states that they lived poorly and miserably, eating "seafood" and roots: some of this may be an exaggeration. Their main activities were fishing, hunting, canoe-building and war (Torquemada, 1:106). The tribute to Azcapotzalco was made up of "those things which grow in this lake" (ibid., 1:122). Tezozomoc (pp. 24, 62) draws a similar picture. During a quarrel with Azcapotzalco, the Tepaneca chiefs said: "Let us see where they will get the wood which they burn there and the vegetables (crops) which go from our land to Mexico Tenochtitlan to support them" (Tezozomoc, p. 24).

During the reign of Itzcoatl things began to change. Torquemada (1:136) mentions "sementeras" (cultivated fields) as part of Tenochtitlan's tribute to the Tepaneca. The appearance of cultivated chinampas seems to be related to the construction of an aqueduct to bring water from the springs of Chapultepec (Relación del origen..., pp. 51-52). The decisive change took place after the defeat of the Tepaneca of Azcapotzalco, when Itzcoatl "had them call the Tepaneca of Azcapotzalco, those of Cuyuacán together with the Xochimilcas and told them: now you have to build, together, a paved highway and road, all of heavy stone, fifteen brazas wide and two estados high. After the order was heard, it was carried out and there resulted the present Xololco entrance to Mexico City " (Tezozomoc, p. 68). It seems as if this was the first major public work of the Tenochca, planned not only as a means of communication but also as a dike to detain the floods.

Actually, the measures taken by Itzcoatl were insufficient. In the ninth year of the reign of Moctezuma the Elder the city was flooded. The Tenochca appealed to the superior hydraulic skill of the Texcocans and under the leadership of Netzahualcoyotl a new dike was built of lumber and stone. The wall was more than four brazas wide and more than three leagues long; the stones had to be brought from three and four leagues away. Moctezuma had to put to work the people of Tenochtitlan, Texcoco, Tacuba, Culhuacán, Ixtapalapa and Tenayuca. The new construction "prevented the sudden blend of salty waters with those sweet ones" (Torquemada 1:157-158). Another time, as during the reign of Itzcoatl, the building of a highway-dike was accompanied by the erection of an aqueduct to take fresh water to Tenochtitlan (Anales de Cuauhtitlán, pp. 53-54).

The volume of water thus transferred was soon inadequate and the new king, Ahuizotl, decided to build another aqueduct, from Coyoacán. It has frequently been said that the waters of the aqueduct were used only for domestic purposes. The thirst of the Tenochca seems incredible. The Anales de Cuauhtitlán (p. 58) report that when the aqueduct of Ahuizotl sprung a leak, Tenochtitlan was flooded and the waters reached Mixquic, Tlahuac and Xochimilco; even Texcoco was within the flood's radius. Another source (Relación del origen..., pp. 91-93) indicates clearly that the waterworks were built "to increase the waters of the lake" (in other words, to maintain an adequate level). Tezozomoc (pp. 379-388) tells us that during this period chinampas could already be found within the city of Tenochtitlan (see also Torquemada 1:291) and that Ahuizotl ordered the chinamperos to plant maize, beans, squash, flowers, chile peppers, tomatoes and trees in "troughs" (camellones) so Mexico would "flourish" and the city "did not look like...a city...but a labyrinth, a flowering garden." This latter aqueduct (built of lime and stone) was erected by the natives of Texcoco, Azcapotzalco, Tacuba, Coyoacán, Xochimilco and "the other four chinampa-using towns." The crowd taking part in the work was so numerous "the Indians looked like ants." When the waters reached Tenochtitlan and Tlatelolco, Ahuizotl received them with the following greeting: "You will be used for human sustenance and as a result of the fruits produced by you, there will come many kinds of provisions and flying birds."

We feel there is little ground left for doubt. The cultivated zone was extended by the dike-highway which contained the floods and created reservoirs; fresh water was brought through aqueducts to "wash" the nitrous soil, for irrigation and to maintain the level of the lake in addition to domestic use. When the Spaniards arrived, the system was functioning. Gómara (1:247-248) says that the paved road separating the fresh from the nitrous waters had "six or seven very large openings" through which fresh waters were channeled. He mentions no way of closing these holes which must have existed for use during the floods of nitrous water. This is confirmed by Cortés (pp.174-175) who, in describing a battle, explains that the Indians opened a "road or dike" from Ixtapalapa to Tenochtitlan and then "the water from the salt lake began to flow with violent force toward the fresh one" (cf. Ixtlilxochitl 1:344). It is obvious that the inhabitants of the Valley (see also Gómara 2:9, 20, for Xochimilco and Jaltocan) had a method of controling the water flow in both directions through openings in the dike-roads and this method was in active use. Most probably the Tenochca did no more than extend a system used much earlier in Jaltocan and Zumpango, in Chalco and Xochimilco.

In conclusion, we view the development of irrigation in the Valley of Mexico not so much as the result of many small-scale initiatives by small groups, but as the result of large-scale enterprise, well planned, in which an enormous number of people took part, engaged in important and prolonged public works under centralized and authoritative leadership. It is uncertain to what extent this was the general norm in Mesoamerica. We tend to think that usually irrigation was only of local importance, but in certain regions waterworks were built (even if with different techniques) which were similar to those in the Valley of Mexico. Among them are probably those of Cholula and the valley of Atlixco. Nor should one discard the possibility that local irrigation networks dependent on a common river basin would require the same conditions of cooperation, coordination, planning and authority. This may have been the situation in some parts of Colima, Oaxaca, Guerrero, etc.

V. Some Characteristics of Irrigation and the History of the Valley of Mexico

The case of the Tenochca in the Valley of Mexico was presented as an easily available example, perhaps the culminating one, of the nature and importance of the public works serving irrigation agriculture in Mesoamerica. Nevertheless, it is obvious that the techniques employed were widely used and quite ancient in the Valley of Mexico. It is also obvious that other political units, like Texcoco, Cholula, the Tepanec empire, the Toltecs and certainly Teotihuacan, were in a position to gather and manipulate as considerable a labor force as that which was required by the Tenochca. The volume of human effort and the technical skill represented by the pyramids of Teotihuacan and Cholula are, no doubt, greater than those required for the construction of Netzahualcoyotl's dike (see Armillas, 1951). On the other hand, all during the same period when Itzcoatl began the Mexico-Xololco road, his neighbors of Cuauhtitlán were building a dam to deflect a river and excavating a new bed for it (Anales de Cuauhtitlán, pp. 49-50). The monumental structure of Tetzcutzingo, built by the Texcocans date from the same period.

Another characteristic to which Armillas has drawn attention (1951, pp. 21-22), is the "contrast between [the] relatively low technology and [the] highly developed socio-political structure and intellectual life." This is a real contrast, but not a contradiction. Actually, a strong socio-political organization seems to be the only way open to a people with a poorly developed technology to have and use large-scale public works. Human labor is the only substitute for advanced technology; the less technology the more human effort is required, which means greater coercive organization. The only possible way of constructing the great pre-Hispanic public works (be they dike-highways, aqueducts, canals or monumental pyramids) in a limited amount of time is reflected for us by Tezozomoc's image, when he talks of large crowds working constantly "like ants" (pp. 378-388).

We also have some additional, more detailed, references. The job of detaining the river of Cuauhtitlán and deflecting it into a new channel was assigned by the chiefs to the inhabitants of Tultitlán. The dam was made of beams, joined and upright; its construction lasted two years. To clean an old canal and make it fit for the new river bed took seven years (see Anales de Cuauhtitlán, pp. 49-50). When Cortés asked for the help of Texcoco in order to widen a channel (so as to move the brigantines used in the siege of Tenochtitlan) eight thousand men from the Texcoco kingdom worked daily for fifty days. The finished canal was half a league long (about two kilometers), two estados (twelve feet) wide, and about that deep. This required 400,000 man-days (see Cortés, pp. 205-206; Gómara 2:26). We have seen above the number of villages moved to action by the Tenochca kings for their public works.

How can one mobilize such crowds, make them work in organized fashion and maintain them, without a powerful and efficient social structure? In part, the socio-political organization of Mesoamerica was the result or consequence of the low technology and it may be that the low technical development was perpetuated by a social organization which allowed the ready use of such supplies of human labor. In any case, the foundation of this complex relationship rested on irrigation agriculture, the only type capable, under Mesoamerican conditions, of producing the necessary crop surpluses required to feed the thousands who, from time to time, did not work at producing their own subsistence. These surpluses were necessarily also great enough to maintain the upper classes and the specialized urban population as well as keep up trading activities. The public works which increased the irrigated surface multiplied the surplus-producing capacity which in turn allowed the use of ever greater quantities of human effort for new works, new urban populations and the growing socio-political organization. Still, all this structuring and economic capacity were not used solely for developing irrigation. They could serve to make war, conquer one's neighbors and develop the historically known empires.

In the regions where irrigation did not acquire the importance it had in the Valley of Mexico, we find a different socio-political situation. Instead of the great concentration of power and the formation of empires we find "city-states" whose control reached rarely beyond a limited constellation of satellites. Coalitions sprang up sometimes but mostly they were at war with each other.

The process may be illustrated through a description of events at Yecapichtla, a town which, with its nine satellites, had about 20-25,000 inhabitants, about ten percent of whom were mayeques and one percent chiefs. It had "many good irrigated lands, and in great amounts." Disputes with neighbors over water were frequent. In early colonial days they complained that if "they irrigated, it cost them a great deal of work as the water comes from Cuavecavazco.... and many times it is taken away and shut off and not allowed to arrive." An elsewhere: "and granted that it is irrigated with a bit of water which flows through the town of Jantetelco, it [the water] does not come from this town nor does it rise there, but in Tetela....and many times it is snatched away by the inhabitants of those towns; this causes great need, and through the loss of the said water they have lost and lose many times.... some cotton and fruits which they plant" (Nuevos Documentos....pp. 179, 182, 194, 207).

These circumstances, which can probably be duplicated in many parts of Mesoamerica, may have pushed the "city-states" toward the development of a military organization, slowed down only by the imposition of an "empire" or the formation of temporary coalitions.

The explanation of how the Valley of Mexico could overcome this political situation may possibly be found, not only in the spectacular nature of the public works required for irrigation but also in the easily accessible water transport. The network of lakes made it possible for the Valley to become an economic unit before it was a political one, and to add to itself a part of the valley of Morelos (Armillas,

1951, p. 21). There are countless references in the sources to this special role of the lakes and to numbers and uses of canoes. Gómara (1:248) thinks that there were 200,000 small boats (and perhaps more, as he mentions 50,000 in Mexico alone), carrying people and supplies. When the Texcocans evacuated their city at the arrival of the Spaniards, Gómara counted 20,000 canoes (1:385). Cortés (p. 102) states that most of the trade was carried by boat. Torquemada claims that there was nobody in and around the whole lake who did not have a canoe (1:292)

Much later, at the beginning of the XVIII century, the lakes were still playing a most important role, although land communications had expanded and coaches, horses and mule trains were then in use. A document from Chalco, dated 1806 says: "In this province and town of Chalco, with grief I noted today the great hardships to be seen. it being market day -- everywhere a shortage of victuals for survival this coming week; the peasants could not sell their grains and other seeds; the fruit and other precious things grown in the hot country could not be sent to the capital... The greens and other foods which we lack and off which other towns live, are rotting near Tlahuac, the lumber of the Royal Factory [is] in the water but cannot move all this... occurs because for four days now the royal canal has been traffic-less as its sides have fallen in..." (italics ours). The following is said of Xochimilco: "Since we are in the depths of destitution - not only we ourselves but also our unlucky families - this happening because the royal road is closed on which we communicate with the Capital, whence we receive our daily sustenance...." The petition requests that a new acalote or waterway be opened as the old one had been closed by an earthquake (see Archivo General de la Nación). Earlier, Cortés (p. 198) had noted the existence of these waterways used for transport at Xochimilco.

This extraordinary coincidence of such different circumstances -- some natural and ecological, others geographic, agricultural, technological, political and historic - allowed the Valley of Mexico to become the key area of pre-Hispanic Mesoamerica.

References cited:

Anales de Cuauhtitlán, 1954. *Códice Chimalpopoca*. Imprenta Universitaria, México, D.F.

Archivo General de la Nación, 1806. Ramo de Ríos y Acequias, 3. México, D.F. *Ms*.

ARMILLAS, Pedro, 1949. Notas sobre los sistemas de cultivo en Mesoamérica. *Anales del Instituto Nacional de Antropología e Historia*, 3. México, D.F.

_____, 1951. Tecnología, formaciones socio-económicas y religión en Mesoamérica. *The Civilizations of Ancient America*. XXIXth International Congress of Americanists. The University of Chicago Press, Chicago.

CARRION, Juan de, 1581. Descripción del pueblo y cabecera de Papantla, de la jurisdicción de Huetylalpa. Museo Nacional de Antropología, México, D.F. *Ms*.

COOK, S. F., 1949. *The Historical Demography and Ecology of the Teotlalpan.* Ibero-Americana, 33. University of California Press, Berkeley.

CORTES, Hernán, 1866. *Cartas y relaciones de Hernán Cortés al emperador Carlos V.* Colegidas e ilustradas por Pascual de Gayangos. A Chaix y Ca., París.

Epistolario de Nueva España, 1939-1942. Antigua Librería Robredo, México, D.F. 16 vols.

ESQUIVEL, Diego de, 1905. Relación de Chinantla. *Papeles de Nueva España,* 4. Recopilados por F. del Paso y Troncoso. Rivadeneyra, Madrid.

GAMA, Valentín, 1920. *Memoria para la carta del Valle de México.* Poder Ejecutivo Federal, Dirección de Talleres Gráficos, México, D.F.

GOMARA, Francisco López de, 1870. *Conquista de México.* Imprenta de I. Escalante y Ca., México, D.F. 2 vols.

IXTLILXOCHITL, Fernando de Alva, 1891. *Obras históricas.* Oficina tip. de la Secretaría de Fomento, México, D.F. 2 vols.

KELLY, Isabel, 1951. Etnografía moderna totonaca. V Mesa Redonda de Antropología de México. *Ms.*

———, y PALERM, Angel, 1952. *The Tajín Totonac.* Institute of Social Anthropology, 13. Smithsonian Institution, Washington, D.C.

LEBRON de Quiñones, Lorenzo, 1945. Memoria de los pueblos en la provincia de Colima. Memoria de las huertas de cacao que hay en la provincia de Colima. *Papeles de Nueva España.* F. del Paso y Troncoso, compilador; editados por Vargas Rea. Biblioteca de Aportación histórica, México, D.F.

LOPEZ, Jerónimo, 1940. Memorial que dió por extenso... *Epistolario de Nueva España,* 15. Antigua Librería Robredo, México, D.F.

MOTA Y ESCOBAR, Alonso de la, 1940. *Descripción geográfica de los reinos de Nueva Galicia, Nueva Vizcaya y Nuevo León.* Editorial Pedro Robredlo, México, D. F.

Nuevos documentos relativos a los bienes de Hernán Cortés, 1946. Imprenta Universitaria, México,

PALERM, Angel, 1952. La civilización urbana. *Historia Mexicana,* 2. México, D.F.

———, 1954. La distribución del regadío en el área central de Mesoamérica. *Ciencias Sociales,* 5. Washington, D.C.

PONCE, Alonso, 1872. *Relación breve y verdadera...* Imprenta de la Viuda de Calero, Madrid. 2 vols.

QUIJADA, Hernando, 1905. Relación de Ucila. *Papeles de Nueva España,* 4. Recopilados por F. del Paso y Troncoso. Rivadeneyra, Madrid.

Relación del origen de los indios..., 1944. *Códice Ramírez.* Editorial Leyenda, México, D.F.

Relaciones geográficas, 1905. *Papeles de Nueva España,* 4-7. Recopilados por F. del Paso y Troncoso. Rivadeneyra, Madrid.

SAHAGUN, Bernardino de, 1946. *Historia general de las cosas de Nueva España.* Editorial Nueva España, México, D. F. 3 vols.

SANDERS, W., 1951. The Anthropogeography of Central Veracruz. V Mesa Redonda de Antropología de México. *Ms.*

SAUER, Carl, 1948. *Colima of New Spain in the Sixteenth Century.* Ibero-Americana, 29. University of California Press, Berkeley.

SEARS, Paul, 1951. Pollen Profils and Culture Horizons in the Basin of Mexico. *The Civilizations of Ancient America.* XXIXth International Congress of Americanists. The University of Chicago Press, Chicago.

Suma de visitas, 1905. *Papeles de Nueva España,* 1. Recopilados por F. del Paso y Troncoso. Rivadeneyra, Madrid.

TAMAYO, Jorge L., 1946. *Datos para la hidrología de la República mexicana.* Instituto Panamericano de Geografía e Historia, 84. México, D.F.

TEZOZOMOC, H. Alvarado, 1944. *Crónica Mexicana.* Editorial Leyenda, México, D. F.

TORQUEMADA, Juan de, 1943. *Monarquía indiana.* Editorial Salvador Chávez Hayhoe, México, D.F. 3 vols.

VIVO, Jorge, y GOMEZ, José C., 1946. *Climatología de México.* Instituto Panamericano de Geografía e Historia, 19. México, D. F.

VIVO, Jorge, 1948. *Geografía de México.* Fondo de Cultura Económica, México, D. F.

WEST, Robert, y ARMILLAS, Pedro, 1950. Las chinampas de México. *Cuadernos Americanos,* 50. México, D. F.

WHETTEN, Nathan L., 1950. The Rise of a Middle Class in México. *Materiales para el estudio de la clase media en la América Latina,* 2. Unión Panamericana, Washington, D.C.

Cultural Ecology of Nuclear Mesoamerica

WILLIAM T. SANDERS
The Pennsylvania State University

THE following paper is an attempt to define some of the interrelationships between culture and environment and to demonstrate the value of the concepts of cultural ecology in understanding the process of development of pre-Iron Age civilizations. By cultural ecology I mean simply the study of the interaction of cultural processes with the physical environment. My theoretical position may be stated in the following principles:

1) Each environment offers to human occupation a different set of challenges, and therefore a different set of alternate cultural responses may be expected. There is, of course, some overlapping of both challenges and cultural solutions from environment to environment. One can also say that certain alternative responses are more likely to occur than others. Some of these responses may be technological, others social, and some even religious.

2) In responding to such challenges, cultural response tends to take the path of greatest efficiency in the utilization of the environment.

3) In development of any conceptual scheme in culturology, the environ-

ment should be considered as an active, integrated part of the cultural system not as a passive extra-cultural factor.

To most archeologists the term "civilization" has a relatively restricted meaning. Kroeber uses the term more broadly, and even synonymously with "culture," defining it in terms of his pattern concept, and calling it the "total cultural pattern." In this paper I will use the term in the more restricted sense of the archeologist.

A civilization is a particular kind of cultural pattern; as contrasted to cultures as a whole its pattern is broader, less narrowly restricted, and therefore capable of greater elaboration (see Kroeber 1948:311–43). When one views the growth configuration of a civilization one is impressed by its dynamic quality. All cultures change, but in civilizations change is more rapid, more easily measured, and more apparent to the observer. Certain conditions preclude the development of this type of cultural growth; some of them link specifically with the utilization of the environment. These may be enumerated as follows: (1) an effective utilization of natural resources permitting a relatively dense population; (2) the integration of such resources, natural and demographic, into a relatively large society; (3) a system of social stratification, at least on two levels, in which the surplus production of a large majority is systematically accumulated, controlled, and diverted into culturally specified channels by a small dominant minority.

This third condition seems to be an essential one as we have numerous examples of areas of the world with dense populations, relatively large social groupings, but no systematic manipulation of surplus labor and goods. In the earliest civilizations of the New and Old Worlds, this surplus was apparently controlled first by a priestly bureaucracy and directed towards the construction and glorification of buildings dedicated to the gods. Later periods saw the control exercised by, or at least shared by, a secular ruling class. Archeologists recognize civilizations primarily by the tangible results of the "direction of surplus energy," in the form of permanent architecture and an exceptionally high development of skill in other areas of technology. They use technology as a guide for obvious reasons. There is often a striking difference in the quality of the technology of the folk society that produces the surplus and that of the dominant minority that controls it. Furthermore, although few studies have actually been made, we usually find much greater stability and less dynamism on the folk level.

Before the development of the proletarian metal-iron, and the beginnings of the use of metal tools by both levels in the society, this kind of culture had an extremely limited distribution in the Old World. Its primary area was a large, nearly continuous region embracing the Near East, northwest India, northeast Africa, and southeastern Europe. A secondary, historically derived and later development occurred in North China.

Furthermore, the maximal development of the pre-Iron Age civilizations was in four small areas: the Nile valley in Egypt, the Tigris Euphrates valleys in Iraq, the Indus valley in India, and the Hwango Ho valley in China, in all cases associated with a major river valley. Each of these centers was a relatively small, compact, densely populated area; the entire Old Kingdom of Egypt, for example, embraced only about 10,000 square miles of territory.

If we look at the ecological settings of the early civilizations, certain fundamental patterns emerge. The environments can be classed into two major types; (1) nearly rainless deserts with exotic major rivers, or (2), semi-arid country with low annual rainfall concentrated in a single season. In the Near East the latter climate falls generally into the type called "Mediterranean" with winter rains; in North China the rainy season falls in the summer. Average annual rainfall in the areas of dense population varies from 200-1,000mm. In the Near Eastern center another significant characteristic is that there is a great deal of ecological diversity based on altitude and microvariations in climate.

The geographical conditions that seem to be crucial in these centers of the civilizations were: (1) presence of a fertile soil capable of being intensively cultivated and sufficient water for irrigation, and (2), scanty plant cover which could be easily controlled (conditions (1) and (2) permitted an effective and intensive use of the land by a peasant population with an essentially Neolithic technology); (3) presence of a major river providing a natural transportation artery, and (4), a general deficiency of natural resources other than good agricultural land (acting as a stimulus to trade).

The situation in an area such as Mesopotamia offers a unique set of problems to a farmer equipped with a neolithic technology. It is an ecological region of enormous potential, even with a relatively feeble technology. What it does require for successful utilization is a highly organized and cooperative society capable of mass effort in converting swamps and deserts into irrigated cropland. The most effective way to exploit such an environment is the development of a social system of the type we have defined as civilization.

Following V. Gordon Childe's analysis of the spread of civilization from the river valleys into the semi-arid highlands and small coastal plains of the rest of the Near East (1951, 1954), it seems to have occurred primarily as a response to ecological condition number (4). The lack of resources in the major river valleys, he argues, led to the establishment of major trade routes, towns grew up at their termini which in turn were the foci of the extended Near Eastern civilization. Furthermore, the expansion occurred into an area where the environmental conditions permitted intensive and/or specialized (olives, dates, grapes, etc.) agriculture, on a small scale.

In the Old World another process developed hand in hand with civilization—urbanization. We have purposefully kept the two processes separate for reasons to be made explicit later.

I define urbanization as a process of evolution of rural communities into urban communities and further define an urban community as possessing the following attributes:

(1) Nucleation—in my analysis of modern urban communities in Mexico, all have population densities exceeding 2,000 persons per sq. km.

(2) Relatively large size—in another study, based on modern Mexico (Sanders 1956), I use a specific figure in defining towns and cities, but precise population sizes would not apply to all areas of the world. I would generally state that urban communities would have at least 2,000 to 3,000 inhabitants, and reserve the term city for those with populations exceeding 10,000.

(3) Most of the population are nonfood producers, or at least only part-time food producers, and the majority of the population is composed of part and full-time specialists in the production and distribution of technology, regulation of social interaction, or administration of services to the supernatural.

(4) A great deal of social differentiation based on occupation, status, control of power, and in some cases, ethnic diversity. In the early development of urban centers in the Near East, the larger communities were political and religious centers, as well as commercial and industrial communities, and the growth of cities was a process directly linked to the growth of the state.

Having set the stage, in terms of basic concepts, definitions, and events in the Old World, I will now attempt to apply these concepts to the New World. As far as present research indicates, the civilizations of the New World developed independently from those of the Old World, from the same kind of folk technological base, thus providing us with a good laboratory test of the above concepts.

Cultures possessing the attributes of civilization occurred in the New World in two regions, the Mesoamerican and the Andean. The fundamental ecological patterns in the Andean region, in terms of the essential factors that permit the development of a civilization comparable to that of the Near East, correspond to a striking degree. In Peru, the heart of the Andean region, there are three primary, parallel, narrow, north-south ecological strips. To the east is a humid, slope and foothill zone with exuberant tropical forest cover. In the center is a high mountainous region with numerous small and large valleys and basins varying in altitude from 5,000 to 13,000 feet above sea level. All over this strip the climatic type is similar to our type (2) in the Near East, light to moderate rainfall concentrated in the summer season. Average rainfall over the area varies from 500–750 mm. a year. To the west is a nearly rainless desert crossed east to west by some 25 streams which have their sources in the mountains and flow to the sea, each providing water for a small, compact irrigated plain and isolated from other systems by intervening deserts. The Andean civilization centered in the mountain and desert strip and apparently never penetrated the eastern forest with any degree of success. The ecological principles of the Old World apparently may be applied very successfully to the Andean area, and along the coastal desert, at least, urbanization correlated in its development with civilization.

I will now turn to my primary area of interest and research—Mesoamerica. Here the interrelationships between environment and culture are much more complex. The area is ecologically much more diverse than any other region where pre-Iron Age civilizations have developed. Rainfall varies from

300 mm. in southeastern Puebla to over 5,000 mm. in the northeastern escarpment of Chiapas. Altitude varies from sea level to 2,800 m. (in the area of dense human population) with a corresponding great range of temperature. Vegetation varies from near desert conditions to lush tropical rain forest, soils from siernozems to laterites, hydrography from no surface drainage to small flood season streams, to great rivers with huge tributary basins and extensive flood plains. Within this over-all diversity, in terms of problems faced by neolithic farmers, two well defined ecological patterns emerge: (1) a Lowland pattern with heavy rainfall, exuberant vegetation, lower density and more scattered population, with slash and burn cultivation of basic foodstuffs and orchard cultivation of commercial crops; and (2), a Highland pattern with low rainfall, scanty vegetation, dense population living in larger nucleated communities and practicing intensive agriculture.

In actual fact, parts of the Lowlands have subhumid climates, and parts of the Highlands, humid climates, and any detailed analysis of the area should consider these exceptions.

In 1519, the Mesoamerican variant of civilization occurred over the entire region in all of the various ecological zones, including both Highlands and Lowlands. Urbanism, however, has been demonstrated as a corollary trait only in the Highland province, and in reality only definitely in the Central Plateau or Mesa Central of Mexico. In a more expanded paper, to be published in the projected Handbook about Mesoamerican Indians, I have analyzed in detail the role of this area in the development of urbanism and civilization in Mesoamerica. We will present here some of the results of this analysis and apply our basic concepts from Old World archeology.

Within the plateau is a small, compact, centrally located zone we will call the Nuclear Area because of its cultural dominance in the history of Mesoamerica. It includes the Valley of Mexico, Valley of Morelos, and the upper Atoyac-Nejapa drainage basin in Tlaxcala—Western Puebla, an area of approximately 20,000 km. In 1519, 20 percent of the population of Mesoamerica resided in this demographic heartland, approximately $2\frac{1}{2}$ million people. Both Pan-Mesoamerican empires, Aztec and Toltec, had their capitals in this area, and earlier Teotihuacan seems to have been the center of a third, similar state. It is also one of the main contenders for the scene of the origins of American Indian agriculture and Mesoamerican civilization.

The annual rainfall in the area of heavy human occupation is everywhere below 1,000 mm., generally ranging from 500–800 mm., most of which falls in the summer months. Vegetation cover is sparse and presents no serious challenge to primitive farmers. Within the fundamental unity is a great deal of diversity based upon altitudes ranging from 800 m. to 2,800 m. above sea level, in some parts of the area over a distance of only 50–60 km. Every agricultural plant in the Mesoamerican complex may be grown in some part of the area, and agricultural specialization has probably always been a distinctive feature. Soils generally are classed by Mexican agronomists as Chestnuts or Chernozems and with relatively simple techniques of soil restoration have sustained nearly continuous cropping for at least 3,500 years. The ecology generally is similar to type (2) in the Near East. There is no single great river system (although most of the area is drained by tributaries of the Balsas river) that could have served a single integrated irrigation system or provided a single transportation artery. In the Valley of Mexico, however, where two-thirds of the population resided in 1519, there was a chain of lakes that played the same role as the rivers in Old World centers of civilization.

Having described the general environmental factors of the area, let us now examine them as operational factors in the evolution of urban civilization. In the discussion we will refer back to our previous definitions of urbanization and civilization, and here, as in the Near East, the two processes were correlative and simultaneous.

(1) The ecological conditions noted above are optimal for the development of an intensive system of agriculture. Studies by Palerm (1954, 1955), Wolf (1955), Millon (1957), Armillas (1949, 1950) and myself (ms) have demonstrated conclusively that agriculture in 1519 was as intensive as in the great centers of the Old World civilizations. The combination of low rainfall, easily controlled natural vegetation, fertile soils, water resources (lakes, springs, flood water, melt water from glaciers), and generally limited flat terrain made almost imperative the development of such techniques of soil and water conservation as permanent irrigation, chinampas, flood water irrigation, cajete planting, stone and maguey terracing, and fertilization. In the strip above 2,000 m. the possibilities of early frost and retarded rainy season made irrigation necessary for really effective cultivation, even though 500–800mm. of summer rains would ordinarily be ample. The application of this body of practices resulted in an extremely dense population as contrasted to other areas of Mesoamerica. I have postulated that civilizations with a Neolithic technological base can only develop with a relatively dense population. I furthermore insist that urbanization can develop only under even more demanding demographic conditions, especially in Mesoamerica, with hand tillage. I doubt that the neolithic farmer with hand tools can produce more than a 20 percent surplus. A city of 100,000 population would require a rural population of 500,000 to support it. In the history of the Nuclear Area, two cities, Tenochtitlan and Teotihuacan reached that size.

(2) One of the attributes of an urban community is nucleation. In Gordon Childe's analysis of Mesopotamia (1954), he discusses the process as one of increasing size and social complexity from the Neolithic village to the Copper Age town to the Bronze Age city. In this concept the process begins with a small nucleated community. In terms of the *origin* of urban societies the presence of a rural population living in nucleated as opposed to dispersed communities seems to me a necessary requirement for such a development. Furthermore, in the transition period of growth from village to city, agriculture continued as the primary base, so that intensive agriculture would seem to be a necessary condition for such demographic growth, since the agricultural land still remains relatively accessible even when the population runs into the

thousands. My analysis of rural settlement patterns in modern Mesoamerica, and documentary and archeological studies of the pre-Hispanic periods, suggests that the rural settlement pattern in our Nuclear Area from the early pre-Classic to the modern period was basically one of nucleated villages. In the Nuclear Area today the degree of nucleation of the rural community correlates directly with the intensity of agriculture.

(3) One of the characteristic features of our Nuclear Area, as was stated previously, is ecological diversity. This is true of most of the Mesoamerican Highlands. At the time of the conquest and in some of the Highlands today we find an intensive development of regional trade and specialization on a rural community level. As Sol Tax (1952) has pointed out, in the Highlands of southwestern Guatemala, rural communities depend as much on trade for their livelihood as do cities. Although geographical diversity is of course not the only factor involved in this development, certainly it has acted as a powerful stimulus. If we argue that urbanization developed basically out of the agricultural folk society that supported it, and economic specialization is one of the most characteristic traits of urbanization, then the process by which urbanism evolved in Central Mexico seems apparent. Some urban communities grew up at crucial places, in terms of transportation, such as lake shore termini (Chalco) and altitude strips on the border of the Tierra Templada-Tierra Fria. Furthermore, in terms of the origins of cities and towns as centers of trade and craft specialization, the closeness of ecological zoning in Mesoamerica was an important precondition because of the primitiveness of land transportation.

(4) One of the major problems in Mesoamerica as a whole in the support of urban communities was the feeble development of transportation technology. By land, all cargo was hauled by human carriers so that only the closeness of ecological zoning permitted a relatively close spacing of markets and a heavy volume of trade. The chain of lakes in the Valley of Mexico provided a powerful stimulus to trade and undoubtedly was one of the crucial factors in the development of urbanism.

(5) Palerm, Wolf, Millon and Armillas in various papers have attempted to apply the concept of the Irrigation State to the Nuclear Area, but, thus far, with inconclusive results. One of the major problems in setting up a theoretical construct is purely archeological, the lack of data on the age of irrigation in the area. We know, on the basis of documentary and archeological evidence, that it was of great significance during the Aztec period; but it has not been specifically established for the Teotihuacan period where we have evidence for the first large state and urban community in the area. One important difference between our area and the center of Old World civilization is in the hydrographic pattern. In the Nuclear Area there are a great number of separate systems, each of which during the Aztec period provided water for a small, distinct, integrated irrigated system. Of interest with respect to this is the fact that the city state, made up of a small urban town and its dependent villages, was the largest *stable* political grouping. This is in contrast to Egypt where the normal pattern was political unification of the entire river valley. Supra-city

state aggregations did occur several times in the Nuclear Area, but the constituent city states maintained their separate political and social structure and were never integrated into a state of the Egyptian type.

I am not arguing here, of course, that political states of the size of ancient Egypt, or even larger, could not exist in the environment of Central Mexico (the case of the Inca of Peru obviously makes this position untenable). What I am saying is that, in this type of ecology, city-state political integration is the largest level that one can link directly with ecological factors. Palerm and Wolf, in a brilliant essay on the rise of the state of Acolhuacan on the east shore of the lake in the Valley of Mexico, have pointed out the subtle inter-relationships between environment, agricultural technology, and socio-political systems (Wolf and Palerm 1955). In this case they postulated the integrative effects of irrigation on the state, but went further and demonstrated, in this area, that the state, once created, regardless of the factors that produced it, acted as a sponsor of extensive irrigation works and as a mechanism of producing a surplus to strengthen its power and further integrate the socio-economic system.

(6) The Nuclear Area is chronically one of overpopulation, a characteristic feature of mountain countries. Population clusters are isolated by high ranges and barren hills into separate compartments. Good flat land is premium land and never abundant so that the topography has always presented serious obstacles to an expanding population. This problem was met by improvement of agricultural technology, but, I suspect, that by Teotihuacan times the basic inventions had all been completed, except probably chinampa agriculture. It could also be met by social techniques, such as a thorough integration of the population by a system of centralized control for the construction of hydraulic works, terraces, and expansion into marginal lands.

Trade itself is one way of meeting the problem, since maguey, a staple food, can grow on even the most barren hillsides, and specialization of crop production would further increase the efficiency of land use. Spanish descriptions of the control of agriculture by the state suggest that, in fact, by 1519 such social techniques were practiced. Another response is, of course, war, conflict, and conquest between the city states and the expropriation of lands or systematic taxation of conquered groups. This in turn would of course strengthen the power of the state and was one of the factors responsible for the growth of towns into cities. Cook, in an article on Mesoamerican demography, considered war as a demographic safety valve along with human sacrifice.

It has only been in relatively recent times that the concepts of Old World culture history have been applied to Mesoamerica, under the leadership of Julian Steward in the United States and Pedro Armillas in Mexico. H. J. Spinden (1928) anticipated this recent development in the 1920's, but he remains a lone pioneer. The lack of such attempts between the years 1930–1950 demands some explanation, since this period was an exceedingly productive one in basic research in Mesoamerican archeology. The primary reason was undoubtedly the development of research in the Maya Lowlands, where archeological exploration revealed the presence of an extraordinarily rich regional variant of Mesoamerican civilization in a humid forested lowland plain. This discouraged attempts to relate the growth of the civilization to environmental factors. Such research developments furthermore tended to obscure the fact that most of Mesoamerica is, in fact, a sub-humid area. Excluding most of the Yucatan Peninsula, parts of the Gulf Coast, narrow strips of escarpment, a few small segments of the Pacific coast, and parts of the Guatemala Highlands, rainfall over most of this huge area is either less than 1,000mm. a year, or is so irregular from year to year that some techniques of humidity conservation are necessary for an effective enough system of agriculture to provide the demographic basis of a civilization.

The primary agricultural system in most of Lowland Mesoamerica is one called variously in the literature slash and burn, swidden, shifting cultivation, and, in Mexico, roza. It is a system practiced all over the world in tropical areas and, even where iron tools are used, it tends to be correlated with a low population density and a simple folk rural society residing in small, socially autonomous communities. This generalization is even more valid if we apply it to cultures with neolithic technologies. A variant of it was apparently practiced by neolithic societies in humid northern environments as well (northern and central Europe, eastern U. S.) (Childe 1951).

In the New World, outside of Mesoamerica, this system of farming was practiced all over the lowlands of eastern South America and around the Carribean; and nowhere in this huge area was it the base of a culture of the type we are calling civilization.

The occurrence of Mesoamerican civilization in the tropical lowlands of Mesoamerica, based on slash and burn agriculture, is a unique one and demands further explanation. On the basis of published settlement pattern studies in the Peten and my own studies in northern Yucatan, Tabasco, central Vera Cruz, and the Huasteca, one can say that urbanism was not a correlative trait with civilization in those areas. The density of housemounds at sites such as Tikal, Uaxactún, Chichén Itzá, and the Puuc sites is well within the range of a rural, or at least suburban, population. Bullard (1960), in his survey of a large area of the northern Petén, found a surprising lack of correspondence of house clusters to major ceremonial complexes. Apparently the settlement pattern was composed of two basic social levels: (1) a ceremonial center with a small resident priest-craftsman population as the dominant level, and (2) hundreds of small dependent rural hamlets occurring in a nearly continuous distribution between the ceremonial centers. This demographic and social pattern clearly relates to slash and burn agriculture and the primitiveness of Mesoamerican transportation. Apparently the system will permit a dense enough population to support a civilization of the Mesoamerican type but not urbanism, and the demands of this system for space tend to produce a dispersed agricultural population.

In recent years there has been a gradual crystallization of two opposed theoretical positions in the interpretation of the culture history of Mesoamerica: (1) in one position the area of the birth and early development is thought to have occurred in the humid lowlands based on slash and burn agriculture; (2) in the other, the development of civilization is seen as a corollary process with urbanization and occurring first in some part of the sub-humid highlands with intensive agriculture. It is postulated that it then spread into the humid lowlands where, because of the ecological conditions, the development of urbanism was aborted.

Archeological data per se cannot, at the present state of knowledge, resolve the conflict one way or the other. I have, of course, as the previous discussion indicates, accepted this latter approach. Specifically my position may be elaborated in the following points:

(1) Mesoamerican civilization developed first in Central Mexico as a corollary process with urbanization.

(2) This kind of culture which we are calling civilization must have its roots in the folk society, that was its basal level and required the special kind of folk society that intensive agriculture produces. I see very little in the character or personality of a slash and burn folk society or economy that would lead to the development of civilization.

(3) The spread of Mesoamerican civilization into the lowlands was a process directly related to the regional pattern of specialization and symbiosis we discussed previously. As civilizations expanded in the highlands and immediate lowland strips, then the trade orbits were extended all the way to the coast and all of the lowland province shared in the general civilization. This did not occur in the Andean region, primarily because there was a lowland strip along the Pacific coast which had the proper ecological conditions for intensive agriculture. In Mesoamerica, subhumid lowland areas were more restricted in extent and so the humid areas were incorporated.

(4) The spread of Mesoamerican civilization into the humid lowlands was only a partial success, as the spectacular collapse of the Petén Maya civilization demonstrates. The fall of Maya civilization was qualitatively different from the fall of the contemporary Classic civilization of Teotihuacan. In the case of the latter, newer and equally vigorous civilizations replaced it, and the collapse occurred only in the upper, urban level. All of the evidence, archeological and documentary, in the Petén demonstrates that there not only the upper level but the folk agricultural society collapsed as well. There is very little evidence of a post-Classic population in the area, and Spanish records give one the impression that the population in the 16th century was nearly as sparse as the modern.

REFERENCES CITED

ARMILLAS, PEDRO
    1940 Notas sobre los sistemas de cultivo en Mesoamerica. Anales del Instituto Nacional de Anthropologia y Historia, No. 3, Mexico.
    1950 Teotihuacan, Tula y los Toltecas. *In* Runa Vol. 3:37–70. Buenos Aires, Archivo para las Ciencias del Hombre.

BENNETT, WENDELL C. and JUNIUS B. BIRD
    1949 Andean culture history. Handbook series No. 15. Americal Museum of Natural History.

BULLARD, WILLIAM R.
    1960   Maya settlement patterns in north eastern Petén, Guatemala. American Antiquity 25:355–72.

CHILDE, V. GORDON
    1951   Social evolution. New York, Henry Schuman Inc.
    1954   What happened in history. London. Pelican Books.

COOK, SHERBURNE F. and L. B. SIMPSON.
    1958   The populations of Central Mexico in the sixteenth century. Berkeley. University of California Press.

KROEBER, ALFRED L.
    1948   Anthropology. New York, Harcourt, Brace, and Company.

MILLON, RENE
    1957   Irrigation systems in the Valley of Teotihuacan. American Antiquity 23:160–66.

PALERM, ANGEL
    1954   La distribucion del regadio en el area central de Mesoamerica. Ciencias Sociales, Notas e informacione. 5:2–15, 64–74. Union Pan Americana.
    1955   The agricultural bases of urban civilization in Mesoamerica. *In* Irrigation civilizations: a comparative study. Pan American Union, Social Science Monographs.

SANDERS, WILLIAM T.
    1956   The central Mexican symbiotic region: a study in prehistoric settlement patterns. Viking Fund Publication, no. 23:115–28.

SEARS, PAUL
    1951   Pollen profiles and culture horizons in the basin of Mexico. *In* Civilization of ancient America. XXIX International Congress of Americanists. University of Chicago Press.

SPINDEN, HERBERT J.
    1928   Ancient civilizations of Mexico and Central America. American Museum of Natural History. Handbook series No. 3, 3rd and rev. ed.

TAX, SOL
    1952   Heritage of conquest. Glencoe, The Free Press.

WEST, ROBERT and PEDRO ARMILLAS
    1950   Las Chinampas de Mexico. Quadernos Americanos, año 9, No. 2:165–82. Mexico.

WITTFOGEL, KARL A.
    1956   Hydraulic civilizations. *In* Man's role in changing the earth. University of Chicago Press.
    1957   Oriental despotism. Yale University Press.
    1958–59   Contemporary China. Hong Kong University Press.

WOLF, ERIC R. and ANGEL PALERM
    1955   Irrigation in the old Acolhua Domain, Mexico. Southwestern Journal of Anthropology 11:265–81.

ARCHEOLOGY

Mexico. MICHAEL D. COE. (Ancient Peoples and Places, Vol. 29.) New York: Frederick A. Praeger, 1962. 244 pp., bibliography, index, 32 line drawings, 8 maps, 75 plates, 1 chronological table. $6.95.

Reviewed by WILLIAM T. SANDERS, *Pennsylvania State University*

This book by Michael Coe is a welcome addition to the all too few general syntheses of Mesoamerican culture history for the lay and professional reader. It covers all of Mesoamerica west of the Maya, but the entire Maya area is excluded. This omission of one of the most spectacular regional variants of Mesoamerican civilization (and one of the best documented) is perhaps the major defect.

The book is organized primarily by culture stages, with chapters on "Early Hunters," the "Archaic Period," the "Formative Period: Early Villagers," the "Formative Period: Early Civilizations," "The Classic Period," "The Post Classic Period: Early Militaristic," and "The Post Classic Period: The Aztec Empire."

My general impression is that the first four phases are much more adequately covered than the latter three. I am particularly unhappy about the persistence of a number of outmoded viewpoints that few researchers, especially specialists in the Central Plateau, would accept today. One of these is the uncritical acceptance of the documentary references to migration legends that refer to the Post Classic Period. At times the documentary history resembles a gigantic chess game—a historical picture greatly at variance with what we know about peasant society. This leads Coe to accept what to me has always been an incredible fable: the destruction of cities by "Chichimec"

Reprinted from AMERICAN ANTHROPOLOGIST 65, 1963. pp. 972-974.

hunters, and the myth of the miserable, barbarous Aztec migrants who come into the valley as foreigners and are finally civilized by the remnants of older peoples. The model of the contrast of the peaceful Classic to the warlike Post Classic is still supported by Coe, although with reservations. Coe to the contrary, Classic art is full of war symbols and his point as to the lack of Classic fortifications is extremely misleading; Monte Albán has one of the most spectacular defensive settings of any Mesoamerican site, Xochicalco with its hilltop location and series of moats and walls is Late Classic in time (in a chronological sense), and many major Post Classic centers lack fortifications (Cempoalla, Texcoco, Cholula, Huejotzingo, Mitla, and Tenochtitlán).

The rich ethnographic information on the Aztec, which offers a mine of interpretive data for the archeologist, is scantily treated and although Coe does reject some of Bandelier's hypotheses about Aztec socio-political institutions much of Bandelier's influence can be seen in his reconstruction.

• Xochicalco and Cholula, two of the largest sites in Mesoamerica, are very cavalierly treated; in part this is not Coe's fault since the role of neither has been adequately and fully documented.

One other misconception, which I feel must stem from Coe's greater familiarity with the Maya area, is that true cities are rare in Mesoamerica. Actually, aside from the two described (Teotihuacán and Tenochtitlán), urban communities of all sizes from small towns to great cities were characteristic of the Central Plateau from Late Pre-classic times to the Conquest and were probably found in the Oaxaca Highlands as well.

With respect to the settlement pattern of Teotihuacán, Coe is in error on two points which have been established by recent research, some of it unpublished. The residential area of Teotihuacán is at least double Armillas' estimate of three square miles. Coe has also followed the orthodox procedure of labelling as "palaces" the large residential complexes (that include formally organized room complexes with a central ceremonial-social court) of Tetitla, Tepantitla, Teopancaxco, Yayaguala, Atetelco, Zacuala, and Xolalpan. In reality they are big communal houses each occupying an entire urban block. The bulk of the residential zone is probably occupied by a regular grid of alleys separating these "palaces." The huge, sprawling, disordered aggregation of alleys, courts, and rooms found by Linné at Tlamimilolpa is probably characteristic only of the peripheries of the city.

My major adverse criticism of the book, however, lies in the entire theoretical approach. In Mesoamerican archeology in recent years there have evolved at least two fundamental schools with respect to the origin of Mesoamerican civilization. One group sees the semi-arid highlands as the center of Mesoamerican cultural development. They have attempted to apply the basic principles established by the specialists in the Near East to Mesoamerica, and stress the role of hydraulic agriculture in the evolution of cities and states. The other school sees Mesoamerican civilization as evolving in the tropical lowlands, based on slash and burn agriculture, with religion involving an elaborate Rain God cult, as the vehicle of its evolution. Coe's book is the most convincing and vigorous presentation of the latter view and stands in contrast to Wolf's *Sons of the Shaking Earth*, a major work of the Highland School. As an exponent of the Highland School myself, I of course disagree with many of Coe's points.

I will here voice some of my objections to Coe's handling of this issue.

1. Some of his reasoning sounds circular and inconsistent. He accepts Sears' pollen profile of the Valley of Mexico (which is highly suspect anyway) in which the Classic is visualized as a period of low rainfall, and even suggests that the collapse of Teotihuacán may have been the result of this climatic deterioration. Yet he also unceremoniously denies the role of irrigation in the evolution of the city!!

I agree that direct archeological data for Classic irrigation is skimpy, but indirect data from present day and Post Classic meteorological conditions and agricultural practices (today irrigation is crucial to successful farming and yet the Classic is visualized as drier still!) and Classic settlement patterns suggest the importance of irrigation in earlier times.

2. It will come as a shock to researchers familiar with the Valley of Mexico to discover on p. 71 that life is so easy for farmers in that area, that in Toynbee's terms, no challenge is there and therefore no response! This is part of Coe's argument emphasizing the "marginality" of the Valley in the Pre-classic to the Gulf Coast, the latter area being visualized by him as the heartland. Coe concludes that dense forests in the lowlands offer a great challenge and civilizations evolved there first in Toynbee's terms. Coe here confuses the simple physical challenge offered by forests to cultivators and universally solved by small group cooperation (frequently even on a familial level), with the type of challenge offered by arid regions in which large cooperative groups are necessary for effective manipulation of the environment. The latter ecological system can be easily seen as the basis of civilizational growth, whereas there seems little theoretical rationale behind the concept of such a growth from the ecological system of the lowlands.

3. On p. 78 Coe emphasizes the "fact" that during the Pre-classic the Central Plateau played a "marginal" role and that the "main currents of Mesoamerican Civilization" flowed to the south and east, especially along the east coast. In another section he admits the local roots of Classic Teotihuacán and the tremendous all-pervasive influence of Teotihuacán on all other Classic cultures. This poses a peculiar semantic problem: what are "main currents" and what is "marginality"? If Teotihuacán becomes the dominant Mesoamerican culture during the Classic, and if its roots are in the local Pre-classic, does not the local Pre-classic represent the "main current" of Mesoamerican civilization? This argument is further strengthened by the clearly dominant role of the Valley during the entire Post Classic period. The argument presented by Coe offers a number of exceedingly difficult problems which he does not attempt to answer or even suggest that they exist. Why should the Central Plateau play the role of a dominant center for 2,000 years from the Proto Classic until 1962? Furthermore, since Coe admits the priority of the area with respect to the incipient phases of plant domestication, why then did it play the "marginal" role for 1,500 years of succeeding Pre-classic?

4. The major argument in favor of the Lowland School is based on archeological data from southern Vera Cruz where Coe sees the Olmec culture as the "Cultura Madre," as did Covarrubias before him, in the evolution of Mesoamerican civilization. I still feel however that the geographical setting of the initial place of Olmec culture remains an open question. Olmec sites are abundant in the southern strip of the Central Plateau (southern Puebla, Morelos) and at least two Mexicans (Piña Chan and Covarrubias himself) have suggested this area as the birthplace of the culture.

5. Coe's vigorous defense of the Lowland School has led him to reject perhaps 90 percent of the C 14 dates from the Central Plateau as too early. If taken at their face value they suggest that each of the major ceramic stages of the Pre-classic was several centuries earlier in the Plateau than elsewhere.

6. The major defect of the entire Lowland argument is the complete lack of any functional theoretical system parallel to the Hydraulic hypothesis of the Highland School.

SWIDDEN AGRICULTURE AND THE RISE OF MAYA CIVILIZATION[1]

D. E. DUMOND

IT IS A COMMONPLACE to assert that one precondition for the rise of civilization is a degree of efficiency in the production of foodstuffs, whether stated in terms of economic surplus or of the harnessing of energy. This precondition customarily has been met through some system of agriculture, and it seems frequently to be assumed that the more intensive the agriculture, the more likely it is to produce the requisite surplus. Conversely it has also been argued that civilization has not developed where intensive agriculture did not exist—specifically in cases in which the only support was some form of shifting cultivation.[2] It is this thesis which will be briefly examined here, with special reference to the lowland Maya.

One approach is that of Meggers, who postulated a law to the effect that "the level to which a culture can develop is dependent upon the agricultural potentiality of the environment it occupies."[3] The tropical forest, doomed by natural conditions to be tilled by some method of shifting cultivation, is said thereby to possess a low absolute ceiling for cultural development. She includes the lowland Maya area within this land of little opportunity, and concludes that the lowland Maya

---

[1] Thanks are due R. D. Gastil, T. Stern, V. R. Dorjahn, and L. S. Cressman, who kindly read and commented upon a version of this paper, the L. S. and D. C. Cressman Prize Essay in Anthropology for 1960-61. None, of course, is responsible for its shortcomings.

[2] Civilization as here used refers to societies characterized by the most recognizable of the criteria presented by Childe (1950): the possession of "truly monumental public buildings," to which the concentration of "social surplus," some labor specialization, etc., are assumed to be corollary. Swidden agriculture, slash-and-burn or shifting cultivation, is defined after Pelzer (1945, p. 17), as involving rotation of fields rather than crops; clearing by means of fire; use of human labor only; lack of manuring; use of dibble or hoe; use of short periods of cultivation alternating with long periods of fallow.

[3] Meggers, 1954, p. 815.

developed civilized knowledge and skills before their arrival in the Petén, and subsequently spent their most spectacular era in a recessionary decline to which the system of agriculture was causal. Swidden agriculture as a basis for civilized developments is held in similar low esteem by others. Barrau, for instance, indicates it can provide only for subsistence.[4] The FAO staff assert that under such a backward system no concentration of population, and hence no urbanization, is possible.[5] Palerm and Wolf state flatly that "slash and burn agriculture . . . could not provide a stable economic basis for the growth and existence of Maya civilization."[6]

But the objection made is not necessarily based upon a lack of productivity, in terms of the return for an hour's labor. On the contrary, efficient swidden farming is seen by many students to be capable of producing a definite surplus. Although this potentiality seems fairly well established, a short review may be in order. It must be emphasized, however, that data are generally scanty, often unreliable, and that efficiency of shifting cultivation practices varies tremendously.

In Mexico, Lewis indicates that yields per acre from maize swiddens of Tepoztlán farmers average twice as high as those from continuously cropped lands.[7] Kelley and Palerm report that Tajín Totonac swidden farmers as a whole tend to produce a small amount more than they consume.[8] LaFarge and Byers state that the swidden farmers of Jacaltenango, in western Guatemala, raise enough maize to carry on a considerable export business.[9] Figures provided by Villa Rojas suggest that in 1935-36—a better-than-average year—the X-Cacal Maya harvested almost three times their annual requirement of maize, and that without farming to capacity they are able to develop and maintain a surplus sufficient to tide them over two or three lean years.[10] Various other studies indicate that swidden farms in the Mexican tropics are capable of producing a maize surplus of from 20 to 100 percent of subsistence needs.[11]

In temperate Europe the Finno-Ougrian peoples in the nineteenth century are reputed to have obtained from shifting cultivation a yield of rye three to four times as high as that possible from continuously cropped fields.[12]

4 Barrau, 1959, p. 55.
5 FAO staff, 1957, p. 9.
6 Palerm and Wolf, 1957, p. 26; cf. Palerm, 1955, p. 31, Wolf, 1959, p. 77.
7 Lewis, 1955, p. 155f. Productivity per hour of labor *with oxen* in the continuously cropped fields is about fifty percent higher than that without oxen in swiddens. Such a comparison is of course not valid when applied to pre-Columbian Mexico.
8 Kelly and Palerm, 1952, p. 118.
9 LaFarge and Byers, 1931, p. 71.
10 Villa Rojas, 1945, pp. 60, 65.
11 Morley, 1947, p. 154; Emerson and Kempton, 1935, p. 140; Drucker and Heizer, 1960.
12 Clark, 1952, p. 92.

SWIDDEN AGRICULTURE

The situation reported from southeast Asia is similar. Conklin suggests that production per man-hour in Hanunóo rice swiddens in the Philippines "compares favorably with labor cost figures for rice production under the best conditions elsewhere in the tropics."[13] Figures presented by Gourou suggest that irrigated rice agriculture in the heavily populated Tonkinese Delta is less than half as productive as the Hanunóo swiddens, in terms of expended man-hours.[14] Among the Land Dayak of Sarawak, Geddes reports that irrigated (swamp) swiddens—presumably of higher fertility than would be unfertilized, continuously cropped wet fields in the same area—may not yield more than good upland swiddens.[15] Halpern cites figures from Laos and other portions of Indo-China which "indicate the possibility that hectare for hectare in any given season swidden cultivation can be more productive" than irrigated rice farming.[16] Gourou also points out that a shift from swiddens to "intensively cultivated, permanent fields does not necessarily carry with it an increase of productivity—not if the available arable area is so spacious as to permit suitable fallows and thus evade the risk of soil exhaustion. Tropical cultivators are aware of this." Consequently, he says, swidden agriculturalists may oppose changes in their agricultural systems on purely material grounds:

The peoples of some mountains of West Africa (Atacora Mountains, Bauchi Plateau, Mandara Mountains, Adamawa, etc.) learned relatively intensive agricultural techniques, such as artificial terracing and manuring, in response to a crisis: they had retreated into the mountains primarily for defense against external dangers, particularly against the raids of slavers. The establishment of peace and the suppression of slavery allowed these peoples to abandon their mountains and to clear the surrounding plains where arable areas were plentiful. In the new environment they are forgetting these techniques and returning to *ladang* [i.e., swidden farming], in which they find greater productivity. In the same way, all the efforts made between 1920 and 1940 to lead the Moi Rhade (Annamite Cordillera of Indochina) to utilize the plow and to till inundated rice fields have been wasted. . . . They have observed that permanent rice fields, without manure, gave a lesser output per day of work than *ladang*. . . . Still worse, the Vietnamese colonists of Ban Methuot, Darlac, have turned for the first time to *ladang* and have abandoned the ancestral plow.[17]

Leach has thrown further light on the change from extensive to intensive cultivation, with evidence from North Burma:

---
13 Conklin, 1957, p. 152.
14 Gourou, 1956, p. 342.
15 Geddes, 1954, pp. 65f.
16 Halpern, 1958, p. 33.
17 Gourou, 1956, p. 345.

It is noticeable that in the areas of very low population density where the land was plentiful, shifting cultivation was always the preferred technique; efforts by the government to persuade the population to adopt fixed agriculture was almost completely futile. On the other hand wherever the local population density was high so that land was scarce, terraced agriculture is the standard, traditionally established, preferred technique. There is no cultural difference between the shifting agriculturalists and the terraced field agriculturalists. Precisely the same tribal peoples practice both forms of cultivation. They recognize the two techniques as alternatives and are prepared to discuss the relative merits of both. Terraced agriculture represents much harder work but can be relied upon to produce a moderately good yield. Shifting agriculture on the other hand will produce a very high yield in areas where the forest cover has been thick but a very poor yield in areas of deforestation. There is therefore a perfectly definite economic point at which, from the villager's point of view it becomes advantageous to change from shifting agriculture to terraced agriculture.[18]

Clark indicates that the Danubians of Neolithic Europe probably abandoned their swidden agriculture in favor of more intensive methods of tillage only when the population density was too great to permit the shifting system to operate.[19] This may be of general occurrence. It seems not unlikely, for instance, that in ancient Mesopotamia a similar cause existed for the movement of peoples from the hills where agriculture had begun, down toward the dry Mesopotamian plain itself, about 5000 BC,[20] a movement which seems to have necessitated the first use of irrigation,[21] and perhaps of intensive farming techniques.

Bartlett suggests that "wherever a few colonists of a higher culture have gone into countries of primitive culture, they have largely dropped to the primitive [generally swidden-using] level of agriculture. This is well demonstrated by the history of the colonization of the eastern United States. . . ."[22]

Rather than find swidden farming of doubtful productivity, therefore, it seems reasonable to suggest that for reasons of productivity there is everywhere a tendency to employ patterns of cultivation which rely upon movement of the field when fertility drops from over-cropping, rather than systems of intensive cropping. One might go farther and suggest that such practices of extensive agriculture are normally adhered to until population pressure becomes such that the system ceases to be viable through lack of sufficient land for rotation. Such a tendency toward extensive use would not operate, of course, where soil fertility does not diminish— for whatever reason—after continued cultivation, and might be modified in cases

---

18 Leach, 1959, pp. 64f.
19 Clark, 1952, pp. 98f.
20 Braidwood, 1960, p. 148.
21 Adams, 1955, p. 9.
22 Bartlett, 1956, p. 709.

where use of draft animals makes intensive but less productive cultivation easier in terms of human effort.[23]

But as indicated previously, a lack of productivity per man-hour does not constitute the grounds for the final censure of swidden agriculture. Most critics condemn swidden systems as "a wasteful method."[24] Leach suggests that most criticisms base themselves on the destruction of timber and the dangers of deforestation and erosion.[25] That it is wasteful of forest cover is to an extent clear. In its better examples, however, it seems generally to be conservative of soil fertility: Popenoe, for example, suggests that swidden agriculture in the valley of the Polochic River in northern Guatemala represents a very conservative practice, with the soil exhibiting comparatively high levels of fertility.[26] Many other students agree with him.[27] The significance of this for the support of civilization is clear. A well-balanced system of shifting cultivation should be capable of indefinite duration.

But criticisms of systems of shifting cultivation as foundations for civilizations go beyond productivity and the waste of resources. Meggers states that the shortcomings (for present purposes) of swidden agriculture are notably two: a relatively large amount of land per capita must be available for agricultural use; and settlements cannot remain permanently in one place.[28] Wolf states that "slash-and-burn cultivation usually implies a scattered population, a population unwilling to pay homage to a center of control."[29] Other critics agree.[30]

That settlements are in some instances forced to move to keep up with swiddens is undeniable. It is apparently documented in the case of the temperate zone Finno-Ougrians cited above, even though in preference to moving, lands might be cultivated as much as forty miles away;[31] it is also strongly suggested for the Danubians.[32] It is the case with modern peoples, as for instance with the Djarais of central Vietnam, who reportedly succeed in wrecking each piece of land they utilize by continued burning of undergrowth, and consequently are forced into periodic moves.[33] It is also true in the case of pioneer agriculturalists like some Iban of

---

23 Cf. note 7, above.
24 Childe, 1951, p. 64; also, e.g., LaFarge and Byers, 1931, p. 69, and FAO staff, 1957, p. 9.
25 Leach, 1959, p. 64.
26 Popenoe, 1959, p. 76.
27 As, Barrau, 1959, p. 55; Lafont, 1959, p. 56; Meggers, 1957, p. 81.
28 Meggers, 1957, p. 82.
29 Wolf, 1959, p. 77.
30 E.g., FAO staff, 1957.
31 Clark, 1952, p. 96, with references.
32 *Idem,* p. 95.
33 Lafont, 1959.

Sarawak who exhibit a habitual preference for virgin timber, and move in order to find it.[34]

But this pattern is by no means universal. A great proportion of swidden farmers are in sufficient balance with their environment that they remain sedentary.[35] Both Conklin and Carneiro present formulas by means of which the balance between population and land may be calculated, in terms of the number of people which may be supported permanently in a given area.[36] With his, Carneiro calculates that a swidden farming group of low-average efficiency in tropical South America should be able to support nearly five hundred people in a single sedentary settlement, and that the Kuikuru of the Upper Xingú region of Brazil could support a farming population of two thousand people in a single sedentary village, in place of their present 145. These figures are in terms of manioc cultivation with 0.7 acre to a full acre per person per year in cultivation. This compares with the figure furnished by Drucker and Heizer for the amount of maize land per year per capita needed in the La Venta region;[37] but the fallow time is shorter in La Venta, so that it seems likely that even larger sedentary farming towns could be supported there.

If the compulsion to frequent movement of villages is not found a necessary part of much tropical swidden farming, the need for large amounts of land per capita cannot be avoided. It is this need which provides the limiting factor in swidden agriculture—a limit to productivity per area, rather than productivity per man-hour. The total number of people supportable in a given area is smaller; population density is of necessity more sharply limited.

In the case of some extremely low-density populations, areas of population concentration are possible and usual—as, for instance, in the case of nomadic peoples who come together in a periodic throng, and remain together in certain seasons with the throng moving as a unit. Such mobility is lacking in the case of swidden agriculturalists, for the most part; it seems likely that in addition to supporting a population of limited overall density the tendency will be for the population to be dispersed in small towns or villages—at least that portion of the population directly engaged in agricultural pursuits, and during the period in which agricultural labor is necessary.

This is the situation envisioned by Wolf, when he terms such a system "centrifugal."[38] And it is perhaps at this point that the crucial question has been raised.

---

34 Freeman, 1955.
35 Barrau, 1959, p. 55; Pelzer, 1958, p. 127.
36 Conklin, 1959; Carneiro, 1960.
37 Drucker and Heizer, 1960.
38 Wolf, 1959, p. 60.

It seems clear that the better swidden systems in reasonably adequate areas are capable—in terms of return on labor invested—of producing an amount adequate to support not only ceremonial centers but population centers, and a number of specialists. Emerson and Kempton suggest, for example, that where present agricultural practices in Yucatán and Campeche produce a surplus of about twenty percent over the subsistence needs of the cultivators, the same farming population should be capable of doubling its grain output, "thus making possible the food requirements of a non-productive population four or five times that of the present one" of Mérida and Progreso.[39] To be sure, Palerm argues that such support would be impossible for dispersed farmers to provide under aboriginal conditions, from sheer awkwardness of distribution when transportation depended only upon human carriers.[40] But in spite of this assertion the pre-Columbian city of Mayapán in Yucatán remains an example of a center of concentrated population, traditionally supported for two hundred fifty years in an area for which nobody, so far as I am aware, has suggested the practice of anything but swidden agriculture, with a transportation system depending upon nothing but manpower. Palerm and Wolf state that this particular argument "is deceptive in its superficiality," insofar as it supports the case for development of civilization in swidden farming regions, for "the Northern Maya territory was conquered by war-like groups who settled in nucleated and fortified sites from which they dominated and subjected the rural population. The basic patterns of social, political and military organization, however, were introduced from the Mexican highland."[41] Superficial or not, the example supports the supposition that swidden agriculture and transport by human porters is sufficient to provide for an urban settlement, once it has developed.

The problem remaining, then, concerns the assertion that shifting cultivation is by its nature socially "centrifugal," and hence is inimical to the centralization implicit in any civilization, including the Maya—whether the latter in its Classic manifestations in the Petén involved "urban" concentrations of city dwellers or whether it existed in terms of ceremonial centers supported by a dispersed population. At this point little argument should remain in terms of subsistence economics. The problem is one of social organization.

Kroeber, when discussing the effect of the size of a society on its organization, suggests that urbanism—civilization in the present sense—is more likely in larger societies.[42] Steward argues that high population density without centralization

---

39 Emerson and Kempton, 1935, p. 140.
40 Palerm, 1955, p. 31.
41 Palerm and Wolf, 1957, pp. 27f.
42 Kroeber, 1948, pp. 272ff.

does not produce cities.[43] That is to say, the size of the society, in Kroeber's terms, is a matter of organization; a large society is possible—theoretically, at least—in an area of dispersed population as well as in an area of population concentration. The question to be raised here is whether a measure of social centralization may be achieved by people who live as dispersed as do swidden farmers.

What population densities are possible under swidden agriculture? Pelzer suggests that up to one hundred thirty per square mile may be supported in the Asiatic tropics without soil damage.[44] Ooi Jin-Bee provides a list of carrying capacities of lands under shifting cultivation in tropical areas, varying from eighteen to one hundred sixty persons per square mile, with more than half the eleven figures above eighty.[45] Some of these involve root crops, but more involve the cultivation of upland rice. One citation refers to a maize producing area, British Honduras, with a figure of sixty per square mile. Drucker and Heizer provide figures for La Venta which indicate that one person could be fed indefinitely by a maize production of 3.75 acres.[46] If somewhat less than sixty percent of the total land area is arable—about the proportion found usable in a study at Uaxactún[47]—such a region would support one hundred per square mile. Emerson and Kempton suggest that with farming methods in practice at the time of their study, Campeche and Yucatán could support sixty per square mile, and that the carrying capacity could be increased without drastic or harmful change in methods.[48] Densities such as those mentioned here, one might point out, are not extremely low.

That populations no more dense than these are capable of centralized organization seems evident from the most superficial consideration of evidence from Africa, a continent of relatively light population, but

from the point of view of organization and administration, the political acumen . . . in tribe after tribe equals, where it does not surpass, anything in the nonliterate world. Not even the kingdoms of Peru and Mexico could mobilize resources and concentrate power more effectively than could some of these African monarchies, which are more

---

43 Steward, 1955, pp. 73ff.
44 Pelzer, 1945, pp. 23, 29.
45 Ooi, 1958, p. 113.
46 Drucker and Heizer, 1960, p. 43.
47 Morley, 1947, pp. 313f.
48 Emerson and Kempton, 1935. By way of comparison, Thompson (1954, 29) suggests population figures such that ancient inhabitants of the Petén and Yucatán would not have exceeded one million at their most populous; using Morley's (1947, p. 316) estimate of 50,000 square miles for the habitable (not total) area of the Yucatán peninsula, one arrives at a figure of twenty inhabitants per habitable square mile, or ten per square mile of total area. This seems modest indeed. Morley's more ambitious figure of 13,300,000 inhabitants provides a density of 133 per square mile—probably too high, but no higher than figures from present-day swidden-farming areas of Java, Malaya, and northern Nigeria (Ooi, 1958, p. 113).

to be compared to Europe of the middle ages than referred to the common conception of the "primitive" state.[49]

Although population figures for portions of Africa are notorious for their inaccuracy, at least a rough idea may be gained of certain aboriginal densities. According to figures presented by Forde, estimated census figures for the Yoruba in 1921 were slightly over two million, with those of 1931 running slightly more than three million, an unlikely increase of fifty percent in ten years.[50] Hardly more believable is the increase necessary to achieve the 1952 census figure of more than five million. There are, however, a number of estimates of the size of individual Yoruba settlements, and it seems reasonable that these figures are more apt to be accurate than those for the Yoruba as a whole. Bascom[51] presents figures for a number of large Yoruba settlements which may be compared; summing these for 1911 and for 1952—and excluding figures for the modern city of Lagos—one obtains a suggestion of an increase in these populations of some one hundred percent in the indicated forty years. Bascom's citation of Moloney's estimates of ten city populations of 1890 are higher in total than are the same cities in the 1911 census, perhaps as the result of inaccuracy of estimates in either count, or it may be that in 1890, at the end of a long period of slave wars, the population was more concentrated than it was twenty years later. Allowing for a considerable population decline in the nineteenth century as a result of the wars, or for a modern increase in urbanization, one might rather tentatively suggest an increase of fifty percent in general population between 1850 and 1952. Applying this proportion to figures for population density cited by Bascom from the 1952 census, one obtains an approximate range of 1850 population densities between fifty-five and two hundred forty per square mile.[52] Of these, only the density of Ibadan province (at two hundred forty) exceeds one hundred per square mile, and the city of Ibadan itself, with a population in 1952 of nearly 460,000, is known to have developed principally as a nineteenth century military center.[53] These people are swidden agriculturalists, today raising chiefly yams, maize, bananas, and manioc as subsistence foods.[54] Their penchant for dwelling in big settlements, however, was well

---

49 Herskovits, 1948, p. 332.
50 Forde, 1951, p. 3.
51 All subsequent Yoruba census figures are from Bascom, 1959, pp. 31-33.
52 In a personal communication, William Bascom generously provided suggestions of means for tentatively estimating 1850 Yoruba population density, emphasizing that all such estimates must remain somewhat questionable for lack of sufficient and reliable data. His assistance is greatly appreciated, but it should go without saying that he can in no way be held responsible for any untoward results.
53 Bascom, 1959, p. 35.
54 Forde, 1951, p. 6.

developed at the time of the first European contact. Such centers are reported from early in the sixteenth century. In the 1850's they were estimated to have at least nine settlements with populations between twenty and seventy thousand, with craft specialization and social stratification.[55]

Less spectacularly, the Azande of Sudan are estimated at 231,000, in figures cited by Baxter and Butt.[56] The Zande district of Sudan, as mapped by de Schlippe, cannot include more than twenty thousand square miles.[57] The density, therefore, should not exceed twelve per square mile. The Azande maintain dispersed settlements, and their traditions and swidden agricultural operation—the latter utilizing millet, maize, sorghum, rice, pulses, and some oil seeds[58]—are such that moves of homesteads are fairly frequent, some of them motivated by soil depletion, but others brought about by other causes.[59] This is an indigenous pattern, yet the indigenous organization was markedly centralized, with a pyramidal organization headed by a king from a hereditary ruling clan, to whom were owed services and tribute. In some areas at least, the number of people under a semi-independent chief, subordinate to a king, might reach or exceed ten thousand.[60]

In sum, although it seems reasonable that shifting cultivation should tend to produce scattered populations, such scattering is apparently not always the result, and even when it does occur it may not preclude the support of a centralized social or political organization. Parenthetically, Kroeber's citation of Mooney's figure for the population density of the federally-bent five Iroquois tribes is less than one per five square miles.[61]

---

55 Bascom, 1959, pp. 31, 38ff. The Yoruba base much of their subsistence upon root crops, and it seems possible that such crops may produce more heavily than will cereals or maize. Barrau (1959, p. 54), for instance, indicates that in Melanesia generally about one quarter acre of garden suffices to feed one person for one year, and that a total of about two and one half to five acres suffices to feed one person indefinitely. Figured as above, with about sixty percent of the area cultivable, one finds that in Melanesia between about seventy-five and one hundred fifty people could be supported per square mile. It may be noted, however, that anthropologists have not always agreed on the potentiality of root crop cultivation: Palerm and Wolf (1957, p. 28) suggest that large sedentary populations may be supported by root crops in tropical areas more easily than by maize; Meggers (1957, pp. 82f) suggests the reverse—that root crop cultivation is more centrifugal than cultivation of temperate crops, because the lack of a single season of maturation means that farm work is more constant, hence dispersed fields must be tended more frequently. At any rate, with the exception of those for the Ibadan area, the Yoruba densities arrived at above seem in general accord with the carrying capacity of land in the lowland Maya area as estimated by Emerson and Kempton (1935) and others.

56 Baxter and Butt, 1953, p. 13.
57 De Schlippe, 1956, p. 5.
58 *Idem*, pp. 48ff.
59 *Idem*, pp. 191ff.
60 Baxter and Butt, 1953, pp. 48ff.
61 Kroeber, 1939, p. 140.

That some patterns of shifting cultivation do militate against social cohesion in terms of supra-village units, is not denied. This must certainly be the case with peoples who are still "pioneers"—breakers of virgin soil—as in the case of the Iban of Sarawak mentioned above. Here, on rather poor land, is possible a density of thirty-five to forty people per square mile, although present density is much less as the population continues to spread in search of virgin timber, utilizing techniques which are generally destructive of soil.[62] In this area there is still new land to be gained. Here, village long-house communities are the only groups with any cohesion above the nuclear family, having functions in the sphere of religion and the settlement of land claims, but without productive economic role.[63]

The situation is somewhat changed among the Land Dayak of Sarawak, however. Here Geddes reports a heavier population, having little virgin timber land available.[64] When villages multiply through a process of hiving off, daughter villages may continue to pay allegiance to the mother village.[65] And this situation is important to the present argument, for in the maintenance of such ties may be found the seeds of a later centralized development.

Lacking such affective ties, village units might be united by warfare. Herskovits suggests that,

> In all West Africa, the early organization seems to have been that of village autonomy or, at most, the rule of several neighboring settlements by the head of the largest village, so that the number of petty kingdoms which existed before the time of their consolidation into great kingdoms such as Dahomey, Benin, Ashanti, and others, was extensive.[66]

The extent to which warfare was causal, however, is not certain. Bascom, for instance, indicates that "we cannot say either that the early Yoruba cities did or did not develop as defensive or predatory centres, as Ilorin, Abeokuta and Ibadan did in the 19th century. But urbanism clearly antedated the slave trade to the Americas. . . ."[67]

It has been suggested by Willey, based in part on work by the Coes at Nohoch Ek,[68] that even the smallest Pre-classic villages in Mesoamerica may be found eventually to have been constructed around modest ceremonial centers.[69] If the

---

62 Freeman, 1955, p. 134.
63 *Idem*, pp. 8-10.
64 Geddes, 1954.
65 *Idem*, p. 10.
66 Herskovits, 1938, vol. 2, p. 3.
67 Bascom, 1959, p. 38.
68 Coe and Coe, 1956.
69 Willey, 1957, p. 1.

situation is such that new villages retain some allegiance to the ceremonial centers of parent villages, the seeds of centralization have been sown.

Pre-classic remains are not plentiful in the lowland Maya area, to judge by excavations to date. It seems possible that during Pre-classic times small, more or less autonomous villages spread through the lowland Maya area, perhaps in search of virgin land. As the land was filled, migrations became less frequent, and ties between related villages became stronger, with ceremonial relationships elaborated. From this developed the centralization of Classic times, aided, perhaps, by a little warfare here and there. The result of such a process should be very close to the organization of the Maya as formulated by Willey.[70]

The foregoing should not be construed as an argument that Classic Maya civilization in the lowlands was never supported by anything but swidden agriculture. The question as to what was in fact the basis of subsistence can be answered only from work in the field. Rather, this paper is intended to suggest that the development of a centralized, stratified system such as seems indicated for the Classic Maya is by no means impossible under conditions of shifting cultivation. Indeed, present indications of intensive agriculture in ancient Mesoamerica are not demonstrably as early as the rise of notable ceremonial centers at the beginning of the Classic and earlier. Consequently, on the basis of present evidence and in spite of the argument of Palerm that concentration of resources and major ceremonial centers are impossible under conditions of rainfall agriculture in Mesoamerica,[71] it seems only reasonable to conclude that the development of such concentrations and such centers began under conditions of extensive—as opposed to intensive—agricultural practices, probably largely swidden agriculture. It is further suggested—although a consideration of the question has not been attempted here—that a similar development may have occurred in other areas generally conceded to have supported civilizations, at least in those areas in which rainfall agriculture is possible at all.[72] In areas where feasible, however, the growth of population would shortly have made the practice of some form of intensive agriculture necessary.

That is to say, it seems likely that centralization and urbanization tend to pre-date the appearance of intensive cultivation and of heavy population growth. Although a discussion of the mechanisms involved is again outside the scope of this paper, it seems likely that by increasing the chances of human survival such

---

70 Willey, 1956.
71 Palerm, 1955, p. 31.
72 Pelzer (1945, p. 20), for example, cites suggestions to the effect that swidden agriculture was basic, or at least extremely important, to other tropical civilizations, specifically that of Angkor, in Cambodia, and that of Anuradapura, in Ceylon.

centralized organization may stand in a causal relation to population growth, rather than vice versa.

BIBLIOGRAPHY

ADAMS, R. M.
  1955 "Developmental Stages in Ancient Mesopotamia" (in *Agricultural Civilizastions: a Comparative Study*, Pan American Union, Social Science Monographs, no. 1, Washington).

BARRAU, J.
  1959 *The "Bush Fallowing" System of Cultivation in the Continental Islands of Melanesia* (Proceedings, Ninth Pacific Science Congress, 1957, vol. 7, pp. 53-55, Bangkok).

BARTLETT, H. H.
  1956 "Fire, Primitive Agriculture, and Grazing in the Tropics" (in *Man's Role in Changing the Face of the Earth*, W. L. Thomas, ed., Chicago: University of Chicago Press).

BASCOM, W.
  1959 *Urbanism as a Traditional African Pattern* (The Sociological Review, n.s., vol. 7, pp. 29-43, Keele: University College of North Staffordshire).

BAXTER, P. T. W., AND A. BUTT
  1953 *The Azande and Related Peoples of the Anglo-Egyptian Sudan and Belgian Congo* (Ethnographic Survey of Africa, East Central Africa, pt. 9, London: International African Institute).

BRAIDWOOD, R. J.
  1960 *The Agricultural Revolution* (Scientific American, vol. 203, pp. 130-148.)

CARNEIRO, R. L.
  1960 "Slash-and-burn Agriculture: a Closer Look at Its Implications for Settlement Patterns" (in *Men and Cultures*, A. F. C. Wallace, ed., Philadelphia: University of Pennsylvania Press).

CHILDE, V. G.
  1950 *The Urban Revolution* (Town Planning Review, vol. 21, pp. 3-17).
  1951 *Man Makes Himself* (New York: Mentor Books).

CLARK, J. G. D.
  1952 *Prehistoric Europe: the Economic Basis* (New York: Philosophical Library).

COE, W. R., AND M. D. COE
  1956 *Excavations at Nohoch Ek, British Honduras* (American Antiquity, vol. 21, pp. 370-382).

CONKLIN, H. C.
  1957 *Hanunóo Agriculture* (FAO Forestry Development Paper, no. 12, Rome: FAO).
  1959 *Population-Land Balance under Systems of Tropical Forest Agriculture* (Proceedings, Ninth Pacific Science Congress, 1957, vol. 7, p. 63, Bangkok).

DRUCKER, P., AND R. G. HEIZER
   1960   *A Study of the Milpa System of La Venta Island and Its Archaeological Implications* (Southwestern Journal of Anthropology, vol. 16, pp. 36-45).

EMERSON, R. A., AND J. H. KEMPTON
   1935   *Agronomic Investigations in Yucatán* (Carnegie Institution of Washington Yearbook, vol. 34, pp. 138-142, Washington).

FAO STAFF [FOOD AND AGRICULTURE ORGANIZATION OF THE UNITED NATIONS]
   1957   *Shifting Cultivation* (Unasylva, vol. 11, pp. 9-11, Rome: FAO).

FORDE, D.
   1951   *The Yoruba-Speaking Peoples of South-Western Nigeria* (Ethnographic Survey of Africa, Western Africa, pt. 4, London: International African Institute).

FREEMAN, J. D.
   1955   *Iban Agriculture* (Colonial Office, Colonial Research Studies, no. 18, London).

GEDDES, W. R.
   1954   *The Land Dayaks of Sarawak* (Colonial Office, Colonial Research Studies, no. 14, London).

GOUROU, P.
   1956   "The Quality of Land Use of Tropical Cultivators" (in *Man's Role in Changing the Face of the Earth*, W. L. Thomas, ed., Chicago: University of Chicago Press).

HALPERN, J. M.
   1958   *Aspects of Village Life and Culture Change in Laos* (Special Report for the Council on Economic and Cultural Affairs, Inc., New York: Council on Economic and Cultural Affairs, Inc.).

HERSKOVITS, M. J.
   1938   *Dahomey: an Ancient West African Kingdom* (New York: J. J. Augustin, 2 vols.).
   1948   *Man and His Works* (New York: Alfred A. Knopf).

KELLY, I., AND A. PALERM
   1952   *The Tajín Totonac: Part 1, History, Subsistence, Shelter and Technology* (Smithsonian Institution, Institute of Social Anthropology, Pub. 13, Washington).

KROEBER, A. L.
   1939   *Cultural and Natural Areas of Native North America* (University of California Publications in American Archaeology and Ethnology, vol. 38, Berkeley: University of California Press).
   1948   *Anthropology* (New York: Harcourt, Brace and Co.).

LAFARGE, O., II, AND D. BYERS
   1931   *The Year Bearer's People* (Tulane University Department of Middle American Research, Middle American Research Series, Pub. 3, New Orleans).

LAFONT, P.-B.
   1959 The "Slash and Burn" (Ray) Agricultural System of the Mountain Populations of Central Vietnam (Proceedings, Ninth Pacific Science Congress, 1957, vol. 7, pp. 56-59, Bangkok).

LEACH, E. R.
   1959 Some Economic Advantages of Shifting Cultivation (Proceedings, Ninth Pacific Science Congress, 1957, vol. 7, pp. 64-66, Bangkok).

LEWIS, O.
   1955 Life in a Mexican Village (Urbana, Illinois: University of Illinois).

MEGGERS, B. J.
   1954 Environmental Limitation on the Development of Culture (American Anthropologist, vol. 56, pp. 801-824).
   1957 "Environment and Culture in the Amazon Basin: an Appraisal of the Theory of Environmental Determinism" (in Studies in Human Ecology, Pan American Union, Social Science Monographs, no. 3, Washington).

MORLEY, S.
   1947 The Ancient Maya (Stanford University: Stanford University Press).

OOI JIN-BEE
   1958 The Distribution of Present-Day Man in the Tropics: Historical and Ecological Perspective (Proceedings, Ninth Pacific Science Congress, 1957, vol. 20, pp. 111-123, Bangkok).

PALERM, A.
   1955 "The Agricultural Bases of Urban Civilization in Mesoamerica" (in Irrigation Civilizations: a Comparative Study, Pan American Union, Social Science Monographs, no. 1, Washington).

PALERM, A., AND E. R. WOLF
   1957 "Ecological Potential and Cultural Development in Mesoamerica" (in Studies in Human Ecology, Pan American Union, Social Science Monographs, no. 3, Washington).

PELZER, K. J.
   1945 Pioneer Settlement in the Asiatic Tropics (American Geographical Society, Special Publication 29, New York: Institute of Pacific Relations).
   1958 Land Utilization in the Humid Tropics: Agriculture (Proceedings, Ninth Pacific Science Congress, 1957, vol. 20, pp. 124-142, Bangkok).

POPENOE, H.
   1959 The Influence of the Shifting Cultivation Cycle on Soil Properties in Central America (Proceedings, Ninth Pacific Science Congress, 1957, vol. 7, pp. 72-77, Bangkok).

SCHLIPPE, PIERRE DE
   1956 Shifting Cultivation in Africa (London: Routledge and Kegan Paul).

STEWARD, J.
   1955 "Some Implications of the Symposium" (in Irrigation Civilizations: a Comparative Study, Pan American Union, Social Science Monographs, no. 1, Washington).

THOMPSON, J. E. S.
    1954   *The Rise and Fall of Maya Civilization* (Norman, Oklahoma: University of Oklahoma Press).

VILLA ROJAS, A.
    1945   *The Maya of East Central Quintana Roo* (Carnegie Institution of Washington, Pub. 559, Washington).

WILLEY, G. R.
    1956   *The Structure of Ancient Maya Society: Evidence from the Southern Lowlands* (American Anthropologist, vol. 58, pp. 777-782).
    1957   *Selected Papers of the Harvard Middle American Archaeological Seminar, 1955-56: an Introduction* (Kroeber Anthropological Society Papers, no. 17, pp. 1-6).

WOLF, E. R.
    1959   *Sons of the Shaking Earth* (Chicago: University of Chicago Press).

UNIVERSITY OF OREGON
EUGENE, OREGON

An Agricultural Study of the Southern Maya Lowlands

URSULA M. COWGILL
Osborn Zoological Laboratory, Yale University

DURING the Classic Period of Mesoamerican prehistory (ca. A. D. 300 to 900) the cultural area corresponding roughly to the present Department of the Peten, Guatemala, and including British Honduras, was the setting of a high civilization characterized by monumental architecture, high artistic achievement, elaborate systems of writing, astronomy, calendrical computations, and at least a certain degree of social complexity. Partial decipherment of inscriptions and evidence of physical types indicate that the Classic Period population spoke a language belonging to the Mayan family and physically resembled modern Mayan speakers. The area is more or less that which was referred to as the Maya "Old Empire" (Morley 1946). At present it seems preferable to refer to it as the Southern Maya Lowlands; a term which does not make any inferences about the nature of Classic Period political organization.

At the close of the Classic Period the manifestations of cultural complexity mentioned above disappeared rather abruptly in the Southern Maya Lowlands. The area has long been known to have been sparsely populated since prior to first European contact in the 16th century, and recent archeological work (Willey 1956b; G. Cowgill 1959) tends strongly to confirm the suspicion that a sharp decline in population accompanied the cultural decline, or at least followed shortly thereafter.

A variety of explanations has been offered for these events. Some, such as disease or earthquakes, are unsatisfactory both because there is no evidence for any increase in these factors at the close of the Classic Period, and because populations remained high in the subsequent Postclassic Period in other areas equally or more susceptible to disease (e.g., northern Yucatan) or earthquakes (e.g., the Valley of Mexico). What evidence there is concerning climate suggests that there has been no appreciable change since the Classic Period (Hatt et al. 1953:39). A peasant insurrection against elite rulers would account for the disappearance of elaborate culture elements but not for the fact that the bulk of the population also disappeared, as Willey (1956b:781) has pointed out. Foreign invasions remain a strong possibility, but, as in the well-established early Postclassic invasions from Central Mexico into northern Yucatan, one would expect them to cause cultural changes but no marked long-term decline in population. Insurrections or invasions may have occurred at the close of the Classic Period, but in themselves they can hardly provide the full explanation for decline in both population and cultural complexity which lasted for a good half-millennium before European arrival in Mesoamerica.

Reprinted from AMERICAN ANTHROPOLOGIST 64, 1962. pp. 273-286.

Other explanations depend on the environmental adequacy of the Southern Maya Lowlands: in particular, on the feasibility of providing subsistence for the large part-time labor forces implied by the scale of Classic Period construction, and the smaller numbers of talented full-time specialists implied by achievements in art, astronomy, and mathematics. Recently Meggers (1954, 1957) has argued that the Southern Maya Lowlands, a tropical forest area now exploited by shifting slash-and-burn (swidden) agriculture, did not offer an adequate environmental potential. She suggests that Classic Period culture must have been developed in more favored areas and from the beginning in this tropical area was doomed to decline and eventual collapse. Coe (1957) has criticized this view on the grounds that there is no good evidence that Classic Period culture was not developed locally, and that the archeological record clearly indicates internal growth toward a climax near the end of this period rather than a continuous decline from the beginning. Still more recently, Ferdon (1959) has argued that the Southern Maya Lowlands are in fact an area of comparatively high subsistence potential.

These conflicting interpretations of prehistory in the Southern Maya Lowlands, as well as interest in its possible future, suggest a more critical examination of its subsistence potential, and, particularly, that it be asked under what conditions, and in what ways, food production might either fail or be increased.

Specifically, it would be desirable to know how many people per unit area could be fed by swidden agriculture on a long-term basis, what fraction of the total labor supply could be used for purposes other than food production, and whether any system more productive than swidden agriculture might have been feasible during the Classic Period.

A number of studies more or less relevant to these questions have been made, but the results are inconclusive for several reasons. Perhaps the most serious reason is that, with the exception of a few observations by Lundell (1937), these studies have been made in northern Yucatan. This environment differs from the Southern Maya Lowlands, notably in its considerably lower rainfall, and has had a decidedly different cultural history. While undoubtedly more relevant than data from the Guatemalan highlands, the data from northern Yucatan (Kempton 1935; Emerson n.d.; Emerson and Kempton 1935; Steggerda 1941; and Hester 1951, 1952, 1953, 1954) could be considered at best only suggestive, not conclusive, as far as the Southern Maya Lowlands are concerned.

Furthermore, these studies have been to some extent inconsistent in their conclusions about population density and division of labor permitted by swidden agriculture in Yucatan. While Kempton (1935) concludes that shifting of fields is necessitated by loss in soil fertility, and hence presumably could be avoided only through the application of fertilizer, Steggerda (1941) found no evidence for rapid loss in fertility and concludes that shifting is necessitated mainly due to the encroachment of weeds, particularly grasses.

Prior to the work of Hester, at least two different interpretations of the situation in the Southern Maya Lowlands seem to have been compatible with the data from Yucatan. Cook (1921) and Lundell (1937) have suggested that intensive swidden farming in late Classic times led to the conversion of large areas of forest into heavily sodded grasslands which could not have been worked with stone tools. On the other hand, Cooke (1931) and Ricketson (1937) have postulated nonshifting, intensive agriculture, and eventual disastrous erosion. Hester (1954), however, suggests that at least in northern Yucatan the environment was potentially capable of supplying an adequate and stable subsistence for the pre-Columbian population.

In order to obtain data which pertained specifically to the Southern Maya Lowlands and which might be more conclusive than previous work, the author (an agronomist by professional training) carried out field work in 1959 in the vicinity of Lake Peten, Department of the Peten, Guatemala.[1] This lake is near the center of the Southern Maya Lowlands; the range in topography, altitude, vegetation, soils, temperature, and rainfall encountered in the vicinity seems representative of most of the cultural area, although certain atypical environments, e.g., valleys of permanent rivers (such as the Belize or the Usumacinta) or low mountains (as in southern British Honduras), are not included.

Methods and results will be summarized and their implications discussed here. A report of the work and detailed comparison with data from Yucatan has been published elsewhere (U. Cowgill 1961).

Forty farmers in eight localities within the vicinity of Lake Peten were visited in their fields and asked if they were willing to provide data on their agricultural practices. In all cases permission was granted, and they were interviewed concerning their agricultural techniques, proportion of productive to fallow years they considered usual, actual number of years their present field had lain fallow, yields considered normal, yields in specific cases of re-using a field after a given number of fallow years, sizes of fields, times spent in the various steps of the agricultural cycle, types of maize and other plants grown, amount of harvest consumed by household, by animals, or sold, amount of maize purchased (if any), and size of household. At the same time their fields were observed, particularly with respect to size, slope and drainage, and appearance of soil. Crops, weeds, and trees were counted. Density, size, and evidence for disease, insects, and signs of deficiencies in nutrients or water were observed. One hundred and fifty-two soil samples were collected from planted fields, plots which had not been cultivated for a known number of years, areas to be employed in the following year, and climax forest.

With a few exceptions which will be noted below, the resulting data are applicable to conditions during the Classic Period, since there is no evidence for any appreciable climatic change within the area nor for any new agricultural tools or techniques other than the replacement of stone implements by steel knives and axes.

Needless to say, not all interview responses were identical, nor can yield estimates be considered more than good approximations. Nevertheless, there is high internal consistency in the interview data, and from it and direct observations alone, several conclusions are clear.

Agriculture is of the shifting slash and burn type. A plot of forest is cut, allowed to dry, and then burned. A dibble stick is employed to make holes at regular intervals into which maize and other plant seeds (beans, cucurbits, and others) are dropped without other working of the ground. After one or two years the plot is abandoned to forest for some years of rest before being used again for a crop. Since relatively large areas of resting land are needed in proportion to the land actually under cultivation at any one time, this method usually requires much land for the permanent support of each household. Probably the most significant result obtained by interview and observational data is that the length of the necessary rest period is unusually short in the Peten. Of those who plant a single crop before moving to another location, three-fifths asserted that only two years of rest would be needed before the land could be used again, another fifth favored a three year rest, and the remainder gave replies from one to five years. Of those who plant two crops in succession, three-fifths said that five years rest is needed, one-fifth said three years, and the remainder gave from two to six years. Data on the actual number of years that fields being used in 1959 had rested indicated that, in general, actual rest periods were somewhat longer than those indicated in local theory. This, in itself, might be attributed to the fact that there is no shortage of land at present, so that a farmer may allow land to rest somewhat longer than he feels is strictly necessary. However, another method of determining length of the agricultural cycle is to take the 39 cases of yields reported after a given number of years of rest and plot scattergrams of yields as a function of years of rest. Separate plots were made for rest after a single crop and for rest after two crops in succession. In the first case, a linear correlation coefficient of 0.551 (significant beyond the 1 percent level by the t-test) was obtained, and, for two crops the linear correlation coefficient was 0.383 (significant beyond the 10 percent level). In each case, linear regression lines were fitted by the least squares method. For rest after one crop, the line reached the level of reported average yield from new plots after four years' rest, and, for two crops, after six to seven years' rest.

Summarizing these three lines of evidence, it is conservative to conclude that stable swidden agriculture can be carried out on the basis of four years' rest after a single crop, or six to eight years' rest after two successive crops. It is interesting to note that Drucker and Heizer (1960) have recently published data which indicates that an even shorter cycle is possible on La Venta Island.

It is clear that it is misleading to think of tropical forest swidden agriculture as being nearly the same everywhere. Very often conditions are such that rest periods of 15 to 20 years or more are needed (Kempton 1935; Emerson n.d.; Emerson and Kempton 1935; Steggerda 1941). Lower estimates of agricultural potential in northern Yucatan are due to a very large extent to the longer rest period apparently needed there.

The 40 farmers interviewed reported yields from first year plots averaging 1,425 lb. per acre and yields from second year plots averaging 1,010 lb. per acre. In five cases in which farmers reported experience with three years of successive planting, third year yields averaged 417 lb. per acre. These figures do not differ strikingly from those for northern Yucatan, which run from 930 to 1,400 lb. per acre for first year fields and from 460 to 1,100 lb. per acre for second year fields (Kempton 1935; Emerson n.d.; Steggerda 1941), although the Lake Peten figures tend to be slightly higher.

Average reported daily consumption of maize, for people of all ages, is 1.7 lb. per person per day. Again, this figure agrees well with estimates ranging from 1.3 to 2 lb. per person per day which have been made by other workers for the Peten (Higbee 1948), Yucatan (Kempton 1935; Benedict and Steggerda 1937), and highland Guatemala (Stadelman 1940). It amounts to an average annual consumption of 636 lb. per person. However, this figure refers to shelled maize, while yield reports refer to weight of maize on the cob. It was found that 100 lb. of cob maize is roughly equivalent to 55 lb. of shelled maize. Hence, average annual consumption amounts to about 1,155 lb. of maize as harvested. To find the land area needed to produce such a yield one must of course take into account the total cycle, both years of production and years of rest. Where only one crop is grown at a time an effective yearly yield per acre can be found by dividing the average yield during the one year of planting by the number of years of rest, plus one for the year of planting. Where two crops are grown in succession, the effective annual yield can be found by taking average yield of a first year crop, plus average yield of a second year crop, and dividing the total by total years of rest, plus two for the two years of planting.

Since three means of estimating the needed rest period were used, three sets of calculations are possible. If we take rest periods reported as standard, 2.4 acres per person are needed when one crop is grown at a time, and 3.0 acres per person when two successive crops are grown. If rest periods actually reported in 1959 are used instead, the results are about 4.15 acres per person for single crops, and about 3.25 acres per person when two successive crops are grown. Finally, if the regression line data is used, the result is about 4.1 acres per person, whether one crop is grown at a time or crops are grown two years in succession.

Taking all three approaches into account, a figure of 3.25 to 4.3 acres per person seems a generous allowance. This amounts to about 150 to 200 persons per square mile. However, some areas are either unsuitable or of inferior quality for agriculture, and it seems that some allowance should be made for occasional periods of poor crops. It can be concluded that throughout most of the Southern Maya Lowlands, swidden farming could permanently support a population of 100 to 200 people per square mile.

On the basis of reported time required for agricultural work, it appears that one man, with some assistance from his wife and children, can care for up to 13 acres under cultivation in any one year. This is enough to supply the maize requirements of 12.6 people, and since reported size of household averaged 5.78 people, this implies that more than half the total labor supply is potentially available for construction of monumental centers and specialist activities.

It is important to note that the use of stone rather than steel tools would not imply any difference in the total population which could be fed. It only implies that a somewhat smaller proportion of the total labor supply would be available for tasks other than food production. Hester (1952) found that it took twice as long to clear a plot of land using limestone chips as with steel tools. Few operations other than clearing would be much affected by the absence of **steel** tools.

Another result which emerged quite clearly from observation is that there exists considerable evidence against the idea that excessive exploitation of the land leads to invasion by grass in the Southern Maya Lowlands. There are some savannas not far south of Lake Peten, but archeological sites are rare in them and are characteristically found in what is today forest rather than grassland. Since the statement that these savannas are "environmentally unaccountable" has become embedded in the literature and is still being repeated (Ferdon 1959:17), it is well to emphasize that they are clearly a natural phenomenon and not man made. Soils in these savannas are quite different from those in the regions covered by forest, and while forest areas are generally hilly and well drained, the savannas are flat and poorly drained. Limestone hummocks in these savannas often constitute isolated islands of forest vegetation surrounded by grass. On the other hand, there is probably no district in all the Peten which has been more continuously under cultivation than the very areas near Lake Peten where the data on which the present study is based were gathered. These are being most heavily used at present, and yet there is no tendency for grass to be a problem.[2]

From all these results two further conclusions can be drawn. First, since at least the Postclassic Period, the population of the Peten (which is about 1.5 persons per square mile today) has never even remotely approached the limit set by swidden farming. Had agricultural failure alone been the cause of depopulation at the end of the Classic Period, one would have expected a gradual recovery in population as the land itself recovered.

Second, swidden farming can very comfortably account for the labor supply implied by the scale of Classic Period ceremonial centers. It has been estimated that it would have been physically possible for a population of as little as 30 people per square mile to have built all the ceremonial centers in the Southern Maya Lowlands during the course of 600 years (G. Cowgill 1957). While this is an extremely rough calculation, there is no doubt that a population anywhere near 100 per square mile would have been ample.

It seems, then, that agricultural failure is not likely to have been a major factor and certainly was not the only factor in the collapse of Classic Period culture and the subsequent persistent sparse population of the Southern Maya Lowlands.

There are, however, two points which call for caution. First, the actual density of population at various times before, during, and after the Classic Period is still not well known. This cannot be estimated from the size and number of ceremonial centers, but only from careful surveys of dwelling sites over substantial areas, together with quite close chronological control through associated pottery or other means. This is a formidable task which has hardly been begun. At Uaxactun a large (2,273,920 sq. meters) cross-shaped area was cleared and house mounds counted. Assuming that all mounds were occupied simultaneously by households averaging five people and that the density of mounds in the sample is representative of the area as a whole, a population on the order of 1,000 per square mile is indicated (Ricketson 1937:15-24).

Bullard (1960) presents valuable material on settlements in the northeastern Peten, but concentrates more on the general distribution of house ruins and major and minor ceremonial centers than on quantitative population estimates. In one count of house mounds in a 215,000 square meter area at Dos Aguadas, a density of 2,300 persons per square mile was indicated, again assuming five people per mound and simultaneous occupation of all mounds (Bullard 1960:366).

As both Bullard and Ricketson have pointed out, the actual figures may have been much lower. Only by careful excavation and dating of occupations in a number of mounds might the number actually occupied at any one time be estimated. Furthermore, Bullard points out that, although Classic Period settlements are broadly dispersed, there is some tendency toward clustering, and Uaxactun and Dos Aguadas, both major ceremonial centers, probably have a density of house mounds that is higher, by some still very uncertain amount, than the over-all density for the Southern Maya Lowlands as a whole.

At present it seems distinctly possible that population in the Southern Maya Lowlands never exceeded the subsistence potential of swidden agriculture. But it is also quite conceivable that future work will demonstrate a growth in population during the Classic Period leading to temporary overstrain of the agricultural resources which might then be a factor in the initial population decline, if not in its persistence.

A second point requiring caution is that even if the subsistence requirements of the population can be shown never to have demanded anything other than swidden agriculture, this still does not mean that no other form was ever practiced. It would be quite interesting to know whether any more productive methods were workable—particularly whether any methods might have been used which would have *demanded* some substantial degree of socio-political integration and development of a managerial class—in contrast to slash and burn agriculture which *permitted* such elaborations but does not seem to have demanded them in any way.

This **raises** questions which cannot be answered by observation and interview **data** alone; in particular, the problem of determining precisely why there is **a decline** in yields upon successive use of a plot, and a recovery of agricultural potential when native vegetation has been permitted to return. Among factors which, singly or in combination, might account for decline in yields are: decline in soil fertility; competition of weeds with cultivated crops either for sheer space, nutrients, or water; and increased prevalence of insect or other pests.

If weed competition were the major factor, one could imagine the carrying capacity of the land being raised considerably above present values simply by more laborious weeding. If, on the other hand, decline in soil nutrients were the major factor, some form of manuring or fertilization would be needed to increase productivity. Without domesticated animals, it is hard to see how the Maya could have effectively fertilized more than a few small garden plots.

Workers in Yucatan (Kempton 1935; Emerson, n.d.; Emerson and Kempton 1935; Steggerda 1941; Hester 1951, 1952, 1953, 1954) have also been concerned with the cause of yield decline and while Kempton (1935) suggested that loss in fertility was the main factor, most people seem to have felt that weed competition was more important. In particular, Steggerda (1941) had annual chemical analyses performed over a period of several years on four plots that were subjected to differing treatments, which made it appear that weed competition must be the important factor. However, if Steggerda's data are plotted in graph form, it becomes clear that for some years all plots are low for a given element and for other years all are high. This situation strongly suggests variations in laboratory technique from year to year rather than real variations in the samples, and hence data from one year cannot properly be compared with data from another. In an attempt to make Steggerda's data somewhat more useful, one can take his plot D, which was forest left untouched during the years of the experiment, and which should not vary significantly from year to year in soil chemistry, and calculate values for each item measured in each plot as a percentage of those in plot D for each year. When this is done, there is still no obvious trend with increasing years of cultivation for nitrate nitrogen, carbonate carbon, calcium, magnesium, potassium, phosphorus, and manganese. There is slight evidence for a decrease in total nitrogen with successive crops, but no clear evidence for an increase in nitrogen with rest. Organic carbon, however, shows a consistent decrease with continuing cultivation and possibly an increase with rest. Organic matter, as measured by loss of weight on ignition, gives strong evidence for decrease with cultivation and increase with rest.

Thus, awareness of the possibility of variations in laboratory techniques leads one to a very different interpretation of the data than does the assumption that every figure emanating from a laboratory is to be taken as absolute truth. It appears that Steggerda's data in fact rather strongly indicate that loss in soil fertility is an important factor in yield decline in northern Yucatan.

It was in order to obtain data specific to the Lake Peten district and with the hope that more conclusive results could be obtained when more samples were used and when all analytical work was done at one time and place by one person, that the 152 samples of soil were collected while in the field. The needed analyses were completed by the author during the winter of 1960.

Oxidizable organic matter (Walkley 1947; Walkley and Black 1934), total nitrogen (Jackson 1958), plant available phosphorus (Truog 1930; Jeffries and Thomas 1960), exchangeable sodium, potassium, calcium, and magnesium (Kolterman 1952) and pH (Reed and Cummings 1945) were determined for all samples. The results were analyzed by a tri-factorial nonorthogonal statistical design (Stevens 1948) wherein the effect of three different factors, i.e., slope of land, location within eight geographical subregions around Lake Peten, and the agricultural cycle, were isolated.

Table 1 shows the corrected means obtained for samples drawn from each stage of the agricultural cycle of use and rest. "Climax" forest in this paper refers to land that has rested at least 25 years. These means have been corrected to remove the effects of slope and geographical subregions.

TABLE 1. CORRECTED MEANS FOR THE AGRICULTURAL CYCLE

Treatment	pH	N %	o.m. %	P ppm	K	Na	Mg	Ca
					milliequivalents/100 gms			
First year	7.48	.496	7.16	9.03	.46	.102	3.38	75.56
Second year	7.38	.467	6.68	8.87	.37	.071	3.26	64.30
Resting since 1958 after 2 crops	7.47	.481	6.83	6.42	.35	.060	2.69	73.33
Resting since 1958 after 1 crop	7.58	.486	6.99	7.28	.38	.074	3.48	78.56
Resting since 1957 after 2 crops	7.36	.472	6.76	7.77	.32	.069	2.96	69.19
Resting since 1957 after 1 crop	7.49	.481	6.85	11.08	.40	.081	3.53	86.17
Resting slnce 1956 after 2 crops	7.83	.466	7.47	7.43	.29	.033	1.82	35.90
Resting slnce 1956 after 1 crop	7.85	.499	7.93	11.33	.37	.047	2.53	74.04
Resting since 1955	7.56	.455	6.68	8.91	.85	.027	3.38	50.30
Resting since 1954	7.32	.519	7.36	9.10	.25	.106	3.45	73.15
Resting since 1953	7.41	.393	5.76	12.44	.17	.050	2.18	65.97
Resting since 1951	7.00	.503	7.58	6.44	.23	.090	3.01	55.18
Resting for 10 to 12 years	7.06	.499	7.41	7.18	.30	.105	3.58	67.70
"Climax"	7.47	.570	8.75	9.54	.30	.096	3.18	79.73

Employing the F-test, the differences between means for different stages in the cycle are significant beyond the 0.1 percent level for pH, organic matter, total nitrogen, and exchangeable potassium; beyond the 1 percent level for exchangeable sodium; beyond the 5 percent level for plant available phosphorus and exchangeable magnesium; and beyond the 10 percent level for exchangeable calcium.

The comparatively low significance level for calcium and magnesium, indicating that the agricultural cycle has comparatively little effect on these elements, is not surprising since limestone is the parent material of the soils in the Lake Peten district and supplies these elements in great quantities. It is possible that the somewhat low significance level for phosphorus is a result of the fact that archeological remains were irregularly scattered in many of the plots sampled. The phosphorus content of human occupation sites tends to be high.

If the corrected means for "climax" forest are used as a control and subsequently compared with the corrected means for first year plots, certain conclusions can be drawn about the effect of burning. Exchangeable sodium and pH are not affected. Exchangeable potassium and exchangeable magnesium increase with burning. It is to be expected that exchangeable potassium would increase since it is a normal component of charcoal. Organic matter, nitrogen, phosphorus, and exchangeable calcium all decrease with burning. It would be expected that both organic matter and nitrogen would decrease on burning, the amount of decrease being greater for hotter fires than cooler ones. Generally the fires used to clear fields leave black to gray ashes, indicating lower temperatures than those at which white ashes are produced.

There is no obvious reason why exchangeable calcium should decrease with burning, while one would expect plant available phosphorus to increase. It seems likely that the effect of burning on phosphorus was masked by the sporadic presence of archeological sites, a factor which could not be corrected for by the experimental design employed.

The effect of cultivation may be examined by comparing the results of first year plots with those of the second year. All items studied are present in smaller proportions in the second year, and it may be added that in the one third year plot sampled there was a significant decrease in all items measured as compared with the second year plots.

Taking first year means as 100 percent, second year means show a decrease of about seven percent in organic matter, six percent in total nitrogen, two percent in plant available phosphorus, and 20, 30, 4, and 15 percent for exchangeable potassium, sodium, magnesium, and calcium, respectively. The pH becomes slightly lower, i.e., more acid, but since the values are near the neutral range, the change is not important. The pH is in the optimum growth range for most cultivated crops.

The cumulative effect of the declines in the items measured would be enough to cause the corresponding decrease in yield that is apparent when a plot of land is subjected to two successive years of cultivation. It should be noted that leguminous plants had been grown in many of the fields included in this study.

In general, all items measured except pH increase during rest. Two crops tend to extract more from the soil than one in an absolute sense, and the effect of this is still evident in the chemical analyses after at least three years of rest. This result is consistent with the farmer's experience that a longer period of rest is needed after two successive crops than after one.

Examination of the data in more detail indicates that results for the sixth year of rest are rather odd. They are derived from determinations on only five samples, and if they are averaged with those of the fifth year, the results are less anomalous. The depth of the soil layer was not measured in any of these plots and in some cases may account for the rather large variations in percentages of elements during the rest periods.

The density of weeds on both first and second year plots was recorded and no significant relationship was found between density of weeds and years of cultivation.

Agriculture of the Maya Lowlands

Undoubtedly, insect and other types of damage cause some yield decline. In no first year plot examined was corn borer or any other form of insect damage found, with the exception of very small colonies of leaf-cutting ants, while both corn borer and leaf-cutting ants were prevalent in a few second year plots. However, it seems likely that these insects are a minor factor in yield decline compared with loss in soil fertility which was found sufficient to account for the observed decline.

In summary, the following points have been established:

1) Swidden farming is comparatively productive in the Southern Maya Lowlands and could support a population of 100 to 200 people per square mile. This contrasts with northern Yucatan where, mainly because of the necessity for a longer rest period, it seems that the estimated population limit is closer to 60 per square mile (Hester 1954).

2) Swidden farming with stone tools in the Southern Maya Lowlands would leave something close to half the total labor supply available for other tasks. Such a labor supply would suffice for construction of the monumental ruins of the Classic Period.

3) Nevertheless, Classic Period population may quite possibly have exceeded the limits set by stable swidden agriculture. Further work on settlements is needed in order to indicate whether or not this was the case.

4) Whatever the situation in other tropical forest areas, it is clear that grass invasion was not a problem in the Southern Maya Lowlands.

5) The supply of nutrients in the soil decreases when successive crops are grown on a plot and increases when plots are left uncultivated. It is felt that the decrease is large enough to account for observed declines in yields.

6) The present system of agriculture appears to be the most efficient possible for the present environment.

7) Since some time prior to the earliest European influence in the Southern Maya Lowlands, the population has remained something like a hundredth of the limit set by swidden farming.

8) Agricultural failure cannot be ruled out as a possible contributing factor in the collapse of Classic Period culture, but it can hardly account for the persistent and extreme depopulation of the area. The author is inclined to feel that the causes of cultural collapse and population decline were complex, and probably not due to any single factor.

NOTES

[1] This article is a revision of a paper read at the Annual Meetings of the American Anthropological Association in Minneapolis, November 19, 1960. The fieldwork was supported by the Henry L. and Grace Doherty Charitable Foundation, Inc. The laboratory facilities and equipment were provided through the kindness and generosity of G. E. Hutchinson of Yale University. Among numerous people who were of assistance in Guatemala, the author is particularly indebted to Mr. Dana Condon of the United Fruit Company and to the Rev. and Mrs. Stanley Storey of the Nazarene Mission in Santa Elena, Peten, Guatemala. My husband, George Cowgill, collected many of the soil samples, ground most of them by hand, provided useful discussions of Mayan cul-

ture history, drew my attention to some historical sources, and made other valuable suggestions which I gratefully acknowledge.

² Ferdon (1959:17) has suggested that these savannas may be the results of agriculture by the relatively small indigenous population found around Lake Peten in the 16th and 17th centuries. Cortes (MacNutt 1908: vol. 2:270–76) makes it clear that in 1525 these people had farms very close to the lake, in areas which are today forested or the site of present-day farm clearings. The savannas were already in existence and while there is an ambiguous reference that may mean there were some farms in them, it is clear that they were mainly grassland and used for hunting. Cortes' records on the distances he covered, alternately in savanna and forest, agree remarkably well with the present-day dimensions of these grasslands as determined from aerial photographs.

REFERENCES CITED

BENEDICT, F. G. and MORRIS STEGGERDA
    1937   Food of the present-day Maya Indians of Yucatan. Carnegie Institution of Washington Publication 456:155–88.

BULLARD, W. R.
    1960   Maya settlement pattern in northeastern Peten, Guatemala. American Antiquity 25:355–72.

COE, W. R.
    1957   Environmental limitation on Maya culture: a re-examination. American Anthropologist 59:328–35.

COOK, O. F.
    1921   Milpa agriculture, a primitive tropical system. Annual Report of the Smithsonian Institution for 1919:307–26.

COOKE, C. W.
    1931   Why the Mayan cities of the Peten district, Guatemala, were abandoned. Journal of the Washington Academy of Science 21:283–87.

COWGILL, G. L.
    1957   Culture and environment in the northern Peten region. Seminar paper, Harvard University. (Summarized by W. W. Howells *in* The application of quantitative methods in archaeology, R. F. Heizer and S. F. Cook, eds. Viking Fund Publication 28:158–85. 1960).
    1959   Postclassic Period culture in the southern Maya lowlands. Paper given at Annual Meeting of American Anthropological Association, Mexico City, 1959. Ms.

COWGILL, U. M.
    1961   Soil fertility and the ancient Maya. Transactions of the Connecticut Academy of Arts and Sciences 42: 1–56.

DRUCKER, P. and R. F. HEIZER
    1960   A study of the milpa system of La Venta Island and its archaeological implications. Southwestern Journal of Anthropology 16:36–45.

EMERSON, R. A.
    n.d.   A preliminary study of the milpa system of maize culture as practiced by the Maya Indians of the northern part of the Yucatan Peninsula. Cornell University. Ms.

EMERSON, R. A. and J. H. KEMPTON
    1935   Agronomic investigations in Yucatan. Carnegie Institution of Washington Yearbook 34:138–42.

FERDON, E. N., JR.
    1959   Agricultural potential and the development of cultures. Southwestern Journal of Anthropology 15:1–19.

HATT, R. T., et al.
    1953   Faunal and archaeological researches in Yucatan caves. Cranbrook Institute of Science Bulletin 33. Bloomfield Hills, Michigan.

HESTER, J. A., JR.
- 1951 Agriculture, economy, and population density of the Maya. Carnegie Institution of Washington Yearbook 51:266–71.
- 1952 Agriculture, economy, and population density of the Maya. Carnegie Institution of Washington Yearbook 52:288–92.
- 1953 Maya agriculture. Carnegie Institution of Washington Yearbook 53:297–98.
- 1954 Natural and cultural bases of ancient Maya subsistence economy. Doctoral dissertation, University of California, Los Angeles.

HIGBEE, E.
- 1948 Agriculture in the Maya homeland. Geographical Review 38:457–64.

JACKSON, M. L.
- 1958 Soil chemical analysis (pp. 183–190). Englewood Cliffs, N. J., Prentice-Hall, Inc.

JEFFRIES, C. D. and R. J. THOMAS
- 1960 Use of long chain polymers in preparation of soil extracts for soil testing. Science 131:660–61.

KEMPTON, J. H.
- n.d. Report on agricultural survey. Carnegie Institution of Washington Report to the Government of Mexico, 12th year of Chichén Itzá Project and Allied Investigations. Ms.

KOLTERMAN, D. W.
- 1952 Flame photometric determination of potassium, sodium, calcium, and magnesium in soil, plants and other materials. Doctoral dissertation, University of Wisconsin.

LUNDELL, C. L.
- 1937 The vegetation of Peten. Carnegie Institution of Washington Publication 478.

MACNUTT, F. A.
- 1908 Fernando Cortes: his five letters of relation to the Emperor Charles V. (2 vols). Cleveland, The Arthur H. Clark Company.

MEGGERS, B. J.
- 1954 Environmental limitation on the development of culture. American Anthropologist 56:801–23.
- 1957 Environmental limitation on Maya culture: a reply to Coe. American Anthropologist 59:888–90.

MORLEY, S. G.
- 1946 The ancient Maya. Stanford, Stanford University Press.

REED, J. F. and R. W. CUMMINGS
- 1945 Soil reaction-glass electrode and colorimetric methods for determining pH values of soils. Soil Science 59:103.

RICKETSON, O. G. and E. B. RICKETSON
- 1937 Uaxactun, Guatemala, Group E-1926–1931. Carnegie Institution of Washington Publication 477.

STADELMAN, R.
- 1940 Maize cultivation in northwestern Guatemala. Carnegie Institution of Washington Publication 523.

STEGGERDA, M.
- 1941 Maya Indians of Yucatan. Carnegie Institution of Washington Publication 531.

STEVENS, W. L.
- 1948 Statistical analysis of a non-orthogonal tri-factorial experiment. Biometrika 35:346–67.

THOMPSON, J. E. S.
- 1930 Ethnology of the Mayas of southern and central British Honduras. Field Museum of Natural History, Anthropology Series 17, No. 2. Chicago.

TRUOG, E.
>1930 The determination of the readily available phosphorus in soils. Journal of the American Society of Agronomy 22:874–82.

WALKLEY, A.
>1947 A critical examination of a rapid method for determining organic carbon in soils—effect of variations in digestion conditions and of inorganic soil constituents. Soil Science 63:251–64.

WALKLEY, A. and I. W. BLACK
>1934 An examination of the Degtjareff method for determining soil organic matter and a proposed modification of the chromic acid titration method. Soil Science 37:29–38.

WILLEY, G. R.
>1956a Problems concerning prehistoric settlement patterns in the Maya lowlands. *In* Prehistoric settlement patterns in the New World, G. R. Willey, ed. New York, Viking Fund Publications in Anthropology 23.

>1956b The structure of ancient Maya society; evidence from the southern lowlands. American Anthropologist 58:777–82.

AGRICULTURE AND THE THEOCRATIC STATE IN LOWLAND SOUTHEASTERN MEXICO

ROBERT F. HEIZER

ABSTRACT

Shifting cultivation, which is the technique commonly followed by tropical agriculturists, while wasteful of land use in requiring a long fallowing period, will support variable population densities depending upon crops grown, farming tools used, and soil fertility. Twenty persons per square kilometer is accepted as the density for the region around the Preclassic La Venta site which was begun about 800 B.C. and abandoned about 400 B.C. The occupation area of the La Venta culture group is believed to lie between the Coatzacoalcos and Tonalá rivers and amounts to about 900 square kilometers, thus yielding a population figure of about 18,000, of which 3600 are family heads. The total man-days of labor required to build the La Venta site is estimated to be 1,100,000, and the four major rebuildings of the site features are suggested as having been done at completion of 52 and 104 year calendar rounds.

THIS ARTICLE summarizes the procedures involved in the specialized system of cultivation practiced in the Mexican Gulf lowland tropics and concludes that this agricultural method provided sufficient economic support and surplus to make it possible for the theocratic or religious state to develop. The illustration chosen for the Preclassic theocratic state is one of the earliest of the great ceremonial centers of Mexico, that one called La Venta, which was built in the lowland jungles of southeastern Mexico early in the first millennium before Christ.

It is generally believed that New World higher civilization is a local, indigenous development (Willey 1960), that the inventions of plant domestication, complex religions, exact calendars, pottery-making, monumental sculpture, architecture, hieroglyphic writing, true-loom weaving, metallurgy, and the like, which might be called the aspects of high or advanced culture or civilization, were inventions made in America by American Indians.

The invention of agriculture constituted the first major revolution in man's existence, since it provided for a significantly large segment of humanity a means of economic security, settled life, production of surplus foods, and heavier populations which had more free time available which might be diverted into non-subsistence activities, and from which could develop specialization of skills (Boas 1912; Childe 1946; Kroeber 1923; 1948: 690). Eric Wolf, in his recent book on Mexico (1959: 51), says that agriculture

was certainly a major step in giving man greater control of his environment, toward making him its master rather than its slave. For a hunter and gatherer of wild food is a slave to his food supply; if his game or wild food crop is abundant, he may live the life of a savage Riley; if it decreases or vanishes, he may face extinction with it. In controlling the growth and maturation of plants . . . man still makes use of natural processes. But [in his role as a farmer] he assumes some of the functions of nature herself, replacing the natural controls over plant maturation and growth with his own.

Precisely when and where maize, or corn, the main food plant of the North American Indian farmers, was first domesticated is not yet known. Archaeologists have recovered in the dry deposits of Bat Cave in New Mexico and La Perra Cave in Tamaulipas in northeastern Mexico a very primitive form of cultivated corn. The Bat Cave corn is dated at 3600 B.C. and the La Perra Cave corn at 2500 B.C. Analysis of the food refuse in the dry cave of La Perra enabled MacNeish, who performed the excavation, to compute that the diet of the cave occupants of 4500 years ago consisted of 76% wild plant foods, 15% animal food, and 9% cultivated plants, thus providing an economic picture of a hunting and gathering people who were only just beginning to practice farming (MacNeish 1958). By 1500 B.C., about 1000 years later, the same area of Tamaulipas was fully settled by village farmers. Since the oldest known occurrence of cultivated maize in Peru dates from about 700 B.C., it is assumed that the maize plant diffused southward through Central America to western South America. Future research will perhaps answer the question of whether maize might have first developed genetically from its wild ancestor in southern Middle America (Willey 1960: 81) and then diffused to the north into the southwestern and eastern United States, and to the south into South America, or whether its original home lay somewhat farther north (MacNeish 1958).

Although we have no direct evidence of corn in the form of cobs or seeds, it can be stated with practical certainty that maize was being grown (presumably by the slash-and-burn method) in the tropical forest lowlands of southeastern Mexico by 900 or 1000 B.C. A. V. Kidder (1940: 121) has suggested that maize growing in lowland Mexico was preceded by the South American type of tropical agriculture derived from the Amazon-Orinoco region, with the starchy root called manioc as the main cultivated plant (compare Willey 1960: 82). For this theory there is, however, no evidence, and the oldest archaeological remains of settled farmers in lowland Mexico indicate, by the presence of metates, that maize was being grown. Kidder's proposed pre-maize farming complex is analogous to the "vegeculture" stage which precedes true field agriculture in the economic series suggested by Braidwood and Reed (1957: 21–2).

The tropics have been defined by Gourou (1956: 336) as the area of the earth where the average of the coldest month does not descend below 18° C., where the yearly total rainfall is greater than 750 mm., and where agriculture is possible without irrigation. This definition is a special one, and is particularly suited to our present inquiry. The agricultural potential of the tropical portions of the earth is variable, since the efficiency of exploitation depends in part upon variable cultural factors such as tools available for cutting the forest, implements for weeding fields, as well as the agricultural system employed and the crop plants, such as maize, rice, or rootcrops like manioc or taro, which are grown. Thus tropical Asia comprises eight million square kilometers and holds 650 million people, whereas the rest of the earth's tropical regions encompass 30 million square kilometers and hold only 190 million people.

There is one method of cultivation which is best suited to hand-farming (digging-stick or hoe-agriculture) in the tropical forest. This method has various names (Bartlett 1956: 693), the most common being "shifting cultivation" and "slash-and-burn." See Bartlett (1956: 704–8) for a discussion of how permanent cultivation can develop in tropical forest areas. For an exhaustive bibliography of published references on shifting cultivation see Conklin (1959b). In Mexico shifting cultivation is usually called the "milpa" system; for good descriptions of the system see Cook (1921), Lundell (1937), and Steggerda (1941).

A field is measured off in the standing forest and the woody vegetation consisting of trees, shrubs, and vines is cut down, stacked in piles, allowed to dry, and then burned. All this is done according to a strictly observed calendar — for example, the woody plants are most easily cut in the rainy season when they are full of sap, and the slash must have time to dry in order to burn up completely. The best drying occurs in the hottest part of the year which just precedes the onset of the rainy season, and the planting of the maize seeds should come just before or with the first rains. Thus, a miscalculation in timing of even as little as a week in the performance of any of these necessary acts may prevent the jungle farmer from realizing a crop with which to feed himself and his family. A field carved out of the jungle with such effort can grow only one, or at most two, crops. That is, after one or two years a field is abandoned to revert to natural growth and only after an extended time, which may be called the fallowing period, is it again cleared for a milpa.

Computations have been made of the amount of land which a family needs in order to support itself by annual or biennial clearing of a field of a certain size while at the same time observing the proper fallowing period. The modern Totonac of central Veracruz require 19 acres to support a family of five under their system of land rotation which employs a fallowing period of 12 years. The Maya of the village of Chan Kom need 35 acres of land to support a family of five, the fallowing period here being seven years. At Chichén Itzá in Yucatán the modern Maya require 59 acres to support a family of five. Such figures could be cited for many tropical Mexican groups, but this is unnecessary because it is clear from those given that the total amount of land needed to support a family varies, and that where the amount of land is small the yield is large and where the amount of land is large the yield is relatively less. If the land is not very productive and the fallowing period is long, the result is a low density of population. Population density estimates run from 7 to 30 persons per square kilometer in the Yucatán peninsula and lowland Maya area of the department of Petén of Guatemala (Termer 1951: 105; Hester 1953: 290). Twenty persons per square kilometer has been suggested as the density figure for the southern part of the state of Veracruz (Sanders 1953: 51; compare Foster 1942: 4–5).

So long as there are not too many people trying to support themselves off a given amount of land, the agricultural system of shifting cultivation by the slash-and-burn technique will be a successful one. But, as Cook (1921: 310) pointed out 40 years ago, if the land is cleared and burned too frequently, the trees and other woody vegetation may be killed off and the land become subject to erosion or covered with tough grass which cannot be farmed with the simple tools possessed by American Indians. It is also noted that the bush takes longer to renew itself after each cutting and burning, and this is attributed to the decreasing soil fertility. The clearing of fields by fire apparently has a long-term effect of reducing the soil fertility by burning out the humus which is converted to soluble mineral salts in the form of ash which percolate through the thin soil and thus is lost (Hester 1953: 291; Cook 1921: 314). The first year milpa has some weeds and suckers or shoots which come up from the stubs and roots of the cut-off trees. In the second year, even though the field has been cut and burned over again, the corn plants face severe competition from the forest growth and the yield is usually 20–25% less than the first year's crop. If the roots are dug out to clear the field, grass takes over (Kelly and Palerm 1952: 102, 114, 149; Cook 1921; Sanders 1953: 64), so it is on the whole easier, and an adequate maize crop is more assured, if a new milpa is cleared from land which has lain fallow for eight or ten or 12 years.

The demographic effects of the milpa system have been aptly termed "centrifugal" (La Farge and Byers 1931: 70; Wolf 1959: 60) since its lavish use of land inhibits population concentrations and encourages mobility and scattering of people. Let a village of 200 or 300 persons increase to 400 or 500, and there is pressure for conveniently located farm land. In Guatemala and Yucatán fields may be 20 to 30 miles away from a man's home (Cook 1921: 315; Steggerda 1941: 125) and in this situation the inevitable result is the formation of a daughter or offshoot colony some distance away where land is available. When the available free land becomes scarce and the population pressure continues to increase, the unavoidable result is to upset the delicate ecological balance between man and his environment in terms of the agricultural system. The dangers of over-use of land by too frequent clearing and burning will lead to declining production through decreasing soil fertility and invasion of grass, with the final result that the land cannot support the population (Palerm 1955: 28–9). (For a most interesting suggestion on a method of calculating critical population limits under a tropical forest agricultural economy, see Conklin 1959a.) This is one widely held view to account for the abandonment (Willey 1956: 113), about A.D. 900, of the great southern Maya cities and ceremonial centers of lowland Guatemala (Wolf 1959: 273–4; Cook 1921; Ferdon 1959: 13–17).

The amount of time required to clear a field by cutting the bush, drying the slash, burning, planting the crop, weeding the field, and harvesting the maize also varies from region to region in tropical Mexico. The Totonac of central Veracruz need 133 days to produce a crop; in Yucatán 190 days of labor will produce 168 bushels of shelled corn, of which only 64 are needed to support a family of five. The 104 bushels raised but not eaten are sold. The modern Indian group at La Venta on the Veracruz-Tabasco border needs 120 days to produce 150 bushels of maize, but a family of five requires only 100 bushels for food. In each case, only part of the year is expended in agricultural labor, and this expenditure of time produces not only sufficient maize for minimum dietary needs, but a surplus as well. In ancient times some portion of the extra time available, which might range from five to eight months per year, would have been usable for other than subsistence activities.

Over large parts of Mesoamerica, by which I mean here the area extending from central Mexico southward to Honduras, the early part of the first millennium before Christ saw the transition of simple village farmers into regionally organized groups who were under the influence of a special priesthood whose operations were performed at religious or ceremonial centers. These centers are the sites of the oldest large-scale architectural constructions in Mexico, and in general are characterized by arrangements of mounds or pyramids, and plazas. (For discussion of Preclassic platform mounds, see Drucker, Heizer, and Squier 1959: 261; Wauchope 1950; Willey 1955: 573, 582–83; Lowe 1959: 11). In highland Guatemala there was such an early ceremonial center at Kaminaljuyú by 400 B.C.; the occupants of the Valley of Mexico were building similar centers at about the same time or slightly later. The oldest known such ceremonial center, and it is a large and impressive one, is the Olmec culture site of La Venta in northern Tabasco which was built about 800 B.C. La Venta is too large and elaborate a site to be the first of its kind, and although it is the most ancient ceremonial site of its size and complexity known at present in Mexico, there must surely be older and simpler ones yet to be found and excavated.

The La Venta site lies on a small island comprising 2.1 square miles of dry land in the sea-level coastal swamp area of northern Tabasco, on the right bank of the Tonalá River, which, 18 miles below the site, empties into the Gulf of Campeche. The Tonalá River forms the boundary of the state of Veracruz to the north and Tabasco to the south. Heavy tropical forest covers the area except where there are wet swamps. The land is flat, low-lying, and without stone outcrops since these lie deeply buried under alluvial sands and clays. The annual rainfall amounts to about 120 inches per year, and there is one main dry season of about four months which begins in February and ends in late May. The La Venta site (Drucker 1952; Heizer 1957; Drucker, Heizer, and Squier 1959) consists of a linear complex of constructions made of heaped-up clay, the alignment of the site being 8° west of true north, with main mounds bisected by the centerline and secondary ones lying equidistant on either side of the line.

The site is about half a mile long, but only in its northern half is there a concentration of structures. First, proceeding from south to north, comes the great pyramid which is a flat-topped clay construction measuring 240 by 420 feet at the base and standing 110 feet high. Then come two long, low mounds on either side of the centerline, a low mound in the center, a rectangular open court or plaza surrounded by a wall of stone columns set side by side in the top of a low adobe brick wall, and finally, along the centerline at the far north, a large terraced clay mound. Scattered about in the central complex just described, as well as to the north and to the south of the pyramid, are many large stone monuments, some of them weighing 40 tons. These are flat-topped altars, great stelae or flat-surfaced stone slabs with ornate sculpture on one face, five of the famous colossal heads which stand 7–8 feet high, and a score of minor sculptures. Covered now with heavy jungle, this dead religious center which was abandoned 23 centuries ago is still impressive. Nine radiocarbon dates show that the site was built about 800 B.C. and abandoned about 400 B.C. (Drucker, Heizer, and Squier 1957).

The original site plan was maintained faithfully through three major rebuildings when mound and pyramid structures were enlarged, the court floor was successively raised, and monuments were relocated. The average span of time between each construction phase was, therefore, about one hundred years, and in view of the common practice in Mesoamerica of periodic enlargement of ceremonial structures, we may assume that a regular, rather than accidental periodicity of refurbishing is thus evidenced. The so-called Maya calendar system appears among the Maya in fully developed form about A.D. 300, but older dates inscribed on Olmec monuments are known, and most authorities now attribute to the Olmec of southern Veracruz the invention of this time-reckoning system (Coe 1957; Stirling 1940; Thompson 1954: 50, 158). Various time cycles, notably the 20-day month, a 260-day period, the 365-day solar year, and the 584-day Venus year were all correlated so that grand revolutions, at which time great ceremonies were performed, fell in cycles of 52 and 104 years (Thompson 1950, 1954: 137–59). If the La Venta group did observe the 52- and 104-year calendar rounds, as seems highly probable, but thus far unproved (Thompson 1950: 5), we may have here some hint as to the time span separating each of the series of rebuilding phases of the La Venta site.

The ceremonial or ritual nature of the site is obvious. It is surely not a city where large numbers of people lived. A recent study of the modern agricultural system practiced by natives on La Venta island (Drucker and Heizer 1960) shows that not more than 150 persons can support themselves here under slash-and-burn farming of maize, so that a large, self-supporting resident population on the island is not possible. No living trash or occupation refuse occurs in the main site area. There are some refuse deposits scattered about around the borders of the site, and these, we believe, are the trash heaps of the priests and attendants who lived here and performed the ritual activities at the religious metropolis.

The isolated position of the island of La Venta and its religious center by that name clearly indicate that it is a detached center occupied by a corps of priests and attendants, and that it was built and economically supported by a population living some distance away. This supporting population did not live to the east, where there is only a vast stretch of low, swampy ground unsuitable for occupation and farming. To the west, between the Tonalá and Coatzacoalcos rivers, is an area of low hills which amounts in aggregate to some 900 square kilometers (about 350 square miles), and which forms a unitary topographic region lying between the two great rivers (Fig. 1). This area seems a likely one for a small, politically organized group to occupy, and is strategically so situated that the La Venta site may have been its vital center (compare Sanders 1953: 59). While we do not know the present number of peasant farmers in this area, it is known that there occur here a large number of small population concentrations, some of which run to 300 or 400 persons. Local settlements dating from the La Venta period are known to occur in this area, but their size, number, and distribution remain to be determined. It may be supposed that each such local grouping had its own shrine, and an indication, however slight, of such local ritual centers may be seen in the isolated classic Olmec sculpture reported by Nomland (1932) from Arroyo Sonso (the present village of Moloacán). The village of Moloacán, incidentally is comprised of 60 families, of which 15 live in the central *ranchería* and the rest are scattered about in and on the edges of the small valley.

If we accept the figure of 20 persons per square kilometer as the aboriginal density, this area would hold a population of 18,000 persons. Let us now, having assumed that the La Venta ceremonial center served as the religious, and probably administrative, center of a dispersed village population living in the elevated section between the two rivers, inquire into the possibility that a population of 18,000 could have built and maintained the center over a period of 400 years. If we assume a nuclear family of five, there would be 3600 able-bodied male family heads.* Careful calculations have been made of the number of men which would be needed to excavate and refill each of the large offering pits in the La Venta site, and these run between 120 and 300, on the assumption that the work day was 8 hours and the work period was 100 days. The pyramid, which contains 4,700,000 cubic feet of earth, would require 800,000 man-days to construct. Extrapolating from the few examples where we have some basis for believing that we can secure time and labor figures of the proper order of magnitude, to the man-days of labor needed to build all of the constructions in the site and import the stones for monuments and columns, we get a grand total of 1,100,000 man-days. To satisfy this requirement, only 25 man-days per year for 400 years would be needed, but archaeological information tells us that the work was not carried out by yearly bits, but in at least four major efforts. Since the dry season of about 100 days maximum is the only convenient period for such earth-moving activity, the total man-days required would have been 275,000 per year for four years, or 2750 per day for the 100-day work period for each of the four years. But we cannot assume that the great pyramid, with a mass of nearly five million cubic feet of earth, was built in four stages, and it is proposed that at the end of every 50-year calendar round the pyramid was added to, and that every 100

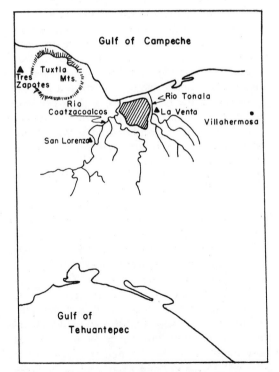

Fig. 1. Location of the three main Olmec sites. Hatched area is suggested occupation region of the La Venta population.

---

* Since this paper was written the important work of S. F. Cook and W. Borah (The Indian Population of Central Mexico, 1531–1610, *Ibero-Americana*, No. 44, Berkeley, 1960) has appeared. Their figure (p. 38) for average family size is 3.3 persons, and I accept it as more accurate than my estimate of 5 persons. Using the 3.3 figure there would be 5450 family heads.

years the other mound constructions to the north of the pyramid were rebuilt.

Let us, therefore, separate the construction of the pyramid from the rebuildings of the mounds and ceremonial court or plaza to the north. When we do this, we note that the pyramid, which requires, in round numbers, 800,000 man-days of labor, could be built in eight 100-day work periods. The labor requirement for each of the eight work periods is 100,000 man-days, or 1000 men working for 100 days. The mound rebuildings and court refurbishing, plus procurement of the stones for the monuments, come to an estimated 300,000 man-days. With a 100-year cycle, four work periods of 100 days each would require 75,000 man-days per year or 750 men working for 100 days. Thus, every 50 years 1000 men would be put to work on the pyramid, and every 100 years the work crew would expand to a total of 1750 to work on the pyramid and the mounds and court area to the north, a number which comes to only one-half of our estimated available labor force of 3600 family heads. If the period of labor service was fixed at two 20-day months, two work gangs of 875 men, each devoting two months of 20 days to the service of the gods, could have done the job.

While these figures are crude estimates, they are nonetheless based in each case upon how much earth a man can dig and carry, and upon time-reckoning periods which we have reason to believe the Olmecs knew (Thompson 1950, 1954) and upon which they conducted their affairs. In other words, while I do not believe the figures are accurate in that this is how the Olmec of 2500 years ago actually planned their work, nevertheless it is reasonable to believe that this is how they may have done it. And even more to the point of the present problem, if the Olmec of this ancient date had practiced slash-and-burn maize agriculture, they would have possessed the free time and economic surplus to carry out the work which I have outlined above. While admitting that I have not explained why the theocratic state came into being, I have at least shown the means by which this development was permitted to exist.

As to why the La Venta site was abandoned after 400 years of use, we have no clear evidence and are forced, therefore, to rely upon speculation. It is perfectly possible that when the site was first built the intention was that it should serve its function for a predetermined span of time, such as eight 50-year periods or four 100-year cycles. Or, the people and the site and its priests may have been conquered by an invading group of another religious persuasion. If the La Venta culture group lived in peace and flourished, they may have expanded their numbers to the point of overpopulation, which placed undue pressures on the land through frequent clearing so that economic suicide became inevitable through decreasing production and increasing demands. Or, if the spiritual and temporal power of the priests increased during their four centuries of control, there may have come a point beyond which the common people refused to go to meet the intolerably heavy demands for their services and time. A bare suggestion of this in the La Venta site is the occurrence in its final phase of large tombs which might be interpreted as the ultimate development of class differences evidenced in the burial of high priests within the ceremonial area (Drucker, Heizer, and Squier 1959: 127). A mutilation of 24 of the 40 sculptured monuments at the La Venta site indicates some religious reaction. The mutilation varies from battering off the heads of sculptures, or the despoiling of the facial features of priests or deities portrayed on stelae or altars, to the outright destruction of whole monuments whose remains now comprise only fragments bearing bits of sculpture. One could interpret such evidence as due either to a succeeding people who were engaged in a program of destroying the religious art of their predecessors, or to the reaction against the old religion by a disillusioned people imbued with iconoclastic fervor. A still further possibility is that a succession of natural catastrophes leading to disruption of the agricultural production system caused disillusionment among the population of the priestly leaders and the religious leadership was overthrown. No evidence of this can be cited, but it is recorded that in the 300-year period from 1535 to 1835 no fewer than 15 great famines were experienced in Yucatán (Steggerda 1941: 130).

The La Venta culture group shared, probably by the mutual processes of both receiving and dispensing, basic features of what are already recognizable, but are to become increasingly manifest as the distinctive characteristics of the Mesoamerican type of civilization (Drucker, Heizer, and Squier 1959: 258). It is because La Venta lies clearly in what Armillas

(1958: 47) has called the "gestation period" of this unique experiment in man's history, so brutally extinguished by the Spanish conquest in the 16th century, that it is of importance to the study of the growth of human culture. While the idea of the theocratic state's emergence early in the first millennium is not a new one (Wauchope 1950, 1954; Willey 1960; Wolf 1959), to date the La Venta site, by reason of its age, isolated position, and restricted population-support area, constitutes the earliest specific example of a Preclassic priest-dominated society maintaining a major ceremonial center. We may hope to learn some of the answers to the problem of how man converted himself from a hunter and gatherer to a civilized being with the advanced arts by squeezing as much interpretation as possible from ancient archaeological sites and by judging the prehistoric data in the light of what we know to have developed later, a method which Bernard Berenson, an art historian, spoke of as the "sense of antecedent probability" in dating and attributing a painting to a certain artist. The anthropologist A. L. Kroeber (1948: 148) refers to the intellectual training of anthropology as consisting of "learning to discriminate between better and worse judgments and better or worse evidence." The present attempt to blend fact and hypothesis is such an exercise in judgment based upon evidence.

ARMILLAS, PEDRO
 1958 Program of the History of American Indians. Pan American Union, Social Science Monographs, 2. Washington.

BARTLETT, H. H.
 1956 Fire, Primitive Agriculture, and Grazing in the Tropics. In *Man's Role in Changing the Face of the Earth*, edited by W. L. Thomas, pp. 692–720. University of Chicago Press, Chicago.

BOAS, FRANZ
 1912 The History of the American Race. *Annals of the New York Academy of Sciences*, Vol. 21, pp. 177–83. New York.

BRAIDWOOD, R. J. AND C. A. REED
 1957 The Achievement and Early Consequences of Food Production: a Consideration of the Archeological and Natural-Historical Evidence. *Cold Spring Harbor Symposia on Quantitative Biology*, Vol. 22, pp. 19–31. Cold Spring Harbor.

CHILDE, V. G.
 1946 *What Happened in History*. Pelican Books, New York.

COE, M. D.
 1957 Cycle 7 Monuments in Middle America: A Reconsideration. *American Anthropologist*, Vol. 59, No. 4, pp. 597–611. Menasha.

CONKLIN, H. C.
 1959a Population-Land Balance Under Systems of Tropical Agriculture. *Proceedings of the Ninth Pacific Science Congress, 1957*, Vol. 7, p. 63. Bangkok.
 1959b *A Preliminary Bibliography of References on Shifting Cultivation*. Mimeographed, 59 pp., Department of Anthropology, Columbia University.

COOK, O. F.
 1921 Milpa Agriculture, a Primitive Tropical System. *Smithsonian Institution Report for 1919*, pp. 307–26. Washington.

DRUCKER, PHILIP
 1952 La Venta, Tabasco: A Study of Olmec Ceramics and Art. *Bureau of American Ethnology, Bulletin 153*. Washington.

DRUCKER, PHILIP AND R. F. HEIZER
 1960 A Study of the Milpa System of La Venta Island and Its Archaeological Implications. *Southwestern Journal of Anthropology*, Vol. 16, No. 1, pp. 36–45. Albuquerque.

DRUCKER, PHILIP, R. F. HEIZER, AND R. J. SQUIER
 1957 Radiocarbon Dates from La Venta, Tabasco. *Science*, Vol. 126, No. 3263, pp. 72–3. Washington.
 1959 Excavations at La Venta, Tabasco, 1955. *Bureau of American Ethnology, Bulletin 170*. Washington.

FERDON, E. N., JR.
 1959 Agricultural Potential and the Development of Cultures. *Southwestern Journal of Anthropology*, Vol. 15, No. 1, pp. 1–19. Albuquerque.

FOSTER, G. M.
 1942 A Primitive Mexican Economy. *Monographs of the American Ethnological Society*, No. 5. J. J. Augustin, New York.

GOUROU, P.
 1956 The Quality of Land Use of Tropical Cultivators. In *Man's Role in Changing the Face of the Earth*, edited by W. L. Thomas, pp. 336–49. University of Chicago Press, Chicago.

HEIZER, R. F.
 1957 Excavations at La Venta, 1955. *Bulletin of the Texas Archaeological Society*, Vol. 28, pp. 98–110. Austin.

HESTER, J. A., JR.
 1953 Agriculture, Economy and Population Densities of the Maya. *Carnegie Institution of Washington, Yearbook 52*, pp. 288–92. Washington.

KELLY, ISABEL AND ANGEL PALERM
  1952 The Tajin Totonac, Part I. *Smithsonian Institution, Institute of Social Anthropology, Publication* 13. Washington.

KIDDER, A. V.
  1940 Archaeological Problems of the Highland Maya. In *The Maya and Their Neighbors*, pp. 117–25. Appleton-Century, New York.

KROEBER, A. L.
  1923 American Culture and the Northwest Coast. *American Anthropologist*, Vol. 25, No. 1, pp. 1–20. Menasha.
  1948 *Anthropology*. Harcourt, Brace, New York.

LA FARGE, OLIVER AND D. S. BYERS
  1931 The Year Bearer's People. *Tulane University, Middle American Research Series, Publication* 3. New Orleans.

LOWE, G. W.
  1959 Archaeological Exploration of the Upper Grijalva River, Chiapas, Mexico. *Papers of the New World Archaeological Foundation*, No. 2. Orinda.

LUNDELL, C. L.
  1937 The Vegetation of Peten. *Carnegie Institution of Washington, Publication* 478. Washington.

MACNEISH, R. S.
  1958 Preliminary Archaeological Investigations in the Sierra de Tamaulipas, Mexico. *Transactions of the American Philosophical Society*, Vol. 48, Part 6. Philadelphia.

NOMLAND, G. A.
  1932 Proboscis Statue from the Isthmus of Tehuantepec. *American Anthropologist*, Vol. 34, No. 4, pp. 591–3. Menasha.

PALERM, ANGEL
  1955 The Agricultural Bases of Urban Civilization in Mesoamerica. In "Irrigation Civilizations: A Comparative Study," pp. 28–42. *Pan American Union, Social Science Monographs*, 1. Washington.

SANDERS, W. T.
  1953 The Anthropogeography of Central Veracruz. In "Huastecos, Totonacos y sus Vecinos," *Revista Mexicana de Estudios Antropológicos*, Vol. 13, Nos. 2–3, pp. 27–78. Mexico.

STEGGERDA, MORRIS
  1941 Maya Indians of Yucatan. *Carnegie Institution of Washington, Publication* 531. Washington.

STIRLING, M. W.
  1940 An Initial Series from Tres Zapotes, Vera Cruz, Mexico. *National Geographic Society Contributions, Technical Papers, Mexican Archaeological Series*, Vol. 1, No. 1. Washington.

TERMER, FRANZ
  1951 The Density of Population in the Southern and Northern Maya Empires as an Archaeological and Geographical Problem. In *Selected Papers of the XXIXth International Congress of Americanists* [New York, 1949], Vol. 1, *The Civilizations of Ancient America*, edited by Sol Tax, pp. 101–7. University of Chicago Press, Chicago.

THOMPSON, J. E. S.
  1950 Maya Hieroglyphic Writing: Introduction. *Carnegie Institution of Washington, Publication* 589. Washington.
  1954 *The Rise and Fall of Maya Civilization*. University of Oklahoma Press, Norman.

WAUCHOPE, ROBERT
  1950 A Tentative Sequence of Pre-Classic Ceramics in Middle America. *Tulane University, Middle American Research Records*, Vol. 1, No. 14, *Middle American Research Institute, Publication* 15, pp. 211–50. New Orleans.
  1954 Implications of Radiocarbon Dates from Middle and South America. *Tulane University, Middle American Research Records*, Vol. 2, No. 2, *Middle American Research Institute, Publication* 18, pp. 17–40. New Orleans.

WILLEY, G. R.
  1955 The Prehistoric Civilizations of Nuclear America. *American Anthropologist*, Vol. 57, No. 3, pp. 571–93. Menasha.
  1956 Problems Concerning Prehistoric Settlement Patterns in the Maya Lowlands. In "Prehistoric Settlement Patterns in the New World," edited by G. R. Willey, pp. 107–14. *Viking Fund Publications in Anthropology*, No. 23. Wenner-Gren Foundation for Anthropological Research, New York.
  1960 New World Prehistory. *Science*, Vol. 131, No. 3393, pp. 73–86. Washington.

WOLF, E. R.
  1959. *Sons of the Shaking Earth*. University of Chicago Press, Chicago.

UNIVERSITY OF CALIFORNIA
Berkeley, Calif.
April, 1960

PROBLEMS CONCERNING PREHISTORIC SETTLEMENT PATTERNS IN THE MAYA LOWLANDS

By GORDON R. WILLEY

SETTING AND PROBLEMS

MAYA civilization had its most brilliant rise and dramatic decline in the lowland jungle regions of the Guatemalan Petén, adjacent Mexico and Yucatán, British Honduras, and the western fringes of Honduras. An estimated date of 1500 B.C. does not seem excessive for the first evidences of a pottery-making, agricultural people inhabiting the forests of the Petén during the Mamom phase of the Maya Formative period. The Formative period is terminated at about A.D. 300,[1] the date at which fully developed forms of Maya architecture, art, and the Initial Series calendrical dating appear. These traits mark the Maya Classic period (Tzakol and Tepeu phases), which lasted from A.D. 300 to approximately 900. The cessation of the Initial Series system of dating and the desertion of the great sites of the southern part of the lowlands provide a break in the sequence dividing the Classic and Postclassic periods. The Postclassic, a time at which nearly all lowland Maya activity was focused in northern Yucatán, is the final period, ending with the Spanish conquest of 1519–40. Throughout this entire time span of Maya prehistory, life was based essentially upon the cultivation of maize by jungle farming. With this background in mind—a 3,000-year history of agricultural civilization in a forested, tropical environment—we turn to settlement patterns.

A great many problems surround the matter of Maya settlements in the lowlands, but the two which we shall consider in this brief essay seem most fundamental at the present stage of research. The first problem, or question, is a double-barreled one, but it is impossible to treat the two halves separately because their interrelationship is obvious. What were the size and composition of the Maya living community, and what was the relationship between the living community and the ceremonial center? As will be evident in the ensuing discussion, this question cannot be answered satisfactorily at the present time, but it is basic to all research into prehistoric settlement in the area. The second question is a demographic one: What changes, if any, occurred in population size and grouping throughout the full run of Maya prehistory?

1. Dates for the opening and close of the Classic period follow the 11.16.0.0.0, or Goodman-Thompson, correlation of Mayan and Christian calendars.

Reprinted by permission of the publisher from PREHISTORIC SETTLEMENT PATTERNS IN THE NEW WORLD by Gordon R. Willey. Copyright 1956 Johnson Reprint Corporation.

THE FORMATIVE PERIOD

Most of the accumulated knowledge of field archeology in the Maya lowlands derives from investigations of major sites, where large pyramids, platform mounds, and imposing architectural remains (hereafter referred to as "ceremonial centers") have attracted attention. This has resulted from the difficult conditions of tropical vegetation cover—in which small mounds and building foundations are extremely hard to locate and examine—rather than any lack of interest on the part of the archeologists. Well over a hundred large ceremonial centers have been surveyed and explored in the lowland area (see Morley, 1946; Thompson, 1954), and, undoubtedly, there are a great many more which are smaller and unrecorded. Most of the ceremonial centers, at least as far as their principal edifices can be dated, belong to the Classic period; however, we know that platform mounds, pyramids, and temple or palace-type buildings make their appearance in the latter part of the Formative. The A-I structure at Uaxactun in the Petén clearly dates from the late Formative, and the E-VII-submound may be this early (A. L. Smith, 1950; Ricketson and Ricketson, 1937). To the north, in Yucatán, the mound at Yaxuná is Formative, as may be others at Santa Rosa Xtampak (Brainerd, 1951).

Concerning the nature of the living community during the Formative period and its relationships to these ceremonial or large mound centers, Brainerd (1954, pp. 15 ff.) states that all or part of Maya settlements at this time may have been of substantial size but that there have not been sufficient excavation and survey to prove this. On the other hand, Shook and Proskouriakoff (this volume) contend: "So far as we can tell, in Meso-America we are dealing at the outset with patterns of town settlement rather than with purely agricultural village communities." The data are too limited to resolve this difference of opinion, but what evidence there is from the lowlands does not indicate large Formative period settlements. At Uaxactun the early Formative, or Mamom, period occupation of that site appears to have covered little more than the top of the knoll of what later became E Group, an area about 200 meters in diameter. For the late Formative, or Chicanel, phase there is again evidence that the E Group knoll was occupied, as was the somewhat larger A Group hill (about 350 meters in diameter). On the latter location the previously mentioned small ceremonial mound, A-I, was constructed. A Chicanel house mound was also discovered at a distance of about 800 meters from the Group A section of the ceremonial center (Wauchope, 1934). These Uaxactun data give the impression of very small villages or hamlets rather than towns. Such small villages became the seats of special or ceremonial buildings in the late Formative, and at this time at least some houses were occupied as much as a half-mile away from what may have been the "main" or "parent" community.

Recent work in the Belize Valley, at Barton Ramie (Willey, Bullard, and

Glass, 1955), affords some additional information on this question of the size of Formative living communities. No ceremonial mounds have been identified with the Formative period at the Barton Ramie site, but several house-mound locations have been dated, tentatively, as of this period. These mounds are rather widely spaced over a square mile of alluvial bottom land, with the implication that Formative period settlement at that site was in small hamlet clusters or isolated houses rather than in a densely occupied town.

Turning to the second problem, that of changes in population size, there are only occasional clues from the Formative period. Shook and Proskouriakoff (this volume) have noted that there is no valid case for increasing populations throughout the Formative period in the Guatemalan highlands. For the lowlands there are some few suggestions that such an increase may have taken place. The Uaxactun excavations reveal more extensive occupational and architectural debris for Chicanel than they do for the earlier Mamom phase; and at Barton Ramie the stratigraphic digging in house mounds gives us three or four times as many Chicanel house occupations as those dating from Mamom. Moreover, lowland sites and ceramic materials of a late Formative or Chicanel-like identification are reported in greater numbers than those for the early Formative.

THE CLASSIC PERIOD

Although there is considerably more knowledge of Maya sites of the Classic period than for the Formative, the question of the size and form of the living community and its relationships to the ceremonial center is still a matter for dispute. Both Morley (1946, pp. 312–13) and Shook and Proskouriakoff hold that the ceremonial centers, with their temple and palace mounds grouped around rectangular courtyards, were nuclei of true cities or towns, with dwellings clustered in or closely around them. In this view they seem to be strongly influenced by Landa's sixteenth-century accounts of Yucatecan town or city life:

> Before the Spaniards had conquered that country, the natives lived together in towns in a very civilized fashion . . . in the middle of the town were their temples with beautiful plazas, and all around the temples stood the houses of the lords and priests, and then most of the important people. Thus came the houses of the richest and of those who were held in the highest estimation nearest to these, and at the outskirts of the town were the houses of the lower class.

Brainerd (1954, pp. 70 ff.) disagrees that this Yucatecan town pattern of the conquest time can be projected back into the Classic. It is his feeling that the town, as both a reality and a concept, was a Toltec-Mexican introduction into Yucatán and a phenomenon of the Postclassic period. He visualizes the Classic settlement pattern as that of scattered single houses or hamlets, with the inhabitants of these dwellings gathering together to support, or celebrate in, the ceremonial centers. In this he is supported by Thompson (1954, pp. 43 ff.).

In this argument it is interesting that Brainerd and Morley each quote the Uaxactun house-mound survey to bolster their respective points of view. The former is of the opinion that the Uaxactun data indicate a dispersed, rural population, while the latter feels that they demonstrate a loosely compacted urbanism. This Uaxactun house-mound survey (Ricketson and Ricketson, 1937) revealed a total of seventy-eight house mounds in an area totaling 0.3 mile of the habitable terrain surrounding the ceremonial precincts at the site. This is a dense occupation on a house-per-acreage basis even if one follows Ricketson's assumption that only one-quarter of the house mounds were in use at any one time; however, it must be kept in mind that the actual distribution of the seventy-eight mounds extended over an area of 2 miles in both north-south and east-west diameters.[2] Perhaps the difficulty here is a matter of definitions: What is a village? A town? What is "densely settled"? My own thinking tends to coincide with Brainerd's in seeing the Uaxactun settlement as scattered rural rather than as an urban concentration.

Another lowland region where house-mound surveys have been carried out, the Belize Valley, presents a picture of ceremonial-center–dwelling-site relationships that differs somewhat from either of the two afore-mentioned conceptions, although it is somewhat closer to the Brainerd interpretation (Willey, Bullard, and Glass, 1955; Willey and Bullard, n.d.). In this valley the house mounds are found along the alluvial terraces in groups varying in size from five or six up to three hundred. Such house-mound groups may lie immediately adjacent to a ceremonial center, as at Baking Pot (Ricketson, 1929), or may be as much as 7 or 8 miles from any important center. It is a logical possibility that the inhabitants of several such dwelling groups may have acted in concert to build and maintain a religious and political center on the order of the nearby centers of Baking Pot or Benque Viejo (Thompson, 1940). In this case the settlement could hardly be considered to be a "city" but rather a series of near-contiguous villages, or even towns, focusing upon a major ceremonial center. It is interesting to note that in each group of a dozen or more house mounds there is at least one mound, or mound-plaza unit, that is appreciably larger than the others and whose presence suggests that some local and small-scale politico-religious activities were carried on within the small dwelling groups as well as in the great centers.

In attempting to sum up this problem of ceremonial-center–dwelling-site relationships for the Classic period, there seem to be three logical and abstract settlement-type possibilities: First, there is the one in which (Type A) the ceremonial center is surrounded by dwellings which are so closely spaced that their inhabitants could not have farmed immediately adjacent to them (Fig. 1). This is nearest the conception of Morley, Shook, and Proskouria-

---

2. The Uaxactun house-mound survey was made in a great cruciform zone, each arm of the cross being 400 yards wide and 1 mile long. The ceremonial precincts were situated near the center of the cross.

koff. In the second type (Type B) the ceremonial center is without dwellings, and houses of the sustaining population are scattered singly over a wide surrounding area. The extent of such a sustaining area is unknown, but Ricketson offered an arbitrary estimate of a 10-mile radius for Uaxactun. This seems reasonable, particularly in regions where foot transportation was the only means of going to and from the ceremonial center. This type would seem to be closest to Brainerd's views. The third idealized type (Type C) is similar to B in that there is no appreciable population concentrated in the

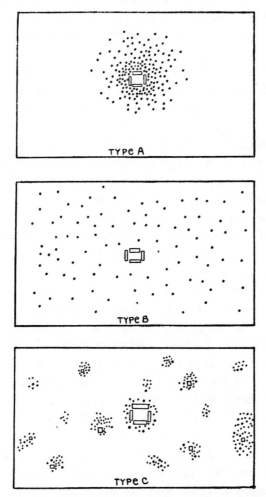

Fig. 1.—Idealized settlement types of the lowland Maya, A, B, and C, showing relationships of ceremonial center to house mounds or locations. Major ceremonial centers indicated by small rectangles in plaza arrangement, houses by dots. There is no exact scale for these diagrams. In Type A, houses are packed in close to the ceremonial center; in Type B houses are dotted over the landscape at a half to a quarter of a mile apart; in Type C houses are grouped in hamlet or village clusters, with some near the major ceremonial center but many others in outlying hamlets. The small rectangles in some of the larger hamlet clusters of the Type C pattern represent small ceremonial constructions whose importance is assumed to be local and subsidiary to that of the major center.

ceremonial center, but the sustaining populations are spotted through the surrounding country in hamlets or small villages rather than in individual houses. It is further suggested that some of these hamlets maintained small ceremonial buildings in their own midst. This may be the type of settlement in the Belize Valley, with, however, the significant modification that the hamlets and villages are distributed "ribbon-wise" along the river. In such a case river travel would have been the obvious means of transport.

It should be emphasized that these are only projected ideal types for prehistoric settlement in the Maya lowlands. There is no reason why combinations of these types might not be nearer actuality, nor need any type have prevailed throughout the entire area and Classic period. Thompson (1954, pp. 43 ff.) and others have described the modern Maya pattern of a town center with church, plaza, and market, around which were the houses of its citizenry. These houses were occupied seasonally, on market days, or during fiestas, while several miles distant from the town were the scattered bush houses in which the same people lived while working their milpas. Such would be a combination of Type *A* with Type *B* or *C*. For the present, however, these types are but working hypotheses. The task facing the archeologist is to check house concentrations, or lack of same, in the immediate environs of ceremonial centers and to plot their occurrences and spacings in the miles of jungle that surround these centers—no mean chore!

The question of lowland Maya population increase between Formative and Classic or within the Classic period is also a moot one. The fact that many more Classic ceremonial centers are known than are reported for the Formative is by no means conclusive as to population growth. Ceremonial-center construction was undoubtedly greater in the later period, but it is also a strong probability that many of these sites were also occupied in the earlier period. As to house-mound counts, only five of the Uaxactun small mounds were excavated and are, therefore, datable by their ceramic contents (Wauchope, 1934); one of these was Formative, the other four Classic. In the Belize Valley, at Barton Ramie, we have sampled the pottery in thirty-nine house mounds (as of 1955) out of a group which numbers over three hundred. A preliminary appraisal of these ceramics shows an increase of about four-to-one between Classic and Formative house occupations. Further, late Classic occupations by far outnumbered those of the early Classic. The stability of the community is attested to by the fact that many of the mounds had been used as house platforms continuously from Formative to Classic times. This is very limited evidence upon which to base any generalizations as regards population changes in the Belize Valley as a whole, let alone the entire Maya lowlands; still the trend revealed in this sampling is that of steady increase.

THE POSTCLASSIC PERIOD

One of the most startling settlement phenomena of Middle American prehistory occurs with the change from Classic to Postclassic. This is the apparent abandonment of the southern Maya lowlands. This abandonment is noted in all the southern ceremonial centers, where construction and stelae dates cease after about A.D. 900. And, from the data available, the events of the ceremonial centers appear to be paralleled in the domestic sites. Ceramics or other materials datable as Postclassic are rare in the Petén and the Belize Valley. As is well known, the only great Postclassic sites of the lowlands are in the plains of northern Yucatán. Chichén Itzá is an old Puuc Classic ceremonial center, considerably enlarged under Toltec influence. The urban quality of the site is not fully known, but there are many house mounds in the immediate vicinity. Mayapan, which reached its zenith somewhat later than Chichén, is an urban zone. Three by 2 kilometers in extent, it is encircled by a great wall within which are some four thousand house mounds (Jones, 1952). The houses are arranged in random fashion, but at the center of the site is a ceremonial center with plazas and pyramid mounds. There is, then, some indication that the Postclassic Maya of northern Yucatán were urbanized and that the concept of the city or town as a fortified position had come into vogue. This, as Brainerd and others have suggested, may well be the result of Toltec and Mexican influences. Yet the walled city is not common in Yucatán. Tulum (Lothrop, 1924), on the east coast of Quintana Roo, is the only other notable example, and the wall inclosure here does not appear to embrace the great house-mound concentrations found at Mayapan.

There is no information on population size change between lowland Classic and Postclassic. Chichén Itzá and Mayapan appear larger than the Puuc ceremonial centers which preceded them in the northern lowlands, but nothing has been reported upon the size or form of Puuc domestic settlements. Populations may have been more densely concentrated in the Postclassic, but there is nothing to indicate that they were, in an over-all sense, larger.

COMMENT

Prehistoric settlement in the Maya lowlands is still a matter for speculation and debate rather than for statement of fact. Ceremonial centers, with temple and palace mounds, were obvious nuclei for the ancient populations of these regions from the latter part of the Formative period, if not earlier. The question as to just how the population grouped itself around these centers—whether in concentrated town fashion, in a dispersed rural manner, or in scattered hamlets—cannot be answered without extensive field surveys and excavations. There are some indications that the population increased more or less steadily from early Formative to late Classic times; but this trend needs checking in many different localities. Following the desertion, or near-desertion, of the southern part of the lowland area, building activity was concentrated in northern Yucatán, a region which also came under strong Mexican influence after A.D. 900. The concept of the town, as a tight population grouping around a ceremonial center, sometimes fortified, may have been introduced into Yucatán from Mexico. Or this concept, as reported upon by the early Spanish, may have been the final expression of an old and deep tradition of the Maya lowlands.

Until we have more real knowledge of Maya settlement, the archeologist will be in no position to attack the problems of demography or of prehistoric agricultural techniques and productiveness. Arguments of milpas versus intensive farming (Ricketson and Ricketson, 1937) will remain insoluble until we can pin down the facts of habitation.

FACTS AND COMMENTS

THE KHMER SETTLEMENT PATTERN: A POSSIBLE ANALOGY WITH THAT OF THE MAYA*

There has recently been increased attention paid to the nature of the settlement pattern of Classic Maya civilization. It now seems likely that Classic Maya "cities" were not secular, urban communities in which large numbers of people were grouped together in close proximity. On the other hand, if these were merely ceremonial centers in which the populace gathered for certain rituals, then the political and religious organization of these centers, and the actual socio-political structure of the entire Maya area, are as yet undetermined.

Archaeological reconstruction proceeds mainly by analogy. It may therefore be of interest to Mayanists to summarize what is now known of the settlement pattern of that other great tropical forest civilization, the Khmer Empire, which bears so many puzzling similarities to the Classic Maya. The Angkor, or Classic, period of the Khmer Empire lasted over 600 years, from A.D. 802 to 1431, during which the capital was at or near the site of Angkor itself. Although the Khmer development took place in a rain forest environment, it should be kept in mind that the economy, unlike that of the Maya, was based on intensive agriculture: the raising of wet rice in paddy lands irrigated from large artificial lakes and canals.

The investigations of the École Française d'Extrême Orient have clarified to a considerable extent the nature of Khmer "cities". A great deal of eyewitness information is also to be found in the report of Chou Ta-Kuan, commercial attaché in the Chinese embassy which arrived at Angkor in 1296 (Pelliot 1951).

The ruler of the Khmer Empire was a priest-king, the intermediary between his royal ancestors and his realm. During his lifetime, he caused a great temple-mausoleum to be constructed; on death, his remains were entombed in this edifice, to which his successor came to worship his progenitor, now God-King. It is likely that most of the great Khmer monuments, including the enormous Angkor Wat, were in function both tombs *and* temples, for which Coedès (1947: 84) proposes the name "funerary temples." In other words, the bulk of the stone architecture visible at a site like Angkor consisted not of civil architecture but religious edifices, dedicated to the royal cult. These sacred cities were microcosms of the divine world: the central structure, with its characteristic 5 towers on a temple pyramid, represented the holy Mount Meru, the center of the universe; the surrounding walls were the rock wall which enclosed the universe; and the water-filled ditch bounding all was the great ocean. Regardless of whether the state religion happened to be a Siva cult or Mahayana Buddhism, the essential nature of Khmer cities remained unchanged.

The king and his entourage evidently did not reside in any of these imposing edifices, but in a palace of wood roofed with tiles. Chou Ta-kuan relates that the king had 1000 to 2000 servants and 3000 to 5000 girls and concubines (Briggs 1951: 245). The nobility lived within the city, and were also entitled to tile roofs. There was a sizeable group of merchants within the city walls, including some from foreign countries. In addition, each of the great temples had its own priests, retainers, and dancers.

According to Chou Ta-kuan, there were over 90 provincial capitals subject to

---
*Gordon R. Willey and Sophie D. Coe gave me the benefit of their advice in this paper.

the Angkor king; each had its own "mandarins" and each was surrounded by a wooden palisade. The great mass of the people lived in the villages; every village had its own temple. However, it is evident that many, if not most, villages were grouped together administratively as ecclesiastical properties belonging by frank-almoign to the great temples of the central capital and provincial centers. (Frank-almoign was a kind of spiritual tenure in feudal England whereby a religious corporation held lands in perpetuity. It is here proposed that this term be extended to include all socio-political systems in which religious centers are supported by the tenants and produce of ecclesiastical lands.) For instance, the temple of the Ta Prohm group at Angkor, consecrated in 1186, was granted by its charter 3140 villages for its support; the total number in its service thus was 79,365 persons. Prah Kahn, another group at Angkor, was inaugurated in 1191 and had 5324 villages and a total of 97,840 persons available as food producers and corvee labor (Coedès 1951: 193-4). By 1191, there were 306,372 persons living in 13,500 villages devoted to the support of the Khmer temples and their cults—a figure that surely must have represented a large part of the Khmer population at that time.

The Classic Khmer settlement pattern, then, consisted of a large rural population scattered in villages throughout Cambodia, supporting ceremonial centers with rice and corvée labor. The Khmer "city" is not at all cognate with fully urban communities like Tenochtitlan, Mohenjo-Daro, Akkadian Uruk, or Rome; rather, it seems to have been a cult center supported by the produce and forced labor of the hinterland. Inside the city were the royal court, the nobility, the priesthood and temple retainers, and some merchants, but with the activity largely directed towards sacred, rather than secular, ends.

Perhaps the situation in the Maya area was not very different. Tikal could have been the major capital, with jurisdiction over provincial capitals like Uaxactún, Copan, and Palenque. In these "cities," the majority of the edifices were probably entirely ceremonial (including the so-called "palaces"), with the administrative hierarchy living in perishable structures. The bulk of the Maya population lived in villages, the distribution of which was based on the availability of arable land. Possibly these villages, as in the Khmer Empire, were organized into frank-almoign territories devoted to the support of temples in both the major capital (Tikal?) and in the provincial centers. In view of the fact that there seems to be no marked increase in the frequency of house mounds close to, and even within, Maya ceremonial centers, this may be a plausible explanation of the nature of the Maya "cities" and settlement pattern.

Briggs, L. P.
   1951 The Ancient Khmer Empire. *Transactions of the American Philosophical Society*, Vol. 41, Pt. 1. Philadelphia.

Coedes, G.
   1947 *Pour mieux comprendre Angkor*. A. Maisonneuve, Paris.

Pelliot, Paul
   1951 *Mémoires sur les coutumes du Cambodge de Tcheou Takouan*. A. Maisonneuve, Paris.

Michael D. Coe
Harvard University
Cambridge, Mass.
December, 1955

Settlement Pattern and Social Structure in the Southern Maya Lowlands during the Classic Period

William R. Bullard, Jr.

THIS PAPER will review implications of recent settlement pattern studies for interpretation of Classic Lowland Maya social and political structure and the function of the large ceremonial center ruins of the region. The data are drawn primarily from an area of the lowlands which was the subject of a survey made by the writer in 1958 (Bullard, 1960). Many of the ideas expressed have also been included in a article on lowland Maya settlement patterns written for the Handbook of Middle American Indians (Willey and Bullard, ms.).

The area discussed lies in the northern part of the Guatemalan Department of Petén. It includes a tract of over 2 000 sq. km. lying northwest of Lake Petén, stretching from the British Honduras border to approximately the longitude of Uaxactún and Tikal. This area includes several of the largest Classic ceremonial ruins, and the settlement pattern here is believed to be typical in its essentials of the Lowland Maya during the Classic periods.

Environmentally, the area is heavily forested limestone country. There is but little doubt that the ancient economy was based on shifting *milpa* cultivation, the form of native cultivation best adapted to the country and universally practiced today in the lowlands of the Yucatán peninsula. Physiographically, the terrain is composed of rolling uplands interspersed with areas of intermittant swampland known as *bajos*. Since the *bajos*, which compose roughly 50% of the land area, are completely uninhabitable, the ancient settlement was limited to the uplands. Water supply was another important limiting factor. Surface water sources such as lakes and rivers are comparatively scarce and dry-season dessication is a problem. The ancient Maya overcame the problem to a large extent by the construction of reservoirs to retain rain water through the dry season.

The outstanding remains of the ancient occupancy are the great ceremonial centers. Within the area under discussion the largest is Tikal, but others which approach first rank in extent and amount of construction are Uaxactún, Nakum, Naranjo, Yaxhá and Holmul. Somewhat smaller, but nevertheless of impressive size, are Benque Viejo, El Gallo, Dos Aguadas, as well as others. These are

---

Reprinted from paper presented at the 35th International Congress of Americanists, Mexico, August 1962.

the major ceremonial centers which were the focal points of Maya religeous and intellectual life, and quite certainly of political and social life as well. Most of the older interpretations of Maya culture and society result from studies made in ruins such as these.

The buildings of the major ceremonial centers were well-built, often elaborately ornamented, and the total amount of construction is appalling. Numbers of temples, both large and small, stand on lofty substructures. Multi-roomed buildings, called for convenience "palaces," contain often dozens of rooms and are not infrequently grouped into extensive compounds. Ball-courts are usual features and were used for a game of ritual significance. Stelae and altars, often sculptured with hieroglyphic texts and elaborately adorned human figures, stand in the plazas. The buildings, the art, the hieroglyphics and the artifacts demonstrate a high degree of specialized craftsmanship and intellectual knowledge. There is evidence of trade with foreign lands. Elaborate tomb burials and human portrayals in the art indicate high social status for some individuals. Moreover, Proskouriakoff (1960) has recently adduced evidence for something comparable to hereditary royal leadership.

Studies in the ceremonial centers themselves lead easily to the inference that they were cities ruled by divine or near-divine kings, supported by a priestly nobility and a corps of craft specialists and minor functionaries. This concept also implies a host of peasantry of inferior status, who raised the food, carried the building stones, and stood in awe of their social and intellectual betters.

However, studies focused on Maya ceremonial centers alone can give only a restricted and one-sided picture of their function and the nature of the society which supported them. Settlement pattern studies, alhough still in an elementary stage, offer a means of widening the perspective. Attention will therefore be turned to the sustaining areas of the major ceremonial centers, where the subordinate populations lived and raised the crops on which Maya civilization was based. To be considered specifically are the size of the sustaining areas, the distribution of settlement within them, the community groupings into which the settlement was organized, and the size of the population which the sustaining areas must have held.

*

The area of northern Peten with which we are specifically concerned has been well explored over a period of many years and there is but little doubt that the locations of all of the larger ceremonial centers and most of the smaller ones are known. From the spacing of these centers and their relationship to habitable upland, we can estimate with fair accuracy the average amount of terrain which must have pertained to a single major center. While some sustaining areas were certainly larger than others, the average cannot have been greater than approximately 100 sq. km. (38 sq. miles) of upland, within which the population lived and the crops were grown. This area seems surprisingly small relative to the amount of elaborate construction in ceremonial centers such as Uaxactún, Nakum, Naranjo and others. It is small enough so that most Maya farmers living within the area could walk either to the ceremonial center or to their fields and return home again the same day. The native provinces of conquest-period Yucatán comprised from several hundred to six or eight thousand square kilometers (Villa Rojas, 1961: 23). It is clear that the Petén major ceremonial centers represent political units of a different order of magnitude from those.

The survey work in Petén has shown that the major ceremonial centers of the Classic Period were not "cities" in the sense of a compact nucleus of settlement. Instead, residential structures were dispersed in rather loose aggregates throughout the sustaining area. The locations of these aggregates were determined primarily by topographical factors. Well-drained sites in the vicinity of a source of water were preferred, and nearness to good *milpa* land was also a factor. The important thing is that domestic settlement was not significantly greater in the immediate vicinity of the major ceremonial centers than it was in the more distant parts of the sustaining areas.

*

The smallest independent unit of settlement is what in a previous paper I have called a "house," but it is better described as a "household unit." It is a small court group containing usually two or three separate building platforms. These units may have contained more than a single family dwelling as well as utility buildings such as kitchens. In composition they seem very similar to the post-Classic household units of Mayapan as well as to those of the modern Maya (Pollock, Roys, Proskouriakoff & Smith, 1962: 165-320). The family groups which dwelt in them must have been similar also.

The household units do not occur in isolation. Not infrequently they occur in hamlet-like clusters of from 5 to 12, sometimes with a larger structure suggesting a shrine or a building with some public function. Almost always these clusters are located near other clusters, and in some areas examined during the survey they could not be defined at all.

A larger community unit into which the household units fall, and of which the clusters —when they occur— are segments, is the aggregate of an estimated 50 to 100 household units which I have previously termed a "zone." The household units of the "zone" scatter over an area of about one square kilometer. Some "zones" are geographically isolated; others are contiguous and blend spatially with one another, according to the nature of the terrain. Consistently associated with each "zone" is a small ceremonial center of from one to several buildings, including often more than one temple mound. These minor ceremonial centers may be similar in layout to the major centers, but they are very much smaller and they lack stelae and ball-courts.

How many of these community units called "zones" were subordinate to a major ceremonial center? While this question cannot be answered with any pretention to exactness, a rough estimate based on observation and knowledge of terrain conditions suggests that the number should be about 10 to 15 for the sustaining areas of major centers such as Yaxhá and Naranjo.

*

An important factor in interpretation of Classic Maya social and political structure is the total size of the population subordinate to the major ceremonial ceners. There are two lines of approach to this problem, one based on the settlement estimates given above, the other on potential agricultural productivity.

Some of the household units in Petén probably held one nuclear family, others two or even more. Let us assume an average of 7 individuals per household. A "zone" comprised 50 to 100 households, which would give us an estimated population range of 350 to 700 persons or an average of 575. With 10 to 15 "zones" estimated for the sustaining area of a major ceremonial center, we emerge with a total population of 5 750 to 8 625 persons. Of course, not all house structures may have been occupied at one time, which would tend to lower the figures. On the other hand, the estimate of 7 persons per household unit may be too low, which would tend to raise the figures.

In a recent agricultural study in northern Petén, Ursula Cowgill (1961) concluded that *milpa* farming could permanently support a population of 100 to 200 people per square mile. Applying this figure to the approximately 38 sq. miles (100 sq. km.) which comprised the sustaining area of a major ceremonial center, we reach a potential population limit of from 3 800 to 7 600 persons, a range slightly lower than but overlapping the figures obtained from settlement pattern estimates.

Without doubt these very elementary estimates will be further modified and refined, but, at least, they give us an indication of the population magnitudes with which we must dealing discussing Maya social structure and the function of the major ceremonial centers. Ricketson once estimated a sustaining population for Uaxactún of nearly 50 000 persons (Ricketson & Ricketson, 1937: 21). It would now appear that we are dealing with a few thousands rather than the tens of thousands once contemplated.

*

To summarize the conclusions so far, the sustaining areas of the large major ceremonial centers of northeastern Petén comprised areas of about 100 sq. km. (38 sq. miles) with populations of between 3 000 and 10 000 persons. The population lived dispersed through the sustaining area in 10 to 15 communities of from 50 to 100 households, representing several hundred persons. Associated with these communities, here called "zones", are minor ceremonial centers. The zones may be segmented into smaller community units of from 5 to 12 households which, at least sometimes, had their own religious or public building.

The general pattern of settlement described above is believed to be representative of the southern Maya Lowlands during the Classic Period, although local geographical conditions would have required modifications in detail. A generally similar pattern was found along the Belize Valley in British Honduras (Willey, Bullard, Glass & Gifford, in press). In Quintana Roo, Sanders (1960) reports that the Late Classic ceremonial center of Tancah had comparatively few house ruins close to it, and that most of the community, instead of being nucleated, was scattered in small house groups west of Tancah. There is evidence that the general dispersed pattern existed in parts of Yucatán until the Spanish Conquest, and it is found today in at least the Chiapan highlands. Thus Villa Rojas (1961: 28) states that in some provinces of conquest-period Yucatán, communities included a *pueblo* proper, but that most of the populace lived scattered in small *parajes* and *rancherias* and came into the *pueblo* only occasionally for religious, commercial or administrative purposes.

A striking parallel to the settlement pattern which we have described for Petén is provided by Vogt's data from the Tzotzil *municipio* of Zinacantan in highland Chiapas (Vogt, 1961). The entire *municipio* of Zinacantan includes 177 sq. km. and has a total population of 7 600, a somewhat larger area than we are estimating for Classic Petén ceremonial center sustaining areas, but with a population of similar size. Only about 6% of this population lives in the town of Zinacantan itself, which Vogt refers to as a ceremonial center. The others live scattered through the *municipio* in smaller communities known as *parajes* and visit the ceremonial center for religious, political and commercial purposes. The *parajes* are rather loose aggregates of household units comprising from about 50 to over 1 000 persons each. They would seem comparable to the Petén "zones" for which I have estimated several hundred people. The *"parajes"* are further divided into "waterhole groups" which may in a general way be comparable to the Petén "clusters" of from about 5 to 12 household units each. The smallest Zinacantan settlement unit is the patrilocal extended family *sitio* which is surely equivalent to the Petén household unit. Not only does the general organization of settlement in Zinacantan seem comparable to that in Classic period Peten, but the dispersal of the households and the apparent spacial blending of some "waterhole groups" with others and some *parajes* with others resembles the Petén situation also.

Vogt, in noting some of these similarities, suggests an historical connection, and that the Maya tended "to activate a basic type of settlement pattern whenever military and geographical circumstances permitted, whether this was in the highlands or lowlands" *(ibid,* p. 142). He goes further to suggest that some of the same mechanisms which integrate Zinacantan society may also have integrated Classic Maya society: specifically, a system of graded ranks whereby men who were normally corn farmers came in to the ceremonial center to serve a term in priestly office, then returned to their *parajes* to accumulate resources enough to ask for the next higher position in the system. As Vogt observes, this would mean that the gulf between priest and peasant was less than has been supposed.

*

Older interpretations on work in ceremonial centers and knowledge of conditions in conquest-period Yucatan have tended to view Maya society as strongly stratified into classes of priestly nobility and peasantry (for example, see Thompson, 1954: 81). As mentioned, the evidence from the ceremonial centers supports such a concept: the skilled art and workmanship, the display of intellectual knowledge, the suggestions of royal lines and high status of individuals, and the sheer size of the major ceremonial centers themselves. On the other hand, emerging knowledge of ancient settlement patterns and analogies with at least superficially similar modern Maya patterns have suggested a more equalitarian society with considerable social mobility. Let us now consider additional facets of this problem which are reflected by settlement patterns and related aspects of the culture.

Agricultural studies such as that of Ursula Cowgill in Peten (1961) have demonstrated that *milpa* agriculture in this region is productive and that one man can raise well above the needs of his family and still have a good deal of time left over for other activities. This means that a surplus was available to support non-food-producing classes, such as a priesthood, and that a farmer had time sufficient to perform labour tasks in the ceremonial centers. But it alsomeans that the farmer himself was able to engage in at least part-time specialist activities, and that he had the economic means to acquire products, both necessities and luxuries, produced by others.

The residence pattern of the Classic period has been described as follows: "the Maya nobility almost surely resided on the outskirts of the city, and the peasant and working population lived further away in small scattered settlements" (Thompson, 1954: 67). The survey work in Peten failed to find evidence of significant concentration of larger and more elaborate house ruins, such as might have been occupied by an upper class, closer to major ceremonial centers than further away. Both large and small house ruins occur both close to major centers and in the most distant communities. While this may reflect a situation whereby persons of high rank lived scattered in the outlying settlements among the general populace, as in parts of post-Classic Yucatan (Villa Rojas, 1961: 28), it does argue against the concept of an upper class holding themselves apart both residentially and socially from the peasantry.

A complicating factor in determining social residence pattern are the large so-called "palace" structures of the ceremonial centers. Many investigators seem to feel that these multi-roomed buildings would be unsuitable for regular residential purposes (Thompson, 1954: 57, 58), although some have been the chosen camping places of archaeologists themselves. Probably the palaces had several purporses, but the possibility remains that some may have been residential and that they were, in fact, the palaces of a noble class.

Excavations into house ruins located at a distance from major ceremonial centers have demonstrated that possession of articles such as handsomely decorated and well-made pottery and carved jades and other ornaments was not unusual among the general populace (Willey, 1956), although such burials are not comparable in wealth to some tomb burials encountered in major ceremonial centers. Moreover, one is impressed by the house ruins themselves. In contrast with the rather shoddy masonry work found today in wall footings and other occasional masonry features of modern Maya houses, the Classic house platforms were well-built and arranged, with hard plaster floors and well-laid and cemented stone retaining walls. Not only were the skills necessary for such building common among the populace, but the traditions of high quality workmanship and pride in impressive appearance were deeply ingrained through all levels of the society.

Another factor is total population size. Whereas a strongly stratified society if feasible for large population aggregates, how feasible is it for a total population of only a few thousand, a large proportion of whom would be children?

Population size leads to the problem of the labour requirements for the great ceremonial centers themselves. Excavations have shown that most, if not all, major ceremonial centers in Peten were founded in pre-Classic times and that construction continued throughout the Classic periods. The ruins which we see today represent at least a millenium of building and enlargement of structures. They would seem to imply not so much a large and tightly organized labour force as a persistent one under skilled direction.

The major ceremonial centers were not the only foci of ceremonial activity. The communities of several hundred persons called "zones" also had their ceremonial centers which, although minor compared to the major centers, nevertheless represent considerable labour and must have served important ritual and social purposes. And the smaller hamlet-like clusters seem also to have had their religious structures. Thus it appears that the complex ritual life of the Classic Maya extended down through all community levels. As Willey has noted (1956: 778), this situation seems incompatible with the notion of a priestly aristocracy aloof from and dominating the general populace. It would accord better with a system in which individuals drawn from the general populace progressed by intermittant stages from local poltico-regious office to positions of larger responsibility in the major ceremonial center.

*

While some of the factors discussed above support different interpretations, the settlement pattern data as a whole tend to indicate that Maya society was mobile rather than rigid, that the general populace enjoyed a relatively high "standard of living" and that they partook to a greater extent than has sometimes been supposed in the material wealth and rich ceremonialism of Classic culture. Conceivably a rotating system of office, such as Vogt describes for Zinacantan, was a factor in the integration of their society. Nevertheless, undeniable evidence exists for high politico-religious status, comparable to royalty, for some individuals, and the complexity of such intellectual attainments as the calendrical knowledge implies long training and a greater specialization than one would expect from a part-time priesthood. The problem has many aspects and is not to be easily solved, but settlement pattern studies are offering wider perspectives and opening new leads.

This paper has so far concentrated on the major ceremonial centers and their sustaining areas. What about larger territorial units? Certainly there is abundant evidence —for example, the similarities in the calendar and in hieroglyphic writing— that these centers were in close and easy contact with each other. The dispersed nature of the settlement pattern is only one argument that conditions were militarily peaceful. It is not unlikely that the major ceremonial centers were joined in some sort of provincial organization, perhaps a confederacy. In the region of northern Peten in which the survey was conducted, Tikal is somewhat larger than the other major centers and it is not unreasonable to suppose that it may have exercised political and religious suzerainty over the rest. If so, its ceremonial and administrative functions would have been greater, labour and officials might have been drawn from considerable distances away, and the settlement distribution in the vicinity might reflect a more complex social situation.

It is not impossible that certain temples in major centers of the region had an especially important status and reputation and that pilgrimages were made to them from distant points. Still another possibility is that certain individuals of high position held supreme religious authority over a large area, but poltical authority only over the sustaining area of their own ceremonial center — a suzerainty somewhat similar to that exercised by the Roman papacy during the Middle Ages. But concerning such possibilities we may never be able to do more than speculate.

References

BULLARD, W. R.
    1960   "Maya Settlement Pattern in Northeastern Peten, Guatemala", *American Antiquity*, Vol. 25, N° 3, pp. 355-372.

COWGILL, URSULA M.
    1961   "Soil Fertility and the Ancient Maya", *Transactions of the Connecticut Academy of Arts and Sciences*, Vol. 42, pp. 1-56. New Haven.

POLLOCK, H. E. D., R. L. ROYS, T. PROSKOURIAKOFF, & A. L. SMITH
    1962   *Mayapan, Yucatan, Mexico* (Carnegie Institution of Washington, Publication 619). Washington.

PROSKOURIAKOFF, T.
1960 "Historical Implications of a Pattern of Dates at Piedras Negras, Guatemala", *American Antiquity*, Vol. 25, N° 4, pp. 454-475.

RICKETSON, O. G. and E. B. RICKETSON
1937 *Uaxactun, Guatemala. Group E* — 1926-1931 (Carnegie Institution of Washington, Publication 477). Washington.

SANDERS, W. T.
1960 *Prehistoric Ceramics and Settlement Patterns in Quintana Roo, Mexico* Carnegie Institution of Washingon, Publication 606, Contribution N° 60). Washington.

THOMPSON, J. E. S.
1954 *The Rise and Fall of Maya Civilization*. University of Oklahoma Press, Norman.

VILLA ROJAS, A.
1961 "Notas sobre la tenencia de la tierra entre los mayas de la antigüedad", *Estudios de Cultura Maya*, Vol. 1, pp. 21-46. México.

VOGT, E. Z.
1961 "Some Aspects of Zinacantan Settlement Patterns and Ceremonial Organization", *Estudios de Cultura Maya*, Vol. 1, pp. 131-145. México.

WILLEY, G. R.
1956 "The Structure of Ancient Maya Society: Evidence from the Southern Lowlands", *American Anthropologist*, Vol. 58, N° 5, pp. 777-782.

WILLEY, G. R., W. R. BULLARD, J. B. GLASS, & J. C. GIFFORD
"Pheristoric Maya Settlements in the Belize Valley", in *Peabody Museum Papers*, Harvard University. (In press.)

REVIEWS

Map of the Ruins of Tikal, El Peten, Guatemala. Robert F. Carr and James E. Hazard. Tikal Reports No. 11, Museum Monographs, The University Museum, University of Pennsylvania, Philadelphia, 1961. iv + 26 pp., 1 fig., 10 folded maps in pocket. $5.00.

The great Maya ruin of Tikal has at last been mapped in detail, and the results constitute an admirable contribution to American archaeology. Maudslay, Maler, and Tozzer and Merwin explored the site at various times; and for many years the Tozzer-Merwin sketch map of 1910 has been the most complete cartographic record of this stupendous aggregate of temples, palaces, and lesser mounds. Now, thanks to the University of Pennsylvania field party, under the direction of Edwin M. Shook, we have a detailed instrument map that covers a zone three kilometers square and includes the major buildings at the center of the site and hundreds of minor ones on the outskirts.

The Tikal map represents the culmination of the efforts of several archaeologists and surveyors. Carr and Hazard assumed responsibility for bringing the work to a successful conclusion and for giving us the final version of the map together with a descriptive accompanying text. They are to be congratulated for an achievement in Maya lowland archaeological mapping that in magnitude and quality is rivaled only by the Morris Jones map of Mayapan.

There are nine quadrangle sheets, each devoted to a single square kilometer of the central section of the Tikal zone. The maps are about 19 inches square, and they are drawn at a scale of 1:2000. The tenth pocket map is a master sheet of the entire zone, embracing 16 square kilometers. It is a composite of the detailed maps of the central 3 by 3 kilometer section plus a more rapidly surveyed 500 meter strip bordering all four sides of this central section. The scale for the master sheet is 1:6250, and the size of the map itself is about 25 inches square.

The detailed Tikal mapping was done with plane table and telescopic alidade, supplemented with a transit. The bordering 500-meter strip was surveyed with Brunton compass, tape, and with the aid of aerial photographs. The individual kilometer quadrangles of the detailed maps are topographic presentations with 1-meter contour intervals. Contour lines and all natural features are rendered in brown. All archaeological structures and monuments are in black line drawings and symbols. The effect is both clear and attractive. The master sheet for the entire zone employs 5-meter contour intervals in brown and schematically depicts structures in black. The detailed quadrangles are conveniently referred to the master sheet by marginal diagrams on both. All maps treat only of surface features and surface-observed archaeology. Subsurface structures and features, as revealed by excavations, are reserved for appropriate excavation unit reports.

A descriptive text accompanies the maps. Appendices to this text include a table, by William A. Haviland, giving new structure numeration equivalences to previous designations of buildings and features in the earlier literature; another table, compiled by Shook, that lists carved stelae and altars by numerical designation and gives location data; and a third table listing the cubic capacities of the 13 Tikal water reservoirs.

In the text Carr and Hazard offer a number of interesting observations. Virtually all Tikal structures, large and small, have an orientation to within 10 degrees of cardinal directions. Curoiusly, these cardinal directions are those derived from magnetic and not true north. Isolated mounds are rare. Both impressive ceremonial buildings and small mounds are nearly always found grouped around leveled rectangular courts or raised plazas. Aside from this, no planned or organized grouping of mounds—particularly the small or "house" mounds—is detectable. The site of Tikal has no known limits. Swamps, or *bajos*, in which no mounds are found, border the east and west sides of the surveyed zone; but beyond these swamps mounds are again seen in numbers. To the north and south of the surveyed area mound density (apparently small mounds) continues at about the same ratio per square kilometer as within the peripheries of the surveyed area. The lesser centers of Chikin Tikal and Uolantun lie some 3 and 5 kilometers distant to the west and south, but it is not known if small mounds continue with high frequency between Tikal and these centers.

The authors compute a figure of 275 mounds per square kilometer for the nine central square kilometers of the Tikal detailed survey. This includes both large "ceremonial" buildings and small "house" mounds. This density suggests urban proportions to the authors. It might be pointed out, however, that near Dos Aguadas, on the opposite side of the Bajo de Santa Fe from Tikal and some 27 kilometers distant, Bullard (Maya Settlement Patterns in Northeastern Peten, Guatemala, *American Antiquity,* Vol. 25, No. 3, pp. 355-72, 1960) recorded 89 separate small platform units in a zone of 215,000 square meters, or between one-fifth and one-fourth of a square kilometer. Projecting these figures to a square kilometer would result in a count of over 400 separate mound platforms. At Barton Ramie, in the hamlet clusters along the Belize River, several kilometers distant from the nearest major ceremonial center at Benque Viejo, we have a count of 106 mound units per square kilometer. But these Barton units appear to be composed of more than one platform each. In effect, they are more like the little court or plaza arrangements of two, three, or four platform mounds seen on the Tikal map. Thus, a multiplication of the Barton Ramie figures by two or three, to give an approximate separate mound count figure, would bring the density of structures at that site to proportions approximating those of Tikal.

It is too early to interpret what all this means. Certainly, the term "urban" needs clarification and better definition, and the functions of Maya mounds and buildings, of any size, are but little understood. For the time being, however, I would like to hold to the argument that the density of small mound structures is just as great in localities at some distance from ceremonial centers as it is in close proximity to such centers—even in close proximity to Tikal. Perhaps, eventually, it may be demonstrated that many large and medium-sized buildings in the great centers—such as the palaces and many of the middle-sized platmorms at Tikal— were dwelling units. If so, I admit that this would make a difference in favor of the urban center proposals.

These questions, however, lead us away from the accomplishment of the map itself which is a basic datum of such value that I have only the highest praise for it.

Gordon R. Willey
Harvard University
Cambridge, Mass.

THE DEVELOPMENT OF FOLK AND COMPLEX CULTURES IN THE SOUTHERN MAYA AREA

STEPHAN F. DE BORHEGYI*

TWO generations of intensive archaeological work conducted in great part by the Carnegie Institution of Washington in the Southern Maya area have resulted in a wealth of factual information and the establishment of a fairly comprehensive and continuous cultural sequence. In spite of the many facts, few attempts have been made by Middle American archaeologists to synthesize this data and present it within a coherent conceptual framework. The reluctance of Middle Americanists to extract from the factual data theories regarding the recurring regularities of human behavior may be due in part to the feeling that such "theorizing" is purely speculative and unscientific. The picture is further complicated by the fact that in the Maya area the great bulk of the archaeological material collected and studied consists of artifacts from the excavations of mounds and tombs in the large ceremonial and urban centers. This material understandably does not represent the totality of the culture concerned. It is generally recognized, however, that the content of science is not made up entirely of facts. Facts, themselves, are simply piles of bricks which alone, although impressive, have no meaning until assembled to make up a building. The general tendency among archaeologists is to favor the brick makers and to scorn the masons, in spite of the obvious fact that no building is possible without the efforts of both. This is not to say that "theorizing" has been completely neglected in the writings of Middle American archaeologists. Many pages have been devoted to discussions of the uniqueness of certain important events in Maya or Aztec history, but few further inferences have been drawn to explain what trends there have been toward universal similarities in human behavior. That studies of this kind are so few may be due to the fact that it has not always been recognized that the same conceptual tools used for historical reconstruction can be used equally well for a scientific approach to the interpretation of human behavior.

Recognizing this "conceptual poverty" in the writings of Middle American archaeologists, Kluckhohn (1940: 43) warns us that

. . . unless archaeologists treat their work quite firmly as part of a general attempt to understand human behavior they will, before many generations, find themselves classed with Aldous Huxley's figure who devoted his life to writing a history of the three-pronged fork.

Since I have devoted much of my time to writing the history of the "three-pronged incense burner" (de Borhegyi 1950b, 1951a, 1951c, 1955), I feel particularly uncomfortable with Kluckhohn's comparison. However, after a prolonged study of these ceremonial vessels which were used throughout the history of the Southern Maya, I came to the conclusion that the inferences gathered from this study may present us with a provocative culture and sociological problem. These incense burners, along with other cult objects such as figurines, effigy whistles, and "rimhead" vessels, were probably used in connection with a simple agricultural, nature, and fertility cult. They formed what I believe to have been the core of a simple animistic *folk cult* and are in great contrast to the more sophisticated and stylized objects used in the complex religious rituals of the later periods. They were, in all probability, the prized private possessions of families and kin-

---

* This study, prompted by Kluckhohn's stimulating article (1940), has profited from the constructive criticism of A. V. Kidder, Erik K. Reed, and Sol Tax as well as from many informal and stimulating discussions with the members of the Carnegie Institution of Washington in Guatemala. The study in its incipient form was first presented in 1953 at the 52nd Annual Meeting of the American Anthropological Association at Tucson, Arizona, and in this form was published in 1954 by the Pan American Union in *Ciencias Sociales*. Research on the subject was conducted under a Bollingen Foundation (New York) grant-in-aid.

group heads and may have been used in a personalized way to attract, control, and placate the supernatural forces. The fact that these ceremonial vessels and cult objects persisted throughout the history of the Southern Maya but have so rarely been found within the sacred confines of the ceremonial precincts suggests that they were favored by the folk component of the society and frowned upon by the more sophisticated members of the upper classes. There must, therefore, have existed in the Southern Maya area communities composed of both a folk and a complex component. Within the community each component with its distinct culture apparently lived side by side over a time span of more than 2 millennia without too greatly influencing the patterns of beliefs and values of the other. Through a study of

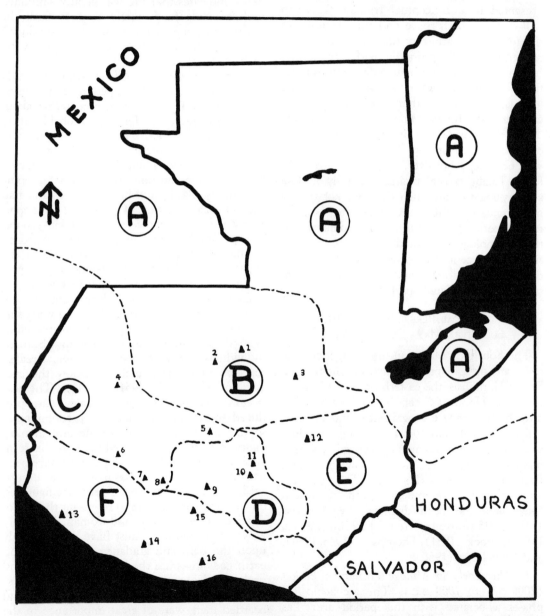

FIG. 107. Map of the southern Maya area. A, tropical rain forest area; B, hilly middle country (1, Chama; 2, Chipal; 3, Chipok); C, western volcanic highlands (4, Zaculeu; 5, Zacualpa; 6, Salcaja; 7, Chuitinamit; 8, Chukumuk); D, central volcanic highlands (9, Terrenos; 10, Kaminaljuyú; 11, Chinautla); E, semi-arid eastern lowlands (12, San Augustín); F, Pacific coastal plain (13, Champerico; 14, Tiquisate; 15, El Baul; 16, Finca Arizona).

these cult objects we may learn more about the development of folk and complex cultures in general and the inferences gained thereby may give us a better understanding of the factors which govern human behavior under specified conditions.

To best present the various stages in the development of folk and complex cultures in the Southern Maya area, this synthesis will be presented in a conceptual framework which will embrace both space and time factors. In the following 6 arbitrary time divisions I have concerned myself primarily with the central highland section of Guatemala. This limitation has been imposed not so much because the area is more typical than the others but because it is much better known archaeologically, due to the considerable number of scientifically controlled excavations. Occasional reference will be made, however, to the tropical rain forest, Pacific coastal plains, and hilly middle country regions, although they are not of primary concern to this study. The dates assigned to each period follow, with slight modifications, the chronology presented by Shook (1952), since the recent implications of radiocarbon datings in other areas of Middle America are still tentative (Wauchope 1954).

HISTORICAL PERSPECTIVE IN THE SOUTHERN MAYA CULTURE AREA

The Southern Maya culture area, including the state of Chiapas in Mexico, Guatemala, British Honduras, the eastern parts of El Salvador, and Honduras, can be divided roughly into the following 6 geographical and cultural units: tropical rain forest area, hilly middle country, western highlands, central volcanic highlands, semi-arid eastern lowlands, and Pacific coastal plains (Fig. 107). The historical and cultural development of the Southern Maya area has been discussed by Armillas (1948, 1951), de Borhegyi (1950a, 1954a, 1954b), Shook (1951), Thompson (1943, 1954), and Wauchope (1950).

1. *The Early or Village Formative Period (2000 B.C. to 1000 B.C.).* The archaeological phases associated with this period are: Las Charcas, Arevalo, Majadas, Providencia (Valley of Guatemala); Zakat, Xaraxong (Almolonga Valley); and Salcaja 1 (western highlands).

By 2000 B.C. there was, in the Southern Maya area, a sedentary way of life based on a primitive method of agriculture. Cotton and various food plants, primarily corn and beans and later squash and avocado, were cultivated. Stone metates and manos for grinding grain as well as clay griddles (comales) are present in the earliest archaeological strata discovered to date in the area. Although the archaeological evidence indicates that life was greatly simplified with a stable food supply thus assured, the labors and plans of these early food producers were still thwarted by natural events beyond their control.

In time, a simple, realistic form of family or kin-group ritual developed to control and placate these forces of nature centering about agriculture, rain, and fertility. Probably every manifestation of nature had its local spirit and many were venerated individually by means of special rituals. These rites were conducted to ensure the multiplication and safekeeping of animals, plants, and human beings and had the practical function of providing an opportunity for the periodic reunion of kin groups. The personalized and individualistic approach to the supernatural can be inferred from the appearance of the cult objects and vessels produced during this Early Formative period.

Examples of these cult objects are the frequently spike-decorated incense burners surmounted by 3 effigy prongs. Most of the effigy prongs seem to represent aged and bearded individuals, many of them with "tear streaks" represented by deep incisions below the eyes (de Borhegyi 1950b, 1951a, 1951c). The tear streaks very likely symbolized rain. Also produced in abundance were the predominantly solid, hand-modeled clay female and monkey figurines as well as effigy whistles in the form of birds or animals. These latter may have been used in magical ceremonies to ensure a successful hunt. The usually nude pregnant figurines, on the other hand, seem to represent the reproductive power of nature and woman. The early Maya food producers must have relied heavily upon the help and guidance of the rain and earth gods to assure the local food supply, and understandably the representations of these gods, depicted on the effigy prongs as aged and bearded men, were of great importance to the community. The help of these gods was probably invoked by means of sympathetic magic during family and communal ceremonies.

It is important to note that these cult objects were made in a decidedly individualistic and realistic manner. Although certain features common to all of them (such as the beard, tear streaks, or a swollen abdomen in the case of the female figurines) must have been magical properties considered essential for the proper functioning of these objects, no two have been found to be identical or even very closely alike. It is fair to assume that through these objects, the individual farmer, village shaman, or kin-group head thought to contact, conciliate, and control the supernatural, probably more often for individual than for communal ends. If the many and varied cylindrical and flat clay stamps produced during the same period were used to mark private ownership, this would also indicate that personal needs were of more immediate concern to the individual than was the well-being of the community as a whole. From the large quantity of these cult objects it can be inferred that they played an important role in the everyday life of these simple, sedentary food producers and eventually formed an integral part of the self-contained way of life referred to earlier as a folk culture.

The sedentary life of these early food producers provided opportunities for improved housing conditions and paved the way for village planning. The settlement pattern of this formative period was probably the unplanned autonomous village unit. Although no house mounds have yet been excavated, we know that in the Guatemalan midwestern highlands, dwellings were made of pole and thatch with walls partially daubed with adobe (Shook 1951: 97). These huts were probably arranged at random throughout the village area. Near these village concentrations 3 to 4 m.-deep cone- or bottle-shaped pits with circular orifices were dug through the sterile surface soil into the underlying volcanic ash. Some may have served the villagers as sweat baths for ritual purification, but more probably they were food storage chambers to house the growing larder of agricultural products. While many were left empty, others were filled with household debris and occasionally even with simple burials. Apparently no burial mounds were constructed during this period. The few pit burials found are sparsely furnished with food containers and personal ornaments and give no indication of accumulated wealth. The struggle for livelihood could have permitted little if any social stratification but the fairly diverse archaeological inventory of stone and clay artifacts and jade, bone, and shell ornaments along with traces of basketry and extensive obsidian workshops, suggests the emergence of a class of specialists, the first men to be supported out of a surplus of foodstuffs.

The growth of these early food producing communities was eventually limited by their own economy. The expansion in numbers involved expansion in space. Additional families could be supported only if more arable land was available for cultivation. Thus each self-sufficient village unit gradually put forth more and more daughter villages.

It is difficult, however, to speak of a uniform "Early Middle American Formative Culture." It would perhaps be more accurate to think in terms of a multitude of different local formative or folk cultures all on the same level of cultural complexity. Practically every village unit must have represented an adaptation to a specific environment with an ideology more or less indigenous to it. The archaeological inventories of tools and culinary objects testify to this fact. The relative abundance of clay comales in the earliest archaeological strata in the highlands and their complete absence in the rain forest and hilly middle country seem to indicate regional variations in the preparation of basic food products or possibly even completely different dietary habits. On the other hand, the archaeological list of ceremonial paraphernalia, as discussed previously, shows sufficient uniformity to indicate that the pooling of human experience had been accelerated by intercommunication in the Southern Maya area at least as early as 1000 B.C.

2. *The Late or "Urban" Formative Period (1000 B.C. to A.D. 200).* The archaeological phases associated with this period are: Miraflores, Arenal, Santa Clara (Valley of Guatemala); Terrenos Altos (Almolonga Valley); Chukumuk 1 (Late Atitlan); Salcaja 2 (western highlands); Chama 1A (Chixoy drainage, west); Finca Arizona, Champerico (Pacific coast).

The beginning of this period saw the appearance of large and elaborate burial and temple mounds arranged along narrow, elongated, rectangular plazas. The 2 parallel plazas were separated by a row of buildings and were oriented roughly northeastward. These platform mounds or earthen pyramids, some of them as high as 20 m., were built of puddled adobe without the use of stone or lime mortar (Shook and Kidder 1952). They were covered with brightly colored adobe plaster and supported perishable structures which probably served as temple shrines. At several highland sites plain stone monuments have been found, usually located to the east of the main pyramid. Although these monuments are plain, they may have been used for marking time, a preoccupation which never seems to have achieved the magnitude in the highlands that it did in the tropical rain forest area.

The organized planning of the mounds and plazas shows the definite concept of a ceremonial precinct, a sacred enclosure from which the village life seems to have been excluded. Within these mounds the bodies of important personages were interred in rectangular burial chambers, sometimes superimposed one upon another. These death chambers, roofed and supported by posts and cross beams, contained the principal body on a wooden platform, many lavish offerings together with the bodies of sacrificed animals and, frequently, human retainers. The existence of these temple mounds presupposes a probably small but active priestly group and a considerable engineering knowledge while the presence of rich burial furniture argues for accumulated wealth concentrated in the hands of certain individuals. The development of these apparently socially sanctioned customs definitely indicates the beginning of social stratification among the Southern Mayas and suggests speculation to a considerable degree on a life after death, the inevitable result of man's quest for immortality. These customs also seem to argue for the presence of organized and directed ceremonies, probably following an annual pattern based on the agricultural or life cycle. The foundation of these advanced concepts must have been an abstract philosophy. Such a philosophy could have developed only in a society whose subsistence was based on intensified local food production, the preservation and storage of surplus food and commodities, and organized trade. The more efficient form of agriculture was undoubtedly made possible in great part by the evolving concept of a calendar.

At this time there is noticeable among the material remains such a variety of elaborate containers and tools that a considerable number of individuals must have been engaged in nonfood producing activities. Priests, craftsmen, and traders were most probably completely withdrawn from direct food production and eventually formed a separate class. Thus we can see elements of complexity developing within the culture.

The fact that the ceremonies and rituals were organized, and that the gods were being standardized, is evident from the changed appearance of the cult objects and ritual vessels of the period. The 3-pronged incense burners, handmade "archaic" figurines, and effigy whistles manufactured at this time were much more conventionalized and one can easily find duplicates among them. The spiked decoration disappears, the prongs are plain, and the walls of the censers depict conventionalized grotesque and even monstrous forms with thick upper lips and overhanging fangs, believed to be feline (jaguar) or reptilian deities. This is obviously at variance with the realism of former days. An offshoot of the 3-pronged incense burner, the highly standardized "rimhead" vessel, also came into use (de Borhegyi 1950b, 1951c). None of these cult objects were found in tombs, however, suggesting that although they had become more conventionalized and widely accepted they were still essentially the property of the folk and were probably rejected by the developing upper classes.

It seems that the individualistic religious approach to the supernatural, at least within the sacred enclosures, was replaced by a more rigid, depersonalized ceremonial discipline. Security was no longer in the hands of the individual. Both the future and earthly existence of man was controlled by a small group of specialists who had achieved a monopoly of magical power and were regarded as intermediaries between god and man. This profitable occupation permitted the concentration of wealth within a specialized class and easily permitted the organization of a theocratic state.

During this period monumental building activities were carried out in the service of the supernatural and the dead. Great labor battalions must have been readily available for such extensive public works as the erection of huge earthen pyramids. This manpower could have been recruited only from an expanded population which allowed the individual sufficient free time to perform such nonfood-producing and not immediately rewarding activities. These enormous cooperative tasks in which several thousand people must have participated were possibly motivated by religious zeal and by the desire on the part of the rising priestly class to keep the growing population occupied.

At the end of the period theocracy, with all its complexities, was in full swing and was a suitable matrix for the reception of diffused traits. The priestly representatives of this complex and incipient urban culture ceased to look inward upon their own community but instead gazed beyond their boundaries seeking new ideas and problem solutions from other cultures. The growing complexity of this theocratic and urban culture was equipped for and most receptive to outside influences. Thus the tight, inwardly turned, or "vertical cultural" interest characteristic of folk cultures became loosely knit, horizontal, and cosmopolitan, a sign of urbanization in the making.

3. *The Early Classic Period or the Rise of the Theocratic City States* (A.D. 200 to 600). The archaeological phases associated with this period are: Aurora, Esperanza (Valley of Guatemala); Terrenos Bajos (Almolonga Valley); Chukumuk 2 (Lake Atitlan); Chama 1B-2 (Chixoy drainage, west); Atzan (Zaculeu); Balam (Zacualpa); Lato (middle Motagua); and San Francisco (Pacific coast).

Some time close to the beginning of this period new religious concepts emanating probably from Teotihuacan, Mexico, spread throughout Middle America and were felt everywhere with varying degrees of intensity. In the Southern Maya area they soon became fashionable with the cosmopolitan upper classes and many of the new religious abstractions and innovations were readily incorporated into the philosophy of the Maya urban theocrats. These ideas were most probably carried by itinerant merchants who dispersed them along with trade goods.

Some of these luxury and ceremonial objects were not only traded but were imitated locally, and they were probably used exclusively by the upper classes, since none of these objects have been found outside of the ceremonial precincts. Rimhead vessels and 3-pronged incense burners disappear completely from the archaeological picture. This suggests that they may have been considered rustic and "old fashioned" and were probably discarded by all but the most conservative members of the society. They were replaced by new types of incense burners characterized by a protruding "loop nose," many of which represented double headed feline or reptilian monsters while others depicted the Mexican rain god, Tlaloc (de Borhegyi 1951b, 1951d). Figurines and effigy whistles are also lacking in the material excavated from the ceremonial and urban centers, but the Teotihuacan type of elaborately stuccoed and painted cylindrical tripod vases with apron covers, the "thin orange" ware bowls, small cult vessels shaped like cream pitchers, and "candle-holders" are relatively abundant among the rich burial offerings.

Utilitarian pottery and household utensils remained much the same. This would suggest that the radical changes were brought through new ideas rather than a migration of people (Kidder, Jennings, and Shook 1946). Unfortunately, the great wealth of archaeological material from this period comes almost exclusively from the excavation of the large ceremonial and urban centers. Figurines, effigy whistles, and 3-pronged incense burners may still have been made and used during this period by the farmers and food producers but in that case they would be found only in the less conspicuous house mounds. To date, however, little attention has been devoted by archaeologists working in the area to these humble and not easily found dwellings.

The settlement pattern of the Early Classic period shows a tendency toward the establishment of more centralized locations and closely knit court assemblages for ceremonial observances and ritual ball games. These ball courts were open at both ends and were built with sloping side walls. The earthen mounds of this period were frequently faced with volcanic pumice blocks set in adobe, were sometimes faced with white plaster, and occasionally contained as many as 8 superimposed structures. Narrow stairways led to the summits of these mounds where stood shrines or altars of perishable materials. Within these mounds the deep burial chambers were roofed with logs and lined with mats, and were filled with rich offerings and sacrificed retainers. Judging from the large number of these burial mounds the society of this period might be labeled "grave-oriented."

Pilgrims who came to offer their devotions to the images of the gods or who gathered in the ceremonial centers for burial rites and feast days were also probably pressed by the priestly class to contribute to the building of new shrines and temples. Thus there was a constant supply of free laborers from the ranks of devotees. The populace living in modest thatched dwellings in the outlying areas must have devoted much of their time and energies to the repair and construction of the large and ornate buildings in the ceremonial centers.

The plazas within the ceremonial centers must also have been the scene of regular market gatherings. Although there is no decisive evidence of the existence of a form of currency at this time, some standardized medium of exchange may have been devised to facilitate the many and varied trading and marketing activities.

The social system that best fits a culture of such complexity must have possessed a reasonably complex stratification consisting of commoners, kin-group heads, warriors, political officials, bureaucrats, clerks, artisans, merchants, and, on the top of the ladder to coordinate all of them, a priestly ruling class. The existence of a slave element recruited from war prisoners is doubtful but possible. All these classes were governed by the economy and the rules of the religious center and every individual no matter how humble was affected by the way of life. All this seems to indicate that within the orbit of the ceremonial center the face-to-face individualistic and personal relationship between man and the supernatural was changed into a complex of abstract, formalized theories and astronomical and mathematical calculations. This esoteric knowledge, however, was not shared by every member of the community. Such advanced concepts could not have been understood or appreciated by the simple farmers who undoubtedly felt much closer to the spirits of the earth and nature than to a far removed and abstract heavenly pantheon. I believe, therefore, that the reason the Early Classic period gives such an appearance of uniformity is due to the cosmopolitan pattern and horizontal world view of the governing upper classes; not because every member of each community understood or contributed to its cultural complexities. Perhaps the picture would be considerably different had more of the outlying and smaller village units or house mounds been excavated.

4. *The Late Classic Period or the Culmination of the Theocratic City States* (A.D. 600 to 1000). The archaeological phases associated with this period are: Amatle, Pamplona (Valley of Guatemala); Pompeya, Portal (Almolonga Valley); Chama 3-4, Chipal 1 (Chixoy drainage, west); Chipok, Seacal (Chixoy drainage, east); Chinaq (Zaculeu); Pokom (Zacualpa); Magdalena (Middle Motagua); and San Juan, Tiquisate (Pacific coast).

For a while, at least, this period seems to have followed the cultural trends established during the Early Classic. If anything, the culture became more complex and the religion more abstract and formalized. The foreign influences from Teotihuacan were fully absorbed and integrated. Regional division of labor must have been quite extensive because some areas show craft centers where one type of pottery or artifact was made to the exclusion of others. In order that these regional products could be traded from one area to another, organized transportation and the building of road networks became important. As trade increased the highly-prized self-sufficiency of the village units was gradually sacrificed and the villagers became dependent upon many imported goods which were no longer luxury objects but vital necessities in the changed village life. Obsidian from the highlands proved to be superior to chert, the material previously used for spearheads in the rain forest region. Volcanic stone was better adapted to grinding corn than anything available in the limestone country. Prior to this time corn had been prepared in different ways in the lowlands but with the introduction of new eating habits metates and manos became vital necessities and were brought to many regions from the highlands. Shell objects were traded from the Atlantic and the Pacific to satisfy the magical and esthetic desires of folk and upper classes alike. Such large scale activities must have been the result of a greatly increased population. The growth of the population during this period may have been due to more highly organized agricultural activities, accurately regulated by calendric calculations, or to such new inventions as irrigation and agricultural terracing (Armillas 1948: 106-7; Ricketson and Ricketson 1937: 2-12).

Toward the end of the period in the volcanic highlands, building activities seem to have slowed down and the large burial mounds were replaced by low platform mounds arranged around small plazas and rectangular ball courts. By this time the ball courts were closed at both ends.

The settlements, although smaller, were still in open country close to arable land, but seem to outnumber the sites of the previous periods. A reorientation of the cultural goals also seems obvious from the changed cultural inventories. The previously fashionable and ornate Teotihuacanoid ceremonial vessels disappear from the archaeological scene and in their place are found again the familiar ritual objects of the folk cult. Figurines, effigy whistles, rimhead vessels, 3-pronged incense burners, and spiked incense burners all came back into popular usage although, as would be suspected after such a long period, in slightly changed forms. Many of these figurines, effigy whistles, effigy prongs, and rimheads were made in clay molds, a convenient and cheap form of mass production. In this way, even without the knowledge of the potter's wheel, they could be turned out rapidly to meet the needs of a large population. From the foregoing it seems obvious that the folk cult must gradually have regained its original importance in the culture. But at the very end of the period the peaceful scene shows signs of turmoil followed by marked sociopolitical changes. Many of the ceremonial and urban centers located in the rain forest region and in the fertile open valleys of the highlands were abruptly abandoned, never to be repopulated. It is fascinating to speculate on how this abrupt change may have come about and just what reason was behind this drastic mass displacement. Exhaustion of cultural potentialities, disease, economic crises brought on by climatic changes, or the collapse of an unsatisfactory agricultural system have all been postulated as causal factors. Recent evidence however points toward the possibility of a revolt of the food producing classes against the exploitative abuses of the theocrats. This may have come as the result of discontent and loss of faith in the power of the priests and could have been brought on or accelerated by any one of or a combination of the above factors. The revolt seems to have started a chain reaction which spread throughout the Maya area and reached the various ceremonial centers in different years and with greater or less violence. The Bonampak frescoes and the mutilated sculptures and thrones of Piedras Negras in the rain forest region are probable signs of violent revolt, whereas in other areas the evidence points to a more peaceful and gradual readjustment to the old ways (Thompson 1954: 88). The fact that by the end of this period practically all of the great ceremonial and urban centers were abandoned for good, the jealously guarded esoteric knowledge and the hieroglyphic writing of the upper classes were largely forgotten, and the temples were left to crumble and decay, indicates a singular lack of respect for the previous world order.

5. *The Postclassic Period or the Rise of the Militaristic City States* (A.D. *1000 to 1524*). The archaeological phases associated with this period are: Ayampuc, Chinautla (Valley of Guatemala); Primavera, Medina (Almolonga Valley); Chipal 2-3 (Chixoy drainage, west); Samac (Chixoy drainage, east); Quankyak, Xinabahul (Zaculeu); Tohil, Yaqui (Zacualpa); and Chuitinamit (Lake Atitlan).

After the turmoil had died down, Maya society began to reorganize itself. In the rain forest area many groups, like the ancestors of the present day Lacandones, went back to the dim forest regions to continue a peaceful fishing, hunting-gathering, and simple slash-and-burn farming existence with the use of the digging stick. In the security of the dense rain forest they gradually elaborated on their folk ritual. They manufactured, as some of them still do today, effigy incense burners and figurines and approached the spirit world in a personalized form according to their ancestral traditions. Other communities, living in the fertile intermontane valleys of the highlands, moved to the mountain slopes or hilltops where some of them found relative but short-lived security. The wide distribution of the 3-pronged incense burners in these marginal areas tends to confirm this hypothesis (de Borhegyi 1951c: 176, map). They had, however, little time to enjoy their newly regained independence. Several waves of foreign migratory groups entered the Southern Maya area from Mexico. Some probably followed the course of the Usumacinta river while others may have traveled along the Pacific coastal plain. Their legendary leaders claimed Tula (Tollan), the famous Toltec capital, as their original home.

These warlike groups, led by a professional soldiery and equipped with superior weapons such as the bow and arrow, settled down in the highlands of Guatemala and must have been a constant threat to the native population until eventually they had brought most of it under their yoke. However, they were unable to uproot the agricultural, religious, and commercial traditions of their predecessors.

The Mexican groups introduced the cult of the feathered serpent, Quetzalcoatl, named Kukulcan or Gucumatz by the Mayas, and the cult of the war and solar gods, along with "idolatry," a sacrificial cult centering about the worship of temple images foreign to the Mayas. They must have brought an end to the manufacture of 3-pronged incense burners and "rimhead" vessels since none have been found in the excavation of Postclassic sites. The cult connected with the figurines and effigy whistles lived on, however, as it lives today, in modified form. The fashionable censer types of the period became the ladle censers and the crude effigy incense burners made after Mexican (more specifically Mixteca-Puebla) models. Metallurgy, previously unknown in the Southern Maya area, was also introduced during this time although it was never practiced to any great extent (Thompson 1943). The malleable copper and copper alloy tools and weapons were first known only as luxury objects but later became necessities desired by all classes. With the subjugation of the native population, the Mexican groups brought into existence a strong militaristic urban middle class with relatively high living standards which must have depended greatly for survival on the agricultural produce of their Maya subjects.

During the Postclassic period, the settlement pattern had changed from the open land or valley site to easily defended hilltop or fortress sites, many of which were surrounded by deep ravines. Temples and pyramids, occasionally serving as burial mounds, were still constructed but usually as a part of urban concentration. "Twin temples" placed on a single substructure, multichambered, spacious dwellings or "palaces," some supported by massive columns, paved courts, and skillfully constructed drainage systems, suggest a growing emphasis on city living although a good part of the population must have continued its previous farming existence. The formerly sacred ball courts were now built in the shape of the letter "I" and may have been used to a great extent for entertainment whereas the sacred enclosures or plazas became the scene of secular market gatherings. In accordance with urban economy trade and specialization were extensive and widespread. Before long a mobile and prosperous class or guild of merchants and artisans came into being, enjoying the benefits of a concentrated surplus of wealth and social standing.

There are no reasons to believe that the population increased at this time, especially since intertribal warfare became a common feature of the period. The secular aspect of life prevailed over, or at least balanced, the power of the priestly class. Religion became an implement in the hands of the secular rulers and war chiefs who may have used it as the rationale for their expansionistic and imperialistic ventures. There are even reasons to believe that some of the itinerant merchants served as spies and informers for their employers while on business in other areas. Most of the conquests reveal economic rather than religious motives. The tribal aim became the possession of the best agricultural lands, markets, and such industrial regions as the salt and cacao producing Pacific lowlands or the flint and copper abundant regions of the highlands. The intensive warfare, large-scale territorial expansion, and colonization led toward social heterogeneity and away from the homogenous folk-type society. That this way of life was not particularly satisfactory to most of the Maya populace can be seen from the great amount of interregional petty warfare. There was a constant economic struggle between the various Mexican dominated political confederacies (the Quiche, Kakchiquel, Zutugil, Mam, and Pipil) for a monopoly of power and land and for commodities such as the cacao beans, which served not only to provide a luxury drink but also as a socially established form of currency. During these "Dark Ages" one or the other of these competing confederacies gained temporal supremacy or local independence only to be shortly thereafter succeeded by another (Thompson 1943; de Borhegyi 1950a). Throughout this period a slow process of "Mayanization" seems to have gone on, together with a growing attachment to the folkways and their associated cults. By the time the Spanish conquerors arrived in Guatemala, most of the Mexican groups were thoroughly "Mayanized," their language was to a great extent forgotten, and Kukulcan or Gucumatz was not even a name to be remembered.

6. *The Colonial and Industrial Period* (A.D. 1524 to the present). With cross and sword the Spaniards introduced to the Mayas an equally abstract and formalized religion, a greatly different economic and political interest, and a complex social structure in which the conquered existed at the lowest level. In spite of constant exposure to these many new ideas, the Maya farmer seems to have been as little affected by them as he was by the pressure of theocracy, or by the Mexican invasions. The strong desire for a direct and individualistic ritual form in which the supernatural could be addressed personally did not abate, and even today it prevails among most of the Guatemalan highland communities. In time they incorporated the cross and made of the saints a form of sacred effigy cult. They amalgamated their old censers with the new ones of the Catholic church and made of the rather impersonal, formalized, and abstract Christian faith a simple family and nature cult that might be labeled "folk catholicism."

The Concept of Folk and Complex Society

The archaeological evidence presented here shows how certain ritual objects and related ideas characteristic of a folk cult persisted through centuries of change and oppression in the Southern Maya area. Although the ceremonial and cult objects themselves underwent certain modifications, the ideology or folk mentality behind them remained practically unchanged (Fig. 108). The conceptual interpretation of the archaeological data argues for a long-lived coexistence of folk and complex cultures in the Southern Maya area with different and frequently opposing world views and mentalities. Not only did each subculture maintain its individuality but over a span of at least 2 millennia it had little, if any, influence on the socioreligious structure of the other. This fact indicates that certain recurring regularities in human behavior can be traced through archaeological data and also calls for a revision of some of the concepts concerning so-called folk cultures, a subject much debated in the literature to date.

According to Redfield's (1947) ideal conception, folk societies are small, isolated, nearly self-sufficient homogeneous groups where a face-to-face personal relationship is preferred, the family or kin group plays an important social role, behavior is traditional and uncritical, and the sacred prevails over the secular. However, the archaeological evidence from the Southern Maya area suggests that folk societies are not necessarily isolated or even small. During the early Formative each folk society was an isolated and self-contained unit, but in later periods it formed a vital part of the total culture and existed in a symbiotic relationship with the more complex urban component. If Termer's calculations are correct (1951: 106), the folk component in the Southern Maya area made up at least 75% of the total populations. He estimates a minimum of 300,000 people as the total population of the area, a density of 6.6 per square kilometer. Of this number it is assumed that only about 75,000 people were connected with the religious cults. According to Redfield (1941: 343), "When folk societies undergo contact and communication with urbanized society, they tend to change in the direction of the opposite of these characters (i.e. the cluster of elements characteristic of folk societies)." The archaeological evidence shows that, in spite of the long and close contact with urbanized society, folk cultures tend to retain their distinct character and resist change toward the opposite direction. Foster (1953: 163), recognizing the inherent limitations of Redfield's hypothesis, describes folk society as a

... "half society," a part of a larger social unit (usually a nation) which is vertically and horizontally structured. The folk component of this unit bears a symbiotic spatial-temporal relationship to the more complex component, which is formed by the upper classes of the pre-industrial urban center. In this sense folk and urban are not polar concepts; rather they are both integral parts of the definition of a certain type of socio-cultural unit in which the pre-industrial city is a focal point. Far from threatening the folk society, this type of urban unit is a precondition for its existence.

According to Steward (1950: 111), "Folk societies and cultures do not entirely disappear but they are modified and acquire new characteristics because of their functional dependence upon a new and larger system."

The definitions of Foster and Steward more closely approach the archaeological picture in the Southern Maya area because both make use of historical depth, a concept greatly lacking in Redfield's "ideal type" of folk society. Foster, after carefully distinguishing between *folk culture* and *folk society*, postulates the 2 stages of development of a folk society as the *pre-industrial*, which appeared with the urban revolution, and the *postindustrial*. He assumes that in the later stages folk cultures disappear according to the degree of industrialization. He does state, however, that "in Latin America large segments of the urban population are more typically folk than anything else." Oscar Lewis (1952) found that Tepozteco families living in Mexico City continued their "folk-like existence" to a surprising degree. Neither Foster nor Lewis have tried to analyze or give reasons for this persistence of "folk qualities," however, nor have they attempted to explain why this "folk ideology" tends to perpetuate itself in the face of strong outside influences. Tax (1941: 29) on the other hand has offered an explanation for this phenomenon. In his description of highland communities in Guatemala he states that the Indians of a municipio "think of themselves as a distinct group of people, biologically and socially." Each group has a relatively exclusive local set of customs and practices. Each municipio has its own economic and social values, its own saints, own fiestas, and standard of living. In spite of the continuous intercommunication, trade relations, and even intermarriage, among the municipios and the realization and acceptance of the fact that different customs and beliefs exist among other groups, they still feel indifferent to them and tend to perpetuate their own sets of beliefs. A medicine or an herb which is good for the neighboring group will not necessarily be accepted in the home community. Tax explains this indifference to the cultural values of other people by attributing it to "the impersonal character of all kinds of social relations." The impersonal character of social relations, according to Tax, "is a form of isolation that restricts communication and borrowing." Because the impersonal type of trade or commercial relationship is generally accepted as a characteristic ascribed to complex cultures he concludes that "a civilized type of social relationship does not necessarily develop together with a civilized type of world view." This picture closely coin-

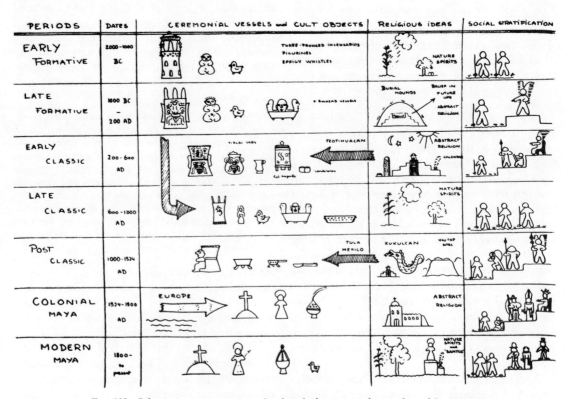

Fig. 108. Schematic representation of cultural changes in the southern Maya area.

cides with the archaeological evidence. The "folk mentality" centering about the agricultural and life cycle, and interwoven with a preferred "face-to-face" relationship with the supernatural, at least in the Southern Maya area, has remained virtually unchanged from the Village Formative period up to the present. It was not greatly affected by the urbanization process nor by the process of general secularization during the Militaristic or Postclassic epoch. While money economy (if cacao beans were really such) and a widespread system of organized trade was well received by most members of the folk culture by virtue of their impersonal nature they left unchanged the basic folk mentality. Tax's conclusions are of considerable importance in the understanding of the folk mentality of the Guatemalan highland communities. He leaves unexplained, however, the basic causal factors for their conservatism. Through an analysis of the integrated goal and value structure of both folk and complex cultures we may better understand why the former tend to perpetuate themselves and the latter are subject to constant change.

In the following list I have presented certain general observations and concepts concerning folk and complex cultures. These observations are based primarily on the conceptual interpretation of the archaeological data in an attempt to discover universal regularities in human behavior. It is to be expected that some of these statements are repetitions of earlier observations made by Redfield (1940, 1941, 1947), Steward (1950), King (1953), and Foster (1953). On the whole, however, I believe this much debated subject will profit by the addition of historical perspective.

Folk Culture

Definition

Generally organized around the local food supply, local institutions, and simple or complex associations with nature. It develops in dispersed self-contained settlements or on the outskirts of urban and/or ceremonial centers.

Characteristics

1. Basically homogeneous, more static than flexible, is usually self-directed and tends to be ethnocentric and perpetuative in its world view.

2. Depends mostly on a self-produced food supply to support its members and the few part-time specialists.

3. Basically realistic, regional, and nationalistic in its philosophy and artistic expression.

4. Prefers a personal "face-to-face" individualistic approach and control of things and the supernatural.

5. Offers few cultural facets and few alternatives, thereby giving a feeling of optimum security to the individual.

6. Prefers a commonly shared, stable way of life with a deeply integrated goal and value system which is ultimately satisfying and rewarding for the individual.

7. Basically nonaggressive and noncompetitive, usually resists new ideas passively, but may rise in violence when threatened by total destruction.

8. Less inventive and less susceptible to cultural influences. Regards them with an implicit suspicion as potential dangers to its group unity, stable goal and value structure, and system of group security.

Complex Culture

Definition

Generally organized around sacred or secular associations, organized trade, money economy, and politico-religious administration. It develops in ceremonial, urban, and/or industrial centers.

Characteristics

1. Basically heterogeneous and dynamic, is usually government directed, and tends to be cosmopolitan and flexible in its world view.

2. Depends mostly on an outside or artificial food supply to support the great number of non-food-producing specialists.

3. Basically abstract, formalized, and cosmopolitan in its philosophy and artistic expression.

4. Prefers an impersonal group approach and control of things and the supernatural.

5. Offers many cultural facets and alternatives, only a few of which can be realized, thereby causing frustration and insecurity for the individual.

6. Prefers a flexible way of life with multiple choices of goals and values which leaves the individual unsatisfied, unrewarded, and seeking satisfaction.

7. Basically aggressive and competitive, seeks new ideas constantly and attempts to disseminate them, if necessary by forceful methods.

8. Inventive and eager to accept cultural influences. Regards them as possible problem solutions, through which the uprooted group unity, stable goal and value structure, and stable system of group security might be regained.

These observations may be summarized as follows: Folk cultures, whether past or present, can exist independently or as distinct subcultures within a more complex cultural unit. They tend to maintain their cultural distinctness because, through the sum total of their satisfying problem solutions, they give the utmost security and reward to their members. As a consequence, they do not readily incorporate new ideas, goals, or values into their cultural structure.

This principle can be applied to many of the present day Maya communities in the Guatemalan highlands. The Maya farmer of today is motivated by an implicit desire for group security in his dealings with other individuals and his philosophy of living. He is generally noninventive, noncompetitive, nonaggressive, and tends to look with suspicion on modern technology and innovations introduced to him by his government or by international agencies. He has made of the abstract and formalized Catholic religion a simple family or kin-group cult through which he approaches the supernatural directly and personally. He prefers the stable way of life that gives him maximum security because of its minimum number of alternatives. As a result he is frequently regarded as backward and stubborn. Time and again anthropologists are asked to explain why the Maya Indian no longer seems to be capable of producing the "grandiose achievements" for which his ancestors are popularly known. In answer to this query, it has been suggested (La Farge 1940; Beals 1952) that the Indian has suffered greatly from the initial shock of the Conquest and that his "degeneration" (or backwardness) is due in part to the many years of humiliating submission and virtual slavery. The archaeological evidence shows us however that neither the Theocratic period nor the Mexican and Spanish conquests brought about drastic changes in the "folk mentality" of the Maya farmer. He probably understood and appreciated neither the intricate glyphic and calendric system nor the abstract philosophical religion imposed upon him by Maya and Mexican theocrats, or by the Church of Rome. Then, as now, the achievements of the ruling upper classes seem to be mere incidents in the life of the Maya farmer. How the increasing pressure of industrialization, scientific farming, and politics on a nation-wide scheme will affect these folk cultures cannot yet be judged in proper perspective.

ARMILLAS, PEDRO

1948 A Sequence of Cultural Development in Mesoamerica. In "A Reappraisal of Peruvian Archaeology," assembled by W. C. Bennett. *Memoirs of the Society for American Archaeology,* No. 4, pp. 105-11. Menasha.

1951 Tecnología, formaciones socio-económicas y religión en Mesoamerica. In "Civilizations of Ancient America," edited by Sol Tax. *Selected Papers of the XXIXth International Congress of Americanists* [New York, 1949], pp. 19-30. University of Chicago Press.

BEALS, RALPH

1952 Notes on Acculturation. In *Heritage of Conquest,* edited by Sol Tax, pp. 225-32. Free Press, Glencoe.

DE BORHEGYI, S.F.

1950a Estudio arqueológico en la falda norte del Volcán de Agua. *Revista del Instituto de Antropología e Historia de Guatemala,* Vol. 2, No. 1, pp. 3-22. Guatemala.

1950b Rimhead Vessels and Cone-shaped Effigy Prongs of the Pre-Classic Period at Kaminaljuyu, Guatemala. *Carnegie Institution of Washington, Notes on Middle American Archaeology and Ethnology* (CIW, NMAE), Vol. 4, No. 97, pp. 60-80. Cambridge.

1951a A Study of Three-pronged Incense Burners from Guatemala and Adjacent Areas. *CIW, NMAE,* Vol. 4, No. 101, pp. 100-24. Cambridge.

1951b Loopnose Incense Burners in the Guatemala Museum. *CIW, NMAE,* Vol. 4, No. 103, pp. 143-58. Cambridge.

1951c Further Notes on Three-pronged Incense Burners and Rimhead Vessels in Guatemala. *CIW, NMAE,* Vol. 4, No. 105, pp. 162-76. Cambridge.

1951d El Incensario de Guayasco. *Revista del Instituto de Antropología e Historia de Guatemala,* Vol. 3, No. 2, pp. 41-4. Guatemala.

1954a A Brief Essay on the Development of Maya Art. *El Palacio,* Vol. 61, No. 1, pp. 1-7. Santa Fe.

1954b Cultura folk y cultura compleja en el área Maya meridional. *Ciencias Sociales,* Vol. 5, No. 26, pp. 50-63. Washington.

1955 Comments on Incense Burners from Copan, Honduras. *American Antiquity,* Vol. 20, No. 3, pp. 284-6. Salt Lake City.

FOSTER, G. M.

1953 What is Folk Culture? *American Anthropologist,* Vol. 55, No. 2, pp. 159-71. Menasha.

KIDDER, A. V., J. D. JENNINGS, AND E. M. SHOOK
1946 Excavations at Kaminaljuyu, Guatemala. *Carnegie Institution of Washington, Publication* 561. Washington.

KING, A. R.
1953 A Note on Emergent Folk Cultures and World Culture Changes. *Social Forces,* Vol. 31, No. 3, pp. 234-7. Chapel Hill.

KLUCKHOHN, CLYDE
1940 The Conceptual Structure in Middle American Studies. In *The Maya and Their Neighbors,* edited by C. L. Hay and others, pp. 41-51. Appleton-Century, New York.

LA FARGE, OLIVER
1940 Maya Ethnology: the Sequence of Cultures. In *The Maya and Their Neighbors,* edited by C. L. Hay and others, pp. 281-94. Appleton-Century, New York.

LEWIS, OSCAR
1952 Urbanization Without Breakdown: A Case Study. *The Scientific Monthly,* Vol. 75, pp. 31-41. Washington.

REDFIELD, ROBERT
1940 The Folk Society and Culture. In *Eleven Twenty-Six: A Decade of Social Science Research,* edited by Louis Wirth, pp. 39-50. University of Chicago Press.
1941 *The Folk Culture of Yucatan.* University of Chicago Press.
1947 The Folk Society. *American Journal of Sociology,* Vol. 52, No. 4, pp. 293-308. Chicago.

RICKETSON, O. G., JR., AND E. B. RICKETSON
1937 Uaxactun, Guatemala, Group E, 1926-1931. *Carnegie Institution of Washington, Publication* 477. Washington.

SHOOK, E. M.
1951 The Present Status of Research on the Pre-Classic Horizons in Guatemala. In "Civilizations of Ancient America," edited by Sol Tax. *Selected Papers of the XXIXth International Congress of Americanists* [New York, 1949], pp. 93-100. University of Chicago Press.

1952 Lugares arqueológicos del Altiplano meridional central de Guatemala. *Revista del Instituto de Antropologia e Historia de Guatemala,* Vol. 4, No. 2, pp. 3-40. Guatemala.

SHOOK, E. M. AND A. V. KIDDER
1952 Mound E-111-3, Kaminaljuyu, Guatemala. *Carnegie Institution of Washington, Publication* 596, *Contributions to American Anthropology and History,* Vol. 9, No. 53, pp. 33-128. Washington.

STEWARD, J. H.
1950 Area Research, Theory and Practice. *Social Science Research Council Bulletin* 63. New York.

TAX, SOL
1941 World View and Social Relations in Guatemala. *American Anthropologist,* Vol. 43, No. 1, pp. 27-42. Menasha.

TERMER, FRANZ
1951 The Density of Population in the Southern and Northern Maya Empires as an Archaeological and Geographical Problem. In "Civilizations of Ancient America," edited by Sol Tax. *Selected Papers of the XXIXth International Congress of Americanists* [New York, 1949], pp. 101-7. University of Chicago Press.

THOMPSON, J. E. S.
1943 A Trial Survey of the Southern Maya Area. *American Antiquity,* Vol. 9, No. 1, pp. 106-34. Menasha.
1954 *The Rise and Fall of Maya Civilization.* University of Oklahoma Press, Norman.

WAUCHOPE, ROBERT
1950 A Tentative Sequence of Pre-Classic Ceramics in Middle America. *Middle American Research Records,* Vol. 1, No. 14, pp. 211-50. Tulane University, New Orleans.
1954 Implications of Radiocarbon Dates from Middle and South America. *Middle American Research Records,* Vol. 2, No. 2, pp. 17-40. Tulane University, New Orleans.

UNIVERSITY OF OKLAHOMA MUSEUM
Norman, Okla.
February, 1955

The Structure of Ancient Maya Society: Evidence from the Southern Lowlands

GORDON R. WILLEY
Harvard University

IT HAS been a somewhat generally accepted opinion of Maya scholars that the structure of old Maya society was severely dichotomized into a village folk and a ceremonial center, or urban, elite, Obviously, there is much to support this view. The great politico-religious centers of the Late Formative (ca. 1000 B.C. to 200 A.D.) and Classic (ca. 200 to 900 A.D.) periods with their impressive temple and palace architecture, elaborate tombs, and the records of calendrical science and hieroglyphic texts carved on stone, stand in dramatic contrast to a jungle village of thatched huts. It is not my purpose to argue here that there was no gulf whatsoever between the Maya farmer of Classic times and his theocratic betters. Such a separation did exist. It is the profundity of the split that I question. There is, it is true, a reasonable continuity and parallel between the life and culture of the common Maya villager of the past and his present-day counterpart. On the other side, there is also a partial analogy between the Spanish urban-Catholic church tradition and the prehistoric Mayan theocratic tradition. Both represent centers of authority toward which the village Indian faced or faces; both were nuclei of civilizations and ideologies which penetrated in a less than full manner into the world of the simple farming communities. I think, however, that the qualification *partial* should be emphasized. An overstress on this analogy has perhaps been responsible for a too ready acceptance of ancient Maya social structure as but an image of historic and modern times.

Recent archeological data from the Maya lowlands of the Belize Valley, British Honduras,[1] and the inferences drawn from them, lead me to believe that the relationship between rural village and ceremonial center may have been considerably more tight-knit than the conventional picture would have it. These new data pertain to systematic field work on prehistoric settlements of small dwelling mounds. To date, there has been relatively little investigation into the problem of settlement patterns in the Maya lowlands (Ricketson and Ricketson 1937; Wauchope 1934; Ruppert and Smith 1952). This is particularly true of studies on the remains of what appear to be ordinary domestic buildings, and the distribution and relation of these domestic sites to the ceremonial units. Because of this lack it has been difficult to compare and contrast village community with ceremonial center.

To begin with, the very nature of the Belize Valley village sites supports the theory that the majority of the Classic period Maya from this region were at least a semisophisticated peasantry rather than a rustic and primitive folk. The settlements are found as clusters of small house mounds dotted along the alluvial terraces of the river or on nearby hillslopes. These house-mound

---

Reprinted from AMERICAN ANTHROPOLOGIST, 58, 1956. pp. 772-782.

clusters run in a more or less continuous distribution from the Guatemalan frontier for a distance of some 30 airline miles to the north and east.[2] Mound clusters will range from groups of a dozen or so to 300 or more. The mounds themselves are small oval or oblong tumuli of earth and rocks. They are the result of the construction of successive and superimposed house platforms. Refuse of general living is found in and around them, and burials have been made under the floor levels or in the mound slopes. In most clusters there are usually found one or more mounds of larger size, suggesting a pyramid base for a small temple or a high platform for a palace-like structure. At the Melhado site (Willey and Bullard 1956) a group of a dozen small house platforms surround a little pyramid mound near the center of the cluster. The site of Nohoch Ek, on a hilltop bordering the river valley, consists of a plaza group of ceremonial buildings and a number of small mounds, presumably house platforms, on the nearby hillside (Coe and Coe 1956). At Barton Ramie (Willey, Bullard, and Glass 1955), where we mapped over 250 mounds within an area of about one square mile, there is a single pyramid, 12 meters high, located near one end of the house-mound distribution. There are also several other Barton Ramie mounds, larger than the small house tumuli, which may have been residential units built around small plazas or may have been platforms for buildings of some public function. This occurrence of what appear to be minor ceremonial mounds in the village house-mound clusters would seem to strengthen the case for a relatively widespread distribution of a ritual and religious life that had some association with temple buildings similar to those of the major centers. We cannot tell, of course, just how much the content of the ceremonial life of the villages had in common with that of the greater centers. Yet the continuous riverine and hillslope settlement of the Belize Valley—with its house mounds clustered around small special buildings, with at least three ceremonial sites of middling size (Banana Bank, Baking Pot, Cahal Pech; see Ricketson 1929; Satterthwaite 1951), and with its one impressive ceremonial center at Xunantunich (Benque Viejo; Thompson 1940)—creates the impression of a large but well-integrated network of theocratic stations and substations, all supported by a peasantry indoctrinated with many of the values of urban life.

Ceramic and other remains from the Belize Valley small house-mound settlements also imply a relative "worldliness" for Maya village society and culture of the district. For example, burials found in house refuse and dating from the Early Classic (Tzakol, 200 to 600 A.D.) period are accompanied by basal-flanged polychrome bowls of fine quality and by Teotihuacan-like tripod jars. Such specimens are virtually identical to "luxury" finds from ceremonial centers. Furthermore, the refuse sherds under floors or in debris dumps off the flanks of the mounds include a substantial percentage of Early Classic polychrome pieces as well as numerous slab-footed tripod jars. This situation seems to be in marked contrast to one noted recently by S. F. de Borhegyi (1956:348) in the Guatemalan highlands. There, the Teotihuacan-like pieces did not occur outside of the ceremonial precincts, and Borhegyi sees in this an urban, upper-class possession of luxury trade goods, or imitations of such exotics, and their absence in the life of the village farmers. The British Honduras occurrence of these items in what is clearly a rural context, several miles from a ceremonial center of any size or significance, suggests that these people were, in Redfield's (1953:31) definition of the term, "peasant" rather than "folk." They were, moreover, a peasantry participating in an appreciable amount of the wealth and, perhaps, the ideology of the associated urban culture of the time.

In the succeeding Late Classic (Tepeu) period (600 to 900 A.D.) the Teotihuacan-like pottery disappears from the Belize Valley sites, but there are still good indications of intimate connections with the urban world. A burial found in a plaza floor of a small mound complex had as furniture a ceremonial celt, a monolithic axe, and a curious wrench-shaped object, all of polished stone. On the axe was a faint and rather badly scrawled Ahau glyph. Around the neck of the individual in the grave, an adult male, a small but handsome gorget of carved jade had been placed. This and other Late Classic burials found in the Belize Valley house mounds had fine pottery in association, and polychrome figure-painted ware as well as vessels with elaborately carved designs were found in domestic refuse.

All of these British Honduras discoveries add up, I think, to a conception of a Maya peasant class that was reasonably prosperous and participating in a cultural tradition not markedly apart from the inhabitants of the great religious centers. The essential differences between rural village and ceremonial center in the Belize Valley, insofar as these differences can be seen archeologically, is that the latter possess the great architecture, monumental art, and writing. The somewhat poorly rendered glyph on the monolithic axe found with the burial of the distinguished villager is a nice proof that the hieratic learning of the theocratic circles had not gone unnoticed in the peasant sphere, and that within this sphere an appreciation and value was placed upon this symbol of learning, even though the owner of the axe and his friends may have had not the slightest notion of what it meant.

In his analysis of prehistoric Maya society, in referring to Spanish and later impingements upon the Maya village, Borhegyi (1956:352) states:

"In spite of constant exposure to these many new ideas, the Maya farmer seems to have been as little affected by them as he was by the pressure of theocracy, or by the Mexican invasions.'"

If I understand him correctly, he sees the old ceremonial center urbanism of Classic Maya civilization and the Toltec-Mexican militaristic urbanism of later prehistoric times, as effecting no more change upon the basic folkways of the Maya farming village than did the later urbanism of Europe or of the modern industrial age. This, in my opinion, overstates the case for the division within ancient Maya society. Borhegyi's data are, of course, largely from the Guatemalan uplands, and it would be unwise to assume that highland and lowland Maya would necessarily follow the same course of development in this regard. Yet as regards both regions, it should not be forgotten that the urbanism of Spain was an alien force in the Maya land. Its roots and traditional hearth lay thousands of miles away in another hemisphere. Its policies were foreign, and in a determined effort to mold the Maya in its own image its acts must have had, or appeared to have, a harsh and arbitrary quality. Possibly the invading Mexicans and their ideology also had a strangeness that would alienate the conquered and widen the breach between peasant and ruler. But the Maya theocratic leadership was, as far as we can tell, a local development.[3] It had arisen from the ancestral peoples and culture of the small village life of the Early Formative or even unknown earlier periods. It drew its form and content from the Maya heritage. Its powers could, of course, have become oppressive to the governed; but one would presume there would be less of a strain between the component parts of a society in such an historical situation than in one where the upper class ideology was relatively new and foreign.

We have little in the way of an exact idea as to how the bonds between peasant and urban segments of Classic Maya society were maintained, but it is likely that the ceremonial centers recruited artisans, retainers, and even some levels of the priesthood from peasant groups. The numerous ceremonial type constructions referred to in the Belize Valley, ranging all the way from a major site, such as Xunantunich, down to the small temple buildings in the villages or hamlets, suggest that a hierarchial ordering or priestly chain-of-command probably existed, and that certain individuals may have found their way up or down the line of the system. There is evidence, too, that as the Classic period progressed, an increasingly greater homogeneity was obtained in Maya culture. Borhegyi (1956:349–350) has described how the elements of the old village religious cults, as exemplified by the three-pronged incense burners, figurines, and animal effigy whistles, once again appeared in the ceremonial centers, and this same trend is also true of the lowlands. It can be interpreted as the passing of peasant beliefs and influence into the metropolitan sphere, and of a wider social participation in the formulation of religious ideology for the culture as a whole. In fact, it must have been in just such a close symbiosis between center and peasant community that urbanism and civilization came into being in Classic Maya times. For the formal demographic requirements of urbanism, in the strictest sense, do not seem to be present in the Maya lowlands in Classic times. Except on a late Postclassic level, at places like Mayapan and Tulum, there are no large, densely packed population concentrations known for the lowlands. Yet lacking this, the Maya achieved city life in the broader sense, for many of the attributes of civilization, as defined by Childe (1950) or Redfield (1953: Chapters I and III), are clearly present. It is doubtful that such accomplishments as writing, monumental public works, the beginnings of astronomical science, and a privileged ruling class could have come into being within a society whose component parts were as seriously riven as was the case in the Maya regions during the Spanish Colonial period. Maya civilization was the creation of a society which, for the very fact of its dispersed physical settlement, was necessarily linked together by unusually strong ties.

Finally, this leads us to the question of the collapse of Maya civilization. Various explanations have been offered, and these will not be recounted here.

One theme, though, that has been frequently considered is that of social breakdown or internal revolt, possibly triggered by crop failure, drought, or soil exhaustion, but made inevitable by the basic schism between theocrat and farmer. This may have been what happened, but I believe this interpretation is less attractive in the light of current evidence. If we accept the internal revolt theory, it would be reasonable to expect that life, albeit on a somewhat reduced scale, continued in the Maya villages after the abandonment of the great lowland ceremonial centers of the south at the close of the Classic period. Not a single one of the numerous test excavations in the Belize Valley has brought to light ceramic or other evidence that would demonstrate a Postclassic period occupation of any of the village house mounds. If collapse occurred—and, indeed, something did occur—Maya priest and peasant collapsed and vanished together.

NOTES

[1] From a four-year survey (1953–56) conducted by the author under auspices of the Peabody Museum, Harvard University, and financed largely by the National Science Foundation.

[2] Our survey was confined to this river valley section. Mounds begin in the limestone hill country, some 40 miles back from the coast, and extend to the Guatemalan line. They probably extend on west and south, but our survey was terminated at this point.

[3] Most authorities feel that the hierarchic elements of Maya civilization were developed within the Maya area, either highland or lowland. This usually assumes that the peoples of the earlier Formative periods were of Maya race and speech and that their various cultures were an important source for Classic civilization. One significant dissent has been raised by Meggers (1954) who believes that an unfavorable jungle environment could not have permitted the original development of Classic Maya in the lowland regions.

REFERENCES CITED

BORHEGYI, S. F. DE
    1956   The development of folk and complex cultures in the Southern Maya area. American Antiquity 21:343–356.

CHILDE, V. GORDON
    1950   The urban revolution. Town Planning Review 21:3–17.

MEGGERS, B. J.
    1954   Environmental limitation on the development of culture. American Anthropologist 56:801–824.

REDFIELD, ROBERT
    1953   The primitive world and its transformations. Ithaca, New York, Cornell University Press.

RICKETSON, O. G., JR.
    1929   Excavations at Baking Pot, British Honduras. Carnegie Institution of Washington, Pub. No. 403, Contributions to American Archaeology vol. 1, no. 1.

RICKETSON, O. G., JR. and E. B. RICKETSON, et al.
    1937   Uaxactun, Guatemala. Group E—1926–1931. Carnegie Institution of Washington, Pub. No. 477.

RUPPERT, KARL and A. L. SMITH
    1952   Excavations in house mounds at Mayapan. Carnegie Institution of Washington, Current Reports no. 4.

SATTERTHWAITE, LINTON, JR.
    1951   Reconnaissance in British Honduras. University of Pennsylvania Museum Bulletin, vol. 16, no. 1.

THOMPSON, J. E. S.
    1955 Late ceramic horizons at Benque Viejo, British Honduras. Carnegie Institution of Washington Pub. No. 528, Contribution No. 35.
WAUCHOPE, ROBERT
    1934 House mounds of Uaxactun, Guatemala. Carnegie Institution of Washington Pub. No. 436, Contribution No. 7.
WILLEY, GORDON R. and W. R. BULLARD, JR.
    1956 The Melhado site, a prehistoric Maya house mound group near El Cayo, British Honduras. American Antiquity vol. 22, no. 1.
WILLEY, GORDON R., W. R. BULLARD, JR., and J. B. GLASS.
    1955 The Maya community of prehistoric times. Archaeology 8:18–25.

THE LORDS OF THE MAYA REALM

By TATIANA PROSKOURIAKOFF

We Mayanists spend an inordinate amount of time deciphering half obliterated hieroglyphic texts. Often it seems that our results are not worth all that effort; but now and again some minor fact that hardly seems worth mentioning at the time can be used to pry open a chink in the wall of obscurity that surrounds the past, and suddenly we get a new and exciting glimpse of events that have left their traces on the old stones of Maya sites. When, in 1943, J. E. S. Thompson changed the date of Stela 14 of Piedras Negras, Guatemala, from A.D. 800, given it by Morley, to A.D. 761, the correction seemed of purely academic interest. The stela was on loan at the University Museum since 1933, and Satterthwaite, by the use of studio-quality photographs, was able to substantiate the new readings. Epigraphers made a note of them in their notebooks for future reference, and there the matter rested.

Thompson had described the stela and others like it as showing "gods seated in niches formed by the bodies of celestial dragons" (Fig. 1), and remarked in passing, without ascribing any special importance to the fact, that the correction of the date made Stela 14 the first monument to be erected in front of Temple O-13. One day, several years later, while wondering what the niche and celestial dragon motif might mean, I noticed that Stela 33, though it has no niche, presents a similar scene, and realized for the first time that the new reading of Stela 14 made all monuments of this type the first to be erected in a given location. Monuments with other motifs were then set up every five years in the same place until another similar group was started near another temple. Thus there were distinct sets of monuments, each beginning with a "niche" stela. My first thought was that the "niche" motif represented the dedication of a new temple, and that the ladder marked with footsteps ascending to the niche symbolized the rise to the sky of the victim of sacrifice, whose body was sometimes shown at the foot of the ladder. It occurred to me that if I searched the inscriptions for a hieroglyph peculiar to these stelae, I might find the glyphic expression for human sacrifice. What I found instead started an entirely new train of thought and led to surprising conclusions.

True enough, there was a record of a date just prior to the erection-date on each "niche" stela, and this date of some immediately preceding event was always followed by a hieroglyph that Thompson, with one of his delightful flashes of humor, has dubbed "the toothache glyph" (Fig. 2). Anniversaries of the event were often subsequently recorded, but only on monuments of the same group. What I had not expected to find was that the only dates that any two groups of stelae had in common were some that marked the ends of conventional time periods, and even this happened rarely, though the recorded dates of two contiguous groups invariably overlapped in time. Evidently each group of monuments presents an independent set of records. Moreover, it is not the "toothache glyph" date that is the earliest in each set, but another that is anywhere from twelve to thirty-one years earlier and is always

---

Reprinted by permission of the publisher; EXPEDITION MAGAZINE; Fall 1961; pp.14-21; by Tatiana Proskouriakoff, Carnegie Institution of Washington. Copyright 1961 The University Museum.

Fig. 1. Stela 14 at Piedras Negras. The young lord sits in an elevated doorway or "niche" ascended by a ladder draped with a cloth or carpet with footprints that symbolize his ascent. Above the curtained doorway is a band of astronomical symbols, and at the very top, a bird with serpent-heads on its wings, wearing a grotesque mask and holding a serpent in its mouth. On the jambs are masks of the sun god, and just below, the two heads of the double-headed celestial dragon. In front stands a woman wearing a jaguar headdress and holding a feathered object of unknown significance. At the lower right is a somewhat eroded representation of human sacrifice.

This lord acceded in A.D. 761, just after the Bat-Jaguar of Lintel 3, and ruled less than five years. It may be that Lintel 3 commemorates the restoration of his dynasty after the untimely overthrow of his reign. The correction of the date on this monument led to the discovery of the significance of its motif and to the formulation of the "dynastic hypothesis," which sees the figures on Maya stelae as portraits of reigning lords.

accompanied by the so-called "upended frog glyph" (Fig. 3). This earlier event could not have had much public importance when it happened since no notation was made of it at the time. It was first recorded after the "toothache glyph" event occurred, and only then began to be celebrated by anniversaries.

Doubtless there are various events in history that are paired in this way, but surely the most common is the birth of some person who in his mature years acquires great prestige or political power. But if the "upended frog" date is a birth date, the fact that it was celebrated for only a limited period suggests that that period was the person's lifetime, and effectively refutes my original notion that the "toothache glyph" expresses the human sacrifice shown on "niche" stelae. More likely, these stelae portray the accession of a new ruler, the "seating on high of the Lord," as the Maya books put it. Subsequent stelae, too, are probably portraits of the lord.

To test this new idea, I calculated the length of time covered by each set of records. There were only three sets whose full span was known, and the figures were 60, 64, and 56 years. These are reasonable lifetimes for rulers who lived at a time when the ordered setting up of monuments suggests tranquil conditions. I was greatly encouraged, feeling that at last I might be on the right track.

The next step, of course, was to identify the names of the lords, or at least to make sure that the birth and accession date referred to the same individual. If so, the "upended frog glyph" (birth date), and the "toothache glyph" (accession) of each set of records would be followed by the same glyph, which would differ for every set. This actually proved to be the case, though the name was expressed by three or four glyphs, and sometimes a glyph was omitted or substituted by another. After all, an important lord is bound to have various honorifics and titles. The first glyph was always the same after both dates, and I felt confident that my identification of the name phrases was correct. But did these "names" refer to the sculptured figures?

I was convinced that they did when I examined the texts on Stelae 1 and 2. These stelae are eroded on the front, where the portrait of the lord appears, and on the sides, but on the back each has a complete text and a sculptured figure dressed in a long robe. Many Mayanists had believed that the robe was a priestly garment worn by men, but here both texts record the same birth date followed by the same two name glyphs with a prefix which is clearly a face of a woman, identified by a black (cross-hatched) spot or a lock of hair on the forehead (Fig. 4a). What is more, on Stela 3, which shows a small figure seated beside the one in the robe, the text contains a second birth date, thirty-three years later than the first and only three years earlier than the final date on the stela. This later birth date is followed by a different set of name glyphs (Fig. 4b), though they, too, are prefixed by female faces. How can one reasonably doubt that both robed figures are portraits of the same person, that the person is a woman, and that her little daughter, not yet born when Stela 1 was erected, is shown on Stela 3 (Fig. 5)? The theme of family suggested by this woman and child is quite consistent with the theme of dynasty in which questions of marriage and descent are always involved, but it would be difficult to reconcile it with a theme of Maya religion.

In retrospect, the idea that Maya texts record history, naming the rulers or lords of the towns, seems so natural that it is strange it has not been thoroughly explored before. The reason is that the only substantial progress made in the decipherment of texts dealt with astronomical and calendrical notations, and these form such a large part of the inscriptions that there appeared to be no room left for historical narrative. The Maya, however, had a conception of history different from ours. Even in colonial times their historical statements were very cryptic and were often mixed with prophesy, for they believed that every event casts its shadow on the future. Thus, if we accept the "dynastic hypothesis," as it is currently called, we may yet find that the birth date of the

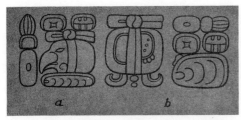

Fig. 2. Two forms of the "toothache" or "accession" glyph. This glyph indicates the accession to power of the lord named in the glyphs that follow it. The date of this accession and the birthday of the lord are often repeated on subsequent stelae and celebrated by anniversaries.

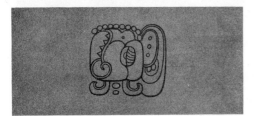

Fig. 3. The "upended frog" or "birth date" glyph. This glyph follows the earliest date associated with the group of name glyphs immediately after it. If the name is that of a lord, this birth date may be repeated on later monuments.

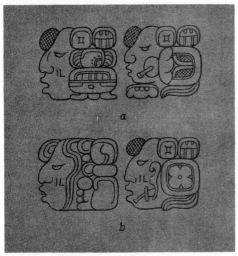

Fig 4. The "name" glyphs of the woman and her daughter depicted on the back of Stela 3. The woman's first name "Katun" is the designation for a twenty-year period, but is known also as a part of a feminine name or title in Yucatan. Women's names are always prefixed by a profile face, identified as that of a woman by the cross-hatched oval or lock of hair on the forehead.

Fig. 5. The back of Stela 3, Piedras Negras. The woman sitting on the throne is named in the inscription above, as is the child beside her. Their birth dates are 33 years apart. The front of this monument, portraying the ruling lord, is badly eroded. His name probably appears on the sides, together with the date of the erection of the stela, A.D. 711.

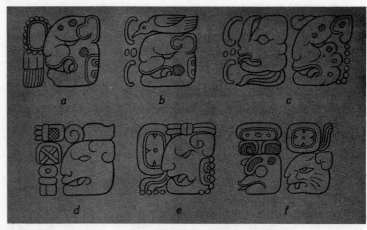

Fig. 6. Various combinations of the jaguar glyph.
 a: The Shield-Jaguar, one of the "names" of a lord who ruled at Yaxchilan early in the eighth century.
 b: The Bird-Jaguar, who succeeded him in A.D. 752.
 c: The Bat-Jaguar, whose accession is recorded at Piedras Negras.
 d: The jaguar glyph from the "jaguar-protector" lintel of Temple I at Tikal.
 e: The corresponding glyph, Kin-Jaguar, from a similar lintel in Temple IV.
 f: The "relative?" of the Kin-Jaguar, named on Stela 1, Aguateca. (After a drawing by Ian Graham.)

lord and his accession date were not inscribed for historical purposes alone, but mainly to provide a base for the prognosis of the fortunes of a given reign. This may explain the emphasis on astronomical data given with the dates. In any case, it is well to remember that the hypothesis is still far from being established to everyone's satisfaction. A great deal remains to be done before a crucial test of it can be made. One of the first tasks will be to study the structure of all the purported "name phrases," so that we can separate proper names from titles, lineage designations, and other epithets applied to the lords and their dependents. The identity of some of the persons or entities mentioned in the texts is still clouded with complications and contradictions, and doubtless will continue to trouble us for some time.

There is one group of hieroglyphs in particular for which I have not found a satisfactory explanation. This group comprises jaguar-glyphs with varying prefixes and super-fixes (Fig. 6). Two of the combinations appear to be names of lords who ruled Yaxchilan, a city up-river from Piedras Negras and on the opposite bank. Here, on Lintels 29 and 30, are clearly recorded the birth and accession dates of a certain Bird-Jaguar (Fig. 6b), who also has additional designations. His accession in A.D. 752 is recorded again on Stela 11, where he is shown wearing a sun-mask before three prisoners (Fig. 7). Above him (in the sky?) are two seated figures, a man and a woman, with their names inscribed at the sides. The man's name includes a Shield-Jaguar glyph (Fig. 6a), and elsewhere appears on earlier Yaxchilan lintels, so that even without having the accession date we may suppose that the Shield-Jaguar is the predecessor and perhaps the progenitor of the Bird-Jaguar lord. So far everything is clear and consistent with our hypothesis.

But on Stela 12, which was apparently erected at the same time as Stela 11, the accession date of the Bird-Jaguar is followed not by its usual expression, but by a variant form and then by an unusually complicated name phrase including a Jaguar glyph preceded by a Bat (Fig. 4c). There is some possibility that the Bat-Jaguar is named here as the heir-apparent to the Bird-Jaguar lord, or as a co-ruler or high official. What is curious is that his accession date does not appear at Yaxchilan, but at Piedras Negras, where it is incised on the background of Lintel 3, next to a throne on which a chief holds audience before a group of people (Fig. 9). The precise date of this accession is uncertain (probably A.D. 757, five years after the accession of the Bird-Jaguar, and seemingly during his reign), and it is not recorded on any of the surviving stelae. The lintel itself was carved after A.D. 782, but the dates recorded on it cover more than thirty years, and it is impossible to say which of the recorded events is shown in the sculpture. The first date recorded falls in A.D. 749, and is stated to be the twenty-year anniversary of the accession of a ruler portrayed on Stela 11 of Piedras Negras, in front of Temple J-3. About twelve years after this accession, a very unusual and striking motif was carved on Stela 10, which stands in the same group. Here the lord is shown seated on a cushion, and behind him is a huge jaguar, reared on hind legs and with one forepaw extended forward over the head of the seated figure. There are no hieroglyphs surviving except those of the currently completed period. What can be the meaning of this obviously symbolic scene? Is the jaguar a god-protector of the lord? Is he a foreign overlord to whom the ruler of the town is subject? Or does he represent a lineage, symbolized by the most powerful animal known to the Maya? Above all,

#

Fig. 7. Stela 11, Yaxchilan, which records the accession of the Bird-Jaguar, shown wearing a sun-mask, in front of three prisoners. Above are the Shield-Jaguar and a woman, probably his wife.

Fig. 8. The "jaguar-protector" motif on a lintel of Temple I, Tikal. The name of the ruling lord is the same that appears on Stela 16, erected in A.D. 711. The lord is seated, and above him can be seen the head of the Jaguar and one extended paw. This motif is associated with another lord in Temple IV, where the jaguar-figure appears as a man.

is there any significance in the fact that the accession date of the current ruler is linked with the Bat-Jaguar from Yaxchilan on Lintel 3?

According to Satterthwaite's calculations based on radiocarbon dates, near the beginning of the eighth century, probably even prior to the reign of the Shield-Jaguar at Yaxchilan, the motif of the jaguar-protector was carved on a wooden lintel in Temple I at Tikal (Fig. 8). Roughly forty or fifty years later, it was repeated on a lintel of Temple IV, this time with the "protector" in the form of a man, still bearing, however, certain jaguar and sun symbols. The texts of both lintels contain jaguar glyphs (Fig. 6d, e), but not as names of the ruling lords. The rulers' names are known from contemporary stelae, and appear on the lintels linked with the jaguar-glyphs in clauses. On the later lintel, the jaguar glyph is prefixed by the sign *Kin* (day or sun), and this same Kin-Jaguar is mentioned also on Stelae 1 and 2 at the newly discovered site of Aguateca, many kilometers south of Tikal. On these stelae, the Kin-Jaguar glyph is part of a name-phrase, but again is apparently not the proper name of the ruler, for it is preceded by another glyph that seems to indicate some sort of relationship between the lord named and the jaguar (Fig. 6f). On accession of the next lord of Aguateca, in A.D. 741, the Kin-Jaguar is replaced by a turtle-glyph, which is one of the designations of the lords of Piedras Negras. One may note that this is the very year when the jaguar-protector motif was carved at Piedras Negras, but whether this fact has any relevance is not at all clear to me.

Fig. 9. Lintel 3, Piedras Negras. The scene shows a lord probably the Bat-Jaguar, seated upon a throne before a council of elders. At his right is a small group of men; at his left, three children presided over by a woman servant. This scene may present deliberations which placed the young lord shown on Stela 14 on the throne of Piedras Negras. The lintel, carved after 782, may justify the right of succession of the lord who began his rule in 785.

So far, I have been unable to untangle the obscure connections between the jaguar glyphs and the "protector" motif. What may be significant about them is that all the associated dates seem to belong to that period known as "The Period of Uniformity," when many elements of costume and artistic style, formerly local, became widely dispersed through the Maya area, and when all large cities adopted a uniform lunar count. A. V. Kidder once remarked that only under the pressure of political unification is such agreement among a group of clerics conceivable. Perhaps the ubiquitous jaguars of this period hold some clue to the nature of this unification. Is it possible that the lords of Yaxchilan, a city whose militant battle scenes are unique in Maya sculpture, succeeded in subjecting to their will such great and ancient cities of the Peten as Tikal and Piedras Negras, or is it merely that they incorporated in their proper names the designation of a widespread lineage? Was there some political or military alliance that took the name of the jaguar, with member states denoted by varying prefixes?

Such speculation, unfortunately, is just as likely as not to lead us astray. What is needed now is some new fact: perhaps no more than one clarified date, perhaps an observation of some small detail on the sculptures, or some relation between them that has escaped notice. Sooner or later, someone is bound to come upon this crucial little fact that will solve the enigma of the jaguars, and we can take another step forward in the interpretation of Maya texts.

In the meantime, some scholars hold that it won't be long before the electronic computer will solve all the major problems of glyphic decipherment and put our present efforts to shame. One experiment has already been made in Russia, but its results are not published, and its success is therefore still unknown. Much will depend on the validity of the assumptions concerning the nature of Maya writing on which the programming was based. It is not at all certain that a completely linguistic rendering of hieroglyphic passages is possible, but even if it is, we may still be far from understanding their meaning, for known Maya texts of Colonial date, written in Roman characters, are replete with metaphors and allusions completely incomprehensible to us. I hope that no one, relying on the marvels of modern invention, will be deterred from pursuing the more laborious method of minute simultaneous scrutiny of texts and sculptures, which is the only way we can make sure that any reading proposed in the future does in fact express the intention of the text. Even if our most optimistic hopes are fulfilled, the full understanding of Maya hieroglyphic inscriptions will require many years of effort. However, if it is true that they contain history and narrative, we may expect ultimately to gain a far more intimate knowledge of the social and political aspects of Maya life than, until now, we have dared to anticipate, and it will be exciting to explore various paths by which we might approach this goal.

Some Implications of Zinacantan Social Structure for the Study of the Ancient Maya*

Evon Z. Vogt

0. Introduction
1. Social Structure of the Ceremonial Center
2. Social Structure of the Outlying Hamlets
3. Ritual Expression of the Social Structure
4. Implications for the Study of the Ancient Maya

0. The Highland Maya of Chiapas comprise a nucleus of some 150 000 conservative Indians living in municipio units distributed around the Ladino town of San Cristobal Las Casas. Each municipio speaks a distinct dialect of Tzotzil or Tzetzal, possesses distinctive styles of dress, and has local customs that differ in varying degrees from neighboring municipios. Zinacantan with a 1960 population of 7 600 Indians is located just to the West of San Cristobal Las Casas. I have elsewhere (Vogt, 1961 a) described the settlement pattern as typically Maya with ceremonial center and outlying hamlets, or *parajes* as these are called in Chiapas. The ceremonial center contains the Catholic churches, the cabildo, and a plaza where markets are held during fiestas. In and around this ceremonial center are located a series of sacred mountains and sacred waterholes which figure importantly in the religious life. I have also elsewhere provided a brief description of the basic elements of Zinacantan religion (Vogt 1961 a; 1961 b). My purpose, in this paper, is to describe briefly the social structure of Zinacantan, with special focus on the outlying hamlets, and then to explore some implications of these patterns for our study of ancient Maya culture.

---

* My field research is supported by a grant (M-2100) from the National Institute of Mental Health. I am grateful to my colleagues and students — especially Don Bahr, Frank Cancian, Francesca Cancian, B. N. Colby, Lore Colby, George Collier, Jane Fishburne, Robert Laughlin, Mimi Laughlin, Jack Stauder, Susan Tax, and Manuel Zabala Cubillos — who have done field work on the project and have contributed importantly to my understanding of Zinacatan culture. I am also indebted to the Mexican Instituto Nacional Indigenista for hospitality and cooperation in Chiapas. The paper has benefited from comments by David Maybury-Lewis and Frank and Francesca Cancian.

Reprinted from paper presented at the 35th International Congress of Americanists, Mexico, August 1962.

Zinacantan provides an interesting case for this Symposium since we now know that the municipio maintains a number of apparently ancient Maya patterns that promise to illuminate our understanding of the prehistoric Lowland Maya culture of the Peten. As several recent field workers in Chiapas have pointed out (notably Vogt, 1960 and 1961 a; Guiteras-Holmes, 1961; and Holland, 1961), Highland Chiapas is probably one of the crucial regions for the discovery of ancient Maya patterns in relatively undisturbed form. It is closer to the Peten than are the more remote contemporary Maya communities in Northern Yucatan and Quintana Roo; it has probably been subjected to less pressure from Central Mexican invasions in prehistoric times and from the Spanish Conquest in the Colonial Period than either the Yucatec or the Guatemalan Highlands regions, save for the possible exception of the Cuchumatanes area.

1. About 800 people live in the densely settled valley in which the ceremonial center is located; the other 6 800 live in eleven outlying parajes. The most important social structural feature of this ceremonial center is a religious hierarchy with 53 cargo positions in four levels. These cargos are filled on an annual basis with the cargo-holders moving with their families into the ceremonial center to live during their terms in office, then returning to their parajes to farm corn during the rest periods between cargos. Since Frank Cancian's paper (Cancian, 1962) presented in this same Symposium deals in detail with this religious hierarchy, I shall move immediately to a description of the social structure of the outlying parajes.

2. The social structure of the hamlets is based upon the following residential units: (1) the patrilocal extended family; (2) the *sna* composed of one or more localized patrilineages; (3) the waterhole group composed of two or more *snas;* and (4) the paraje. These residential units are cross-cut by descent-based units which I shall call localized lineages, exogamous patriclans, and phratries. Ceremonial life in the hamlets is directed by *h'iloletik* who not only divine and cure individual illness, but also perform rituals for each of the residential units in the social structure.

2.1. The basic kin and residential unit is the patrilocal extended family, occupying a *sitio* as the house compounds are called in Chiapas. The sitio (see Vogt 1961 a, p. 137) is typically enclosed by some type of pole and brush fence and contains two or more houses, a granary for the storage of maize, a sweat house, and in the center, the patio cross that serves ritually as the house shrine for the extended family.

There is, of course, some variation in this general pattern. I can provide some precise data from one of the large parajes, that of Paste' with a 1960 population of 1276, where I have been doing intensive field work. Paste' has 246 married couples, and the residence patterns are as follows:

Residence Type*	Number	Percentage
Patrilocal	199	81
Matrilocal	41	17
Neolocal	6	2
	246	100

Another type of variation is present in the precise living arrangements found at any given point of time. For example, many newly married couples will be found living in the same house with the husband's father; the older married sons will be found in houses located a short distance away from their father's house, sometimes in the same sitio, sometimes in adjacent sitios. There appears to be a developmental cycle here of the type described by Fortes (1958). When a young man first marries, after a long and expensive courtship (see Fishburne 1962), he almost never has his own house, but moves his bride into his father's house. After a few years, he manages to pay off his debts, accumulate some money, and secure his father's permission to build a house on nearby land, either in the same sitio, if there is room, or in an adjacent sitio which he will establish. As his sons come of age and marry, the cycle starts over again, except for one son (usually the youngest) who inherits the father's house and remains in the father's sitio.

2.2. Patrilocal extended families live in larger units which I shall call *snas*. The term *sna* means literally "the houses of," and it is the term the Zinacatencos themselves use to refer to these residential units that are composed of one or more localized parilineages. Before I discuss the structure of the *sna*, I must clarify the nature of the descent-based units in the Zinacatenco social system.

The localized patrilineages have no more than four generations of depth. They live on adjacent lands controlled by the members of the lineage, and they possess some jural authority in the sense that important decisions for lineage members are made by the senior males.

Beyond four generations the ancestors die off, their precise names are forgotten, and exact genealogical connections cannot be traced by informants. What is left that is operationally effective is the system of patronymics. Each Zinacanteco possesses three names: (1) a first name, like Romin (Domingo), Shun (Juan), or Maruch (María); (2) a Spanish surname like Lopis (López), Hernantis (Hernández), or de la Cruz; and (3) an Indian surname like *'akov* (meaning "wasp nest") or *ok'il* (meaning "coyote"), or *chochov* (meaning "acorn"). Both of the surnames are inherited patrilineally from the father and are retained throughout life, even by women after they are married. A given man might be named Shun de la Cruz 'akov, but since the Indian sur-

---

* The matrilocal cases have resulted from husbands who were either orphans or came from families without sufficient land and hence moved to live matrilocally with the wives' kinsmen who did have sufficient land.

names combine only with a given Spanish surname and never with another Spanish surname, it is enough to say "shun 'akov" to identiy the man in question. Zinacantan now has 17 Spanish surnames which combine with at least 62 Indian surnames.*

I do not know what the Spanish surnames mean since they appear to have lost whatever functions they may once have had. It may well be that they are the vestiges of patrilineal units of the type described for Oxchuc by Villa Rojas (1947) who calls them "patrilineal clans" or by Siverts (1960) who calls them "phratries." Guiteras-Holmes (1961) and Pozas (1959) also describe "clans" designated by the Spanish surnames for Chenalho and Chamula. I shall use the term "phratry" to describe these Spanish surname groups in Zinacantan, and reserve the term "patriclan" for the Indian surname groups. For it is clear that the Indian surnames are still functionally important designations of exogamous units. The Zinacantecos have a very strong rule that one should never marry a person of the same Indian surname regardless of whether close genealogical connection with this person can be traced or not.

What is important however in the case of the *sna* is that each contains one or more of the localized lineages in which genealogical connections can be traced. The *sna* takes its name from these lineages. In cases where the unit contains only one lineage, there is no problem. The unit is simply called, for example, *sna 'akovetik,* or "the houses of the wasp nests." In the cases of larger *snas* containing two or more lineages, the unit takes its name from the predominant lineage.** Thus *sna' ok'iletik* "the houses of the coyotes," contains

---

* To be more precise: Perez combines with 21 different Indian surnames; Hernandez with 14 Indian surnames; de la Cruz with 4 Indian surnames; Lopez, Sanchez, and de la Torre with 3 Indian surnames each; Gomez, Mendez, and Jimenez with 2 Indian surnames each; and Montejo, Arias, Martinez, Vasquez, Gonzales, Ruiz, Garcia, and Patishtan (probably Bautista) with 1 Indian surname each.

** From the data now available it seems highly probable that predominant lineage was the first to settle on the land now controlled by the *sna,* and that this fact accounts for its pre-eminent position. This further suggests that the *sna* unit may have been originally a localized patriclan, the waterhole group a localized phratry, and that the contemporary structure resulted from migrations of Zinacantecos from lands that had become part of Ladino latifundia in order to escape serfdom (see Guiteras-Holmes 1961, pp. 68-69). A further complicating factor must have been the marked demographic growth of Zinacantan in recent decades. The resulting land pressure would have certainly made it impossible for many lineages and clans to expand through the generations on adjacent lands.

This possibility for the ancient structure of Zinacantan also suggests a solution for an apparent paradox — if local groups were composed of exogamous phratries, then how could men find spouses as close to home as our data indicate for marriage preferences? For example, we now have precise data for the paraje of Paste' by waterhole groups indicating that mates are found as close to home as possible. Out of 246 married couples, 120 wives (or almost 50 per cent) were reared in the same waterhole group as the husbands; another 75 wives (or 30 per cent) were from different waterholes within the paraje. In other words, fully 80 per cent of the marriages took place within the paraje; almost all of the remaining 20 per cent took place with spouses that were selected from the two neighboring parajes of Elamvo' and Nachih. But if we can assume that the contemporary waterhole group was originally an exogamous phratry subdivided into several patriclans, then we would have a functionally consistent social system in

the coyote lineage, but also contains two smaller lineages that have settled next to the coyotes and intermarried with them.

I do not have to depend merely upon informants' statements and my mapping procedures to describe the boundaries and composition of these *snas*. An observational measure of who's who in the world of *snas* is available in the *k'in krus* ceremonies performed by each *sna* twice a year (in May and in October) for their *totilme'iletik* (meaning "fathers-mothers") who function as ancestral deities and for *yahval balamil* (the "earth owner"). More about these ceremonies later.

Suffice it to say now that *snas* in Paste' vary in size from those containing one lineage and only 4 houses with less than 15 people up to large ones with seven intermarrying lineages living in over 40 houses with 150 people. The determinants of the sizes are still unclear to me.

2.3. The next unit of ascending size in the social structure is what I have chosen to call the waterhole group. The population of Paste' is clustered around five important waterholes.* These five waterholes each have distinctive names and these names are used by the Indians to describe where a person lives within the paraje (see Vogt 1961 a, pp. 134-135). The waterholes are highly sacred, and there are myths about each of them which describe the circumstances under which the ancestors found the water and how the waterhole acquired its distinctive name.

Each waterhole group is composed of two to seven *snas*, the size in this case depending basically upon the amount of water available in each waterhole for household water and for watering sheep and other livestock, such as horses and mules.

Since a *k'in krus* ceremony is also performed twice a year for the waterhole and its ancestral deities, I also have a precise operational measure of the size and composition of each of these groups.

2.4. There is finally the paraje unit which is composed of one or more waterhole groups. Some small parajes, such as Elamvo', are composed of a single waterhole group; but all of the large parajes, such as Paste', Nachih, or Navenchauk, are subdivided into two or more waterhole groups. The parajes are formally recognized by the Mexican government, as, for example, for census-taking purposes. But more important from the Indian point of view is that two *krinsupales* (principales) are selected each year from each paraje to represent the *presidente*. They carry out orders from the presidente in the ceremonial center; they report on paraje affairs and problems to the presidente each week.

---

which a series of exogamous phratries each living around their own waterholes could exchange women with each other and still keep all the marriages within the endogamous local hamlet or paraje unit.

* There are three additional small waterholes from which a few families from the paraje of Paste' carry their water; the other families in these waterhole groups belong to the neighboring parajes of Nachih and Elamvo',

3. While the priestly hierarchy is functioning in the ceremonial center with its complex annual round of rituals, the religious life of the outlying hamlets is essentially in the hands of the *h'iloletik*. The term *h'ilol* means literally "seer," the belief being that while in ancient mythological times all Zinacantecos could "see" into the mountains and observe their ancestral gods directly, now only the *h'iloletik* can accomplish this miracle.* There are at least 100

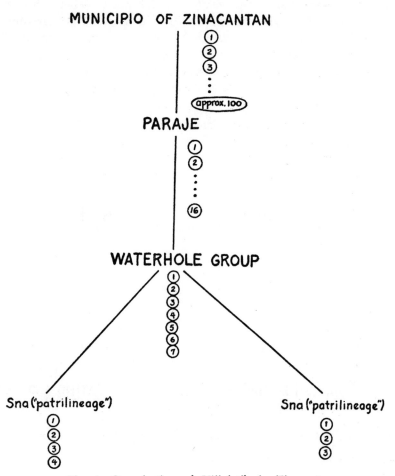

Fig. 1. Organization of H'iloletik in Zinacantan.

h'iloletik in Zinacantan. Most are men, but some are women, and some are as young as 15 years of age. To become an *h'ilol* one dreams three times that one has been called before the ancestral gods in the largest sacred mountain and given the power and knowledge to perform ceremonies. Sometime after the third dream, the novice appears before the highest ranking *h'ilol* in his paraje,

---

* The most important curing ceremony performed by the *h'iloletik* is called *Muk' ta' ilel*, or the "large seeing."

tells his dreams, and asks permission to make his debut. If permission is granted, he goes to Tierra Caliente, cuts himself a bamboo staff, which is the symbol of the office, and is ready to perform ceremonies.

Perhaps the most surprising feature about the *h'iloletik* is that they are all ranked in Zinacantan from 1 to 100 or more. Rank order depends not upon age or power to cure, but strictly upon time in service, i. e., the number of years that have elapsed since the *h'ilol* made his public debut. This organizational feature is shown in Figure 1. Note that the *h'iloletik* are carefully sorted out by rank in each *sna*, in each waterhole group, and in each paraje. Thus in Figure 1, one of the *snas* has three *h'iloletik*, the other has four. When these combine in ceremonies for the waterhole group composed of these two *snas*, then all seven *h'iloletik* are sorted into rank order one to seven, and so on.

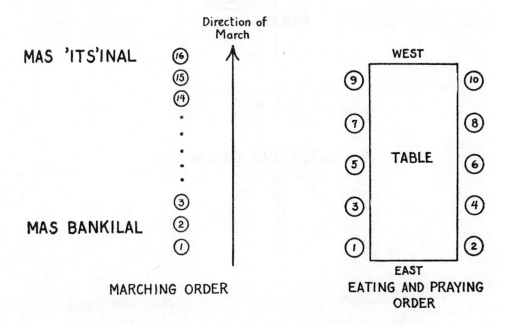

Fig. 2. Operational measures of H'iloletik rank in Zinacantan.

Fortunately, there are reliable operational measures for determining rank in observing Zinacanteco behavior. Note in Figure 2 that marching order in processions and pilgrimages, which are a prominent feature of Zinacantan ritual, is always junior man in front, senior man in the rear. This is expressed by the Indians by whether a man is "mas bankilal" or "mas its'inal" — "more older brother" or "more younger brother" — a concept that is much used in Zinacantan (see Vogt 1960). Similarly, there is a rigid seating order at ritual tables when the *h'iloletik* assemble to eat and pray, and this order is invariably followed regardless of size of ceremony or the table. There is never any doubt about a man's rank in ritual context in Zinacantan.

Just as there exists a social order of ascending scale from the patrilocal extended family, through the *sna* (composed of one or more localized patrilineages), the waterhole group, and up to the paraje, so there is also a ceremonial order of ascending scale that exactly parallels and expresses the social order both in terms of ritual concepts and paraphernalia and in terms of ceremonies of increasing size and complexity. Each of the social structural units I have described is symbolized by shrines composed of crosses that are conceptualized by the Zinacantecos as "doorways," or in other words, as means of communication with the *totilme'iletik* (the ancestral deities living in the mountains) and with *yahval balamil* (the earth god) (Vogt 1960).

3.1. Each Zinacanteco extended family sitio erects and maintains a *krus ti'na,* or "house cross," that serves as the family shrine. When a son moves away from his father's sitio and establishes his own sitio nearby, he invariably erects another cross in the patio to symbolize his new family unit. Ritual entrance into or departure from one of the houses of the family always involves the proper prayers at this *krus ti'na.* While the ceremonies for the extended family, or one of its members, may be quite complex (such as some of the curing ceremonies), they never require the services of more than one *h'ilol.*

3.2. Each *sna* maintains a series of cross shrines; some are erected on hills and designated as *kalvaryos* which defines them as means of communication with the ancestral deities of the lineages making up the *sna*. Others are erected in caves called *ch'ens* and are defined as means of communication with the "earth owner." All of the *h'iloletik* who live in the *sna* assemble in rank to perform the semiannual *k'in krus* ceremonies for the *sna*.

The ceremony has four basic parts: First, there is a formal ritual meal in the house of the *bankilal martomo* (older brother mayordomo) who is selected each year to serve as host. Seated in rank order at the table (always oriented East-West) are the senior male members of the predominant lineage in the *sna,* the *h'iloletik* and the four *mayordomos* (two leaving office and two coming into office). The eating is always accompanied by ritual drinking of *posh* (aguardiente). Second, there is a long prayer over the candles, flowers and incense by the *h'iloletik* who pray in rank order using censers with burning copal. Third, there is an all-night ceremonial circuit, proceeding counterclockwise, around the lands belonging to the *sna* and stopping at various cross shrines, decorated with pine boughs, red geraniums, and other plants, to offer candles, *posh,* incense, music, and appropriate prayers to the *totilme'iletik* of the *sna* and to *yahval balamil.* The ceremony ends the following morning back at the house of the *martomo* with a closing ritual meal.

Many of the men of the *sna* participate as musicians and as other ritual assistants of various types; most of the others attend the meals and make the ceremonial circuit. The women are busy cooking the required amounts of food.

This *k'in krus* ceremony occurs near the time of Santa Cruz in May. But it also occurs at the end of the rainy season in October, and it appears to have little to do with the Christian concept of the cross. Christ and the crucifixion are not mentioned, despite the use of the term *kalvaryo* (calvary) to designate ancestral shrine. Rather, it appears to me that the ceremonial circuit is in effect a symbolic way of expressing the rights of the members of the *sna* in the lands they now occupy which have been inherited from their patrilineal ancestors. In performing rituals for these ancestral patrons, the ceremony not only pays appropriate respect to these deities, but also links together their descendants as common worshippers and occupants of the same *sna* and hence symbolizes the unity of the *sna* as a structurally significant unit in Zinacantan society.

3.3. Similarly, each waterhole group maintains cross shrines for its waterhole. One of these shrines is at the side of the waterhole; another is on a high hill above the waterhole where it is designated as the *kalvaryo* for the whole waterhole group. At this *kalvaryo* the *totilme'iletik* for the members of the waterhole group are believed to assemble and hold meetings to survey the affairs of their descendants and to wait for the semiannual offerings of white candles. This *k'in krus* (performed by all the *h'iloletik* living in the group) follows the same pattern as the ceremonies for the *snas,* but the ceremonial circuit includes rituals performed at the waterhole and at the *kalvaryo* for the waterhole. Ritual respect is paid to *yahavl balamil* who "owns" the waterhole, and to the *totilme' iletik* who "found" the waterhole in the first place.

What this ceremony apperas to express by its ritual forms are the rights which members of the waterhole group have to draw water from a waterhole and their obligations to care for the waterhole properly. Control of rights to water is crucial for human and animal life, especially during the long dry season from October to May when the supplies of water for household and livestock use are strictly limited. Just as the *k'in krus* ceremony for a *sna* expresses rights in land, so the *k'in krus* ceremony for a waterhole group expresses rights in water. In performing rituals for the deities associated with the waterhole, this ceremony links together the *snas* that compose a waterhole group and hence symbolizes the unity of the waterhole group as another structurally significant unit in Zinacantan society.

3.4. Finally, the paraje unit is ritually expressed by two annual ceremonies performed by all of the *h'iloletik* living in the paraje. These ceremonies are called *'ach' hab'il* ("new year") and *slaheb hab'il* ("end of year"), and their function can be conceived of as symbolizing the unity of the paraje and its relationship to the tribal *totilme'iletik* in the ceremonial center. In this case, significantly enough, the two *krinsupales* serve as the *martomos* and play host for the ritual meals which begin and end the ceremonial circuit. This ceremonial circuit does not include sacred places in the paraje, but is rather a pilgrimage to offer candles and prayers to the saints in the churches and the tribal ancestral gods residing in the mountains around the ceremonial center. Just as the *krinsupales* have to report to the presidente, the *h'iloletik* have to pay their respects to tribal gods.

In each case — extended family, *sna,* waterhole group, and paraje — the ritual forms are repeated but in ever-increasing scale and complexity. The culmination is reached in the ceremonial center itself where not only are the priestly cargo-holders performing almost daily ritual for the welfare of Zinacantan as a whole, but also where *h'iloletik* from *all* parajes perform three annual ceremonies called *'ach' hab'il, 'o'lol hab'il,* and *slaheb hab'il*. These ceremonies are for "the new year," "the middle of the year," and "the end of the year." For these ceremonies the *h'iloletik* assemble at a table in the house of the *muk'ta alkalte,* the highest ranking cargo holder (see Figure 3). Hence they involve ritual which emanates from the peak of sacred power in Zinacantan — the highest ranking *h'ilol* sitting in the house of the ranking *muk'ta alkalte* of the priestly hierarchy. From this point the *h'iloletik* make pilgrimages to all of the sacred mountains and caves where they leave offerings of candles and copal incense and plead with the ancestral gods and the earth-owner to make things right in Zinacantan.

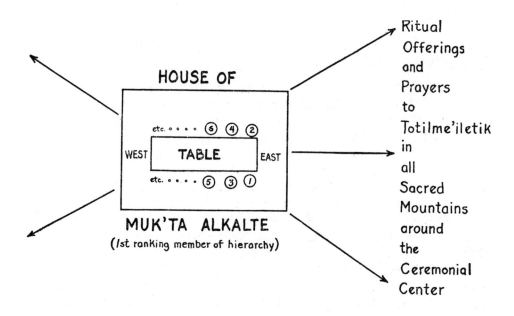

Fig. 3. Articulation of Hierarchy and H'iloletik in Zinacantan.

4. I now wish to advance some hypotheses concerning the possible implications of these data for the study of ancient Maya society.

4.1. I have previously noted (Vogt 1961 a) how closely the settlement pattern for Zinacantan approximates the archeological findings of Willey (1956) from the Belize Valley and of Bullard (1960) from the Peten. In light of my more recent data, I would tend to make the following equations:

Zinacantan	Classic Maya
Sitio (patrilocal extended family)	House group
Sna	Cluster
Waterhole group	Cluster group
Paraje	Hamlet with minor ceremonial center
Cabecera	Major ceremonial center

I would now like to suggest that just as the settlement pattern appears to take the form of an aggregate of aggregates, so the social structure and the ceremonial organization appears to manifest some orderly replications of increasing structural scale from the simple household ceremonies involving only the extended family to the complex ceremonies in the ceremonial center involving the whole tribal unit.

4.2. As I suggested at the Paris meetings in 1960 (Vogt 1960) and in a recent paper (Vogt 1962) for a Burg Warternstein Symposium, there is probably an important relationship between:

(1) the sacred mountains as dwelling places of the ancestral gods in Zinacantan and the steep-sided pyramids in the ceremonial centers of the Maya Classic, and

(2) the ritual performed at cross shrines at the foot and on top of sacred mountains in Zinacantan and the ritual performed at the round altars in front of stelae at the foot of Classic Maya pyramids.

These two hypotheses have recently received some confirmation from Holland (1961) who finds the same concept in Larrainzar.

4.3. I now further suggest that the ceremonial circuit performed for *snas*, waterhole groups, and for the ceremonial center in Zinacantan may have had its counterpart in Classic Maya ceremonial procedure. A comparable kind of ceremonial circuit is described by Landa (Tozzer, 1941: 144-48) who states that its purpose was to ritually establish boundaries and to ritually purify the area and people enclosed by the circuit — an interpretation that would not be out of line for the Zinacantan ceremonial circuits. From a Zinacanteco point of view, all of the ceremonies performed by the *h'iloletik* have the purpose of ritually purifying Zinacantecos by asking pardon from the *totilme'iletik* for their clients whether they be individual patients in curing ceremonies or all of Zinacantan in the large ceremonies held in the ceremonial center for "the new year," "the middle of the year," and "the end of the year."

References

BULLARD, WILLIAM R., JR.
   1960   "Maya Settlement Pattern in Northeastern Petén, Guatemala", *American Antiquity*, Vol. 25, N° 3, pp. 355-72.

CANCIAN, FRANK
   1962   "Some Aspects of the Social and Religious Organization of a Maya Society", Paper presented at the 35th International Congress of Americanists, Mexico, August, 1962.

FISHBURNE, JANE
   1962   "Courtship and Marriage in Zinacantan", Senior Honors Thesis, Radcliffe College.

FORTES, MEYER
   1958   *"Introduction"* to *The Developmental Cycle in Domestic Groups.* Jack Goody, ed. (Cambridge Papers in Social Anthropology, N° 1).

GUITERAS-HOLMES, C.
   1961   *Perils of the Soul. The World View of a Tzotzil Indian.* Glencoe, The Free Press.

HOLLAND, WILLIAM R.
   1961   "Relaciones entre la religión tzotzil contemporánea y la maya antigua", in *Anales,* Instituto Nacional de Antropología e Historia, Mexico, Tomo XIII, pp. 113-132.

POZAS, RICARDO
   1959   *Chamula, un pueblo indio de los Altos de Chiapas, México* (Memorias del Instituto Nacional Indigenista, Vol. VIII).

SIVERTS, HENNING
   1960   "Political Organization in a Tzetzal Community in Chiapas, Mexico", *Alpha Kappa Deltan*, Vol. XXX, N° 1, pp. 14-29.

TOZZER, ALFRED M.
   1941   *Landa's Relacion de las Cosas de Yucatan* (Papers of the Peabody Museum of American Archeology and Ethnology, Harvard University, Vol. VIII).

VILLA ROJAS, ALFONSO
   1947   "Kinship and Nagualism in a Tzeltal Community. Southeastern Mexico", *American Anthropologist*, Vol. 49, N° 1, pp. 18-33.

VOGT, EVON Z.
   1960   "Ancient Maya Concepts in Contemporary Zinacatan Religion", in VIe Congrès International des Sciences Anthropologiques et Ethnologiques, Paris, 30 Juillet-6 Août, 1960, Tome II, Musée de l'Homme. (In press.)
   1961a "Some Aspects o Zinacantan Settlement Patterns and Ceremonial Organization", *Estudios de Cultura Maya,* Vol. I, pp. 131-46. Seminario de Cultura Maya", Universidad Nacional Autónoma de México.

1961b   "A Model for the Study of Ceremonial Organization in Highland Chiapas", Paper presented at the 60th Annual Meetings of the American Anthropological Association, Philadelphia, 1961.

1962   "The Genetic Model and Maya Cultural Development", Paper prepared in advance for participants in Symposium N° 20: "The Cultural Development of the Maya". Burg Wartenstein, Sept. 6-13, 1962.

WILLEY, GORDON R.
1956   "The Structure of Ancient Maya Society: Evidence from the Southern Lowlands", *American Anthropologist*, Vol. 58, N° 5, pp. 777-82.

THE END OF CLASSIC MAYA CULTURE: A REVIEW OF RECENT EVIDENCE

GEORGE L. COWGILL

INTRODUCTION

THE COLLAPSE of Classic Period culture in the Southern Maya Lowlands remains poorly understood after several generations of speculation and research. By "poorly understood" I mean both that no satisfactory explanations have been proposed so far and also that our ideas about what happened—about what, in fact, we are trying to explain—have themselves changed considerably over the years. I do not intend to review the history of the problem in any detail, since this has been ably done in a number of recent publications, including those by Thompson (1954), U. Cowgill (1962), and Sanders (1962). Rather, I wish to give a concise summary of what, on the most recent evidence, the phenomena are that have to be accounted for; and then to evaluate explanations of the cultural collapse in the light of this evidence.

Some of the data presented are derived from my own unpublished fieldwork in Guatemala in 1959[1] (G. Cowgill 1963), but I am less concerned with presenting previously unavailable information than with drawing together material published in the last few years in a number of scattered sources. I have tried to correct some misconceptions, to stress points which are of significance for the comparative study of civilizations, to take stock generally of what I now think we know, and to point out some topics on which more research is important.

One result of this survey is that no previous explanations of the Maya collapse appear very convincing; indeed, most are highly implausible. In the course of writing this paper it occurred to me that forced resettlement may have been a factor in the collapse. I include a discussion of this hypothesis, my justification being that it is, so far as I know, new[2] and that there is no very clear evidence

---

[1] Supported from December 1958 to September 1959 by a Fellowship from the Henry L. and Grace Doherty Charitable Foundation, and from September 1959 to June 1960 by a National Science Foundation Graduate Fellowship. I am indebted to Dr. Ursula M. Cowgill for assistance in archaeological reconnaissance and excavations. Mr. Dana Condon, General Traffic Manager for Central America of the United Fruit Company, was of very great assistance, as were the Rev. and Mrs. Stanley Storey of the Nazarene Mission in Santa Elena, El Peten, and Sr. Carlos Samayoa Chinchilla, Director of the Instituto Nacional de Antropologia e Historia in Guatemala City.

[2] M. E. Moseley has called my attention to the fact that Brainerd (1958:30, 95) suggested that the Puuc region of Yucatan may have been depopulated through forcible resettlement. He did not extend this notion to apply also to the Southern Lowlands, as is done here.

against it. Neither is there strong evidence in its favor. The chief aim of this paper, then, is to provide something in the nature of a progress report on the problem of the Maya collapse; and the notion of forced resettlement is added more as an epilogue than as a logical consequence of earlier sections of the paper.

MAYA CULTURE HISTORY

The Southern Maya Lowlands, roughly comprising British Honduras, the department of El Peten and nearby areas of Guatemala, and some adjacent sections of Honduras and Mexico, is primarily low-lying tropical forest. It is difficult to say what, if any, human activity took place in this region during the long era of incipient agriculture known in the central Mexican Highlands (MacNeish 1961) or during the Early Preclassic Period, when sedentary farming villages appeared elsewhere in Mesoamerica. As early as the Middle Preclassic Period the Southern Maya Lowlands supported at least a moderate population which made sophisticated pottery and must surely have practiced agriculture. The chief evidence is the widely scattered occurrence of ceramics comparable to those of the Mamom Phase at Uaxactun (Smith 1955). While always relatively scarce compared to pottery of later phases, Mamom-like pottery is known at a number of sites, including Nohoch Ek (Coe and Coe 1956) and Barton Ramie (Willey et al. MS) in British Honduras; and Uaxactun (Smith 1955), Tikal (Coe 1962:504), Flores (G. Cowgill 1963:17), and Altar de Sacrificios in the Peten (Willey and Smith 1963). A pre-Mamom phase is also present at Altar. Food production is inferred from the difficulty in imagining that Mamom-like pottery could have been produced by a society exploiting only the hunting and gathering resources of the lowlands, and there is supporting evidence in a report that maize pollen dating from before 800 B.C. has been found in the central Peten (U. Cowgill and Hutchinson 1963a:276). The time limits of the Mamom Phase are not well established, but it surely extends to at least several centuries B.C.

By Late Preclassic times (roughly the last centuries B.C.) population in the Southern Maya Lowlands was substantial. Some recent writers, including Dumond (1961:312), have mistakenly supposed that Preclassic remains are not plentiful. It is easy to form this impression because Classic Period material is given much greater attention in the literature. Actually, most or all major sites contain a great deal of pottery similar to that of the Chicanel Phase of Uaxactun, and both Bullard (1960a) in the northeastern Peten and I in the central Peten have found a profusion of small sites with Chicanel-like pottery. Such diagnostic Classic Maya traits as polychrome pottery (Mamom and Chicanel pottery is mostly monochrome), the typical Classic art style, hieroglyphic inscriptions, and buildings with vaulted masonry roofs are lacking or not yet demonstrated for the Late Preclassic in the Southern Lowlands; but glyphs were surely present elsewhere in Mesoamerica by this time (M. Coe 1957), and a Preclassic vaulted tomb chamber has been found at Tikal (Coe and McGinn 1963). Nevertheless, ceremonial centers with lime-plastered plaza floors and masonry temple substructures were widely distributed and sometimes sizable, as at Tikal (W. Coe 1962:504), where the recent finding of a well-stocked Late Preclassic tomb (Coe and McGinn 1963) implies considerable differentiation in status of individuals. It is difficult to say much about the level of socio-cultural complexity, but quite clearly it was well beyond the self-sufficient "neolithic" little community. At the same time, nothing suggests that the Southern Lowlands were particularly outstanding in comparison with Late Preclassic Period developments elsewhere in Mesoamerica. Indeed, culture here seems to fall well short of some probably earlier manifestations, notably the "Olmec" climax in the La Venta region of the Gulf Coast (Drucker *et al.* 1955).

But, it should be emphasized, small housemounds with Late Preclassic pottery are very widespread in the Southern Maya Lowlands. Chicanel-like pottery is plentiful wherever signs of later occupation have been found, and, so far as one can judge at present, the population must have been just about as large as it ever became during the Classic Period. Furthermore, it seems that the settlement pattern of Classic times was already established, with few or no congested centers of population but with a scattering of dwellings almost everywhere that the land was not too swampy for habitation (a pattern best described by Bullard 1960a). The size of each household and the number of dwellings simultaneously occupied is uncertain, but a population of at least several hundred thousand must be inferred for the Late Preclassic Southern Maya Lowlands. A further implication is that the essential ecological adaptations of the Classic Period must already have been in operation.

Following a short and still little-known Protoclassic transition (the Uaxactun Matzanel Phase of Smith 1955), the Classic Period (about A.D. 300 to 900) sees the full development of a Maya "great tradition" in art, architecture, arithmetic, calendrics, and hieroglyphic writing. The precise sources of many specific traits are still very much a matter of debate, but what is really relevant is that both outside stimuli and local innovations must have been important. Classic culture in the Southern Maya Lowlands has a very distinctive regional flavor when contrasted with the rest of Mesoamerica, and it was necessarily on the basis of local human and material resources that new concepts, of whatever origin, were given physical embodiment, expressed in a characteristically Maya fashion and increasingly elaborated throughout the Classic Period.

Some Classic ceremonial centers are very impressive, but, given the centuries available for their growth by accretion, fairly small populations would have been physically capable of their construction, without excessive labor. They do not *necessarily* imply any highly centralized or bureaucratic political authority (Altshuler 1958, Kaplan 1963). There were still few or no dense concentrations of population, but the ubiquitous scatter of housemounds continues, and a population of at least a few hundred thousand is again implied.

There is no evidence in most of the lowlands for any more complicated subsistence technique than swidden (slash and burn) farming, based chiefly on maize, but with beans, squash, and root crops also important. Terraces are reported for a few districts in British Honduras, but their role in agriculture is not established. Hunting and fishing presumably made important protein contributions to the diet. Swidden farming was once commonly believed to be an inadequate basis for supporting a dense population or an elaborate cultural tradition, but recent studies show that in many parts of the world this has not been true (Dumond 1961). Work by U. Cowgill (1961, 1962) indicates that for the Southern Maya Lowlands, in particular, swidden farming could well support 100 to 200 people per square mile, while full exploitation of the land still leaves a good deal of time for other activities, since periods of peak agricultural work alternate with slack times in the annual cycle. It is certainly not necessary to postulate this large a population to account for Classic ceremonial centers, and probably such a population could account for housemound densities.

Today surface water disappears rapidly into the porous limestone bedrock, and drinking water is scarce during much of the year in the Southern Maya Lowlands, except near a few large lakes and permanent streams. Several Classic centers are known to have had reservoirs which stored runoff water from paved plazas, and such water storage must have been essential for the survival of the large Classic population. Presumably, indeed, reservoirs were already in use in Late Preclassic times.

In the Northern Maya Lowlands, including the present Mexican state of Yucatan and adjacent areas, Preclassic and Classic cultures are broadly comparable in level to those of the Southern Lowlands. Local styles differ considerably from those in the south, and the hieroglyphic stela cult and polychrome painted pottery are much less in evidence, but monumental architecture is extensive and excellent. Swidden farming is relatively productive here too, as shown by a number of studies, but the length of the fallow period is greater than in the south, and Hester (1954) estimates a population ceiling on the order of 60 per square mile. In most of the north, natural sinkholes (*cenotes*) reach below the water table and provide a fairly easy source of water, although this is not true in the Puuc hill country, where cisterns were often used (Brainerd 1956).

In the Southern Lowlands, hieroglyphic inscriptions and monumental building ceased somewhere around A.D. 900. A substantial population may have persisted for a while, but before long the region was nearly or totally deserted (Willey 1956). Although revival of a great tradition obviously was not possible without personnel to support it, this depopulation was not necessarily one of the original precipitating factors in the collapse of Classic Period culture. But no explanation of the collapse is adequate unless it accounts for depopulation.

At about this time the hieroglyphic stela cult (although not all hieroglyphic inscriptions) came to an end in the Northern Lowlands, and northern styles of art and architecture blend with traditions of Mexican origin. At Chichen Itza, which became the preeminent center, there are many close resemblances to Tula, the Toltec capital north of Mexico City, and foreign conquest is clearly indicated (Tozzer 1957). In general Yucatan does not seem to have been depopulated, but the Puuc hills were deserted at about this time or a little later (Brainerd 1956). Whether judged by aesthetic impressions or by scale of monumental building and evidence of craft skills, this Early Postclassic Period in the north is more a time of cultural change than of striking decline.

After some centuries, perhaps around A.D. 1200, monumental building ceased at Chichen Itza, and a little later Mayapan assumed a position of political dominance, well attested by reliable native tradition, which it held until the north broke up into a number of autonomous and often warring political units in the mid-15th century. This Late Postclassic Period is less a time of total cultural collapse than of decadence and impoverishment. Population may not have declined. Yet, not only are architecture and craft products much less pleasing to 20th century archaeologists, but there also seems to be much less technical ability shown in pottery and other artifacts. For the first time true cities (or at least large towns) appear in Yucatan, but the scale of both temples and more or less secular residential structures is diminished (Pollock *et al.* 1962). Precious materials such as jade and gold seem considerably scarcer than in the Early Postclassic. All this suggests to me more than a deterioration of taste; I would argue that even the elite had become relatively poor in a material sense.

This decline in the north is a different phenomenon from that which occurred earlier in the south, and it may be merely a phase in the ups and downs found in any culture area with a long history of civilization. Perhaps the elite had become less able to divert to their own uses the labor potentially available for non-subsistence activities; this situation could have resulted from a weakening of centralized authority, from a greater disaffection of the non-elite, or from both. Possibly also trade had become less extensive and less profitable. Politically prominent Yucatec Maya are known to have been active in long-distance trade even after the fall of Mayapan, but the volume of their business must have been small in comparison to the wealth that was then flowing into Tenochtitlan, the Aztec capital. Indeed, there is a suspicious inverse relationship between the rapid expansion of central Mexican political and economic influence in Late Postclassic times and the apparent impoverishment of Yucatan. I suggest, as a possibility worthy of further investigation, that Chichen Itza may have had control over commerce with many areas, notably the central and southern Gulf Coast, which were lost to the expanding Aztec power during the Late Postclassic Mayapan Period.

Recent and partly unpublished archaeological work in the Southern Maya Lowlands gives us for the first time some worthwhile data (aside from negative evidence) on the quite different situation there in the Postclassic Period (Berlin 1955, Bullard 1960b, Adams and Trik 1961, W. Coe 1962, G. Cowgill 1963). Postclassic pottery is far less universally distributed than is that of the Late Preclassic and Classic Periods, and indicates that settlements were mainly towns and villages, as in Late Postclassic Yucatan, in contrast to the dispersed Preclassic and Classic pattern. Its scarcity is in keeping with Spanish evidence for a population of at most a few tens of thousands in the 16th and 17th centuries. Such a population is far below the most conservative estimates for the Classic Period and far below the limit set by swidden farming.

An extensive comparative study of the pottery (G. Cowgill 1963), whose results can be only summarized here, suggests derivation from the north much more than development from Classic Southern Lowland traditions. The idea of re-occupation from the north is strongly supported by the fact that in the 17th century the language of the Peten differed only slightly from that of Yucatan, while it contrasted considerably with Chol and other Mayan languages to the south, according to the experience of Father Cano in 1695 (Means 1917: 97). The resemblance to Yucatec is much too close to be plausible unless there had been migration between the Peten and Yucatan, and replacement of local dialects in one or the other region at some time later than the Classic Period. A south to north movement is a logical possibility, favored some years ago when the north was believed to have been virtually uninhabited before Postclassic times; but the greater cultural continuity and populational stability in the north makes immigration on a scale large enough to have introduced a new language seem most unlikely. Linguistic and ceramic data corroborate one another in suggesting a north to south movement in Postclassic times.

The date and origin of such a movement are still very uncertain. Postclassic Peten ceramics very possibly changed enough with time to permit recognition of two or more pottery phases, but so far no site has been found where stratigraphic conditions give a firm basis for such a subdivision. Resemblances to northern types are mostly general rather than detailed. Some wares found in the south, such as unslipped effigy incensarios, are believed to be diagnostically Late Postclassic in the north. But many other southern types cannot possibly be derived from the Late Postclassic types of Mayapan (nor from the somewhat different styles of Tulum and other east coast sites); they are much more reminiscent of Early Postclassic northern types, including X Fine Orange, and even the very late Classic or earliest Postclassic "Florescent Phase" wares of the Puuc region. A very few clearly Early Postclassic imports, X Fine Orange and Tohil Plumbate, have been found in the southern lowlands, but never in circumstances where the relationship to local Postclassic types is clear.

On present evidence, local Postclassic pottery is surprisingly similar throughout British Honduras and central and southeastern Peten, including the 17th century ranges of both the Peten Itza and Mopan Maya groups. Topoxte is a conspicuous exception, with closely related but quite distinct pottery types which are somewhat more reminiscent of east coast Yucatec types (Bullard 1960b), and further work may reveal still more local variation. So far the situation in the southwestern Peten and along the Usumacinta and its upper tributaries seems quite different. Central Peten Postclassic types have not been found, while the latest materials at Altar de Sacrificios, the Jimba Phase, suggest a major incursion of newcomers in very Early Postclassic times, not from Yucatan but perhaps from Tabasco (Willey and Smith 1963). It is worth noting that in the 16th century this region was evidently Chol rather than Yucatec-speaking (Scholes and Roys 1948:17).

It is possible, but by no means demonstrated, that there was no real break in the occupation of the central Peten and British Honduras and that movement from the north followed immediately upon the collapse of the Classic culture. It is at least equally likely that there was a distinct hiatus before Postclassic reoccupation. However the number of ceramic traits derived from the Early Postclassic of Yucatan indicates that reoccupation cannot have begun much later than the decline of Chichen Itza. Roys (1962) has assembled a good deal of evidence from native traditions that date such a southward migration to the fall of Mayapan, but other authorities (such as Thompson 1954:118, 128) interpret the same traditions as referring to a migration after the fall of Chichen Itza. The new archaeological data from the Southern Lowlands fit the latter interpretation much more easily, although it is conceivable that some native traditions record a second migration, later than that attested by much of the known Postclassic pottery in the south.

EXPLANATIONS OF THE MAYA COLLAPSE

One major category of explanations for the cultural collapse and depopulation of the Southern Maya Lowlands is that invoking natural disaster or seeking to relate the collapse to some ecological difficulty. Several features of the modern environment have been pointed to as evidence of agricultural disaster. Savannas in some localities have been mentioned as possible remnants of an invasion of grass throughout the whole region as a result of excessive shortening of the swidden cycle in response to population pressure, leading to disaster because grasslands could not be cultivated with aboriginal equipment. But, in fact, savannas are limited at present to poorly drained areas virtually devoid of prehistoric sites, in contrast to the present forest around both ancient and modern regions of settlement (Thompson 1954:86, U. Cowgill 1962:278). Indeed, recent pollen studies indicate that grasses were more prevalent prior to extensive agriculture in the Peten than they have been since (U. Cowgill and Hutchinson 1963a). Others have suggested that modern swamps are the result of disastrous erosion and silting up of former lakes, but again recent evidence shows that sediments in these swamps have accumulated slowly over a long period (U. Cowgill and Hutchinson 1963a). The present-day environmental potential looks adequate for support of Classic Maya civilization, and it will not do to explain its collapse by the suggestion (Meggers 1954) that it never should have existed in the first place.

Postulation of epidemic diseases or a succession of crop failures due to drought, insects, or other causes leaves one unable to explain why just this one region was affected, and affected so disastrously. In particular, the persistence of population in the nearby and agriculturally less productive Northern Lowlands is unaccountable in terms of such theories. On a world-wide basis, pestilence and famine have often caused great loss of life and social disturbance but rarely if ever the wholesale and enduring desertion of entire regions.

MacKie's (1961) recent suggestion of earthquakes as a factor fails to account for the persistence of population in highland parts of Middle America that are far more subject to serious earthquakes. Earthquake damage at certain sites could conceivably have hastened a collapse already under way for other reasons but can hardly be the principal causal factor.

A few years ago I suggested informally that insurrections or invasions may have led to destruction of reservoirs, which in turn forced abandonment of much of the Southern Lowlands. Since this suggestion has begun to be attributed to me in recent literature (Sanders 1962:112), it must be emphasized that I no longer think it very useful; nevertheless, there can be little doubt that reservoirs in the unfortified Classic centers would have been very vulnerable to invaders bent on creating a maximum of distress with a minimum of effort and that the resulting disturbance would have created chaos in well-watered localities also. Disuse of reservoirs by the Postclassic population seems only natural as long as there was more than enough land within reach of natural water sources.

Other recent suggestions are that population may have declined in part because of the evolution of a tradition tending to rejection, and hence less careful nurture and higher death rate, of female children; and also that expansion of population and farmed areas may have meant a relative shortage of wild food rich in protein, possibly having a significant effect on "Maya nutrition, reproductive physiology, and demography" (U. Cowgill and Hutchinson 1963b). Neither of these phenomena have yet been demonstrated for the Classic Period, and the authors propose them only as contributing factors in a collapse which they feel "may ultimately be solved in terms of a multiplicity of small and often non-obvious causes rather than of a single dramatic catastrophe" (U. Cowgill and Hutchinson 1963b:101). But, at least, these hypotheses call attention to the need for examining skeletal material for signs of dietary deficiency. Of four burials from Tikal examined by Dr. Charles Weer Goff, one, the Late Classic burial of a child aged about 15, of undetermined sex, showed signs of "nutritional underdevelopment" (Coe and Broman 1958). It will be of extreme interest to see what results emerge from a study of a larger sample of burials, extending over a wider time span and covering the gamut of Classic Period social status.

A second major category of explanations of cultural collapse in the Southern Maya Lowlands is less concerned with ecology than with internal forces within Maya culture, or the interaction of that culture with its neighbors. One such explanation sees the culture as having somehow run its course, or become "decadent," or exhausted its pattern. This makes some sense when one speaks of a style or cultural tradition, but it has always been difficult for me to understand what is meant when the subject of discourse is a social system. Certainly it does not account for depopulation in the south, although conceivably it should be included with social and economic changes as part of the explanation for shoddy styles in the Late Postclassic Northern Lowlands, where Pollock (1962: 16) speaks of an "internal dry rot" in the culture.

Others, including Thompson (1954:87) and Altshuler (1958), have suggested that perhaps peasants revolted against oppressive priest-rulers. In spite of the size of ceremonial centers and the pomp and splendor of priestly ritual and regalia, it is easy to imagine that throughout most of the Classic Period there may have been relatively little coercion by the elite. Since swidden farming, even with stone tools, permits a household to meet its own subsistence needs and have considerable time left to produce food for specialists or to engage in other activities, all the "great tradition" manifestations could have been achieved without lowering the standard of living of the common people. The peasants very possibly contributed willingly to support a ritual system which they found reassuring and took community pride in the glories of their temples and leaders, a situation not unlike that underlying elite displays of wealth in Polynesia or on the Northwest Coast of North America. However, it is possible that increasingly esoteric priestly religion, increasing pretensions to absolute authority, and increasing demands for labor and tribute led low-status people to change their attitude and perceive themselves as victims of oppression. I know of no real evidence that such a sequence of events actually occurred, but it does seem a perfectly plausible supposition. And, since as far as we can tell the elite were in no way indispensable to management or administration of subsistence activities, it would have been extremely easy to get rid of them, once they ceased to have any ideological value for the non-elite. Unfortunately, as Willey (1956) has pointed out, this theory of peasant revolt does not explain the disappearance of peasants as well as rulers.

Invasions by groups from central or southern Mexico have also been suggested as playing a major role in the collapse of Classic culture in the Southern Lowlands. Since Yucatan was obviously invaded at about this time, it would be strange if the south had been completely untouched. However, even remarkably savage invasions, given pre-industrial instruments of homicide, have not characteristically depopulated entire regions, and Yucatan was certainly not depopulated. It seems that the invasion theory also comes to grief by not being able to account for desertion of the Southern Maya Lowlands, and one is left with no explanation of the Maya collapse that does not at some point come into conflict with the evidence.

One final point is that, once depopulation had occurred, it is not particularly surprising that it persisted in Postclassic times, just as it has in Colonial and modern times. The Southern Lowlands have few resources of value to a pre-industrial culture aside from forest products that could be collected by small parties; and without people already present there, they would not be very strategic either economically or politically. The main factor that would motivate their resettlement would be land shortage elsewhere. Presumably this was what led to their occupation by farmers in the first place. People may have begun to fill the area again when the Spanish impact led to a drastic population decline throughout Mesoamerica and interrupted the process. Since the 1930's population has been increasing in the Peten at about 3½ per cent a year (G. Cowgill 1963:500), at which rate a population of about a quarter of a million (exclusive of British Honduras) will be reached in another 70 years.

FORCED RESETTLEMENT AS A POSSIBLE FACTOR

The unsatisfactory nature of earlier attempts to account for the Maya collapse clearly demands further thought and further research on the problem. I have one suggestion to offer, which as yet has little evidence in its support, but it is, at least, not strongly contradicted by any facts presented here. There may have been a period of Mexican invasions, affecting the entire Maya Lowlands (as well as, perhaps, the highlands), lasting some years, possibly several generations; during this time strife and social disorganization were prevalent, resulting in substantial decline, but not extermination, of population throughout the lowlands. Causes would have been death in warfare, starvation through famine resulting from destruction of crops, and very possibly extensive taking of captives for sale as slaves. The final outcome may have been control over the entire lowlands by a relatively small group of invaders, who then set about to consolidate their power over the Maya survivors, ruling the whole region from a single capital at Chichen Itza. I suggest that the invaders may have more or less forcibly resettled the inhabitants of the whole Maya Lowlands, moving them to localities within relatively easy reach of Chichen Itza. Landa says of the lords of Chichen that they "brought together in those localities a great population of towns and peoples . . ." (Roys 1962:62), and this might refer to deliberate resettlement. The motives would have been similar to those the Spaniards later had for relocating Indians in many parts of the New World—closer political control and greater ease in collecting tribute. Perhaps such a movement was assisted by a northward retreat of the Maya from attacks which struck first at the southern and southwestern parts of the lowlands.

Many Spanish attempts at resettlement were short-lived, perhaps largely because the locations chosen often had no realistic relation to ecological conditions. On the other hand, this hypothetical Chichen-directed resettlement would have made good ecological sense, given a population in the lowlands reduced to considerably below what the land could support, so that the subsistence potential in the north alone would have been adequate for all survivors. Agriculture would not be more difficult or very different in the north than elsewhere, while drinking water could be easily obtained from *cenotes*, in contrast to the difficulties of obtaining water in many parts of the districts apparently deserted at this time.

Certainly the Chichen government could not have prevented the escape of a few fugitives, but it could well have prevented the establishment of any substantial settlements in administratively inconvenient areas. Nor would there have been any strong economic motive to repopulate the Southern Lowlands, so long as the entire remaining population could be kept busy closer to home. In the 17th century cacao was of some importance in limited districts of the Southern Lowlands, such as the Belize Valley, but it would probably not have seemed attractive to the rulers at Chichen to establish cacao plantations there, in view of the greater possibilities in the Chontalpa of Tabasco, and elsewhere. Forest products such as feathers, honey, skins, and copal incense could be extracted by relatively small parties, who would also be quick to detect any sizeable settlements of fugitives.

It might also be assumed that the Chichen government would wish, for administrative purposes, to impose a single language on the ethnically somewhat diverse Mayan groups they had brought together in the north. Remnants of the Classic Period population of the Southern Lowlands may have kept some traditions about their origins, while quickly losing much of whatever they still possessed of any distinctively southern language or culture.

This explanation is consistent with the ceramic evidence, summarized previously, which indicates that the Southern Lowlands were reoccupied from the north, and possibly at about the time that centralized government at Chichen ended. It may be that after a few generations of peace under the rule of Chichen, population in the north had again increased to the point where there was a land shortage in the region easily controlled from the capital, leading to pressure to move into deserted territory. But most important would have been the disappearance of the strong authority which alone could prevent such resettlement, at precisely the time that a return of open warfare between competing factions gave defeated groups a motive for seeking refuge in distant and uninhabited regions. The native traditions, while conflicting as to whether the event took place when Chichen fell or when Mayapan fell, are fairly clear that those who fled southward were the defeated leader of one faction and his followers.

BIBLIOGRAPHY

ADAMS, R. E. W., AND A. S. TRIK
  1961 Temple I (Str. 5D-1): Post-constructional Activities. *Tikal Reports*, no. 7, *Museum Monographs*. Philadelphia: The University Museum.

ALTSHULER, MILTON
  1958 On the Environmental Limitations of Mayan Cultural Development. *Southwestern Journal of Anthropology* 14:189-198.

BERLIN, HEINRICH
  1955 Apuntes sobre Vasijas de Flores (El Peten). *Antropología e Historia de Guatemala* 7:15-17.

BRAINERD, GEORGE W.
  1956 Changing Living Patterns of the Yucatan Maya. *American Antiquity* 22:162-164.
  1958 *The Archaeological Ceramics of Yucatan*. Berkeley: University of California Publications, Anthropological Records 19.

BULLARD, WILLIAM R., JR.
  1960a Maya Settlement Pattern in Northeastern Peten, Guatemala. *American Antiquity* 25:355-372.
  1960b Archaeological Investigation of the Maya Ruin of Topoxte, Peten, Guatemala. *Year Book of the American Philosophical Society, 1960*: 551-554.

COE, MICHAEL D.
  1957 Cycle 7 Monuments in Middle America: a Reconsideration. *American Anthropologist* 59:597-611.

COE, WILLIAM R.
  1962 A Summary of Excavation and Research at Tikal, Guatemala: 1956-61. *American Antiquity* 27:479-507.

COE, W. R., AND V. L. BROMAN
  1958 Excavations in the Stela 23 Group. *Tikal Reports*, no. 2, *Museum Monographs*. Philadelphia: The University Museum.

COE, W. R., AND M. D. COE
  1956 Excavations at Nohoch Ek, British Honduras. *American Antiquity* 21:370-382.

COE, W. R., AND J. J. MCGINN
  1963 Tikal: the North Acropolis and an Early Tomb. *Expedition* 5:24-32.

COWGILL, GEORGE L.
  1963 *Postclassic Period Culture in the Vicinity of Flores, Peten, Guatemala*. Unpublished Ph.D. dissertation, Harvard University, Cambridge, Massachusetts.

COWGILL, URSULA M.
  1961 Soil Fertility and the Ancient Maya. *Transactions of the Connecticut Academy of Arts and Sciences* 42:1-56.
  1962 An Agricultural Study of the Southern Maya Lowlands. *American Anthropologist* 64:273-286.

COWGILL, U. M., AND G. E. HUTCHINSON
    1963a Ecological and Geochemical Archaeology in the Southern Maya Lowlands. *Southwestern Journal of Anthropology* 19:267-286.
    1963b Sex-ratio in Childhood and the Depopulation of the Peten, Guatemala. *Human Biology* 35:90-103.

DRUCKER, P., R. F. HEIZER, AND R. J. SQUIER
    1959 *Excavations at La Venta, Tabasco, 1955*. Washington: Bureau of American Ethnology, bulletin 170.

DUMOND, D. E.
    1961 Swidden Agriculture and the Rise of Maya Civilization. *Southwestern Journal of Anthropology.* 17:301-316.

HESTER, JOSEPH A., JR.
    1954 *Natural and Cultural Bases of Ancient Maya Subsistence Economy.* Unpublished Ph.D. dissertation, University of California at Los Angeles, Los Angeles, California.

KAPLAN, DAVID
    1963 Men, Monuments, and Political Systems. *Southwestern Journal of Anthropology* 19:397-410.

MACKIE, EUAN W.
    1961 New Light on the End of Classic Maya Culture at Benque Viejo, British Honduras. *American Antiquity* 27:216-224.

MACNEISH, RICHARD S.
    1961 *First Annual Report of the Tehuacan Archaeological-Botanical Project.* Andover: Robert S. Peabody Foundation for Archaeology.

MEANS, PHILIP A.
    1917 *History of the Spanish Conquest of Yucatan and of the Itzas.* Cambridge: Papers of the Peabody Museum, Harvard University, no. 7.

MEGGERS, BETTY J.
    1954 Environmental Limitation on the Development of Culture. *American Anthropologist* 56:801-824.

POLLOCK, H. E. D., R. L. ROYS, T. PROSKOURIAKOFF, AND A. L. SMITH
    1962 *Mayapan, Yucatan, Mexico.* Washington: Carnegie Institution of Washington, publication 619.

ROYS, RALPH L.
    1962 Literary Sources for the History of Mayapan. In *Mayapan, Yucatan, Mexico* (Pollock *et al.*). Washington: Carnegie Institution of Washington, publication 619.

SANDERS, WILLIAM T.
    1962 Cultural Ecology of the Maya Lowlands (Part I). *Estudios de Cultura Maya* 2:79-121.

SCHOLES, F., AND R. ROYS
    1948 *The Maya Chontal of Acalan-Tixchel.* Washington: Carnegie Institution of Washington, publication 560.

SMITH, ROBERT E.
   1955   *Ceramic Sequence at Uaxactun.* New Orleans: Middle American Research Institute, Tulane University, publication 20.

THOMPSON, J. ERIC S.
   1954   *The Rise and Fall of Maya Civilization.* Norman: University of Oklahoma Press.

TOZZER, A. M.
   1957   *Chichen Itza and its Cenote of Sacrifice: a Comparative Study of Contemporaneous Maya and Toltec.* Cambridge: Memoirs of the Peabody Museum, Harvard University, nos. 11-12.

WILLEY, GORDON R.
   1956   The Structure of Ancient Maya Society: Evidence from the Southern Lowlands. *American Anthropologist* 58:777-782.

WILLEY, G. R., W. R. BULLARD, J. GLASS, AND J. C. GIFFORD
   MS   *Prehistoric Maya Settlements in the Belize Valley.* Cambridge: Papers of the Peabody Museum, Harvard University (in press).

WILLEY, G. R., AND A. L. SMITH
   1963   New Discoveries at Altar de Sacrificios, Guatemala. *Archaeology* 16:83-89.

BRANDEIS UNIVERSITY
WALTHAM, MASSACHUSETTS

SYSTEMS OF HIEROGLYPHIC WRITING IN MIDDLE AMERICA AND METHODS OF DECIPHERING THEM

J. Eric S. Thompson

RECENT disagreement on the nature of Maya hieroglyphic writing calls for a reappraisal of the historical sources, and an examination of alternative methods of decipherment. Unfortunately, no one has both a thorough grasp of the subject and an unbiased attitude.

Landa's Alphabet

Diego de Landa, bishop of Yucatán and the author of that bible of Maya students, *Relación de las cosas de Yucatán* (Tozzer 1941), written nearly 400 years ago, has stirred up much discord. He fought a series of heavy and acrimonious engagements with his fellow countrymen, lay and clerical; he caused great unrest and bitter feeling among the Maya; and from the grave he has inspired much controversial writing since the rediscovery and publication, 98 years ago, of his *Relación* with its famous — some might say infamous — Maya alphabet. This so-called alphabet (Fig. 1 d) republished in Whorf (1933), in Tozzer (1941) and elsewhere, consists of 27 signs corresponding to the Spanish names of such letters of the alphabet as represent sounds present also in Maya, for it is abundantly clear (Thompson 1953) that Landa pronounced the letters name by name. On the subject of writing and Maya characters he has this to say:

> This people also made use of certain characters or letters with which they wrote in their books their antiquities and sciences, and with these figures and some signs in their figures they understood their things and taught them and made them understood. . . .
>
> Of their letters I will put down here an A.B.C.; their clumsiness does not permit more, for they use a character for all the aspirations [*aspiraciones*], and then they join it to part of another, and thus they come to be *ad infinitum*, as one can see in the following example. Le means "noose" and "to trap game with a snare"; to write le with their characters, after we had made them understand that they are two letters [italics of J. E. S. T.], they used to write it with three, putting for the aspiration of the l [called *ele* and pronounced *aylay* in Spanish] the vowel e, which it has before it, and in this they do not err,

although they may use *e* if they wish, as a curiosity [*por curiosidad*]. Then, at the end they stick to it the joined part. Example: [Fig. 1 *a*].

Ha means water. As h [called *hache* and pronounced *achay*] has an *a* in front of it, they put it down with *a* at the beginning and at the end thus: [Fig. 1 *b*].

They also write by parts, but I would not put down either the one way or the other save only to give a complete account of the affairs of this people: *Ma in kati* means "I do not wish," and they write it by parts in this way [Fig. 1 *c*]. There follows their A.B.C. [Fig. 1 *d*].

This language lacks the letters which are not given here, and it has others added from ours for other things of which it has need, and nowadays they do not use these characters for anything, especially the young people who have learned ours. (Translated from Spanish by J.E.S.T.)

Valentini (1880) quickly established that Landa's informant had drawn for the alphabet signs or glyphs with Maya names corresponding with reasonable closeness to the sounds of the Spanish letters. For *a* one glyph is the head of a turtle, *ac* in Yucatec; for *b* (Spanish *be*) it is a footprint, symbol throughout Middle America for road or journey (*be* in Maya). For *c* (pronounced *say*) the informant drew the month sign Zec (pronounced *sayc*). Unfortunately, a distressingly large number of Spanish letters end in *e*. One of two signs for *l* (*ele*) seems to be a leaf (*le*); for *n* (*ene*) it is probably the tail (*ne*) of a monkey. The head of the god Xipe seems to stand for *p'*, and a vomiting (*xe*) man seems to be the action corresponding to *x*. Some signs are obvious; others are indistinct or escape interpretation.

Several deductions can be made:

1. Correct symbols for road, turtle, the month Zec, the locative *ti*, and the *u* bracket make it certain that Landa's informant was acquainted with the glyphs.

2. Some of the signs the informant drew could not have been in general use for a syllabic or alphabetic writing. For instance, footprints are fairly common in pictures of travel and perhaps have other meanings, but only twice in the whole range of Maya writing does a foot-

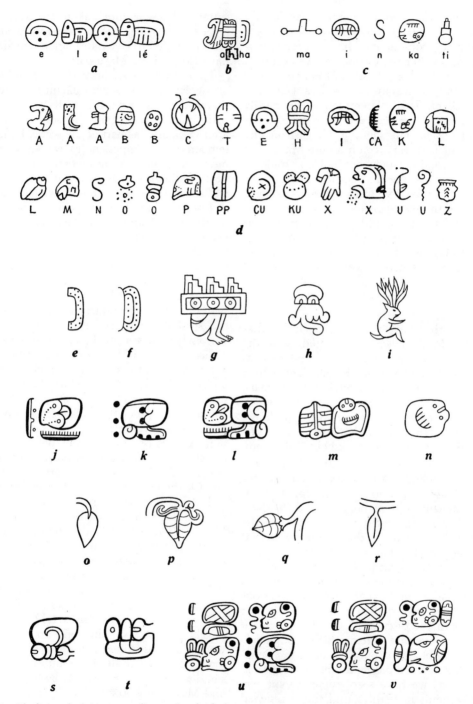

FIG. 1. Glyphs. *a, le,* snare, according to Landa; *b, ha,* water, according to Landa; *c, ma in kati,* I do not wish, according to Landa; *d,* Landa's alphabet; *e, f,* affixes denoting water (*ha*) Chichén Itzá and Palenque (compare with sign for *ha* in *b*); *g,* glyph for Tenantzinco, Codex Mendoza; *h,* glyph for Mixtlan, Codex Mendoza; *i,* glyph for Viceroy Antonio Mendoza, Codex of 1576; *j, k,* augural glyphs for evil (*kas*) and very good tidings according to Thompson; *l, kas* and good tidings glyphs combined; *m,* glyph for dog; *n,* Beyer's gouged eye, sacrificial glyph, Chichén Itzá (note differences from Landa's *l,* in *d*); *o–r,* representations of leaves, Madrid 96 *a,* and Chichén Itzá; *s,* Knorozov's *mut,* Dresden 17 *b; t,* same reversed, with same picture, Madrid 94 *c; u, v,* sentences on Dresden 19 *b.*

print appear as a glyphic element, yet *be* is a component of many Maya words and *b* is a very common consonant. The head for *p*, perhaps, *pek*, dog, for the distinctive eye occurs in one picture of a dog (Dresden 21 *b*), appears as a glyph only twice in the codices (Zimmermann's Glyph 716). Therefore, it can hardly have been in everyday use to represent the sounds *pe* or *p*. The sound *x* (English *sh*, the Arabic *shin*) is very common in Maya, but glyphs of vomiting men are not. Turning to vowels, we may note that both elements given the sound value *o*, two of the three signs for *a*, and one of the two signs for *u* never appear as main signs, as one would expect if there was a system of writing such as Landa describes, for most Maya words are monosyllabic, and the combination consonant-vowel-consonant is commonest. Moreover, the supposed glyphic equivalents of vowels with the exception of the *u* signs are also quite rare.

3. From the above we have concluded that Landa's informant was acquainted with the hieroglyphs, but gave for some common consonants of the alphabet glyphic elements which very seldom appear in surviving Maya texts, and for vowels he supplied elements which are for the most part rare and, in addition, affixes rather than main elements such as one would expect were there an alphabetical system.

We can now make one of three deductions: *a*, the informant did not supply material for reading Maya inscriptions by an alphabetic or syllabic system because none existed; *b*, there was such a system but it was not used in the surviving Maya texts; *c*, the informant wished to deceive Landa. That Landa's system per se cannot be used to read the glyphs is too well known to need comment (I omit the question of modifications and expansions which various authors have suggested in recent years as not pertinent to the discussion). If the informant was giving data on a system which has not survived, the alphabet is purely academic. Deliberate deception is a possibility, but not a probability, for as we have seen, some glyphic elements certainly have the sound values assigned them. We must accept deduction *a*, the informant did not supply an alphabetic or syllabic system because none existed. Landa's informant was probably Juan (Nachi) Cocom, who, he tells us, was very intimate with him and gave him much information on the old ways. This Cocom, a former *halach uinic* (head chief),

certainly knew as much about the Maya hieroglyphs as anyone, and presumably would not have hesitated to give information which would have glorified the Maya past.

Those two words Landa gives, *le* and *ha*, tell us a great deal. It is not difficult to picture the thatch and white-washed walls of *cal y canto* with lizards basking in the sun of the early afternoon, and, as part of the scene, Landa, hot tempered and impatient as we know him to have been, and Cocom mentally digging in his heels. Landa is ploughing through the alphabet, and trying to make Cocom understand what he is driving at. He tries to get from Juan a glyph for the letter *l*, and repeats *"e-le, ele"* — remember that he writes that the Indians had to be told that *l* has two syllables or letters. Cocom finally comes up with *elel*, to burn, and gives Landa the sign of the three hearthstones, symbol for fire in the Maya area from time immemorial. Landa misunderstands, and demands the symbol for *le*, noose or snare, for which Cocom supplies a glyph, very common in the codices (about 100 occurrences). Once it appears over what may be the *elel* element above a picture (Codex Madrid 91 *a*) of a bird caught in a snare. Cyrus Thomas (1893) and Knorozov consider this proof that this element does have the phonetic value *le*, but the same combination appears on the adjacent page 92 *a* above a picture of a deer caught, not in a snare (*le*), but in a deadfall (*petz'*). There is no noose at all. Of the approximately 99 other occurrences of Landa's *le* element, not one seems to belong in the fold with the one occupant pictured on Madrid 91 *a*. On the other hand the *elel* element appears several times above pictures of snares. Landa's *le* may well be both a snare and a delusion, but it cannot also be a deadfall.

To return to our early afternoon in 16th century Yucatán, Landa draws the glyph (Fig. 1 *a*) which now reads *elel-le-elel-le*, a most impossible Maya combination, and which he would have us believe is the Maya way of writing *le*. It is obviously the result of a misunderstanding perhaps brought on by loss of temper and Maya stubborness.

Practically the same thing happened with the attempt to write *ha* water. Landa clearly said *h-a, ha*, but as he pronounced *h* Spanish fashion as *achay* probably with a slight aspirate, he got the head of a turtle, *ac*, a tied-up length of cloth, pretty obviously standing for *hach'*, a term for tying up trousers or skirts with a sash or belt, and for *ha* a badly drawn water symbol as can be seen by comparing it with water symbols at Chichén Itzá and at Classic sites (Fig. 1 *e, f*). Knorozov misidentifies this sign with the distinctive lunar postfix, assigning the latter the phonic value *ha* or, more frequently, *ah*.

Poor Cocom, quite at sea, had produced elements corresponding to *ac, hach'* and *ha* to represent *ha*, water; Landa, equally uncomprehending, had drawn them in his notebook. Cocom probably took the *hach'* sign, like *be* and *le*, leaf, from nontextual sources.

Nevertheless, there certainly is a strong phonetic element in Maya writing, but it is, I believe, very largely a matter of play on homonyms, in other words rebus writing (Thompson 1950: 46-7, 269-70, 289-91; 1958). However, that is a very different matter from an alphabetic or syllabic writing, although with time it might have developed along those lines.

Nahuatl and Hispano-Nahuatl Writing

We turn now to Nahuatl hieroglyphs in the knowledge that Maya culture did not flower alone, particularly in the centuries immediately before the Spanish conquest when deities, plants, elements of social organization and warfare (Thompson 1943: 23-4), and trade goods were increasingly interchanged. With such interchange a writing system approaching alphabetic or syllabic would surely have passed from one area to the other, and, even had it been rejected by the priesthood, it would have been accepted by the merchant guilds and the collectors of tribute. Part of what follows has been published by Valentini (1880), Leon (1900), and Tozzer (1911) but it is worth restating with new deductions.

There is no alphabetic or true syllabic writing in preconquest Mexican codices; this would easily be spotted had it existed because the glyphs are mainly of identifiable places and persons. There is a certain use of rebus writing. Codex Mendoza, an immediate post-Columbian copy in part of the Aztec tribute list, has pictorial glyphs and a few cases of rebus writing. For example, Tenantzinco, place of the little wall, is drawn as a parapet, *tenamitl*, and under it, the lower half of a human body, *tzintli*, to represent the homonym *tzin*, small. The locative *co* is omitted (Fig. 1 *g*). The postfix *tlan*, near, is commonly drawn as two teeth, *tlantli*. Mixtlan, near the clouds, is painted as a cloud, *mixtli*, below two teeth (Fig. 1 *h*). Note that to our European way of thinking the spoken syllables reverse the arrangement of the drawing; we would read it downwards as Tlanmixtli. Under Spanish influence Nahuatl writing showed a great increase in rebus writing, but it also developed in directions of which there are no indications in the pre-Columbian documents.

The present copy of Codex Xolotl, written a decade or two after Landa prepared (about A.D. 1560) his alphabet, well illustrates these processes. The Nahuatl authority Charles Dibble (1940, 1951) has made outstanding contributions to the problems of historical codices by his catalog and discussion of the glyphs in that codex and by his scholarly commentary on the whole codex. He notes (1940: 110-2):

This is the only [nahuatl] codex in which there is an attempt to express a complete thought (phrase) with a series of hieroglyphs. This tendency, to the best of the author's knowledge, does not appear in codices made before the conquest. Codex Xolotl was written toward the close of the century of the conquest and Spanish influence is easily distinguished in the manner of representing objects (sun, moon, stars, flag, trees). This inclines the author to think that the combination of hieroglyphs to express a complete thought is an example of stimulus diffusion. (Translated from Spanish by J. E. S. T.)

Here the various glyphs which form the phrase are in line, just as in Landa's Maya sentence, but they are still pictographic, ideographic, or rebus writing; there is no attempt at anything approaching an alphabet. This same transition is well illustrated in the post-conquest Codex of 1576, which in part derives from the preconquest Codex Boturini, but was written early in the 17th century. Long (1935) made the important points that the former contains far more examples of rebus writing than the latter and that it has the year glyphs, not placed as in Codex Boturini zigzag and often to be read from the bottom upwards, but arranged in blocks to be read from left to right, line by line, in European fashion. One might in passing note a charming example of rebus writing in this codex: the glyph of the great Viceroy of Mexico, Antonio de Mendoza, is a maguey plant, *metl*, over a rabbit (*tochtli*), there being no *d* in nahuatl (Fig. 1 *i*).

A word should be said about Testerian, a form of writing, largely pictorial, used until the 19th century for teaching Christian doctrine, and named after Jacobo de Testera, a Franciscan who reached Mexico in 1529 and is credited with its invention (Leon 1900). Seler (1904:

221-8) illustrates and deciphers one text; Tozzer (1911) illustrates another and gives full citations. Pictures, largely European in design and conception, served to teach the creed, catechism and so on. God Almighty is shown with European orb and scepter, or as a hand, a medieval convention for God the Father. The entrance to hell is the open mouth of a monster as in medieval "dooms," but closely resembling the Aztec cave symbol, the open jaws of the earth monster, a remarkable example of convergence. Ascent and descent are shown by a European ladder. Nevertheless, there are some native elements. The Aztec glyph for heart *yollotl*, stands for heart, and placed in the jaws of hell it may also stand for interior (compare Tepeyollotl, the heart or interior of the mountain).

In Codex Mexicanus 23-24 (Mengin 1952) mixed Testerian and rebus writing occur in an almanac for the year 1570. A fish stands for vigil, a candle over a mummy bundle (!) is the glyph for All Souls Day, a hand and the wounded side of Christ is the glyph for St. Thomas, and a grill by itself represents St. Lawrence, whereas in Europe one would expect the figure of the saint holding the grill. The concept is European, but the design (the mummy bundle, for example) is purely native, as are the rebus elements discussed below.

The friars soon put the Testerian system to general use, painting the pictorial stories on large charts for the instruction of out-door classes, and on folded sheets for individual study. At the same time they adapted the old Aztec hieroglyphic writing to their own needs for the instruction of the new converts, transforming it into a purely rebus system with a less restrictive choice of near homophones. This method had presumably been evolved before 1547, for it is described by Las Casas (1909, ch. 235) who left Mexico in 1547. In any case it was in use before 1555, the year in which Las Casas is generally thought to have completed his *Apologética historia*. Following a short note on pre-Columbian codices which he says he had seen, he writes:

> It happens at times that some Indians forget some words or details of what is preached to them of the Christian doctrine, and as they do not know how to read our writing, they write all the doctrine with their figures and characters, putting down the figure which corresponds in voice and sound to our word. Thus, when we would say *amen*, they paint one like gushing water and then a maguey which in their language resembles *amen* because they call it *ametl*, and so for all the rest. I have seen a great part of the Christian doctrine written in their figures and images, and they read it by means of these as I read a letter by our writing. This is an ingenious artifice by no means unworthy of admiration. (Translated from Spanish by J. E. S. T.)

Las Casas is slightly in error for amen is two syllables. Gushing water corresponds to *atl* (*a* in compounds); maguey is *metl*. In crediting this invention to the Indians, he gives, as always, the benefit of the doubt to the Indian when praise is due. Probably the credit should be shared by Indian and Spaniard, for the friars without much doubt built on Indian foundations.

This form of rebus writing — for example, *pater noster* was written as a flag (*pantli*), a stone (*tetl*, for there is no *r* in nahuatl), a prickly pear (*nochtli*) and again a stone (*tetl*) — is arranged, European fashion, in straight lines like the phrases in Codex Xolotl and in Landa's illustrative material.

Acculturation produced a remarkable burgeoning of hispano-nahuatl writing. Codex Sierra (composed 1550-64), for instance, has a mixture of pre-Columbian glyphs, Testerian writing, and new adaptations (Leon 1933). Year bearers — 7 Tecpatl, 8 Calli, and so forth — are pre-Columbian, but the glyph for Christmas, an open-sided shed or stable straight from Botticelli, is Testerian. The use of the cursive A year symbol with numerical dot to indicate a *period* of one year and the formation of a sign for 10 by slicing in half the flag (nahuatl symbol for 20) and the object over which it flies are mental advances the pre-Columbians never made. A charming example of acculturation in another document is a hand holding a large iron key as the name glyph of Juan Tlatlin, for *tlatlati* means he who hides, shuts up or guards a thing (Seler 1904: 217). In Codex Mexicanus 23-24 (Mengin 1952), alongside Testerian writing, is the head of a bird (*tototl*) below what seems to be a plant (*centzontli*) of maize as the glyph for All Saints Day; *toto centz* is not a bad rendering of *Todos Santos*. Perhaps because of language difficulties this shift of vowel from *e* to *o* marks a very rare deviation from pre-Columbian practice, but in compensation for that laxity the enclosing consonants of the syllable are unchanged. Note the inversion, as in the glyph for Mixtlan, the *santos* being above the *todos* glyph.

The Valades alphabet (Brinton 1886) need not detain us. It was a stillborn child of pure

European parentage, having had no influence on hispanic-American systems. The whole point of the friars' use of rebus and Testerian writing was that an alphabetic writing was something beyond native ken.

In summary: rebus writing, relatively rare in pre-Spanish documents, proliferated when it was taken over and expanded by the friars to spread Christianity. A glyph came then to represent, not a complete syllable, as was the pre-Columbian ideal, but only the opening consonant and vowel (for example, *metl* standing for *men*, *nochtli* for *nos*), but — and this is an extremely important point — even with this relaxation of rules, the maguey (*metl*) glyph, for example, could not stand for the letter *m* alone or the sounds *ma*, *mi*, *mo* or *mu*; it could stand only for *me* plus any final consonant. Very rarely, the vowel could shift, but then the enclosing consonants were inviolate.

Testerian writing, which had its counterparts in pre-Columbian picture writing (for example, shield and spear and burning temple as symbols of war and of conquest) was widely used by the friars. It was accepted by educated Indians and appears side by side with regular nahuatl glyphs and hispano-nahuatl innovations. Of the last several examples have been noted. Old symbols are given extended meanings or undergo modification; glyphic elements are written European style in straight lines; and in Codex Xolotl glyphs express regular phrases.

Hispano-Maya Writing

Landa, unfortunately, is our only source for postcontact Maya writing. Other examples must have existed for Ciudad Real, writing some 20 years after Landa, says that some friars learned to read and even write the Maya glyphs. Assuredly, they were not writing the usual calendar and ritual of the codices, but had evolved a *pater noster* type of writing for indoctrination.

The same tendencies we have noted in hispano-nahuatl are discernible in Landa's hispano-Maya. The manipulations, so far as we can follow them in his alphabet — *aac* (turtle) for *a*; *zec* (month sign) for *ce*; *ne* (tail) for *ene* and so forth — conform to what was happening at the same time in central Mexico. Glyphs are made rebus fashion to represent the sound, but an opening vowel or, as in hispano-nahuatl, the final consonant of a syllable could be ignored. There is no evidence that the rules of this writing, whether invented by native priest or Spanish friar, allowed *be* (road), for example, to stand for *ba*, *bi*, *bo*, or *bu*, or for sounds beginning with *p*. Signs almost unknown in pre-Columbian texts are promoted to "alphabetic" rank, surely a very strong argument for its non-Maya origin.

The hispano-nahuatl arrangement of glyphs in straight lines occurs in Landa's single supposedly Maya phrase. The five glyphic elements corresponding to the Maya *ma in kati*, I do not wish, are not clustered, Maya style, as affixes around one or two main elements, but are in a straight line, a presentation as Spanish as Don Quijote or the Guadalquivir (Fig. 1 c). No Maya could possibly have written them that way; the *ma* and *ti* would have been affixes, the first above or to the left of the main sign, the last below or to the right, but touching the main sign and with changed axis.

We can also detect accultural innovations. Elements are attached to many of the month signs which Landa draws. What these represent is not clear — that before Cumku looks rather like the fire drill glyph — but in Maya usage month signs are always completely isolated except for their numerical affixes. Elements before a Maya month sign are as out of place as a designation in the British peerage before the name of a president of the United States.

Landa's Alphabet as a Rosetta Stone

Landa's *Relación* was published in 1864. In short time several writers had seized the alphabetic key and with it read the hieroglyphs, each to his own, but to no one else's satisfaction. Interpreters were handicapped by failing to realize that the Maya sound corresponded to the name of the letter, not to the letter itself. For instance, *c* could not stand for *c* hard but only for the sound *say* (Thompson 1953). Because of the extreme rarity in Maya texts of several of Landa's alphabetic signs, each interpreter was impelled to supplement Landa's Holy Writ. These numerous attempts to make silk purses out of Landa's sow's ear ended in disaster; the extravagances of the decipherers, growing with each failure, shrouded in clouds of fantasy the three or four reasonable decipherments. Both alphabet and phonetic system were thoroughly discredited. No one, then or since, has taken seriously Landa's queerly constructed glyphs for *le* and *ha*; each accepts his alphabet, but rejects his demonstration of how it is used!

Fifty years later, Benjamin Whorf (1933, 1942), declaring that only a trained linguist could tackle the glyphs, retrieved Landa's alphabet from the attic, and added to it. The Maya, he claimed, would have spelled *cab* with glyphic elements representing *c-a-b* or *ca-b*. The glyphic element *ca* could stand for *ca* or for *c*; it could not, he maintained, be used for *cu, co, ce*, or *ci*. His attempt to read the codices also bogged down in failure. His second (posthumous) paper revealed no noticeable progress in the eight intervening years (Thompson 1950: 311-3), whereas, if a system is alphabetic or syllabic, one must progress with gathering momentum after the first decipherments have been made. Whorf's ideas found no acceptance, and have been forgotten.

Recently J. V. Knorozov (1952, 1953, 1955, 1958a, 1958b) claims to have solved the problem with what he terms a Marxist-Leninist approach, basing his work on Landa's alphabet.

The Knorozov Approach

Knorozov bases his work on the Landa alphabet but he, too, treats it eclectically. Landa carefully distinguished between letters with and without glottal stop, carefully giving glyphs for *p* and *p'* and for the velar and palatal *ka* and *ca* and *ku* and *cu* in accordance with Maya practice; Knorozov discriminates or not as the fancy takes him. He pays no attention to the inescapable evidence that Landa was naming, not pronouncing, the letters of the Spanish alphabet, and so reads the Spanish *c* (pronounced *say*) as a hard *c* and even as a *k* (velar) in *kek*. Landa's *l* (*ele*) is identified as a glyph to which the sound value *lu* is given. Like others, Knorozov ignores the examples of word formation which Landa gives.

Basically, the system is that one constructs a monosyllabic word (to simplify matters I shall discuss only the more numerous consonant-vowel-consonant words) by taking a glyphic element which corresponds in sound to the opening c + v and adding to it a second glyphic element the first letter of which corresponds to the last consonant of the word to be formed. Thus, one would write *cab* as *cat* for *ca* and *bat* for the final *b*, choosing for the final consonant a glyph with the same middle vowel. This is what Knorozov terms synharmonic construction, but there are so many exceptions to it (for example, *mu-ti* read as *mut*, *mu-ca* as *muc*) that it can be ignored.

There are also many exceptions which Knorozov makes to his own rule that the first glyphic element rigidly adhere to the c + v of the sound value. Thus, Landa's *ma* sign is read as *mo* in *mok* and as *na* to make *napahan*; the *yax* affix is read not only as *yax* but as *hal* in *itzhal* and as *hol* in *cahol*; Knorozov's *nal* becomes *mal* in *oxpocmal* and *mol* in *molhal*; his *om* is *om* in *olom*, *an* in *napahan*, and *hun* in *hunabah* (although the Motul dictionary lists *hun* with intensified *h*); *chac* (red) can also be read *ta* as in *takan* (but *chac* does not shift to *ta-* in any Maya dialect); the hand glyph is both the God Chac and *chuc*; the affix read *pidz'* becomes *p'iz* in *et p'izan* (a remarkable shift) and *pedz'* in *pedz'kin*; *kin* becomes *cun* in *yaxcunah* and so on. Clearly, one has much freedom in the matter of the vowel. (Note that in two or three cases Knorozov gives the impression that these variations in spelling are Maya, for example, that *pidz'kin* is a Maya variation of *pedz'kin*. Such is not the case; they originate with Knorozov.)

A doubled element can be read as a single, as in the reading *takan* where two *kan* signs are present, or can be repeated as in *cu-cu* to give *cuc* or *ce-ce* to form *kek*. Phonetic elements can be passed over, as with the *n* element after the name glyph Chac or an affix may be added to reinforce the reading, as the *na* element added to the *tun* sign to indicate the *tun* ends in *n* — *tun-na* equals *tun*.

The order of reading in a system of this nature is obviously of the highest importance, but here, again, there is no hard and fast rule. Normally, the order is left to right and top to bottom, and if there are two postfixes the one below is read before the one to the right. In the case of the glyphic compound read *cutz*, a reversal of order produces a reversal of sound, and the glyph is read *tzuc* (Knorozov 1958: 288). Elsewhere (1958b: 469-70) he tells us that the arrangement may conform to esthetic considerations. The glyph *mu* above *ti* is read *mut*, but the order is not infrequently reversed, and one would suppose it should be read *ti-mu*, *tim*, but this supposition is incorrect; this is to be read *mut* also. If that reversal of order is of no consequence, if one can read it either way and shift an occasional vowel, one is obviously playing the game of decipherment with deuces wild. This brief outline oversimplifies Knorozov's ideas, and in fairness to him readers should read his papers. As Knorozov (1958a: 286) claims to have deciphered the glyphs after a century of others' failure, his achievement merits discussion. I propose: *a*, to review his use of source materials; *b*, to criticize his technique of decipherment; *c*, specifically to compare decipherments of two glyphs as read by him and by me, both being vital to my approach and important to his, and to dwell briefly on a third glyph in the same category; *d*, to discuss two readings equally vital to the Knorozov approach; *e*, to analyze his translation of a single sentence. First, I would urge careful study of the views expressed by Barthel (1958).

Source Materials

Knorozov depends for Maya on the excellent Motul dictionary and the quite unreliable Brasseur de Bourbourg vocabulary, of which Brinton (1882: 75) wrote: "I can say little in its praise. ... it contains about ten thousand words, but many of these are drawn from doubtful sources and are incorrectly given." Among words which Knorozov matches with glyphs and, following de Bourbourg, assigns quite incorrect meanings, are: *bilah, cech, im, in* (in *coch in*) *kahol, moc,* and *tz'anacul.*

Furthermore, Knorozov invents meanings for Maya words. He reads a glyph *cumchabah* (the terminal *ah* is the lunar postfix he wrongly identifies as Landa's *ha* reversed to sound *ah*). This, he tells us, is the same as the modern *cumcabtah*, to seat, citing the Motul dictionary. It is followed by a common maize compound, and he reads the pair as "sows the maize" (Knorozov 1955: 87, No. 141; 94, No. 13). For *cumcabtah* the Motul gives the translation, "set jars, vases, and such like things on the ground." *Cum* is a storage jar, *cab* is earth, *t* is the sign of the agent, and *ah* a verbal termination. Thus the incorporative word for setting a jar on the ground is rendered as sow in reference to maize! *Oczah* is the common Yucatec word for sow; to plant is *pak*.

Knorozov reads the last word in this same sentence (No. 13) as *ti ch'abtan*, which he translates "at a happy time." *Ti* is the locative; five entries in the Motul dictionary cover *ch'abtan*. Four translate it as continence, fasting, penance, abstention from the delights of the flesh, and observant of God's laws; a verb *ch'ab* has the same meanings. The fifth entry, a fortunate thing, has as its illustration a phrase translated "fortunate (*bien aventurado*) the souls of those who keep God's commandments." It is highly probable that the clerical author either made a slip here or used the word because those who had all the Christian virtues comprehended in the word *ch'abtan* necessarily had blissful souls. Knorozov drops no hint that elsewhere there is no association of the word with happiness, and that certainly there is no reason to suppose it could mean happy time.

Again, the meanings Knorozov assigns to *macaan, kinanhal* and *bat u cah* in Examples 12 and 14, on each side of the above citation, are spurious. Space restrictions prevent analysis of these and quite a few other demonstrable distortions of grammar or meanings. Impossible translations of *u muc, ox ocaan, icham,* and *zac ch'up* are discussed below.

Techniques of Decipherment

A number of compound glyphs, all the components of which have been assigned sonic values by Knorozov, do not appear among his decipherments, although they obviously ought to be excellent proof of the soundness of his method if they did make sense. I have tried my hand with some, using Knorozov's sound values, but the results were meaningless. Knorozov himself makes little attempt to see whether the value assigned a glyphic element fits in other contexts; when he does, the meanings may be so forced as to be useless. For example, the suffix in Figure 1 *k* is assigned the value *an* or *aan*. This element is postfixed to the month signs Pop, Zec, Kankin, Kayab, and once to Muan (this case apparently gave Knorozov the reading *an*). To account for these he reads Pop, which means mat and has a mat pattern in it, as *ch'acaan*, chopped down with ax, and this is referred to clearing milpa. Kayab is reread as *aakaan*, fresh or damp, and is said to be month of fresh or green grain. There is not a tittle of evidence for such translations. Moreover, Kayab, month of green corn, falls two months before Pop, when the land is cleared for planting!

This same *aan* element affixed to the *kin,* sun, sign with Ben Ich prefix is the well-known glyph of the sun god. Knozorov reads this as *kinaan*, he who rules. *Kin* can mean to rule; *aan* is a past participle termination. The Motul dictionary gives the meanings something half warmed (sun heated) and a thing which rules, reigns and is prevalent. Use of the word *cosa,* thing, and the example, the pest prevails, illustrating *kinancil,* to reign or rule, make it obvious that this is not personal rule, but is to prevail, one of three meanings given for *reinar* in the Royal Academy dictionary. To translate thing which prevails as he who reigns, is to play ducks and drakes with Spanish and Maya. Another incorrect use of this termination will appear in discussion of *ox ocaan*.

The Subject Matter of Codices Dresden and Madrid

A brief outline of what is known of the contents of the Maya codices is pertinent at this point. Early sources report that the Maya recorded in hieroglyphic books their histories and prophecies, which in the Maya thought pattern are interwoven; Codex Paris carries a series of katun prophecies. Planetary and eclipse tables in Codex Dresden surely have a divinatory function, and the many 260-day almanacs, divided into compartments, which occupy the greater part of the Dresden and Madrid codices have been recognized as divinatory from Förstemann (1895) to Zimmermann (1956). The *Relaciones de Yucatán* (Vol. 2: 210) recount that priests had books of figures indicating times to sow and harvest, to go hunting or to war. This same pattern of interwoven history and prophecy, of astronomy, and of 260-day almanacs listing lucky and unlucky days occurs also in the books of Chilam Balam, the lineal descendants of the hieroglyphic codices. The evidence is overwhelming that the 260-day almanacs in the two codices (they number about 300) give the luck of the day for such matters as hunting, planting, beekeeping and disease. Decipherments of associated glyphs must conform to that pattern.

A Pair of Contrasted Glyphs as Deciphered by Thompson and Knorozov

A few years ago I established, at least to my own satisfaction, that the glyphs in each compartment of most divinatory almanacs conformed to a general pattern (Thompson 1950: 263-73). Students had been working toward this solution for many years, and perhaps my task was to dot the *i*'s and cross the *t*'s. Generally, each compartment holds four glyphs: (1) an action or verbal glyph; (2) the name glyph of the god ruling the days in question, usually the subject; (3) sometimes an object; (4) the last glyph or pair of glyphs recording the augury resulting from the action or influence of the god — abundance, drought, good times, misery, and so forth. There is a clear pattern: certain augural glyphs occur with good gods; others, notably the death glyph and the one I named the *kaz* or evil glyph, occur with the death god and the evil God Q. These associations had been partly perceived by Gates (1931); they were worked out more fully by Zimmermann (1956) with his positive (good) and negative (bad) groupings. Barthel (1953: 45) certainly accepts the general thesis of divinatory almanacs, of action glyphs, and resulting augural good and bad glyphs. There is, therefore, much agreement on this side of the world on the divinatory nature of most almanacs in the codices. Any general interpretation of glyphs should conform to this divinatory pattern or reasons should be given for rejecting these categories which have gained wide acceptance.

The two chief augural glyphs are, according to my interpretation, the symbol for evil or misery and that for what I term very good tidings (Fig. 1 *j, k*).

Schellhas (1904: 13), 60 years ago, said our evil glyph, usually found with Gods A and Q, "relates to death and the death deity." Tozzer and Allen (1910: 338) note "it is the representative in many places of God A, the death god." Gates (1931: 127) saw it as "a determinative of the 'evil' force active." I (Thompson 1950: 268) identified it as the augural glyph of evil and misery, probably corresponding to the Yucatec *kaz*; Zimmermann (1956: 705) lists it in his negative (unfortunate) category. Here is close agreement.

My very good tidings glyph occurs nearly 100 times in the codices, nearly always with benevolent deities such as the rain gods, the maize god and God K; it is never with the death god's glyph or above his picture or with the glyph of death. Gates (1931: 58) noted its occurrence "over 90 times, in connections 'of good omen,'" and suggested the reading *oxtescun*, thrice greeted, a formal salutation in prayer. Zimmermann places it in his positive (favorable) category. I pointed out that the number three, *ox*, in front of the sign was almost certainly to be read as an intensifier, practically our English "very." Rejecting *och*, sustenance, for the Oc main sign, I opted for something like very good tidings (Thompson 1950: 268-9).

Here, then, we have two glyphs shown by their contexts to be exact opposites, bad and good, death and life, or something similar, which appear largely in divinatory almanacs, usually at the close of each section where the luck of the day is to be expected. Clearly, they correspond closely to the *utz* or *malob*, good, and *lob*, bad, or the rarer *kaz*, evil, written beside the days in the divinatory almanacs of the post-Columbian books of Chilam Balam.

Knorozov (1955: 94, 95) reads my evil glyph as *u muc*, this time, and my very good tidings glyph as *ox ocaan*, frequently, or habitually, but his Maya constructions leave much to be desired. *Muc* is a numerical classifier. Beltrán, compiler of a list of numerical classifiers, says that *muc* after a number signifies single, double (*el tanto y el duplo*); the Motul dictionary says times (*veces*) and lists *hun muc*, *ca muc*, once, twice. There is doubt as to whether *ca muc*, for example, signifies two occasions or double because of the ambiguity of Spanish *vez* and English *times*. According to Beltrán it means double. In any case, *u muc* cannot mean this time. *U* before a noun is the possessive, and conceding that *muc* could be a noun, the compound should be followed by the glyph of the possessor, but usually it has no glyph after it; it is the last glyph in the compartment. On the unverifiable assumption that *muc* is also a noun, it could only mean his time (occasion) or her time or, more probably, his multiple. This glyph is never joined to a number which would be its normal use were it, indeed, the numerical classifier *muc*. Knorozov follows early authorities in identifying this little head as that of an owl. As a variety of owl is called Muan he gives the main element the sound value *mu*. He has overlooked a long article by Beyer (1929) with over 100 drawings which showed conclusively that the little head is not that of an owl. Clearly, the reading this time is based on a misidentification of a glyph and misunderstandings of the nature of Maya numerical classifiers and of the *u* element.

The reading of my very good tidings glyph (Fig. 1 *k*) as *ox ocaan*, frequently or habitually, is based on the main element being the day sign Oc. Knorozov follows me in choosing for the numerical three (*ox*) its secondary use as an augmentative, much or very. He reads the postfix as *aan*. *Ocol* is to enter as to enter a house; *ocaan*, its past participle, is something or somebody which has entered, which is inside, and it is used figuratively — sin has entered my heart, or Chac (the rain god) has entered, that is, the rainy season has begun. *Ox ocaan* could perhaps mean much entered, but there is no conceivable reason to suppose it can mean frequently or habitually.

Accordingly, of Knorozov's two readings, *u muc* is meaningless, while *ox ocaan* can be rendered much entered, whatever precisely that may signify, but it cannot be given his interpretation of frequently or habitually. Even were those two readings linguistically acceptable, an explanation should be forthcoming as to why "this time" is confined to phrases involving malignant gods and "frequently" to those associated with beneficent deities. Nor is the combination of the two glyphs on Dresden 65 *a* (Fig. 1 *l*) explained, for this time and habitual sort ill together. In my case the explanation is logical. *Kaz* has a homonym meaning somewhat or partly. Partly good tidings (the *ox* augmentative is here absent) is a perfectly good Maya augury. Indeed, days are thus labeled in almanacs in the books of Chilam Balam.

To dissect in that way every decipherment by Knorozov would quickly exhaust the patience of editor and reader, but I submit that those two readings well exemplify the violence Knorozov does to the Maya language to obtain a meaning, that they reveal his disregard for all that is known of context and subject matter, and make evident his failure to test his translations against other occurrences of the glyph or its elements.

In passing, one may note that Knorozov assigns the sound *mu* also to the spiral element of the glyph which I read as *koch*, disease or divine punishment, and its homonym *koch*, carry on one's head or shoulders (Thompson 1958).[1] Knorozov interprets these signs also as *u muc*, this time; as *mut*, totem, when the locative *ti* is present above or below it. Here is a case where our interpretations meet head on.

Glyphs for Dog and Turkey

In all his papers Knorozov (for example 1958a: 288; 1958b) cites his readings of the long recog-

---

[1] There I overlooked remarks by Napoleon Cordy (1946) on this subject. We both apply *koch*, the only term that fits, to the actions shown in those passages. There the parallel ends. Cordy takes what is for me the locative *ti* as the sign of the vulture, *kuch*, and reads it *cuch* or *koch*; I read the spiral element as *koch*. Cordy was demonstrating that in Maya writing *o* and *u* and *c* and *k* can be interchanged, an approach I oppose; I see the whole as a pictorial and glyphic rebus for *koch*, disease, views Cordy did not touch on.

nized glyphs for dog and turkey as fundamental advances along the path of phonetic decipherment. Let us examine them.

The glyph for dog (Fig. 1 *m*) has two elements. To the first, widely thought to depict the thorax, Knorozov assigns the sonic value *tzu* (from *tzuulbac*, backbone); the second he identifies as Landa's *ele* glyph and reads it as *lu*. The whole forms *tzulu*, that is *tzul*, dog. There are four strong arguments against this reading: (1) *tzul* is a rare term for dog, (2) the element read as *lu* is almost certainly not Landa's *l* (*ele*), (3) the order of the two components is once reversed, (4) there is good evidence the compiler of the Dresden codex assigned the value *pek* to this sign.

The common Yucatec word for dog in general is *pek*; *tzul*, defined as a domestic dog, appears only in the Spanish-Maya part of Motul and in the San Francisco dictionaries, both believed to be rather late compilations. *Tzul* is not the ancient term for dog (*tsi* in most Maya languages), and does not occur in the books of Chilam Balam, where *pek* is invariably used for dog.

The second part of the dog glyph almost certainly is not Landa's *l*, but is Beyer's gouged eye, a common glyphic element (Fig. 1 *n*). Förstemann thought it a symbol of sacrifice, as does Barthel (1955: 17); Lizardi (1948) sees it as the glyph of human sacrifice. It always has the comb element or a cross-hatched area infixed in the middle. Landa's *l* (Fig. 1 *d*) lacks this characteristic infix, but has, instead, a line bisecting the drawing, rather like the medial vein of a leaf. Leaves are not common in Maya art, but I give a selection (Fig. 1 *o-r*). It is a reasonable supposition that Landa's Maya informant drew a leaf (*le*) for the Spanish *l* (*ele*). Whether it is a leaf or not, is not the gouged-eye glyph and should not be confused with it.

Knorozov (1958a: 288), as noted, finding the two elements of his *cutz*, turkey, glyph in reversed order, reads them as *tzuc*, heap or division, and on the next page this decipherment is cited as evidence for the correctness of his approach. On Dresden 39 *a* above a picture of a dog is a damaged but still legible example of the dog glyph, but in reversed order, the supposed *lu* is to the left and the supposed *tzu* to the right. Logically then Knorozov must read this as *lutz*, fish hook, and explain why a fish hook is the name glyph of a dog.

Apart from these arguments against the reading *tzul*, the Chilam Balam of Chumayel supplies excellent grounds for reading the sign as *pek*, the usual term for dog. In the prophecy for Katun 3 Ahau (Roys 1933: 154) we read: "The dog (*pek*) is its tidings. There are rains of little profit, rains from a rabbit sky, rains from a gourd-rattle sky, rains from a woodpecker sky, high rains, rains from a vulture sky." Rain from a rabbit sky is a known expression for drought; gourd-rattle Chacs, still alive in Maya folklore, make much thunder but little rain. Clearly, *pek* is a symbol of drought.

This is confirmed by the entries for Katun 1 Ahau, of which it is said "*pek* is its tidings; the vulture is its tidings." The prophecy continues with prophecies of drought, of pestilence, and of vultures entering the houses (a stock phrase for death sweeping the country). In the small picture of the katun there is a drawing of what assuredly is a dog. Roys (1933: 154) notes that a second meaning of *pek* is water tank or reservoir, and the tidings may have been the water tank because these had to be used in times of drought. *Pek*, dog, therefore stands for its homonym *pek*, water reservoir. On Dresden 39 *a* and 40 *b* this dog glyph appears above pictures of a dog with blazing torch in each paw (the blazing torch is a common symbol for drought and extreme heat). Both are in compartments of almanacs which clearly treat of farmers' weather, for in other compartments there are glyphs for drought and contrasting pictures of the rain god standing or sitting in the rain. One picture is of a vulture in the rain, a graphic parallel to the prophecy of rains from a vulture sky. The dog with his torches must be *pek*, the *pek* tidings of drought, probably rebus writing for the homonym *pek*, water tank, symbol of drought. Read as *tzul*, the drought association is completely lost.

On all four counts *tzul* is a most improbable decipherment. Moreover, if my thesis of disease divination is correct, the dog glyph is used rebus fashion for *pek*, a skin infection (Thompson 1958: 305); there is no *tzul* disease.

The second occurrence of this supposed *tzu* sign is with the Cauac glyph, Landa's *cu*. As this appears once above a picture of a turkey cock (Madrid 91 *a*) Knorozov follows Cyrus Thomas in reading it as *cutz*. The usual Yucatec term for the wild (ocellated) turkey cock is *ah tzo*, found in various Maya languages, or *ah tzo cutz*. *Cutz* and *ixch'ich'* or *ixch'ich' cutz* are names for the hen (*ch'ich'* is a generic term for bird). *Ulum,* now used for the domestic turkey, and *cahmal,* a sacrificial turkey, are other terms. Turkeys are mentioned nine times in the Chilam Balam of Chumayel; *ah tzo* and *ulum* four times each and *cutz* once. There *cutz* is paired with *ah tzo,* and the context (Roys 1933: 39) shows it to be female. The Maya, excellent observers, would hardly have drawn a male bird and labeled it with the glyph for the female.

This ribs glyph is distinctly one of the rarer Maya signs, whereas *tz* is a very common Maya sound. If the glyph does have that sound value, why is it so uncommon? It may be more significant that the only pictures with which it occurs are dog, turkey, and fish, all sacrificial offerings.

Analysis of a Sentence

To conclude this discussion, I shall analyze a sentence translated by Knorozov (1955: 45, No. 23) comprising four glyphs (Fig. 1 *u*) which he reads: (1) *hicham,* the married; (2) *ch'up,* woman; (3) *zac ch'up,* [is] a sterile woman (literally, white woman); (4) *ox ocaan,* frequently.

Glyph 4 is my very good tidings already discussed. Glyphs 2 and 3 have been recognized for the past 70 or 80 years as representing woman or goddess. I regard her as the moon goddess, Ixchel, the mother goddess. Her divinity is apparent in various scenes. For instance, on Dresden 22 *b,* seated at the north, she is one of the four-world directional deities. On Dresden 38 *a* she is in an allegory of the rain god making fecund the earth. Were she mortal the scene would be more Greek than Maya; a Jovian eye for mortal pulchritude is hardly in the Maya tradition. However, this is not a serious disagreement; Knorozov has merely taken the less likely choice between goddess and woman. *Ch'uplal* or *ch'up* is the common Yucatec term for woman in general.

When the *zac* sign, long identified as such, is affixed to the glyph, Knorozov reads it *zac ch'up,* sterile (literally white) woman. *Zac,* white, has a homonym *zac,* pseudo or artificial. I myself have read this affix as pseudo in the glyph *zac cimil,* severe epileptic attacks (pseudo death). *Zac* does not mean sterile. Knorozov seems to have derived that meaning in a wholly unwarrantable fashion from an entry in the Motul dictionary: "*zac yaom,* woman, mare or bitch who appears pregnant because of a large belly, but it isn't pregnancy." *Yaom* is pregnancy; *zac* converts it to false pregnancy. One can't divorce *zac* from *yaom* and read it as sterile when it is with the glyph for woman; *zac ch'up* can only mean a white woman or a pseudo woman, whatever that may be. The Yucatec word for sterile is *ixmaal,* she not child. For me, the glyph is that of the moon goddess, goddess of weaving, one of whose names was Zac Ixchel. *Zac* may refer to her weaving activities as it is the root of *zacal,* to weave.

Knorozov reads Glyph 1 as *hicham* (modern *icham*), married. Elsewhere he assigns the sound *hi* to the affix to left, *ch(a)* to the crossed band element, and *am, om, un, hun,* and *-m* to the suffix. The aspirate occasionally disappears after a consonant, but very, very rarely is dropped at the start of a word. I see no evidence that *hicham* is an early form of *icham;* Yucatec *icham* is not even related to the word for spouse in most Maya languages. Moreover, as Knorozov accepts Codex Dresden as Yucatec, it is a strange supposition that *i* is expressed by the *hi* sign when Landa's *i* was available.

Icham means not married, but husband; *atan* is Yucatec for wife, specifying the husband; *atanbil* is married woman in general. *Icham* can only be applied to a woman in roots carrying the idea of getting her man: *ichamben,* husband worthy, is a marriageable woman (*ben* as a suffix is worthy); *ichamancil,* to take a husband, is intransitive and cannot be converted into an adjectival form; *ah icham,* husband owner, is a term for married women, just as *ah atan,* wife owner, is a term for married men, but here *ah,* related to or owner of, is the key term (*ah* is a gender prefix only with certain categories of words), just as *ben* is in *ichamben* and *ancil* in *ichamancil.* Obviously, *icham,* husband, cannot mean married in reference to a woman, and the supposed glyph for *icham,* without additional qualifying affix, can no more stand for *ah icham* than in English, for example, the word husbandless can be read husband. Furthermore, in other sentences Knorozov reads exactly the same glyph as *icham,* husband. Unfortunately, much space is wasted correcting these many perversions of straight-forward meanings of words. They cannot be due to Knorozov's inability to understand the Spanish of the Motul dictionary, for he has translated Landa from Spanish into Russian.

Incidentally, Knorozov (1955: 77, No. 3) reads a glyph *ah achan* (*ah-a-cha-n*), and this is said to be an archaic form of *ah atan*, married man. I am flattered that elsewhere Knorozov has followed me in my theory that the shift was *t* to *ch*, not *ch* to *t*, as linguistic opinion has supposed, but he can't have it both ways. If *te* becomes *che* in modern Yucatec, *achan* can hardly have been ancestral to modern Yucatec *atan*.

To summarize: (1) the construction of *icham* with an aspirated *hi* affix is very unlikely; (2) *icham* means husband, not married; (3) even were it read *atanbil*, wife, it would not precede the word (and glyph) *ch'up*, woman, any more than we would say wife woman in English; (4) *zac ch'up* cannot be translated sterile woman, but only white woman or pseudo woman; (5) the final glyph, *ox ocaan*, cannot mean frequently, but might be rendered much entered; (6) accepting Knorozov's sound values, the best reading would be: husband of a specified person, woman, pseudo woman, much entered.

The next compartment is the same except that the death god replaces *ox ocaan* as the fourth glyph (Fig. 1 *v*). This must read in the Knorozov system: husband of a specified person, woman, pseudo woman, death god. Even conceding that glyphs and sounds are correctly matched, I am at a loss to comprehend the divinatory aspects of these decipherments.

Examples I have discussed are not weak chinks in Knorozov's armor; they are typical of all his work. I can duplicate or triplicate this whole section with completely different examples of his errors in grammar, in word meanings, and in glyph usage. Linguistic references have been confined to Yucatec because practically all the glyphs discussed above occur only in the codices, not in early texts.

Future Research

No fire-faced prophet brought me word which way behoved me go, as Housman puts it. I can claim neither to have deciphered the Maya glyphs nor to know of any system to replace the one I have attacked, for I suspect that Maya writing, like Topsy, just grew. Rebus writing surely is a most important factor and rebus pictures also. Clearly glyphic elements represent both words and syllables (often homonyms). There are ideographs, glyphs with roots in mythology, and bits and pieces of half a dozen other attempts to write.

Best hope of progress perhaps lies in matching affixes with sounds. This is not an easy matter for clearly the proposed sound must fit wherever the meaning is known of the main sign to which it is attached. The difficulties are best shown by an example.

The postfix on the right of the second glyph (goddess) in Figure 1 *v* is a common glyphic element. In the codices it is most frequently used: (1) postfixed to the head of the moon goddess, as just noted; it is not always present; (2) almost invariably postfixed to the hand which forms the glyph of God B; (3) usually attached to the head variant of the dog; (4) often beneath the *uinal* sign; (5) often below offerings of maize, meat, fish, and so forth. Note that in no case is it indispensable, and it is not used as a prefix in the codices. The problem is to find a value which will fit all five cases.

The best answer seems to be *bil* or *uil*; the two sounds are used because *uil* replaces Yucatec *bil* in some Maya languages in its chief employment, to form a past participle. *Bil*, added to some relationship terms, generalizes them, for *na* is mother; *nabil*, mother without specifying whose. *Nabil* or *Coolelbil*, mistress, fits the glyph of the moon goddess, who was regarded as mother of mankind and is thus addressed. *Kab* is hand and *kabil* is one who is a good sower or beekeeper. God B, whose glyph is the hand, appears sowing in several pictures, and without his rain the crops fail. *Kabil* would be a good name and glyph for him. Presumably the Maya did not object to writing *kabil* as *kabbil*. *Bil* is the Yucatecan term for the hairless dog; this affix might be added to show that the hairless dog was meant. *Uil* means food, and so reasonably the affix could appear below food offerings. It also means month, and so the affix could appear under the *uinal* sign to indicate its use as a month sign, for it is used elsewhere in contexts which call for another meaning.

The score is quite good, but I am not sure it is good enough. Unfortunately, one is left in doubt. *Tzil*, a term of reverence, and *zil*, offering, also fit after a fashion, but I hesitate to make *tz* and *z* interchangeable, for that is a slippery path to descend. We are left in doubt until more evidence is available. *Kat* for the cross bands (Knorozov's *cha*) and *tan* for Landa's *ma* are other possibilities, but in our present knowledge of Maya glyphs, they cannot be made to fit all appearances. Mythological associations might help, did we know them better. Meanwhile, prudence bids us not to smother research with unproved conjecture.

Man always welcomes simple explanations for difficult things and sets of rules for the unruly, but things are never quite what we suppose, and an orderly, logical solution is improbable when dealing with the unregimented Maya.

Summary

The pre-Columbian hieroglyphic system of the Aztec and related peoples made a quite limited use of homonyms, but had no phonetic writing. With Spanish stimulus, rebus writing expanded greatly and old rules were loosened. A glyph which formerly had represented a complete word or syllable now stood only for the opening vowel and consonant. Glyphs were written, European fashion, line-by-line, and to be read left to right. Glyphic affixes were similarly rearranged in line. Landa's alphabet and sample words conform to this hispano-nahuatl style. Alphabet signs are of the consonant and vowel type, and glyphic elements are arranged in a straight line in a thoroughly un-Maya arrangement. This was because Landa, supposing the Maya had evolved a similar system, tried to elicit it from his bewildered informant. The latter, completely at sea, produced the signs demanded, but some were so uncommon they could never have played the parts assigned them in a supposedly phonetic system.

The Landa alphabet has proved a poor crutch. Recently, in the face of the failure of all previous attempts to read the glyphs phonetically, Knorozov has again tried that approach. Results are not promising. Many Maya words Knorozov obtains for his readings do not have the meanings he assigns them. To cite two examples, *cumcabtah* which means to place a jar (*cum*) on the ground (*cab*) is rendered to sow maize; *ox ocaan,* which can only mean much entered, is translated habitually or very frequently. Even readings thus obtained bear no relation to the subject matter. In a key demonstration of his phonetic approach he reads the glyph for dog as *tzul*, a rare term, but there is much evidence it should be read *pek*, the common Yucatec word for dog.

A complete sentence read by Knorozov as "the married woman frequently is sterile" is analyzed. Accepting all his readings, his Maya translation can mean only "husband, woman, pseudo (or white) woman, much entered." In largely monosyllabic Maya it is easy to match sound to glyphic element if one ignores differences between glottalized and non-glottalized sounds, ignores aspirates, postulates without any evidence supposedly archaic forms (for example *mahal* claimed as archaic form of *nohol*) and permits vowel shifts; the difficulty is to make sense of the words thus obtained. It is distressing that there are so many impossible derivations; if a Maya word means one thing, it hardly advances one's cause to say it means something totally different. There is little attempt to test a sound value against all appearances of the glyph in question.

Knorozov believes Maya writing to be a mixture of ideographic and phonetic; his pairings of sound with glyphic element are numerous. He has passed the point at which, if his readings are correct, the rate of decipherment should have accelerated astonishingly, for, as with a code, each new phonetic reading makes solution of the remainder easier. That did not happen with previous essays in phonetic decipherment from Brasseur de Bourbourg to Benjamin Whorf; it has not happened with Knorozov whose conquest of the problem was announced seven years ago. In each case there is a starting gush of unproven decipherments, but they do not swell to a river. Instead they peter out in a bog. For a similar rejection by a glyphic specialist of Knorozov's claims, see Barthel (1958).

In conclusion, the most promising path to decipherment is noted and its difficulties underlined.

Barthel, T. S.

1952 Der Morgensternkult in den Darstellungen der Dresdener Mayahandschrift. *Ethnos*, Vol. 17, pp. 73-112. Stockholm.

1954 Maya Epigraphy: Some Remarks on the Affix 'al.' *Proceedings of the Thirtieth International Congress of Americanists* [Cambridge, 1952], pp. 45-9. Royal Anthropological Institute, London.

1955 Versuch über die Inschriften von Chich'en Itzá viejo. *Baessler-Archiv*, n.s., Vol. 3, pp. 5-33. Berlin.

1958 Die gegenwärtige Situation in der Erforschung der Mayaschrift. *Proceedings of the Thirty-second International Congress of Americanists* [Copenhagen, 1956], pp. 476-84. Munksgaard, Copenhagen.

Beyer, Hermann

1929 The Supposed Maya Hieroglyph of the Screech Owl. *American Anthropologist*, Vol. 31, No. 1, pp. 34-59. Menasha.

1937 Studies on the Inscriptions of Chichen Itza. *Carnegie Institution of Washington, Publication 483, Contributions to American Anthropology and History*, No. 21. Washington.

Brinton, D. G.

1882 *The Maya Chronicles*. Philadelphia.

1886 The Phonetic Elements in the Graphic Systems of the Mayas and Mexicans. *American Antiquarian and Oriental Journal*, Vol. 8, pp. 347-57. Chicago.

Cordy, N.

1946 Examples of Phonetic Construction in Maya Hieroglyphs. *American Antiquity*, Vol. 12, No. 2, pp. 108-17. Menasha.

Dibble, C. E.

1940 El antiguo sistema de escritura en México. *Revista Mexicana de Estudios Antropológicos*, Vol. 4, pp. 105-28. Mexico.

1951 Códice Xolotl. *Publicaciones del Instituto de Historia*, 1st series, No. 22. Mexico.

Förstemann, Ernst

1885 Das mittelamerikanische Tonalamatl. *Globus*, Vol. 67, pp. 283-5. Brunswick.

Gates, William

1931 An Outline Dictionary of Maya Glyphs. *Maya Society, Publication* 1. Baltimore.

Knorozov, Y. V.

1952 Drevnyaya Pis'menost' Tsentralnoy Ameriki [The Ancient Script of Central America]. *Sovietskaya Etnografiya 1952*, No. 3, pp. 100-18. Moscow.

1953 La antigua escritura de los pueblos de la América central. *Boletín de Información de la Embajada de la U. R. S. S.*, Año 10, No. 20. Mexico.

1955 La escritura de los antiguos mayas (ensayo de descifrado). In Russian and Spanish. *Institut Etnografii Akademii Nauk*, Moscow.

1958a The Problem of the Study of the Maya Hieroglyphic Writing. *American Antiquity*, Vol. 23, No. 3, pp. 284-91. Salt Lake City.

1958b New Data on the Maya Written Language. *Proceedings of the Thirty-second International Congress of Americanists* [Copenhagen, 1956], pp. 467-75. Munksgaard, Copenhagen.

de las Casas, Bartolomé

1909 *Apologética historia de las Indias*. Madrid.

León, Nicolás

1900 A Mazahua Catechism in Testera-Amerind Hieroglyphics. *American Anthropologist*, Vol. 2, No. 4, pp. 722-40. New York.

1933 *Códice Sierra. Traducción y explicación*. Museo Nacional de México. Mexico.

Lizardi Ramos, César

1948 Copán y el jeroglífico de los sacrificios humanos. *Honduras Maya*, Vol. 2, pp. 40-3. Tegucigalpa.

Long, R. C. E.

1935 Maya and Mexican Writing. *Maya Research*, Vol. 2, No. 1, pp. 24-32. New York.

Maya codices and vocabularies

See Roys 1933, Thompson 1950, or Tozzer 1941.

Mengin, Ernest

1952 Commentaire du Codex Mexicanus Nos. 23-24 de la Bibliothèque Nationale de Paris. *Journal de la Société des Américanistes*, n.s., Vol. 41, No. 2, pp. 387-498. Paris.

Relaciones de Yucatán

1898-1900 In *Colección de documentos inéditos relativos al descubrimiento, conquista y organización de las antiguas posesiones españolas de ultramar*, Vols. 11, 13. Madrid.

Roys, R. L.

1933 The Book of Chilam Balam of Chumayel. *Carnegie Institution of Washington, Publication* 438. Washington.

Schellhas, Paul

1904 Representations of Deities of the Maya Manuscripts. *Papers of the Peabody Museum, Harvard University*, Vol. 4, No. 1. Cambridge.

Seler, Eduard

1904 Alexander von Humboldt's Picture Manuscripts in the Royal Library at Berlin. *Bureau of American Ethnology, Bulletin* 28, pp. 123-229. Washington.

Thomas, Cyrus

1893 Are the Maya Hieroglyphs Phonetic? *American Anthropologist*, o.s., Vol. 6, No. 3, pp. 241-70. Washington.

THOMPSON, J. E. S.

1943 Pitfalls and Stimuli in the Interpretation of History Through Loan Words. *Middle American Research Institute, Tulane University, Publication 11, Philological and Documentary Studies,* Vol. 1, No. 2, pp. 17-26. New Orleans.

1950 Maya Hieroglyphic Writing: Introduction. *Carnegie Institution of Washington, Publication* 589. Washington.

1953 Review of Y. V. Knorozov—The Ancient Writing of the Peoples of Central America. *Yan,* No. 2, pp. 174-8. Mexico.

1958 Symbols, Glyphs, and Divinatory Almanacs for Diseases in the Maya Dresden and Madrid Codices. *American Antiquity,* Vol. 23, No. 3, pp. 297-308. Salt Lake City.

TOZZER, A. M.

1911 The Value of Ancient Mexican Manuscripts in the Study of the General Development of Writing. *Proceedings of the American Antiquarian Society,* n.s., Vol. 21, pp. 80-101. Worcester.

1941 Landa's Relación de las Cosas de Yucatan. A Translation. *Papers of the Peabody Museum, Harvard University,* Vol. 18. Cambridge.

TOZZER, A. M. AND G. M. ALLEN

1910 Animal Figures in the Maya Codices. *Papers of the Peabody Museum, Harvard University,* Vol. 4, No. 3. Cambridge.

VALENTINI, P. J. J.

1880 The Landa Alphabet; a Spanish Fabrication. *Proceedings of the American Antiquarian Society,* Vol. 75, pp. 59-91. Worcester.

WHORF, B. L.

1933 The Phonetic Value of Certain Characters in Maya Writing. *Papers of the Peabody Museum, Harvard University,* Vol. 13, No. 2. Cambridge.

1942 Decipherment of the Linguistic Portion of the Maya Hieroglyphs. *Smithsonian Institution, Report for 1941,* pp. 479-502. Washington.

ZIMMERMANN, GUNTER

1956 Die Hieroglyphen der Maya-Handschriften. *Universität Hamburg, Abhandlungen aus dem Gebeit der Auslandkunde,* Vol. 62. Hamburg.

HARVARD, ASHDON
Saffron Walden, England
February, 1958

THE TEOTIHUACAN MAPPING PROJECT

René Millon

Abstract

A detailed map of Teotihuacán is being prepared through the use of photogrammetry and ground survey. The city's maximum limits have been circumscribed, and it appears that they surround an area of more than 10 square miles. Part of this area was occupied only during the first phase of the occupation of Teotihuacán (Tzacualli) in the Pre-Classic period; Tzacualli phase Teotihuacán appears to have covered an area of approximately 3 square miles. The maximum area reached by the city during its later phases appears to be close to 9 square miles, but how much of this area was actually occupied during any one period of time remains to be determined. The central 4.5 square miles of the city seem to have been subject to extensive planning (grid pattern, streets, and blocks of uniform size). Teotihuacán appeared as a settlement of great size in the Pre-Classic period and grew to mammoth proportions during the Classic period. No population estimates are yet possible. The Ciudadela now appears to have occupied a central rather than a southerly position in the city. Several Early Classic period Maya pottery fragments were found near the city's eastern border in the immediate vicinity of Tlamimilolpa where similar fragments had previously been found by Linné.

A PROJECT TO MAP the ancient city of Teotihuacán in the Valley of Mexico is in progress. Low-altitude aerial photographs have been made and photogrammetric manuscript maps are being prepared for use in a detailed archaeological survey. Work on the project, which began in June, 1962, made possible delimitation of the maximum size and configuration of the city and also yielded other data of interest. An entirely new area of the earliest phase of occupation of Teotihuacán (dated shortly after the time of Christ) was found to the northwest (Figs. 1–3). This new zone covers an area of more than 1.5 square miles. It shows that Teotihuacán was a center of great size during the earliest phase of its occupation in the Pre-Classic period and that it provided a developmental base for the growth of the metropolis which followed. It also will be possible to trace changes in the size and composition of the city from its beginnings until its fall, thus providing a basis for a developmental study of urbanism at the site. Another result still only partially realized is an increased appreciation of the amount of planning exhibited in the remains in the central 4.5 square miles of the city. In view of the great area seemingly subjected to planning (with streets, blocks of uniform size, and uniform grid pattern), it seems likely that Xolalpan phase Teotihuacán was the site of one of the most extensive experiments in urban planning prior to modern times.

Objectives

The original plan was to map an area of 25 square kilometers. It was expected that this area would include all of the ancient city, and the latter, it was thought, would cover an area of 16–18 square kilometers and would not exceed 20 square kilometers. It was hoped that the map would not only include all the area formerly covered by the ancient city throughout its history, but also place it, to the extent possible, in the surrounding countryside. Work in the field in 1962 forced changes in these estimates.

Instead of a maximum area of 25 square kilometers, our surface reconnaissance to determine the city's maximum boundaries encompassed an area of 53 square kilometers (Fig. 1). The area which we actually walked over and examined in the reconnaissance was 27 square kilometers, in itself more than the originally planned 25, and leaving an additional 26 square kilometers in the center (Fig. 1). Our surface survey established that the *maximum* boundaries of Teotihuacán surround an area of 26–28 square kilometers or 10–11 square miles. Five square kilometers of this area were surveyed during the reconnaissance to determine the city's boundaries (Fig. 1). This major increase in the area found to have been occupied by the Teotihuacanos is further complicated by the fact that the ancient city's boundary is extremely tortured, its perimeter exceedingly irregular (Figs. 1, 2).

The map is being prepared at a scale of 1:2000, with contour intervals of 1 meter. A 500-meter grid is being used, which is oriented to the Street of the Dead rather than to north because so many of the city's buildings and streets are so oriented (Fig. 3). (The Street of the Dead appears to have an orientation of 15°30′ east of north [astronomic] rather than the frequently cited figure of 17° east of north.) The zero point on the grid is the center of the Street of the Dead near the southwest corner of the Ciudadela (Fig. 3). This is close to a

Reprinted from AMERICAN ANTIQUITY, Vol. 29, No. 3, 1964. pp. 345–352.

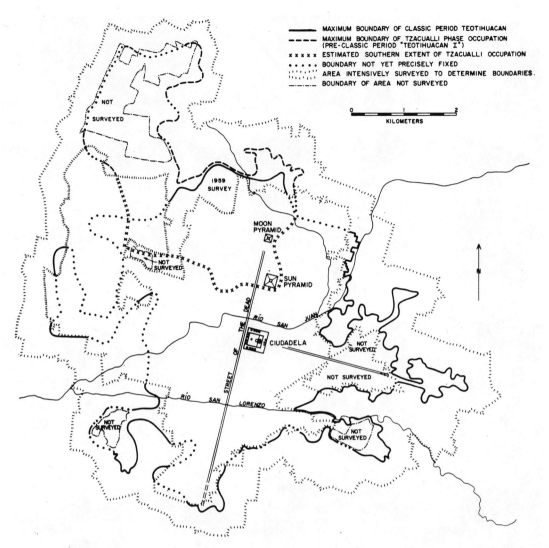

Fig. 1. The limits of Teotihuacán. Known boundaries shown for the Classic period city are maximal and do not necessarily indicate that the city covered all of this area at any one time. Almost certainly it did not.

central position for Classic period Teotihuacán. Selection of this spot as a zero point has several advantages, not the least of which is the fact that it provides a reference point of significance for current and future investigations, not only within the ancient city itself but also in the rest of the Teotihuacán valley. In our opinion the advantages of the system of reference adopted outweigh its disadvantages. Each structure in a given square is numbered, with the structure number preceding the coordinates designating the square in which it is located (examples are cited in captions of Figs. 3, 4).

After the detailed information from our intensive survey is placed on the manuscript maps, final drawings will be made, each covering 1 square kilometer, at a scale of 1:2000 and a contour interval of 1 meter. To include all of the city, approximately 45 such maps will be required, although many of the sectional sheets on the city's margins will bear mapped areas only on portions of them (Fig. 3). It had also been planned to prepare a single map of the entire city, at a scale of 1:5000, with contour intervals of 5 meters. This map would not show the detailed information recorded on the sectional maps, but it would provide the indispensable view of the city as a whole. It may be necessary now to change the scale of this map to 1:10,000.

Fig. 2. Aerial view of Teotihuacán and its limits as shown in Fig. 1. The town labeled "San Francisco" on this mosaic is actually San Martín de las Pirámides. Courtesy Cía. Mexicana Aerofoto, S. A.

The intent is to publish these maps, the main map and the sectional maps, together with selected aerial photographs, both vertical and oblique, and selected drawings of exposed structures previously unpublished. The publication will also include either references to, or reproductions of, previous maps and plans of buildings and room complexes at Teotihuacán.

Field Procedures

The first phase of field work on the project extended from June through December, 1962. Our objective was the definition of the city's perimeter so that we would know how large an area would have to be mapped in detail, both photogrammetrically and on the ground. It had

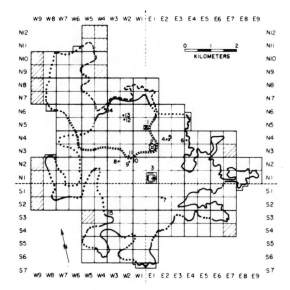

FIG. 3. The grid system for the Teotihuacán map. *1*, Pyramid of the Moon (Structure 1 N5E1); *2*, Pyramid of the Sun (Str. 1 N3E1); *3*, Ciudadela (Str. 1 N1E1); *4*, Tepantitla (Str. 1 N4E2); *5*, Xolalpan (Str. 2 N4E2); *6*, Tlamimilolpa; *7*, Teopancaxco; *8*, Atetelco; *9*, Tetitla; *10*, Zacuala (Palacio and Patios); *11*, Yayahuala; *12*, Oztoyahualco, Plaza 1; *13*, Casa de las Aguilas; *14*, Tzacualli temple platform and fronting terrace; *15*, buried Classic period structures on the edge of the irrigated plain (Fig. 2).

been our hope to complete this phase of the project during the summer. But it soon became clear that this would be impossible, not only because of the greatly increased area occupied by the city but also because of the extreme irregularity of its perimeter. It also became clear that our surface collections of pottery were providing extraordinary information (discussed below) and could not be curtailed.

Our problem was to find the boundaries of the city at their maximum extent in every direction. Since the only boundary of Teotihuacán known was the northwestern corner of the Classic period city, we used this as a point of departure. What we tried to do was record on our aerial photographs the outermost structural remains, without penetrating any more than necessary into the city. Ideally, we wanted to find an outer "ring" of structures beyond which were "empty" fields, with neither structural remains nor pottery fragments of any of the Teotihuacán phases. To be sure that we were really in the presence of a boundary and not a lightly occupied part of the city, we had to survey in detail, field by field, to get a broad band of "unoccupied" land at least 300 meters wide (sometimes slightly less, often much more) (Fig. 1). While we were not always able to accomplish as much as we would have wished, our job consisted of trying to extend this margin of ruined buildings, bounded by a broad band of "unoccupied" land around the entire perimeter of the city, taking pottery samples from the sites located. The total area surveyed in this fashion was 27 square kilometers (Fig. 1).

Results to Date

It has not yet been possible to digest the results of work in the field during the first seven months. Even so, a preliminary look at some of the results gives some indication of the wealth of new data which the map will provide.

Perhaps the most extraordinary result was the discovery that Teotihuacán during the Tzacualli phase ("Teotihuacán I") was much greater than anyone has seriously believed possible (Figs. 1–3). A northwestern extension of the Tzacualli center was found which in itself covered an area of more than 1.5 square miles (more than 4 square kilometers); all of this falls completely outside the Teotihuacán of the Classic period. In addition, a huge area of Tzacualli settlement of approximately the same size (4-plus square kilometers) appears to underlie the city in its later phases (see Figs. 1–3). Thus it now appears that during the earliest recognized phase in the Teotihuacán sequence at the site itself, Teotihuacán already had reached a size of over 8 square kilometers or more than 3 square miles. It is possible that this area will be reduced somewhat during our intensive survey within the city's boundaries, but we do not expect that this will reduce it markedly. Teotihuacán during the first century A.D. must have been by far the largest Pre-Classic period center in Middle America and larger than most Middle American centers at any time in the pre-Hispanic past. We are still not certain how densely settled Teotihuacán was in this initial phase, to say nothing of its social composition. For this reason we are reserving judgment on the degree of urbanization which might have existed in the first Teotihuacán. But by the end of the Tzacualli phase, Teotihuacán was already more than large enough to provide a base for the growth and expansion which occurred in the succeeding phases of the life of the city. (It now appears that the Pyramid of the Sun was built to its

Fig. 4. A section of Teotihuacán which appears to exhibit planned, block construction, at least in part (Fig. 3, N2-3,W2-3). a, Atetelco (Str. I N2W3); b, Tetitla (Str. 1 N2W2); c, Zacuala Patios (Str. 2 N2W2); d, Zacuala Palacio (Str. 3 N2W2); e, Yayahuala (Str. 1 N3W2). The Yayahuala and Zacuala Palacio compounds were recently excavated by Séjourné (1959, 1962). The walls of both compounds measure close to 60 meters on a side. The trees marking the southern edge of Tetitla are approximately 350 meters south of the south wall of Yayahuala. Courtesy Cia. Mexicana Aerofoto, S. A.

present height at the end of the Tzacualli phase or in the transition between the end of the Tzacualli phase and the beginning of the Miccaotli.) The view that no developmental base exists at Teotihuacán for the great city of the Classic period is increasingly difficult to support.

In much of the area of the northwestern extension of Tzacualli phase Teotihuacán, low mounds of varying size predominate. These give the impression of the former presence of structures of pole and thatch and wattle and daub rather than of stone, concrete, and lime plaster, suggesting structures like those associated with earth floors in the Tzacualli phase deposits at Plaza 1 (Fig. 3, No. 12) in Oztoyahualco (Millon and Bennyhoff 1961). A relatively large ceremonial structure belonging to the Tzacualli phase occupation, and apparently not used later, was found near the southernmost part of its northern boundary, just beyond the boundary of Classic period Teotihuacán at this point (Figs. 1, 2, and 3, No. 14). It consists of a temple platform with a broad terrace in front. Its central location in the Tzacualli phase community is worth noting, as well as the fact that it is oriented to the east rather than to the west.

The survey also demonstrated that it is possible to recover a remarkable amount of information concerning areas occupied during the various phases in the life of the city which succeeded Tzacualli. In fact, unless more than the usual number of unexpected snags develop, we expect to be able to trace the history of the occupation of Teotihuacán on a large part of the site from the Tzacualli phase, through the Miccaotli, Tlamimilolpa, Xolalpan and Metepec[1] phases, thus giving a picture of the growth, florescence, and decline of the city. Figs. 1–3 show Classic period Teotithuacán superimposed on the Teotihuacán of the Tzacualli phase. Once the map has been completed and all of Teotihuacán surveyed, we hope to be able to present a sequence of maps for each of the major phases of its occupation. We expect to find that the city during any single phase of its life was smaller than the maximum boundary shown in Figs. 1–3; for example, the maximum boundary for post-Tzacualli Teotihuacán should be conceived as marking the maximum points reached by a series of successive waves, a single maximum beachline taken from successive beachlines which partially but not completely overlap. Areas occupied in one phase may be abandoned in the next, to be reoccupied again still later. "Suburban" islands in one phase may become incorporated in the city in the next, and the like.

If we are able to present this picture of the genesis, development, and death of the city, it should open the way for judgments on a number of problems not now readily accessible to analysis, among them the changing social composition of the city, the changing quality of urban life in it, changing concepts of urban planning, changing urban-rural relationships, and so on. In this regard, the survey has revealed areas of heavy sherd cover within the boundaries of the Classic period city which do not manifest the typical signs of concrete and lime-plaster construction. It is possible that these areas were occupied by the poorer classes, but more information is needed before a determination can be made on this important point.

The extent of planning at the site remains to be determined, but it is clear that it is more extensive than usually realized in the central 12 square kilometers. In some parts of the site, blocks 60 meters square (approximately), or multiples of this, seem to have been laid out. Possible instances of this may be found southwest of the Pyramid of the Sun and far to the east, around Tlamimilolpa (Figs. 2 and 3, No. 6). The newly excavated compound Yayahuala to the west is such a block; the Zacuala "Palace" is another, although modified at its southeast corner (Figs. 3, Nos. 10, 11 and 4, c, d, e). The latter is one block south and one block east of Yayahuala. The intervening blocks are unexcavated. Another unexcavated block lies immediately to the north of Yayahuala (Fig. 4). Still others seem to exist further to the west. Streets have been found at various points both west and east of the Street of the Dead; their orientation is always that of the Street of the Dead or at right angles to it (Fig. 1). It appears that two processes may be seen at work in the growth of Teotihuacán: a high degree of planning in the central region, together with largely planless growth on the city's fringes, as evidenced by the tortuous outline of the city's perimeter (Figs. 1–3). It also seems likely that the area subject to planning was gradually extended during the life of the city, perhaps in a fashion analogous to what we call "urban renewal." Another result of interest in this regard concerns the Ciudadela (Figs. 1, 2, and 3, No. 3), which usually has been thought of as occupying a position near the southern edge of the city. Actually, as may be seen in Figs. 1–3, it is now evident that the large Ciudadela compound occupies a position near the geographic center of Classic period Teotihuacán. If, as Armillas has argued, the Ciudadela was the administrative center for Teotihuacán, it would have been strategically located for that purpose (Armillas, personal communication, 1960).

Another discovery of interest was the location of what appears to be a large, walled, platform enclosure, as large as the Ciudadela compound and apparently of the same form, situated directly across the Street of the Dead from it (Figs. 1, 2). The platform forming the compound does not appear to have borne any structures of great size like those on the Ciudadela walls, which is perhaps why it has received little attention up to now. But it does bear rooms, some of which were exposed in an excavation

---

[1] "Metepec" is the name we are tentatively giving to the phase which succeeds the Xolalpan phase at Teotihuacán itself. It marks the last phase of the occupation of the city before its fall (about A.D. 350–500 ? [Spinden correlation] or about A.D. 600–750 ? [G-M-T correlation]).

carried out several years ago. A plaza at least as large as the plaza within the Ciudadela lies within the compound. But there are no large structures in the parts of it we were able to inspect (the eastern portion). In October and November, construction trenches exposed small structures of concrete and lime plaster, but most of the eastern part of the plaza seems not to have contained permanent structures nor to have been floored with plaster. Its location opposite the Ciudadela, its monumental size, coupled with the apparent absence of large structures aside from the massive platform enclosure itself, the recent discoveries of stacked pottery and figurines in its great plaza, its wide street-level entrance on the Street of the Dead, the apparent presence of a broad street coming into it from the west, all suggest that this plaza may have served as one of the city's markets, perhaps its principal one, and at the same time as a major access to the Street of the Dead for those coming into the city from the west (Fig. 2). (The new museum, restaurant, and living quarters now being built in the archaeological zone are located on the east side of this plaza.)

In the northwestern part of the Classic period city, fragmentary mural paintings were found in very poor condition. The structures involved had been looted recently (since 1959), but exposure to the elements had destroyed the designs. Mural paintings had been known from this zone (for example, Casa de las Aguilas, Fig. 3, No. 13; Noguera and Leonard 1957), but the new discoveries indicate the extensive use of the technique for the decoration of buildings as far as the northern edge of the city. Other fragments of murals were found near the southern extension of the Street of the Dead just south of the Río San Lorenzo (Figs. 1, 2).

The boundary of the city on the north and east is sharp and definite for the most part, with construction and pottery fragments ending abruptly. To the south and west, on the other hand, the boundary is less sharp, small sites are scattered beyond the heavy building concentrations, and the problem of defining the boundary is more difficult. In the south and southwest, interpretation is complicated by the fact that a number of sites are known to have been leveled, and still others are known to be deeply buried beneath several meters of silt on the edge of the irrigated plain (Fig. 3, No. 15).

Just beyond the eastern border of the city, due east of the Pyramid of the Sun, a broad, flat, abandoned canal was found which connects with other similar canals to the east. Whatever may have been its functions, water-carrying or otherwise, when Teotihuacán was flourishing, it and its "tributaries" followed a course which makes it seem logical that it was a major access route to the city from the Otumba region and the passes through which traffic from Tlaxcala, Puebla, and Veracruz would make its way. A short distance to the west of this, within the eastern margin of the city, four Early Classic period Maya pottery fragments (Tzakol) were found on the surface, together with several sherds from Veracruz. All were found a short distance to the south of the site of the great Tlamimilolpa room agglomeration (Fig. 3, No. 6), where other fragments of Tzakol Maya pottery were found previously in excavations by Linné (1942). Only one other Maya sherd (also Tzakol) was found in our survey of the city's perimeter. This was found in 1959 in a looted cemetery on the northwestern edge of the Classic period city.[2] It seems likely that this clustering of foreign and particularly Maya pottery has a special significance. Perhaps there was a sector of Teotihuacán where visitors, envoys, and traders from Veracruz and the Maya area were housed. More work may provide the answer.

---

[2] The identification of all of these sherds as Tzakol was confirmed by Robert E. Smith who examined them in Palo Alto in March.

Acknowledgments. The Teotihuacán mapping project is supported by the National Science Foundation and the University of Rochester and, during 1962–63, by the Center for Advanced Study in the Behavioral Sciences. James A. Bennyhoff, Research Associate, University of Rochester, and Bruce Drewitt, Instructor in Anthropology, University of Toronto, are collaborating with the author on the project. The first field session lasted from June through December, 1962. Bennyhoff remained in the field throughout this period; Drewitt served as a senior field assistant during the summer. The author worked in the field from June through August and for a month in November and December. Beginning in September, Joseph Marino and Charles Fletcher, Pennsylvania State University graduate students, served as field assistants, both having gained much experience in working on the closely related project of William T. Sanders in the Valley of Teotihuacán. The author gratefully acknowledges the cooperation and assistance of Dr. Eusebio Dávalos Hurtado, Director, Instituto Nacional de Antropología e Historia; Dr. Ignacio Bernal, Sub-Director, I.N.A.H., Director of the new Museum of Anthropology and Coordinating Director of the Mexican Government's Teotihuacán Project; Arql. Román Piña Chan, Director of Museum Planning, I.N.A.H.; Arql. Jorge R. Acosta, Director of Monumentos

Prehispánicos, I.N.A.H., and Director of Archaeological Investigations at Teotihuacán; Prof. José Luis Lorenzo, Director of Prehistoria, I.N.A.H.; Arql. Ponciano Salazar, I.N.A.H., assisting Prof. Acosta at Teotihuacán; Robert E. Smith and Florencia Muller, I.N.A.H., in charge of Teotihuacán ceramic analyses; Ernesto Taboada, Chief of the Archaeological Zone of Teotihuacán; H. B. Nicholson and Frederic Hicks, University of California at Los Angeles; Keith Dixon, Long Beach State College; and Matthew Wallrath, University of Montreal. Special debts to William T. Sanders and José Luis Franco are also gratefully acknowledged.

LINNÉ, S.
    1942 Mexican Highland Cultures. *Ethnographical Museum of Sweden, Publication*, No. 7. Stockholm.

MILLON, RENÉ AND JAMES A. BENNYHOFF
    1961 A Long Architectural Sequence at Teotihuacán. *American Antiquity*, Vol. 26, No. 4, pp. 516–23. Salt Lake City.

NOGUERA, EDUARDO AND JUAN LEONARD
    1957 Descubrimiento de la Casa de las Aguilas. *Boletín del Centro de Investigaciones Antropológicos de México*, No. 4, pp. 6–9. México.

SÉJOURNÉ, LAURETTE
    1959 *Un Palacio en la Ciudad de los Dioses: Exploraciones en Teotihuacán, 1955–1958*. Instituto Nacional de Antropología e Historia, México.
    1962 *El Universo de Quetzalcoatl*. Fondo de Cultura Económica, México.

CENTER FOR ADVANCED STUDY
IN THE BEHAVIORAL SCIENCES
Stanford, California
April, 1963

THE INTERRELATION OF POPULATION, FOOD SUPPLY, AND BUILDING IN PRE-CONQUEST CENTRAL MEXICO

S. F. Cook

I

THIS paper is frankly exploratory, designed to test the possibility of applying historical and archaeological evidence to the solution of certain problems in demography and human ecology for which it is impossible to secure data of more conventional character.

The Central Mexican region was selected because it contained for a very long time perhaps the densest population on the North American continent and because the annalistic as well as archaeological information concerning it is remarkably copious. Specifically the area is defined for present purposes as that included in the present states of Vera Cruz, Hidalgo, Tlaxcala, Puebla, Mexico, Federal District, Morelos, Oaxaca, Michoacan, and Guerrero. This territory is not an ethnic or economic entity since it includes both coastal and highland cultures together with numerous independent linguistic stocks. On the other hand it corresponds to the most intensive area of archaeological investigation outside of Yucatan and is more or less coterminous with the so-called "Aztec Empire" as the latter existed in 1520.

II

The lowest archaeological horizons lie at the base of what are variously designated the archaic culture and the Middle cultures. These are represented by the Zacatenco and San Angel horizons in the Valley of Mexico, and Monte Alban I and Tres Zapotes I in Oaxaca and Vera Cruz. The dating of this period is subject to controversy but appears to lie somewhere in the first centuries B.C. Previously there existed what Vaillant and others have called the Early cultures, or which might also be termed the pre-Archaic.

It is generally considered that during the latter epoch, which must have been of very long, although of unknown duration, the country was inhabited by nomadic tribes, or at least by hunting-gathering groups. Concerning their identity, location, and particularly numbers, we have no direct evidence whatever. It is possible however, to make certain inferences by analogy which will at least provide us with a starting point for comparison with subsequent cultures.

Even allowing for a certain amount of arid land the Central Mexican environment cannot have been profoundly different from that of the nondesert portions of California prior to white occupancy. The hill and plateau country still strongly resembles the foothill and valley regions of California, whereas the coastal tropics, although superficially unlike the middle Pacific area, resemble it quantitatively with respect to food supply. It may be concluded that since the ecological status of the two regions was at least not widely at variance, somewhere near the same population density may have prevailed before the appearance of agriculture.

Through the exhaustive investigations of Kroeber (1921) supplemented by my own studies (1943) we know that the aboriginal population of California, exclusive of desert was very close to 133,500. The area involved was 110,330 square miles and the mean density 1.21 per square mile. The Mexican area under consideration includes 143,985 square miles. Using the same density factor the population, when a similar type of culture prevailed, would have been approximately 175,000. If it be held that the greater density in the tropics should be allowed for, we can use the factor for the north coast California tribes, 2.1 persons per square mile. This gives 302,000 for Central Mexico. Without attempting to secure an exact value it may be stated that comparison with California indicates a pre-Archaic population for Central Mexico of 150,000–250,000, say 200,000 as a working estimate.

III

The transition from a strictly hunting-gathering to a sedentary economy coincided with the introduction or development of corn as the basic dietary staple. That this evolution must have occurred sometime toward the end of the Early and the beginning of the Middle period, is supported by reasonably sound evidence. In the first place no artifacts such as figurines, pottery, or religious structures are likely to be found unless the producing civilization is sufficiently settled to remain in one locality for a considerable period of time. This in turn requires an adequate and a predictable food supply, together with periods of leisure, at least for some of the population. The primary crop food fulfilling the necessary requirements in Middle America was corn.

In the second place the importance of corn during the Middle Period is attested by the material remains. Numerous grinding implements, principally *metates* and *manos*, have been reported by Beyer (1921) at San Angel in the Valley of Mexico and Rancho Colorado in Puebla, by Gamio (1929) under the lava at San Angel, by Gamio (1922) at Teotihuacan, by Drucker (1943) at Tres Zapotes in Vera Cruz, by Vaillant (1930) at Zacatenco, by Leon (1903) in Michoacan. Stylistically somewhat primitive, they are entirely usable for grinding corn. Indeed, Vaillant (1941) feels that their presence proves "that the people relied on corn as their principal food." Finally actual pieces of charred corn cobs have also been found (Lozano, 1925; Vaillant, 1941), although the condition of the fragments was such that the type of corn and hence its exact nutritional value could not be determined.

Corn was very early supplemented by beans. Nicolas Leon (1903) in his work on the Tarascans states that the "primitivos pobladores" who very probably extended as far back as the Archaic period "sembraban maiz, chile, frijol ... y fabricaban pulque." According to Palacios (1937), the Middle cultures generally represent the first agricultural horizon, during which in addition to corn there were introduced "frijol, cacao, semillas y frutas." At exactly what stage these were introduced is of course conjectural, but it is safe to say that by the beginning of the Teotihuacan cycle there were available all the chief vegetable components of later and even modern diets: corn, beans, wild seeds, fruits, chile, and pulque. A rapidly expanding variety of staple foods is therefore indicated during the progress of the Middle period. Simultaneously, even with virgin soil tillage and exceedingly crude ploughing and reaping methods, the total available bulk must have been augmented manyfold.

Certain items, however, are qualitatively important, two in particular: vitamins and protein. If the inhabitants generally received a full ration of corn, beans, whole wild seeds, fruit, and pulque, they probably were adequately cared for with respect to vitamins, although the margin between adequacy and at least sub- clinical deficiency must have been dangerously narrow. The question of protein is serious. Linton (1940) holds that it is the protein level, not the total bulk or calorific level which limits the growth of populations. He then states that the vegetable foods of the Middle Americas were as a whole low in protein. But he fails to differentiate between animal protein of high biological value and vegetable protein of low biological value. As to pure quantity, 500 grams each of corn and beans can easily supply 100 grams of protein, a great sufficiency were it not for the high energy cost of utilization and the lack of essential amino acids. On the other hand a relatively small amount of animal protein can so supplement the vegetable as to render the diet quite suitable for maintenance and even growth. It is often taken for granted that the early inhabitants secured no food beyond the staple crops mentioned. This assumption is scarcely warranted. The people of the Archaic period and their successors, were not distantly removed from hunting-gathering, and the latter consumed every animal they could catch. Repeated reference is made by writers on the Nahua civilization to the many unaesthetic and unappetizing items in the native dietary, such as worms, reptiles, insects, pond scum, and the like. The function of such materials is quite clear—to supply animal protein, together with additional vitamins. With respect to both quantity and quality, this source of food was by no means negligible.

Game, in the sense of wild mammals, was obtainable even into colonial times, and at an earlier period was probably quite abundant. Reptiles and amphibia were always numerous. Birds swarmed wherever there were inland lakes. Vaillant (1930) found a considerable number of animal bones in the refuse heaps at Zacatenco and postulates therefrom "a considerable consumption of the flesh of birds and deer." It is noteworthy that the most highly developed cultures (with the exception of the Zapotec) were either lacustrine or coastal. The prodigious influence of the lake in the Valley of Mexico cannot be overestimated. Noguera (1931) emphasizes the importance of Lake Patzcuaro in the latter phases of Tarascan culture. He considers that there was a series of lakes in Michoacan and that the population centers were built around them. Staub (1919) and others have shown that the most densely populated portion of the Huasteca in prehistoric times was the shores of creeks and lagoons in the Panuco-Topila district, waters which furnished good sources of animal protein in the form of fish, waterfowl, and amphibia. The great shell deposits mentioned by Ekholm (1944) are proof that the coastal tribes made heavy use of clams, oysters, and crabs, and it can indeed be shown that this source alone was sufficient to maintain a very large population.

Another factor of importance was trade. The commerce of the Aztecs and their associates in the Valley of Mexico has been the subject of comment since the days of Sahagun. Students of ceramics and buildings have repeatedly pointed out how artistic styles were influenced by ideas brought in from the exterior, even in the earliest known horizons. It is wholly unlikely that intertribal or inter-regional contact would produce such striking results in the aesthetic field without interchange of material commodities on the dietary level as well. Items of high nutritional value and small bulk would have been specially well adapted to such commerce. Cocoa is a good example. Linné (1934) stresses that his excavations near Teotihuacan brought to light the shells of numerous molluscs, mostly from the Pacific Coast. The inhabitants showed "great interest in these animals for decorative purposes." However, it is quite conceivable that the meat, as well as the shell, was sent to the interior in a manner analogous to that employed by the California Indians many centuries ago. On the whole we may hazard the statement that the supply of animal protein was greater than has been supposed, and that it did not constitute a serious limitation on the growth and maintenance of population.

The striking and abrupt appearance in the early Middle period of advanced material artifacts points to the existence of a moderately well developed culture. Accompanying or even preceding the development of this culture was the establishment of a primitive agriculture throughout Central Mexico which furnished support for a very much larger number of people than did hunting and gathering. In the initial stages much reliance was doubtless placed upon the older form of subsistence, but as the period progressed the newer methods must have come to predominance, at least to the extent of permitting some attention to the domestic arts and religious architecture. Simultaneously the population must have undergone a progressive increase of considerable magnitude. It will not be too radical to suggest the ratio of increase at five to one. Accordingly, if we admit a population of 200,000 for the Early period, that at the end of the Middle period for the entire area may have reached 1,000,000.

According to the archaeological data there was no very sudden break between the Archaic and the Teotihuacan periods. Indeed, as has been mentioned, there has even been described in the Valley of Mexico a definite overlap, as if the older and newer forms existed for a whole period side by side. This is in conformity with the probability that the agricultural base upon which all these social organisms rested did not alter in character but at the most merely expanded. Leaving aside the purely cultural differences for which ceramic styles are testimony, it appears that the general economic level rose steadily through the Middle cultures well into the Teotihuacan period. By the latter epoch sufficient material resources, particularly with respect to food and shelter (and perhaps military security), had accumulated to make possible the construction of very elaborate and pretentious public works of a religious and ceremonial nature. In order to divert so much manpower and material resources to such purposes a very considerable population was necessary. I believe, therefore, that an expanding agriculture was followed by increase in population which always crowded the subsistence level and which reached its maximum in the great building period. To allow for this final increase a purely tentative figure of 2,500,000 may be assigned for the entire area at this time.

The later phases at Teotihuacan and Monte Alban under the Zapotecs are characterized generally by some artistic decadence in ceramics and the cessation of heavy construction at the established sites. It may be inferred that the primitive agriculture had now reached its limit of expansion and had actually suffered retrogression in certain regions. Under these circumstances the population would stabilize at such a level that the margin between adequacy of subsistence and actual famine would be very narrow. Moreover, even this margin may well have been nearly if not completely wiped out by the exhaustion of economic reserves through an over-extended construction program. An actual population decline is indicated at the long-established centers such as Teotihuacan itself, and in any case a weakening of the older social structure. Inevitably the existing tribes became less and less able to resist the pressure of external assault and ultimately gave way. Replacing them and absorbing their culture were those peoples known vaguely as Chichimecs, the earlier representatives of whom included probably the historical or dynastic Toltecs. This tribe flourished and went through a relatively brief but brilliant cycle of culture and building at Tula during the Mazapan or early Mixteca-Puebla period. Perhaps at more or less the same time the somewhat decadent Zapotec culture was replaced in central Oaxaca by the Mixtecs, who supported a renewal of artistic effort and building at Monte Alban and at Mitla.

The evidence for the existence of processes which, toward the end of the Teotihuacan period, tended to restrict or reduce food supply, is highly significant, although somewhat scanty. Linton (1940) suggests that soil exhaustion may have been important in the older, heavily populated communities, for example in the valleys of Mexico and Oaxaca. The long cultural sequences at certain restricted sites such as Teotihuacan, Cholula, Xochicalco, Tres Zapotes, and Monte Alban would imply a local population of some magnitude which would depend upon the adjacent territory for crops. In the course of centuries intensive use would naturally induce soil deterioration. But on the other hand solid cultural tradition would militate against the removal to a new and virgin territory. The local civilization would tend to remain static at the cost of less and less efficient food production until starvation forced down the numbers, or the weakened people were overwhelmed by more powerful neighbors.

The ecological status of the plateau country and central Oaxaca very probably underwent considerable change in this era. It is not coincidence that such magnificant ruins as Teotihuacan and Mitla are located in what is now arid or almost desert country. The builders can scarcely have selected such sites even for ceremonial centers in preference to better watered, more fertile ones not too far away. That some alteration occurred is indicated in various ways. From the relative scarcity of stone axes at Teotihuacan, Linné (1934) deduces a lack of heavy forests at the time of this culture. However, Vaillant (1941) points out quite pertinently that tremendous quantities of wood had to be consumed in order to reduce limestone for the cement used in the pyramids and temples. From the weight needed to reduce a unit mass of calcium carbonate it can be calculated that thousands of tons of wood must have been sacrificed. Hence deforestation on a significant scale must have occurred. Erosion would follow, with its well known train of consequences for agriculture and wild food supply.

Another possible bit of evidence pertains to the lake levels. Vaillant (1935, 1938) attempted to correlate changes in the depth of Lake Tezcoco with culture sequences but without much success. He did, however, demonstrate clearly in the hills around Guadalupe that wide fluctuations in the lake level have occurred, some of which may indicate soil and erosional rather than truly climatic alterations. Noguera (1931) was able to show that in Michoacan, populations followed lakes. The earliest was at Zamora and the next at Zacapu. The lakes at these points have now disappeared and the populations with them. Most recent is Lake Patzcuaro which is still in existence and is heavily inhabited. An interesting study was made in the latter region by Deevey (1944) using the new method of pollen analysis. A change from a wet to a relatively dry climate at a remote period was clearly demonstrated together with a drastic realignment in the floral associations. Although this particular change may have been too remote to apply to conditions during the centuries immediately preceding the Spanish conquest, it is highly suggestive in indicating the possibility of material shifts in ecological balance during more recent periods.

Finally the annalists (such as Ixtlilxochitl, Tezozomoc, Annales de Quautitlan) refer to the downfall of "Tollan" in terms of crop failure and famine as well as of religious conflict and war. The tradition upon which their accounts were based no doubt pertained to the decline of Tula, rather than of Teotihuacan, but nevertheless must have its inception in a long-term tendency which was evident even at the time of the abandonment of Teotihuacan itself.

The exhaustion of agriculture was no doubt felt most severely in the highlands but also may have adversely affected the civilizations on the Atlantic coastal strip despite the lower susceptibility to erosion and the greater recuperative power of the tropics. We have little or no direct proof to this effect, but suggestive is the disappearance of the early civilizations at Tres Zapotes (Drucker, 1943) and La Venta and the withdrawal of the Huastecan peoples from the higher ground of San Luis Potosí (Ekholm, 1944). During this intermediate period of **retrogression** and readjustment it is possible that the demographic condition of Michoacan and the coasts remained more or less stable. But the decline of the high cultures of Monte Alban, Cholula, and Teotihuacan, the abandonment of great religious centers, and above all the unanimous statements of the annalists, speak for a definite decline on the plateau. The legend of the destruction or expulsion of the "Toltecs," the description of the empty wastes encountered by the Nahua invaders, surely must have a remote but unequivocal factual basis. If we conceded a previous peak of 2,500,000 people for Central Mexico from coast to coast, then in subsequent centuries it may have fallen to 2,000,000 or even possibly the hypothetical archaic level of 1,000,000.

As they arrived, the successive waves of newcomers gradually assimilated the culture they found—or were assimilated by it. Finally some degree of stabilization was achieved under the dominance of the later Nahua tribes, permitting them to consolidate, economically and politically. Meanwhile, it is likely that some degree of soil and forest restoration was effected, thus permitting a recrudescence of agriculture. Assisting in this process were certain new dietary and agricultural techniques coupled with a very active commerce. Among the former were three of outstanding significance. The first was the control of water supplies for both domestic use and irrigation. This, as much as anything, made possible intensive urbanization. The second was the "chinampa," a device for making land in a lacustrine habitat which had been known among the Middle cultures (Apenes, 1943; Noguera, 1943) but which was brought to a very high state of perfection in the Aztec period. Due to the "chinampa" a highly specialized vegetable truck garden system was evolved. The third was the tortilla, evidently invented during the intermediate period (Leon, 1903; Linné, 1934). By virtue of its ease of preparation, compact form, long-keeping quality, and ready portability, the tortilla became the basic ration of the Central Mexican armies and is perhaps the key to their tremendous endurance in distant and long protracted military campaigns.

Under Aztec and Tezcocan leadership in agriculture and commerce, the entire economic level rose rapidly carrying with it the available food supply and unquestionably the population. It is a safe assumption that the latter attained its previous maximum, say 2,500,000, and reached a far higher figure before it was cut down again by the Spanish conquest. To evaluate the exact situation in the last two centuries prior to 1520 will require special investigation, which is reserved for the future.

IV

Since even the days of Cortes all visitors have been impressed by the size and majesty of the great Mexican ruins, Teotihuacan, Monte Alban, Mitla, Tajin, and Cholula. Many students have felt that in these material remains lay a clue to the size and power of the peoples who constructed them, and yet few, if any, have made a serious effort to utilize this particular type of objective data.

There can be no question that the ponderous edifices constructed in Central Mexico were ceremonial and religious in character. In other words they satisfied the aesthetic and emotional urge of the people, but instead of contributing in any way to their material welfare they constituted a drain upon all the tangible resources of the tribe. Since the economy was almost exclusively agricultural, based on corn and available wild foods, the subsistence level, and hence in the long run the population, was determined and limited by the corn production. However, as suggested previously, in the middle of the first millennium A. D. the agriculture appears to have somewhat outstripped population. As a result there was generated an excess productive capacity such that, while the group as a whole remained at the strict level of bare necessity, certain members could be spared from the active pursuit of food production and their energies devoted to the erection of religious centers. If, now, in any way we could correlate the magnitude of building construction with the labor and food supply, we might be able to deduce the approximate population. For this purpose it appears most satisfactory to concentrate our effort upon the period lying between the end of the Middle times and the beginning of what Mason has called the Mixteca-Puebla period, i.e., the period of Independent Cultures. During this era were constructed some of the most extensive and at the same time most thoroughly studied building complexes, although it will be freely conceded that later centuries saw the completion of numerous important enterprises, such as that at Tula.

Such an enterprise as the Pyramid of the Sun at Teotihuacan, together with the subsidiary structures which were being erected at the time, must have absorbed the energy of the population within a wide radius. Let us assume that the territory included everything within a long day's foot journey of the site, perhaps 50 kilometers with a total area of 8,000 square kilometers. At any one time, during the active construction of a pyramid of such magnitude, the number of laborers must have approached 3,000, particularly if we include those who were engaged in digging dirt, cutting stones, and the like in preparation for the direct use of these materials. In addition there must have been an equal number of laborers and artisans working on other buildings or indirectly contributing to the construction of the pyramid itself. At the same time Teotihuacan was a going concern, carrying on its functions as not only a great religious but a political center. Numerous priests, assistants, nobles, chiefs, and other members of the ruling class, together with their retinue of servants and probably slaves, had to be supported by the people at large. It will not be excessive to estimate this group at 2,500. Finally there were the dependents of the former groups, wives, children, and aged relatives, who had to be carried by the general organization. They must have been at least as numerous as those actually participating. The total then would be 17,000.

According to the principle of economic surplus only the food production over and above the maintenance level of the entire supporting population could be devoted to those engaged in political or religious enterprise, otherwise starvation would collapse the entire system. The question then becomes: what number of people were necessary to produce an excess of food, in corn or its equivalent, sufficient for 17,000 persons? We might make an arbitrary guess that the productive population had to be ten times greater than the non-productive, which would yield 170,000, plus 17,000 or 187,000. However, there is still another method of estimate which may be more accurate, based on the energy requirement of the diet.

Nutritionists today hold without exception that a daily intake of at least 3,500 calories is necessary for an adult who is leading more than a very sedentary life, whereas the need of a laborer is much greater. Yet it has been shown, for example by Gamio (1922) and Llamas (1933), that in modern rural Mexico the average value of the diet is no more than 2,000 calories per day. There is good reason to wonder whether the prehistoric dietary status may not have been better than it is today, and it certainly must have been as good. It is therefore necessary to ascribe a minimum of 2,000 calories for the average individual in Teotihuacan times. In view of the extraordinary ability demonstrated by the tribe, and the clear evidence of their drive and power, it is probably better to raise this value to 2,500 at least.

The energy value of "corn," as given by Rose (1938), is 285 calories per 100 grams or 2,500 for 712 grams. This is only an approximation since the varieties of corn differ in value and we do not know the exact properties of that used by the Teotihuacan people, but it is within the correct order of magnitude. Furthermore, we have to compute the entire prehistoric diet in terms of corn, although other types of food were eaten as well. The corn requirement of the 17,000 non-productive persons was then 12,100 kilograms per day, or 4,420 metric tons per year.

It is impossible to state, naturally, just what was the agricultural surplus available for this group. In late Aztec times, however, when the social order was at a high level of organization and agricultural methods better developed, probably somewhere near one third of the total food production went (in the form of tribute) to the ruling caste. An allowance of one fifth, therefore, seems liberal for Teotihuacan. This means an effective food production, as corn, of 22,100 metric tons. If we add 20 per cent for seed and spoilage, we get 26,500 tons. In English units this is 1,035,000 bushels. Since the mean weight of shelled corn is nearly 56 pounds per bushel and a fair, but not outstanding, production is 40 bushels per acre, we find that the land under cultivation must have been somewhere near 25,800 acres. Under the very primitive conditions existing at the time it is doubtful whether one family unit could successfully cultivate more than one acre. In modern Mexico it often cultivates much less. At the rate of six persons per family this means 155,000 persons, and together with the 17,000 non-productive citizens makes a total of 173,000.

These calculations are admittedly speculative, although based on the best probability, and cannot be taken too literally. Nevertheless the evidence appears good that at least 150,000 persons constituted the religious and cultural unit at Teotihuacan during its period of greatest glory.

Monte Alban was a tremendous establishment. Its buildings alone covered 40 square kilometers (Caso, 1941), as compared to 18 at

Teotihuacan. Caso thinks it was surrounded by numerous towns in which the producing population actually lived. The size suggests a supporting radius twice that of Teotihuacan, an area of 31,400 square kilometers, and an official staff of roughly 25,000, including laborers, slaves, and dependents. The total population may, therefore, have been as high as 250,000.

At Cholula the pyramid contains 1,800,000 cubic meters of earth and stone (Lehmann, 1933), as compared with 993,000 for the Pyramid of the Sun at Teotihuacan. On the other hand there are few remains of other buildings, and furthermore this pyramid was built by several superpositions over a very long period of time. On the whole it will be liberal to assign this religious center an area of 4,000 square kilometers and a population of 75,000 persons.

The Michoacan or Tarascan region is of different character. Here are found small burial mounds (*yácatas*) of variable size but few really large constructions except the level platforms on which the mounds were placed. The mounds, however, are so very numerous (Leon, 1903; Lumholtz, 1902; Caso, 1930) as to represent an amount of labor and upkeep comparable to that of Teotihuacan. In an area of perhaps 20,000 square kilometers centering around Lake Patzcuaro we may then assume a population of 150,000.

Other sites may be mentioned as appropriate to similar analysis, such as the recently uncovered building complex at Tula, other localities in northern Mexico and northern Morelos, and the extensive centers in coastal Vera Cruz excavated by Drucker and by Ekholm. Most of these, however, pertain to post-Teotihuacan time and moreover, merit a more careful and detailed consideration than is possible within the scope of the present paper.

The population densities for the four sites or centers discussed are respectively 18.8, 8.0, 18.8, and 7.5 persons per square kilometer. Collectively the value is 13.3. Since these were the most advanced regions culturally, the intervening territory must have been more sparsely populated, say with one half the density or 6.7 persons per square kilometer. Then, since the area was 310,000 square kilometers, the population would have been 2,075,000. Together with the 625,000 from the four centers mentioned the total would reach 2,700,000, a value greater than the 2,500,000 suggested previously for the period and perhaps too high, but well within the same range. A more detailed study of sites, buildings, and chronology would no doubt provide a much closer approximation.

SUMMARY

The thesis is advanced that the preconquest population of Central Mexico was dependent primarily on food supply. The latter, prior to the Middle cultures, was on the hunting-gathering level and may have supported 200,000 persons. During the Middle and early Teotihuacan periods the development of agriculture, founded on corn and beans and supplemented by wild animal sources, permitted an increase to at least 2,500,000. That this estimate is not too low is indicated by calculations based on the probable economic surplus needed to support the building programs of Teotihuacan and elsewhere. Erosion, deforestation, and possibly soil exhaustion then forced a decline. Recovery occurred after an interval of rehabilitation and infusion of new races. This recovery, aided by more elaborate technical methods, made possible further growth of the population up to the time of the Conquest.

BIBLIOGRAPHY

APENES, O.
    1943. "The 'Tlateles' of Lake Texcoco." AMERICAN ANTIQUITY, Vol. 9, pp. 29–32.

BEYER, H.
    1918. "Sobre antiquedades del Pedregal de San Angel." *Memorias de la Sociedad Científica "Antonio Alzate,"* Vol. 37, pp. 1–16. Mexico.

CASO, A.
    1930. "Informe preliminar de las exploraciones realizadas en Michoacan." *Anales del Museo Nacional de Mexico*, Ser. IV, Vol. 6, pp. 446–52. Mexico.
    1941. *Culturas mixteca y zapoteca*. Mexico.

CASO, A. AND D. F. RUBIN DE LA BORBOLLA
    1936. "Exploraciones en Mitla, 1934–1935." *Publicaciones, Instituto Panamericano de Geografia e Historia*, No. 21.

COOK, S. F.
    1937. "The Extent and Significance of Disease Among the Indians of Baja California." *Ibero-Americana*, No. 12. Berkeley.
    1943. "The Conflict Between the California Indian and White Civilization. I." *Ibero-Americana*, No. 21. Berkeley.
    1943. "The Conflict Between the California Indian and White Civilization. II." *Ibero-Americana*, No. 22. Berkeley.

DEEVEY, E. S., JR.
    1944. "Pollen Analysis and Mexican Archaeology: an Attempt to Apply the Method." AMERICAN ANTIQUITY, Vol. 10, pp. 135–49.

DIAZ LOZANO, E.
    1925. "Cultura postneolithica del Pedregal de San

Angel." *Ethnos*, Ser. 3, Vol. 1, pp. 25–35. Mexico.

DRUCKER, P.
1943. "Ceramic Sequences at Tres Zapotes, Vera Cruz, Mexico." *Bulletin, Bureau of American Ethnology*, No. 140. Washington.

EKHOLM, G. F.
1944. "Excavations at Tampico and Panuco in the Huasteca, Mexico." *Anthropological Papers of the American Museum of Natural History*, Vol. 38, pp. 321–509. New York.

GAMIO, M.
1922. *La población del Valle de Teotihuacan*. Mexico: Secretaria de Agricultura y Fomento.
1929. "Las excavaciones del Pedregal de San Angel." 2nd Edition. *Publicaciones de la Secretaria de Educacion Publica*, Vol. 22, No. 2. Mexico.

LEHMANN, W.
1933. *Aus den Pyramidenstädten in Alt-Mexiko*. Berlin.

KROEBER, A. L.
1925. "Handbook of the Indians of California." *Bulletin, Bureau of American Ethnology*, No. 78. Washington.

LEON, N.
1903. "Los Tarascos, II." *Anales del Museo Nacional de Mexico*, Ser. II, Vol. 1, pp. 392–502. Mexico.

LINNÉ, R.
1934. "Archaeological Researches at Teotihuacan, Mexico." *Publication, the Ethnographical Museum of Sweden*, N.S., No. 1. Stockholm.

LINTON, R.
1940. "Crops, Soils and Culture in America." In *The Maya and Their Neighbors*, pp. 32–40. New York.

LLAMAS, R.
1035. "Alimentación de los antiguos mexicanos." *Anales del Instituto Biológico Mexicano*, Vol. 6, pp. 245–58. Mexico.

LUMHOLTZ, C.
1902. *Unknown Mexico*. 2 Vols. New York.

NOGUERA, E.
1931. "Exploraciones arqueológicas en las regiones de Zamora y Patzcuaro, Estado de Michoacan." *Anales del Museo Nacional de Mexico*, Ser. 4, Vol. 3, pp. 89–103. Mexico.
1943. "Excavaciones en el Tepalcate, Chimalhuacan, Mexico." AMERICAN ANTIQUITY, Vol. 9, pp. 33–43.

PALACIOS, E. J.
1937. "Arqueología de Mexico." In *Enciclopedia Ilustrada Mexicana*. Mexico.

ROSE, M. S.
1938. *The Foundations of Nutrition*. 3rd Edition. New York.

RUBIN DE LA BARBOLLA, D. F.
1939. "Antropología Tzintzuntzan-Ihuatzio: Temporadas I y II." *Revista Mexicana de Estudios Antropológicos*, Vol. 3, pp. 99–121. Mexico.

SAVILLE, M. H.
1909. "The Cruciform Structures of Mitla and Vicinity." In *Putnam Anniversary Volume*, pp. 151–90. New York.

STAUB, W.
1919. "Some Data about the Prehispanic and the Now Living Haustec Indians." *El Mexico Antiguo*, Vol. 1, pp. 49–65. Mexico.

VAILLANT, G. C.
1930. "Excavations at Zacatenco." *Anthropological Papers of the American Museum of Natural History*, Vol. 32, Pt. 1, pp. 1–197. New York.
1935. "Excavations at El Arbolillo." *Anthropological Papers of the American Museum of Natural History*, Vol. 35, Pt. 1, pp. 137–279. New York.
1938. "A Correlation of Archaeological and Historical Sequences in the Valley of Mexico." *American Anthropologist*, N.S., Vol. 40, pp. 535–73. Menasha.
1941. *The Aztecs of Mexico*. New York.

University of California
Berkeley, California
July, 1946

LITTLE MASK OF THE GOD XIPE-TOTEC

READING THE RIDDLE OF ANCIENT JEWELS

An Analysis of the Historical Significance of the Monte Alban Treasure—the Ritualistic Meaning of the Ancient Mixtec Inscriptions

By ALFONSO CASO

Chief, Department of Archæology, National Museum of Mexico

Translated from the Spanish by S. B. and G. C. Vaillant

WITH A FOREWORD BY G. C. VAILLANT, ASSOCIATE CURATOR OF MEXICAN ARCHÆOLOGY, AMERICAN MUSEUM

PHOTOGRAPHS BY THE AUTHOR

FOREWORD

THERE arose great interest last winter when Professor Caso, excavating the ruins of Monte Alban, Oaxaca, Mexico, found a royal tomb with all its treasures intact. Since Professor Caso is the authority in the field of Oaxacan archæology, the historical and scientific data pertaining to the tomb were completely recovered. The rings and necklaces of gold, the cups of crystal, and the other jewels comprising this treasure have been made known through popular articles in the press and current periodicals, but little has appeared as yet to tell us who the makers of the treasure were and when they lived.

It is especially fortunate for the readers of NATURAL HISTORY that Professor Caso, the discoverer of the tomb and one of the foremost authorities on Mexican prehistory, consented to give in these pages his first analysis of the significance of his finds. One of the greatest of Egyptologists said that "Museum collections are but a by-product of history," and in the following article the reader will see that archæology is not merely grubbing in the ground for curiosities, but is instead a method of historical research. Professor Caso uses his magnificent material to tell the story of these forgotten civilizations, not as collateral for personal aggrandizement or romantic interest.

Previous to Professor Caso's work at Monte Alban much digging but little historical research had been done in the State of Oaxaca. As a result considerable collections were amassed but very

---

Reprinted by permission of the publisher; NATURAL HISTORY; Vol. XXXII, No. 5; pp. 464-480; by Alfonso Caso. Copyright 1932 The American Museum of Natural History.

little was known of them. The work of Professor Saville for the American Museum stood out from this welter of pot-hunting, and his Oaxacan collections now in this Museum are among the best documented in the world. Professor Caso, however, has succeeded in distinguishing the culture of the indigenous Zapotec of the State of Oaxaca from the intrusive Mixtec civilization that was closely affiliated to the Aztec or "Mexican" civilization to the north. It is quite conceivable that in future research he may find even earlier civilizations than the Zapotec and may possibly connect them with the Mayas to the south.

In this article he places great reliance on the native inscriptions inscribed on stone and written on leather or paper. Such writing has as yet been found only among the Maya of Guatemala and Yucatan, among the Zapotecs of the Oaxaca region, and in the region occupied by the Mixtecs, the Aztecs, and other culturally affiliated Nahua tribes. Thus the connections and differences between these three styles of writing are of the same significance to a Mexicanist as the Egyptian, Greek, and Roman inscriptions are to a European scholar.

Not only is it a great privilege to welcome to these pages so distinguished a scholar as Professor Caso, but also it is peculiarly fitting to have an article which bears so pertinently upon one of the most important of the Mexican collections in the American Museum, and which gives so clear a picture of American intellectual attainment before Columbus.

—G. C.

※ ※ ※ ※ ※

IN a recent magzaine article I gave a short preliminary explanation of the discoveries made at Monte Alban during the season of 1931–1932, under the patronage of the Ministry of Public Education, the government of the State of Oaxaca, the Panamerican Institute of Geography and History, the National University, and the Messrs. Morrow, Del Valle, Melgar, and Velazquez Uriarte.

Wide World Photograph

THE ANCIENT RUINS OF MONTE ALBAN
Outside the City of Oaxaca, Mexico. The tombs uncovered here contained jewels and other relics of a civilization which flourished before the Spaniards came to America

Wide World Photograph

IN ONE OF THE NEWLY DISCOVERED TOMBS
Professor Caso (left) and Martin Bazan, his assistant, are taking the measure of a copper pot near Professor Caso's right hand. In the foreground at the left are the bones of Mixtec chieftains with pearls resting beside them

I wish, however, in this present article to discuss a specific point, but one very important to the find: To what indigenous civilization do the objects belong?

But before entering into this discussion, let me briefly relate how we found the tomb and made the excavation.

The mound of Tomb 7 at Monte Alban lies immediately next to the western edge of the road which goes from Oaxaca to the place where the ruins are situated. This mound is very little elevated in relation to the general level of the soil, but it is located at the foot of a small hillock which is some four meters high and represents undoubtedly the substructure of a temple. On the other side of the road and in front of the tomb and the temple are the tombs numbered 3, 8, and 9. Next to Tomb 7 is another little mound which shows a depression and doubtless contains another tomb which I could not explore in this season's work, but which I intend to uncover in the next.

We began the exploration of the mound over Tomb 7 by cleaning off the upper part, encountering what seemed to be the remains of the walls of some small rooms located on top of the mound, the floors of which were covered by a thick coating of the stucco used in Monte Alban to surface walls, their sloping bases, stairways, and pavements.

One of the most important characteristics of Tomb 7 was a little ditch approximately 20 cm. wide by 6.85 meters long, situated exactly in the back part of the tomb, parallel to its transverse axis. (See plan on p. 468).

In opening up a vertical pit to find the tomb, we had to break through a second stucco floor, before we encountered the stones forming the vault. We removed two of these vault stones and were then able to descend into the tomb and to measure its interior length, with a view to finding the door. To do this, however, it was necessary to open another vertical pit before we reached a little antechamber, roofless and full of dirt, in which appeared, intentionally broken, three great Zapotec urns with their pedestals, shown restored in the figure on page 467. The central one of these very common urns represents an old god, probably the god of fire, whom the Mexicans call Huehueteotl, and who in their mythology was the lord of the central region of the universe. The urns at either side are representations of the Zapotec god called Cocijo, who, as I have demonstrated elsewhere, is equivalent to the rain god, called Tlaloc by the Mexicans. (*El Vaso de Jade de la Coleccion Plancarte.* Revista Mexicana de Estudios Historicos. Vol. I, p. 7).

After carefully removing the urns and

READING THE RIDDLE OF ANCIENT JEWELS

fragments, we were able to find the entrance to the tomb. It was closed by means of large stone slabs, and when we removed these we discovered that the door was almost completely blocked by a great heap of earth. Between the top of this earth and the lintel of the door there remained only a small opening, which we had to enlarge in order to penetrate to the interior.

None of the stones which sealed the entrance had inscriptions, but on the other hand, forming part of the vault of the antechamber and resting directly on the lintel, we found a stone with the inscription which appears on page 470, and which has about the same dimensions as the doorway, so that it is extremely probable that at first it occupied this position.

The inscription on this stone is indubitably Zapotec and I was able to read on it the year "serpent" and the day "flower," as well as the number 8, formed by a bar and three dots; but I could not say whether the sign ought to be attributed to the glyph "serpent" or to the glyph "flower," although the first seems to me more probable. Beneath the second of these signs there is a glyph which I do not know how to interpret, but it could be the number 4, united to the day sign.

As can be seen on the plan of the tomb, in the longitudinal cross section shown on page 469, there was a layer of earth inside which varied greatly in thickness. In the second room, next to the end of the tomb, it had a depth of merely 30 cm., while at the entrance it almost

hid the door, and we found in the projecting portions of the walls and the lintels, small heaps of dirt which indicated that the layer of earth originally reached that height and later owing to settling, subsided a little until it left, as I have said, a small opening between its upper level and the lintel of the tomb.

Furthermore, after cleaning away the earth which covered the tomb and taking out the objects from the principal burial, there appeared underneath, small clay vessels, a fragment of a Zapotec urn like those found in the antechamber, and a piece of a metate. The little pots are just like those which I found in Mound B during the excavations there, and are of the type which has always been considered Zapotec.

Therefore it seems to me unquestionable that Tomb 7 in Monte Alban was used twice. The first burial was made directly on the floor of the tomb and was accompanied by the vases, metates, etc. which I have just described, and by the Zapotec urns. The door was sealed, probably with the stone which is now in the vault of the first room and which

ZAPOTEC URNS FOUND IN THE ENTRANCE TO TOMB 7

These mortuary vessels represent Zapotec gods. The center one is the Old God while at either side are effigies of the Rain God Cocijo
(See page 466)

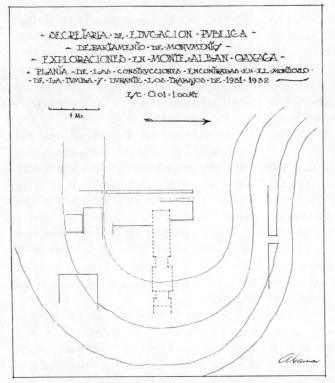

PLAN OF THE MOUND COVERING TOMB 7
The dotted lines represent the plan of the tomb, while the solid straight lines show traces of walls. The irregular lines give the contours of the mound. (See page 466)

was so roofed, as can be seen in the transverse and longitudinal cross sections on page 469.

The second chamber has an angular roof, formed by two inclined stones, as can be seen in cross section AB, on the diagram page 469. We find plane vaulting chiefly in cruciform tombs like those of Mitla and Tomb 3 of Monte Alban. Angular vaulting, on the other hand, is more characteristic of the tombs with niches, like all the others we discovered in Monte Alban in this first season of work.

It seems to me very probable that between the cruciform tomb and the tomb with niches there is a sequential relation. As a matter of fact the niches in the tombs are always three, and are placed one at the end of the chamber and two in the walls. It might follow that these niches are survivals of the arms of the cross, or, if the tomb with niches is earlier, then they have become gradually more important, until they stand converted into the little rooms which form the head and the arms of the cruciform tombs. At the present stage of our knowledge, it is impossible to say if the first method of constructing the tombs was the cruciform type or that with niches, but the two methods of construction seem to me to have a definite relation.

has the inscription of the year 8 "serpent" and the day 4 (?) "flower." Thus both the urns and the inscription show the first burial to have been Zapotec.

Furthermore, the very architecture of the tomb is Zapotec, like others which we found in Monte Alban and which Saville discovered in Xoxo and Cuilapan. (M. H. Saville, *Exploration of Zapotecan Tombs in Southern Mexico*. American Anthropologist, n.s., vol. 1, pp. 350–362). The chambers of the tomb are roofed by the two methods which the Zapotecs used and which we might call plane vaulting and angular vaulting. The first consists of great smooth stones placed horizontally and resting either on the walls of the tomb, or, as in the case of Tomb 7, on stones like brackets which are used to sustain the roof stones. The first chamber

Before entering into the discussion of the objects of the later burial, I wish to define what I mean *archæologically* by the term *Zapotec*. As I showed in my book *Las Estelas Zapotecas* (Zapotec Stelae), there is a great resemblance between the urns thus classified and the stones with inscriptions which have been found at Monte Alban and other places,— Etla, Zaachila, etc.

The urns which have in front a figure usually adorned with great panaches of plumes, have always been considered Zapotec, since they are found only within the territory which this nation used to inhabit. The stones or stelae with inscriptions have a great resemblance to the urns, since, as I have shown, on both are represented the same gods and symbols. The hieroglyphs which are found on the urns and the stelae are consequently Zapotec, and belong to a system of writing unquestionably related, in a general way, to that of the Mexicans and the Mayas, but in reality very distinct. For example, the signs of the days are very different in Zapotec writing, from the Mexican and Mixtec. Even though I cannot yet give the order of the Zapotec hieroglyphs, the day signs appear on page 470. On the other hand, if Mexican glyphs are compared with Mixtec, it will be seen that they are the same, if one excepts the stylistic variations which characterize glyphs as Mixtec without altering their essential form. (Page 470).

The year sign is different in all three: Mexican, Mixtec, and Zapotec writing, and probably also in Maya, but in this last case no year sign has yet been defined.

The Zapotec year sign is the face of the god Cocijo or Tlaloc, who has before his mouth a mask with serpentine attributes, in which the fundamental characteristic seems to be an ornament over the nose made by a disc and a trapezoid, which in the Mexican codices is the representation of the turquoise nose-plug. This adornment acquires greater importance as the glyph is simplified, so that I believe it must be the fundamental part of the sign. (Page 471).

In the Mixtec and Cuicatec codices and inscriptions, the sign of the year is a kind of interlaced A.O., although a trapezoid sometimes appears united to them (bottom, page 471). The A represents the solar ray such as we find in innumerable Mexican monuments, like the so-called Aztec calendar stone for example. The O, and the trapezoid which sometimes appears, represent the same symbol as is found in Zapotec writing, the turquoise in the nose of the god Cocijo. In some representations of this sign one or

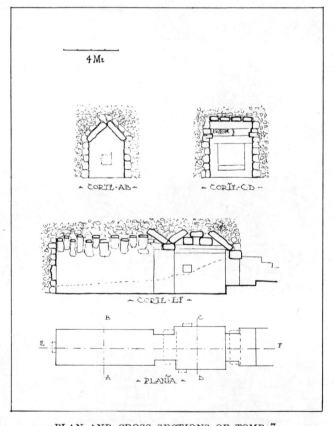

PLAN AND CROSS SECTIONS OF TOMB 7
The dotted line EF marks the height of the earth in the tomb. On top of the earth were found the skeletons and jewels comprising the second (Mixtec) burial, and below, inside the earth, the objects of pottery and stone comprising the first (Zapotce) burial

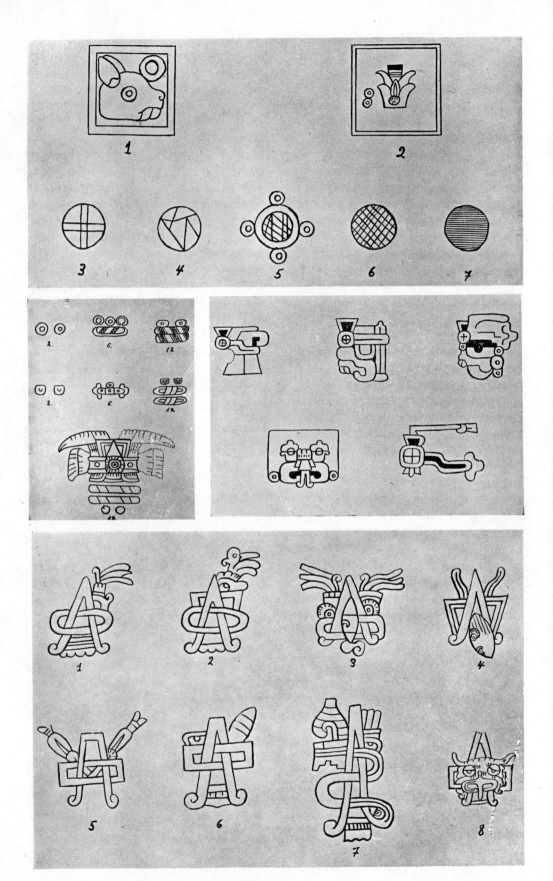

FIGURES ON THIS PAGE

Above. Mixtec and Mexican Day Signs (cf., pp. 469 and 474).

Right. Inscription on the stone now in the roof of Tomb 7, but which originally must have covered the entrance (cf., pp. 467–468).

Bottom. Zapotec Day Signs (cf. p. 469).

FIGURES ON OPPOSITE PAGE

Uppermost Plate. Mexican Year Signs: (cf., p. 472). 1. Teocalli of the Holy War. 2. Bourbon Codex. 3. Clavijero. 4. Aubin Codex. 5. Codex Matritense del Real Palacio. 6. Codex Vaticanus A. 7. Mendoza Codex.

Middle Left. Numerals, Top Row: Maya Numerals (cf., p. 472). Middle Row: Zapotec Numerals. Bottom Row: Glyphs on a Shell from Teotihuacan.

Middle Right. Zapotec Year Signs (cf. p. 469).

Lowermost Plate. Mixtec Year Signs (cf., pp. 469–472) 1 and 2. Colombino Codex. 3. Nuttall Codex. 4. Borgia Codex. 5. Selden Codex. 6. Bodley Codex. 7. Bodley Codex. 8. Vienna Codex.

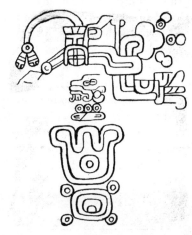

BONE, SHOWING YEAR SIGNS
Reading from right to left, the years 2 Flint, 3 House, 4 Rabbit, 5 Reed in rotation up to 13 (destroyed) Reed. Note the use of the dot system of enumeration and the day sign applied to that of the year (cf., p. 473)

both of the god's eyes are still retained.

Among the Mexicans the year sign is different, since they usually indicated it by the glyph of the first day in the year, enclosed in a square, or by the turquoise. The Mexicans designated with one term, *Xihuitl*, both the year and the turquoise (top, page 471). The representation of numerals is also different, although we cannot here make as neat a distinction as in the preceding cases.

The Mayas, the Zapotecs, and the Teotihuacanos used dots to express numbers up to 5, and a bar or bars to represent 5 or multiples of 5, combining bars and dots for other quantities. (Page 471). In no Aztec monument or codex do we find bars indicating 5, since they used dots to represent numbers as high as 13. On the other hand, in codices and monuments attributed to the Mixtecs we find both systems used; dots and bars combined in some, and in others only dots. Examples of the first are: the Laud, Cospi, and Fejervary-Mayer codices, and the stone of Cuilapan. As examples of the second we shall mention the Vindobonensis, the Nuttall, the Colombino, the Dehesa, etc., and several of the Borgia group as well. It should be noted that in the three codices where the dots and bars are combined,—Laud, Fejervary, and Cospi—*the system of enumeration by simple dots also occurs.* The last is used for the coefficients of the days in the ritual calendar, and, in general, for any calculation of days. With the system of combined dots and bars, other calculations are made which cannot yet be deciphered. The Laud and the Fejervary codices do not seem like the Cospi to have been altered subsequent to the original writing, a fact which demonstrates that both systems could be used at the same time and by men of the same culture, in spite of the proven fact that the Aztecs never used the combination of dots and bars. To summarize: The Zapotecs used the system of dots and bars, the Aztecs that of dots only, and the Mixtecs both.

PECTORAL REPRESENTING A TIGER KNIGHT
Showing the years 10 Wind and 11 House and the day 2 Flint. (cf., pp. 473-474)

We can say, therefore, that in hieroglyphic writing and in artistic style there exists a great difference between the

READING THE RIDDLE OF ANCIENT JEWELS

HEADS OF QUETZALCOATL
The two heads on either side represent Quetzalcoatl. The one in the middle is Tonatiuh, god of the sun. His head protrudes from the open beak of an eagle which in turn projects from a solar disc. Another eagle hangs from the labret of the god. The head on the right dangles a butterfly in its mouth; that on the left a jade, from which hangs an eagle

material which has hitherto been called Zapotec and that designated as Mixtec. On the other hand this latter material is only distinguished from the Mexican or Aztec by the use of the year sign A.O., by the *occasional* utilization of the numerical system of dots and bars, and by less important stylistic variations.

On this basis, then, I am going to analyse some of the objects found in Tomb 7, which, having hieroglyphs, will permit us to study them. These objects are principally the carved bones and the jewels of gold and silver.

THE YEAR SIGN.—The year sign, indicated by an intertwined A.O., appears repeatedly on the carved bones and twice on the gold pectoral representing a tiger knight. It is certain that the first 13 years of the indigenous "century," a cycle of 52 years, are represented on the bone (Page 472), and the signs united to the year glyph are *Acatl* (Reed), *Tecpatl* (Flint), *Calli* (House), and *Tochtli* (Rabbit), that is to say, precisely the signs used by the Mexicans and Mixtecs to name their years. The Zapotecs used *Ehecatl* (Wind), *Mazatl* (Deer), *Malinalli* (Herb), *Ollin* (Earthquake), signs which were characteristic also of the Cuicatecs. It should be noted that the numerical system of simple dots, rather than that of combined dots and bars, is used.

In the pectoral representing a tiger knight (Page 472) we have two dates. The sign A.O. tells us that we are dealing here with two years. In the square on the right the gylph inside the A is undoubtedly

BONES SHOWING DAY SIGNS
The upper bone gives from right to left between the two eagles the first thirteen days of the month, the lower from left to right the first twelve. (cf., pp. 474–475)

Calli, or "House," and outside we have eleven dots which gives us the reading "Year 11 House."

In the square on the left the sign inside the glyph A.O. is the head of the wind god Ehecatl; and ten dots surround the glyph, which gives us the reading "Year 10 Wind." Outside of the glyph also appears another small sign representing a flint knife (*Tecpatl*), and to this are attached two dots.

Now, in this case the two years marked on the two squares of the pectoral *cannot* belong to the same calendric system, since the days *Ehecatl* and *Calli* (Wind and House) are immediately next each other in the sequence of the signs (top page 470) and for two year signs to belong in the same system they must be five, ten, or fifteen days apart. The actual list of days follows:

GLYPHS ON THE BASE OF A CUP OF *tecali* (ALABASTER)

1. CIPACTLI—CROCODILE
2. EHECATL—WIND
3. CALLI—HOUSE
4. CUETZPALLIN—LIZARD
5. COATL—SERPENT
6. MIQUITZLI—DEATH
7. MAZATL—DEER
8. TOCHTLI—RABBIT
9. ATL—WATER
10. ITZCUINTLI—DOG
11. OZOMATLI—MONKEY
12. MALINALLI—HERB
13. ACATL—REED
14. OCELOTL—TIGER
15. CUAUHTLI—EAGLE
16. COZCACUAUHTLI—BUZZARD
17. OLLIN—EARTHQUAKE
18. TECPATL—FLINT
19. QUIAHUITL—RAIN
20. XOCHITL—FLOWER

Since each year begins with one of the above signs, and since the list is repeated in the same order indefinitely and without interruption, after 360 days each of the twenty signs will have been repeated eighteen times, and to complete the 365 days of the year we shall have to count five more days from our point of departure. Thus the first day of one year must necessarily be five days later than the first day of the year before. For example, if a year begins with the day *Ehecatl*, the three-hundred-and-sixtieth day of that year will be *Cipactli*, and the last five days will be *Ehecatl*, *Calli*, *Cuetzpallin*, *Coatl*, and, finally, *Miquiztli*, which will be the last day of the year, causing the next year to begin with the day *Mazatl*. The following year will begin with *Malinalli*, the next with *Ollin*, and the one after that will begin with *Ehecatl* again. In the same way if the year has begun with *Calli*, the following years will begin with *Tochtli*, *Acatl*, and *Tecpatl*, but never in the same calendric system can one year begin with *Ehecatl* and another with *Calli*, as do the years on the pectoral. On the other hand the *2 Tecpatl* (2 Flint) which appears in the left hand square is undoubtedly a day sign, since it is not united to any other year sign.

We know that the Zapotecs, like the Mayas, named their years for the signs *Ehecatl*, *Mazatl*, *Malinalli*, and *Ollin*, while the Mixtecs and the Mexicans named them for the signs *Calli*, *Tochtli*, *Acatl* and *Tecpatl*. Moreover, on the calendar the day 11 *Calli* follows immediately after the day 10 *Ehecatl*, yet both these signs appear on the pectoral.

As a probable hypothesis I suggest that we have here an attempt to correlate the two calendars, the Mixtec and the Zapotec, and that both signs stand for one and the same year, called by the Zapotecs 10 *Ehecatl* and by the Mixtecs 11 *Calli*. The complete reading of the pectoral

READING THE RIDDLE OF ANCIENT JEWELS

would then be as follows: "The day 2 *Tecpatl* (Flint) of the year 10 *Ehecatl* (Wind) in the Zapotec calendar, which is equal to the year 11 *Calli* (House) in the Mixtec calendar."

The Zapotecs, like the Mayas, computed only elapsed time, so that it is quite probable that they should name the year which began with the day 11 *Calli* by the last day sign of the preceding year, that is to say, 10 *Ehecatl* whereas the Mixtecs and the Mexicans computed time while it was actually elapsing, so that they named the year which began with 11 *Calli* precisely by that day sign. (On page VI of the Vienna Codex we have also the Mixtec year sign joined to an owl head, which is also a Zapotec day sign. Cf. No. 8, bottom of page 471). The occurrence on the pectoral of the year sign A.O. similar in every respect to that which appears on the carved bones, proves the jewel to be Mixtec.

THE DAY SIGNS.—In addition to the three day signs which we have mentioned, among all the other signs that appear on the bones and on the alabaster cup (Page 474), *not one is Zapotec*, and furthermore they are in every respect similar to those which appear in the Mixtec and Mexican codices. Note for example the top bone in the illustration on the bottom of page 473, on which from right to left there is first an eagle head, then the first thirteen days of the calendar, from 1 *Cipactli* to 13 *Acatl*, and finally another eagle head. The other bone in this same illustration, on which appear the day signs, must be read, on the contrary, from left to right. It also begins with *Cipactli*, though this figure is almost destroyed, but instead of having 13 days, it has only 12 and ends with *Malinalli*. The dots which occupy the separating brackets between the day signs on this bone have no numerical value. The third bone illustrated on page 472 is the one already discussed, which has the year glyphs, attached to each of which appears one of the four day signs, *Acatl*, *Tecpatl*, *Calli*, and *Tochtli*.

On other bones also there are day signs used either as the names of people or as dates. Thus I have found 4 *Tochtli*, 13 *Cozcacuauhtli*, 8 *Calli*, 8 *Ehecatl*, 7 *Acatl*, 5 *Quiahuitl*, 7 *Ollin*, 4 *Xochitl*, 8 *Ocelotl*. There is not a single day sign which fails to appear somewhere, and there are moreover very important variants which I shall treat in detail in my monograph. Of all the bones and objects with hieroglyphs, *not one* bears a Zapotec sign, and it cannot be said that this is because the Zapotecs made no use of carved bone, since precisely at Monte Alban, from a place on the main highway, one of our guards recovered the three bones figured at the foot of this page, the designs of which are more clearly shown on page 476.

The upper one represents an owl and

CARVED BONES SHOWING THE ZAPOTEC GLYPHS

another hieroglyph that I have not been able to decipher, although it seems to be a place name. The one at the left shows two claws of a bird of prey, perhaps an eagle, and facing them another hieroglyph which I would interpret as a bundle or a knot. The one at the right represents a conventionalized serpent with a great forked tongue and a graticulated body. The rattles of the serpent are carved in the space facing the head.

The three glyphs are of a style completely Zapotec. Note for example the glyphs M and F among the day signs of the Zapotec calendar shown on page 470, representing the serpent and owl heads, taken from Zapotec inscriptions. A mere superficial inspection is enough to convince one that these three carved bones are totally different from those found in Tomb 7.

THE GODS.—Representations of gods are also to be found among the objects of gold and the carved bones. In the former the two heads of *Quetzalcoatl* (page 473) are of particular interest. Each head projects from a solar disc, conceived in the Nahua or Mixtec manner, as we shall see hereafter, and wears over his mouth a sort of bird beak. But what definitely distinguishes these heads as those of *Quetzalcoatl* are the twisted ear plugs which in Mexican (Nahua) are called *epcololli* and which are always worn by the wind god and other associated deities, for example *Xolotl*. In the tomb we found several of

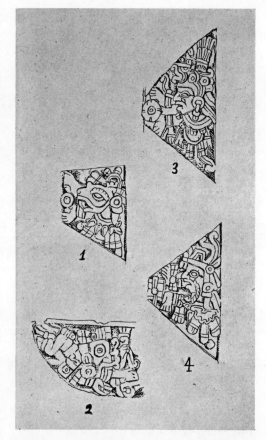

FIGURES OF GODS ON THE CARVED BONES
1. Xolotl, god of monsters. 2. Tlaloc, rain god.
3. Tonatiuh, sun god. 4. Quetzalcoatl, god of life, the wind, and the planet Venus

these ear plugs life-size, three of gold and the rest of shell. Never yet have I discovered a representation of *Quetzalcoatl* thus conceived, in a Zapotec urn or sculpture.

But without doubt the most beautiful image of any deity among all those we found in Tomb 7 is the already famous little mask of the god *Xipe-totec*, "our lord the flayed one," god of spring, of vegetation, and of jewelers (page 464). Although Sahagun tells

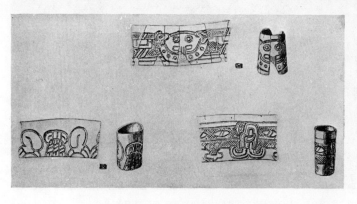

DRAWING OF ZAPOTEC GLYPHS ON BONES SHOWN ON PAGE 475

us that he was a Zapotec god, under his other name Yopi, he seems also to distinguish him as god of the *Yopi* or *Tlapaneca* tribe, who lived enslaved by Mixtec tribes in the region conterminous to the present states of Guerrero and Oaxaca. (See page 427 in Seler's translation.)

As a matter of fact I never remember seeing any Zapotec funerary urn or stela in which *Xipe* appears with the attributes we are used to see in his attire, whereas in Mixtec codices his appearance coincides with that

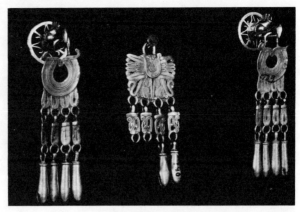

MOON SYMBOLS

On the right and left are eagle heads projecting from solar discs and bearing in their beaks symbols of the moon. In the middle is another representation of the moon

of the little mask. The nose-plug with a cone in the middle and two lateral bands shaped like a swallow tail is found constantly in the representations of this deity.

On the bones we found portraits of *Tlaloc, Tonatiuh, Xochipilli, Xolotl, Huehuecoyotl, Quetzalcoatl,* identical with these gods as they are represented in Mexican and Mixtec manuscripts, but we have had no such experience with the Zapotec urns and sculptures (see page 467). We could add the same of the animals, especially those which are day signs in the *Tonalamatl*, but for comparison one need only see those on the bones here published and to which I referred above.

THE SYMBOLS.—The symbols most common on the jewels of Monte Alban are the sun, the moon, the sky, the butterfly, as symbolic of fire, the *chalchihuite* (jade) the *tlachtli* (ball game), the earth monster, the falling eagle, the mountains, the representation of conquests, etc.

The sun is shown on several pieces of gold, but most significantly on the manysectioned pectoral (at the left). Here, in the second section it is portrayed surrounded by a river of blood and with four rays and four jade pendants; at its center there is a circle with forty-nine dots and a skull. Probably the jeweler meant to

GOLD PECTORAL OF MANY SECTIONS

Above, the *tlachtli* or ball game, representing the sky and the movement of the stars. Next the sun. Next a flint knife representing the moon. Last the toad, symbol of earth

THE CELESTIAL BAND
As shown on the carved bones. The upper carving repeats the design of the sun god set in the celestial band. The lower shows the band extended with faces of divinities between the rays

make fifty-two dots, such as sometimes appear in representations of the solar disc. Again in a small gold disc and others like it from which project eagle heads, *Quetzalcoatl* heads, etc., the sun appears shown after the Mexican or Mixtec fashion.

The moon appears three times in these pendants: twice in the beaks of the eagles and a third time on a bangle. In all three it is shown as in the Mixtec codices (page 477). The celestial band in the Mixtec or Mexican style with the symbol of Venus alternating with flint knives or stellar eyes, also appears many times on the bones illustrated at the top of this page and once on a large shell bracelet shown at the right.

The butterfly as a symbol of fire, and also the jade, are found as pendants in the beaks of the eagles that decorate little plaques and rings of gold and silver (page 479). The *tlachtli* or ball game appears once on the first section of the multiple pectoral (page 477), and again as a place name on one of the bones. The monster of the earth, a toad with his mouth wide open, is also to be found on the last section of the multiple pectoral, and on several bones.

THE CELESTIAL BAND
As shown on a shell bracelet

Conquered towns are indicated by the place glyph crossed out by an arrow, as is the rule in Mixtec codices, see for example the glyphs on one of the bones compared with the codices (top of page 480). On Zapotec stelae the place glyphs are shown (bottom of page 480) by a hill, with the name glyph inside it. The Mexicans use hills, too, but conventionalized after another fashion; and thus we find on one of the Monte Alban bones (top figure at the right, page 480) a conventionalized hill exactly like those in the Mixtec codices.

Lastly, the "falling eagle" or *Cuauhtemoc* is very common on the rings. This is symbolic of the setting sun as we have seen it in any number of Mixtec and Mexican codices, and as it appears also on a gold ring published by Saville (*The Goldsmith's Art in Ancient Mexico.* Plate III, c, d).

To summarize: The year sign, the day signs, the portrayals of gods, animals, and symbols as shown on the objects from Tomb 7 of Monte Alban are similar to those in the Mexican and Mixtec codices, and *totally different* from those which we find on Zapotec urns and stelae. On the

READING THE RIDDLE OF ANCIENT JEWELS

other hand, I have thought I perceived Zapotec style similar to that of the urns and stelae in certain of the gold objects already known; for example, that published by Saville, plate IV, of the above mentioned volume, and the ring (page 480). In these gold objects I seem to note a certain difference from the others already known. On the other hand, it must not be forgotten that the technique of working gold seems to have been the same all over pre-Colombian Mexico, so that it is probable that objects made of that metal, even when they come from places at great distances from each other, should have a similar appearance.

We can say that all the objects found in Tomb 7 show great similarity with Mixtec objects and codices and no stylistic similarity to the style hitherto called Zapotec, that is, that of the urns and stelae. We are forced, then, to accept one of the two following hypotheses:

Either the objects of Tomb 7 are Mixtec, as contrasted with other objects found in Monte Alban and even those placed with the first burial in the tomb, which are Zapotec, or else what we call Zapotec is merely an older style which was replaced later by a new one which we call Mixtec, and as I have already pointed out in my book *The Zapotec Stelae*, this new style may be credited to the influence of tribes of the highlands (Olmecas, Mexicans) in Zapotec art and industry.

FALLING EAGLE
(*Cuauhtemoc*)
Symbol for the setting sun. In his beak he carries a butterfly

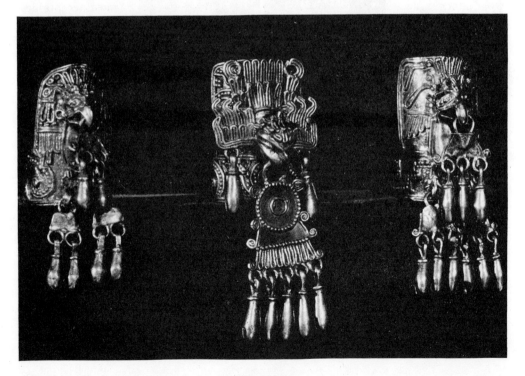

GOLD RINGS
The one in the middle is a falling eagle or *Cuauhtemoc*. He bears in his beak the glyph meaning jade

PLACE GLYPHS, AS SHOWN ON THE CARVED BONES FROM TOMB 7
The first and second glyphs indicate conquered towns, since each sign is transfixed by an arrow. The third glyph is a conventionalized hill. This place glyph is in the Mixtec style, but a similar formula is often used to denote towns in Mexican writing (Cf. p. 478)

But to decide in favor of one of these alternatives we need more excavation and above all stratigraphical excavation. There seems as yet no pressing reason, however, to abandon the first explanation and to assume that what we call Zapotec and Mixtec are two successive phases of one culture rather than coexistent manifestations of diverse cultures; and as long as no new discoveries are made, I think it is meet to consider that the two styles, Zapotec and Mixtec, belong to distinct tribes who jointly occupied Oaxaca, and that in the last centuries before the conquest Monte Alban was a frontier city between these irreconcilably hostile tribes. Thus my hypothesis that the upper or later burial in Tomb 7 must be attributed to the Mixtecs seems to me at present the most acceptable.

In the monograph on Tomb 7 of Monte Alban which I expect to publish at the end of the year, all the jewels we found will appear in illustration, which will provide more data for comparison than are contained in the objects here discussed.

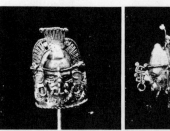

ZAPOTEC (?) GOLD RING
Showing the head of the god Cocijo

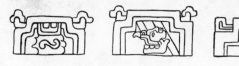

ZAPOTEC PLACE GLYPHS
These glyphs are drawn in a far more rigid style than are the Mixtec signs shown above, but they also represent place names. The designating signs are enclosed within another type of conventionalized hill, which defines these glyphs as locatives (Cf. p. 478)

BOLETÍN DE ESTUDIOS OAXAQUEÑOS

Bulletin of the Centro de Estudios Regionales
Plazuela Antonia Labastida N° 7, Oaxaca, Oax., México

A facility of Mexico City College, A. C.
Km. 16, Carretera México-Toluca, México 10, D. F.

Bulletin No. 10   Editor: Joseph E. Vincent+   November 15, 1958

THE HISTORICAL VALUE of the MIXTEC CODICES
by Alfonso Caso*

The historical value of these manuscripts lies, in the first place, in the fact that the Mixtec scribes were vested with the means for using a glyphic system, pictographic in part and possibly phonetic also, which allowed them to record the more important events in which their princes or rulers took part.

In the second place, we should mention the existence of a functional time count, which allowed them to note exactly when an event occurred, designating the year and the day. We are not certain as to whether they also employed month signs, but it appears very probable.

In the third place, the historical value of the Mixtec codices is strengthened by the fact that we find the same happening set forth independently in several of them; sometimes different types of writing were used, although always within the general style that existed in the Mixteca and, I believe, in other surrounding areas.

Lastly, the historical value of the codices is further supported by the fact that the writing system continued in use after the Conquest and, consequently, we have several documents in which historical events are recorded both in glyphs and in Mixtec or Spanish.

Let us consider more closely these four points which show the historical value of the Mixtec codices.

Mixtec writing.

Without a doubt this type of writing is derived from other earlier styles of which there are, unfortunately, no surviving manuscripts. We do know that these styles existed, however, because mural paintings, glyph-bearing vessels and other utensils and, above all, inscriptions in stone have been discovered which attest to the existence of these writing systems in several places in Mesoamerica.

From the horizon which we designate as the Formative, coming before the Classic and covering approximately the first millenium before Christ, the existence in Mesoamerica of true writing can now be demonstrated. For example, it existed beginning with the Monte Alban I period in Oaxaca[1]; in Tres Zapotes, Veracruz[2]; and in Guatemala.[3]

---

*This paper was presented to the 58th Annual Meeting of the American Anthropological Association in Mexico City, December, 1959. The translation, by Charles R. Wicke of the Mexico City College faculty, is the same one made for that presentation. The paper has been published in Spanish in Cuadernos Americanos, Vol. XIX, No. 2, 1960. The English Version is presented here by permission of Dr. Caso.

Mr. Owens, the editor for this issue, is a graduate student of anthropology at Mexico City College.

[1] Alfonso Caso, Calendario y escritura de las antiguas culturas de Monte Alban, Obras completas de Miguel Othon de Mendizabal. (Mexico: Talleres Graficos de la Nicion, 1947.)

[2] Matthew W. Stirling, Stone Monuments of Southern Mexico. ("Bureau of American Ethnology Bulletin" No. 138) Washington. Smithsonian Institution, 1943.

[3] Walter Lehmann, "Reisebrief aus Puerto Mexico." Zeitschrift fur Ethnologie, 1926.

Just after this Formative horizon, during the Classic, examples abound of the presence of a writing system--in part ideographic and in part phonetic--among the Teotihuacanos[4], Mayas, and Zapotecs, and later during the horizon which we have called Toltec, and which others call Post-classic. From this evidence it can be shown that writing existed in practically all of Mesoamerica.

It seems to us that Mixtec writing is rooted in systems found in older horizons, as we have stated elsewhere.[5] However, the Mixtec writing is known principally from the Mixteca-Puebla culture of the Toltec horizon, because of its abundance in that period. It is from the Mixteca-Puebla culture that the majority of the prehispanic manuscripts have come down to us.

As we have said, this writing is partly pictorial or iconographic. Gods are depicted showing their characteristic attributes. In representing a man or a woman, the figures are painted showing their distinctive features: dress, ornaments, etc. However, it does not appear that in any case an actual portrait of a personage was attempted. Only age and sex are shown. As to age, the child, the adult, and the old are distinguished. Individuals are represented with their jewels and insignia, and at times one's trappings indicate his profession: priest, captain, merchant, or commoner.

Buildings also are represented realistically, although simplified; the same applies to animals, plants, and utensils.

In ideographic form, that is by symbols, such concepts are represented as the year, the days, and perhaps the months. Cities are indicated by hills; rivers and lakes by vessels of water; and the sun, moon, and stars by special symbols.

We think that we have discovered and can show with examples that personal and place names were phonetically written for the most part, as also was the case with Aztec writing. An example is that of the town of Teozacoalco, also called Hueyzacoalco, meaning "large platform" in Nahuatl. This town is called Chiyocanu in Mixtec; chiyo signifies "building platform" and canu denotes "large" or "to fold." Since it would have been very difficult to express "large" by means of glyphs, the place-name of Teozacoalco is expressed by a little man folding a building platform.

The surnames of personages were expressed in this same manner, inasmuch as their proper names, regardless of sex, were those of the days of the calendar on which they were born. For example, one of the most famous kings of Tilantongo was named "8 Deer," since he had been born on the day of this name in the ritual calendar, but his surname was "Tiger Claw," which in this case was expressed pictographically by painting a claw.

Most of the Mixtec codices which have come down to us have mainly a genealogical purpose. They give the calendar name and the personal name of the king; the year he was born; who his parents were and where they ruled; frequently they indicate the date of his marriage; brothers and sisters are mentioned, and at times it is indicated which ones were married and where the husbands and wives of these sisters and brothers came from. They tell who his wives were, and his children by each of them; where the wives came from and who their parents were. Often they mention some of the king's deeds; and they give the day and year of his death.

Other codices are not purely genealogical, but historical, and they tell us of the life of some king or kings. Others recount pilgrimages; and probably, on the obverse of the Vindobonensis, we have a ritual codex.

The Mixtec calendar.

Naturally it would be impossible to sketch a history or a genealogoy which covers eight centuries without the exitence of a perfect calendaric computation, agreed to by a large number of towns. Such

---

[4]Alfonso Caso, "Tenian los teotihuacanos conocimiento del tonalpohualli?" El Mexico Antiguo, IV (1937), Nos. 3-4. Mexico.

[5]_____. "El calendario mixteco," Historia Mexicana, V (1956), No. 4.

was the case in the Mixteca. Just as in writing, in calendaric computation the Mixtecs were the heirs of other peoples who had used a similar computation in earlier times. The fundamentals of this computation were common to all the peoples of Mesoamerica and had been so at least since the Formative horizon.

Fundamentally, it consisted in the combination of two calendars: one ritual, with 260 days, formed by the combination of 20 signs with 13 numbers; the other the 365-day year, made up of 18 twenty-day periods or "months" plus five extra days. The combination of both computations gave the 52-year cycle.

That the count was the same in several cities and that it coincided day by day is proved by the fact that in manuscripts which come from different cities the same event is listed as taking place on the same day and in the same year.

Examining the possibility that the Mixtecs used not only the year and day signs but also the month sign, we note that on a stone which is set in the wall of the monestary at Cuilapan, two Mixtec years are depicted. Two days are shown with one of these years and one day with the other; but with each one there is a symbol that could be interpreted as being a month sign. This supposition is strengthened by the fact that one of these symbols is a flag decorated with transverse bands, and it is precisely a flag decorated in this way that is the symbol for the Aztec month Panquetzaliztli. Glyphs also appear in other manuscripts, especially on the obverse of the Codex Vindobonensis, which may represent months.

Another feature of great interest in the Mixtec calendar is that there are two documents, one a gold ornament and one a codex, on which there appears to be manifested a calendaric correction, establishing a correlation between an old system of Zapotec style and a new system of Mixtec[6] style. This gives some indication of the antiquity of the computation, since we know that calendaric systems are not easily reformed, nor are such reforms frequent.

The Mixtecs had, then, a calendaric system which allowed them to arrange in chronological order the events that they wished to remember, whether because of concern with succession when dealing with genealogies or because of a national or historical interest.

Agreement between different manuscripts.

Some codices have come down to us which record the genealogy or genealogies of just one place, although making constant reference to other places. Manuscripts of a more general nature have also survived in which the genealogies of several Mixtec principalities are set down and elucidated in great detail.

As examples of the first type, we have: (a) The Codex Selden II, which relates the genealogy of a place which Spinden[7] calls "Belching Mountain"; (b) the Becker II[8], which relates the genealogy of an unknown place; (c) the reverse of the Vindobonensis, which mentions the genealogy of Tilantongo.[9]

---

[6] _____. Ibid.

[7] Herbert J. Spinden, "Indian Manuscripts of Southern Mexico," Smithsonian Institution Annual Report for 1933. Washington: United States Government Printing Office, 1935.

[8] Karl A. Nowotny. "Der Codex Becker II," Archiv fur Volkerkunde, XII (1957), Vienna. (The Codices Becker I and II have been published in a new color reproduction, including also Nowotny's commentaries and a summary in English, by Akademische Druck, Auersperggasse 12, Graz, Austria. -- Ed.)

[9] Alfonso Caso, "Explicacion del reverso del Codice Vindobonensis," Memorias del Colegio Nacional, V (1950), No. 5. Mexico.

As examples of the second type, we have the obverse of the Zouche-Nuttall, which gives us not only genealogical information from several places, but historical tidings as well; and above all the Codex Bodley, which takes us back to the year 692 A. D.[10] and contains information about numerous cities.

It follows that the data furnished by one of these manuscripts, the reverse of the Vindobonensis, for example, can be corroborated with those found in the Zouche-Nuttall and in the Bodley. In this case we have three sources that tell the same story, and at times other specimens of secondary importance, such as the Codex Colombino or the Becker I, which may add information that verifies what these manuscripts set forth.

Furthermore, this agreement is not so consummate as to make us suspect that some codices are copies of others. Discrepancies exist which can be important at times. However, this does guarantee us that we are not dealing with copies, even though it often bewilders us as to where lies the truth.

As examples of the second type, we have the obverse of the Zouche-Nuttall, which gives us not only genealogical information from several places, but historical tidings as well; and above all the Codex Bodley, which takes us back to the year 692 A. D.[10] and contains information about numerous cities.

It follows that the data furnished by one of these manuscripts, the reverse of the Vindobonensis, for example, can be corroborated with those found in the Zouche-Nuttall and in the Bodley. In this case we have three sources that tell the same story, and at times other specimens of secondary importance, such as the Codex Colombino or the Becker I, which may add information that verifies what these manuscripts set forth.

Furthermore, this agreement is not so consummate as to make us suspect that some codices are copies of others. Discrepancies exist which can be important at times. However, this does guarantee us that we are not dealing with copies, even though it often bewilders us as to where lies the truth.

At times it may be just a question of simple variations rather than actual discrepancies; for example, the name of a personage might vary, or the day or year of an event. At other times, although fortunately not often, we are left in doubt as to the occurrence itself. For example, while one codex might mention a queen's being the mother of certain princes, another codex will make the princes the children of another of the king's wives.

Some variations are purely representational, with the content being the same. For example, there are two ways of showing the place-glyph for Belching Mountain; there are two also for Tilantongo, which at times is represented by a panel decorated with black mosaic patterns to indicate the name "Black Earth," while at others it is referred to by means of a hill on which rests a temple with a sky-band roof, in order to complete the name "House of the Sky," since the full name of Tilantongo in Mixtec is Notoo-huidadeui, "Black Earth, House of the Sky."

Sometimes the variants are so dissimilar as to indicate different concepts. For example, we have already mentioned that the name of the town Teozacoalco is depicted by a little man folding a building platform, and although this is the general rule, there is a variant in which the name of the town is indicated by a wall which has at one end a flower with four petals. Perhaps the name of this flower also means "large."

In general the Mixtec scribes had plenty of latitude in representing whatever they wished to express. Even glyphs as conventional as those of the calendar, such as day and year signs, show important variants. These cannot always be explained as regional variations or even personal ones, since in the same manuscript and at times on the same page the year sign has squared corners in one place and rounded ones in another, or even varies more radically.

---

[10] _____. "El calendario mixteco," op. cit. (See also Caso's study of the Mapa de Teozacoalco /note 11/ and the major work Interpretation of the Codex Bodley 2858 by Caso, which is also available in Spanish and which is accompanied by a full-size color reproduction of the Codex /Mexico: Sociedad Mexicana de Antropologia, 1960/--Editor.)

Proof of the historical value of the codices.

The events set down in these manuscripts are shown to be true when during the entire 16th century the same writing system continued to be used by the Mixtec scribes. This enables us to verify the happenings represented in the codices by comparison with those gathered by the Spanish chroniclers which are derived from oral tradition.

In several documents which have been preserved in the archives, and which are parts of lawsuits dealing with land or with the succession of indigenous principalities or cacicazgos, we find confirmation of what we are told by Mixtec manuscripts painted before the Conquest. Sometimes these manuscripts are accompanied by pictographic maps or "lienzos," such as those of Coixtlahuaca or Zacatepec.

Without a doubt the postconquest manuscript which most fully corroborates what the prehistoric codices record is the Map of Teozacoalco, which was painted to accompany the report which Hernando de Cervantes made on the ninth of January, 1580 in complying with the command of king Philip II.[11] This record agrees so closely with the data disclosed by the prehispanic codices Bodley, Selden II, Zouche-Nuttall, Vindobonensis, Colombino, and Becker II, that it aided us in translating fully the happenings that these manuscripts set forth.

Thus we have in a document prepared by colonial authorities the conformation and condensation of data which the codices report much more completely. This indicates that 60 years after the Conquest, the art of the Mixtec scribes was still maintained and that the history which they related, with origins going back several centuries, was surely preserved in books which must have been anxiously kept hidden for fear that they would fall into the hands of fanatic monks, who, considering them to be sources of idolatry, would condemn them to the fire, as happened with the many manuscripts that came into the power of Zumarraga and Landa.

Furthermore, agreement is not limited in these documents only to events which refer to Tilantongo and Teozacoalco. Recently I was able to show that three manuscripts--the Codex Selden I, the Lienzo Antonio de Leon, and the Codex Baranda--furnish similar data also.[12] Previously I had shown that the same Codex Selden I, the Lienzo Antonio de Leon, and the Gomez de Orozco Fragment furnish data which agree.[13]

The historical information which the Mixtec codices disclose carries us from 692 A. D. to the end of the 16th century, and, if we include the information from the Codex Muro preserved in the National Museum of Mexico, to the middle to the 17th century.

As we have said, the Mixtecs had a writing system and a calendaric system, which permitted them to preserve the knowledge of events and to fix this in time and space; that is, to set forth true history. The proof of this is that today we are able to read it and translate it into our own language.

For a Mixtec scribe, however, the reading of a codex must have been much richer than it can ever be for us. Actually, it is quite probable that history was expounded in the form of a poem that was chanted as the Aztecs and the Tarascans chanted the deeds of their ancestors in real sagas and epics, and that the manuscript served only to establish those happenings, dates, and names that could have become confused or forgotten.

The manuscripts that have come down to us contain the essence of the historical knowledge in the Mixtecs. They show us the interest that these people had in history, but the rich coloring of the poetic narration disappeared with the men who knew the song.

---

[11] _____. "El Mapa de Teozacoalco," Cuadernos Americanos, VIII (1949), No. 5. Mexico.

[12] _____. "Comentario al Codice Baranda," Miscelanea Paul Rivet. Mexico: Universidad Nacional Autonoma de Mexico, 1958, Vol. 1.

[13] _____. Interpretacion del Codice Gomez de Orozco. Mexico: Talleres de Impresion de Estampillas y Valores, 1954.

THE MIXTECA-PUEBLA CONCEPT IN MESOAMERICAN ARCHEOLOGY: A RE-EXAMINATION

H. B. Nicholson

There is an increasing emphasis in New World archeology on a more precise conceptualization of the vast mass of raw excavational data which has accumulated in recent years. Although a tremendous amount of basic fact-gathering remains to be done, it is recognized that for continuing progress in the field a constant refinement of our methodological and theoretical tools is equally necessary. Occasionally it is also worthwhile to re-examine and, when called for, to reformulate established concepts, particularly where these have been employed somewhat loosely. It is the aim of this brief paper to re-examine and to present suggestions for tightening one such formulation which has had a considerable influence in recent Mesoamerican archeology, the Mixteca-Puebla concept.

Vaillant, in three important studies published between 1938 and 1941 (Vaillant 1938, 1940, 1941) created this construct as a by-product of his attempt to erect a general interpretational scheme for the prehistory of Mesoamerica, with special reference to central Mexico. Boiled down to essentials, Vaillant visualized the development and crystallization of what he variously termed a "culture," "civilization," or "culture complex" in the region of Puebla (especially at Cholula) and the Mixteca of northeastern Oaxaca immediately following the Teotihuacan period, during the "Chichimec" interregnum in the Valley of Mexico. He saw it as diffusing into the Valley, especially at Culhuacan, and providing "the source and inspiration of Aztec civilization" (1941: 83). He also believed that elements of this "culture" were carried throughout Mesoamerica, from Sinaloa in the north to Nicaragua in the south, chiefly by actual migratory movements. So important did he view this impact that he labeled his fifth and final major time division of pre-Hispanic Mesoamerica the "Mixteca-Puebla Period" (1941: Chart 1).

Vaillant never presented a systematic exposition of his concept, but in two brief passages he indicated in general terms its major elements: a carefully defined polytheism, the *tonalpohualli*, 52-year cycle, stylized picture writing, chiefly lineage, formal war, and "characteristic ceremonial practices" (1940: 299; 1941: 84). As sites, areas, and phases which displayed characteristic Mixteca-Puebla influence, apart from late central and southern Mexico in general, he specifically singled out Guasave in Sinaloa, Xochicalco, the Cerro Montoso phase in Veracruz, "the Mexican occupation of Chichen Itza," Santa Rita in British Honduras, Naco in Honduras, and Guatemala, Salvador, and Nicaragua generally. In addition, he felt that "elements of the religion affected tribal communities as far distant as the southeastern United States" (1941: 84).

Applying it to their own findings, Vaillant's Mixteca-Puebla concept was soon accepted by other archeologists. One of the first was Ekholm, who, in his

1942 Guasave report, used it to clarify the source of an important influence in the Aztatlan complex of Sinaloa (Ekholm, 1942: 126–131). In the same year the second Mesa Redonda of the Sociedad Mexicana de Antropología adopted a scheme recognizing four major horizons in Mesoamerica, for the last of which they utilized the label Mixteca-Puebla (Mayas y Olmecas, 1942: 76). Since then the term has passed into common terminological currency. Subsequent to its original formulation, however, the concept has not been the subject of any significant re-analysis. This is all the more surprising in view of a major shift in orientation toward the "Toltec problem" which occurred in the very year that Vaillant's final presentation of the concept appeared and which has since led to the rejection of much of that portion of his scheme which concerns the Teotihuacan-"Toltec" and "Chichimec" periods.

I refer to the Instituto Nacional de Antropología's excavations at Tula, Hidalgo, under the direction of Acosta (beginning in 1940), and the first Mesa Redonda of the Sociedad Mexicana de Antropología, 1941, where it was almost unanimously agreed, after some spirited debate, to effect a final divorce between Teotihuacan and the Toltecs of the traditions. This re-orientation resulted in a recognition that Vaillant's "Chichimec" period (typified ceramically by Mazapan, Coyotlatelco, and Culhuacan-Aztec I) falls almost wholly within the newly defined Toltec period, during which Tula played a dominant political and cultural role in central Mexico. Since Vaillant had classified "Mexican" Chichen Itza as Mixteca-Puebla, the nearly identical parent style of Tula necessarily also fits within his concept. But the picture revealed by the Tula excavations is quite distinct from that drawn by Vaillant, i.e., of a Mixteca-Puebla movement into the Valley of Mexico during a kind of Chichimec time of troubles. Instead, if his chronology on this diffusion is accepted, it would have occurred some time during the Toltec period, in conjunction with the development of the "Mixteca-Puebla" Toltec style itself further to the north. Vaillant's hypothesis of a Pueblan origin for "Aztec civilization" is also greatly weakened by this new alignment, for the essentially Toltec background of the latter is constantly receiving more confirmation.

Do these difficulties caused by our somewhat clearer understanding of the period between the end of Teotihuacan and the rise of Tenochtitlan force the conclusion that Vaillant's Mixteca-Puebla notion has lost its conceptual utility? I think not, but I also believe that a certain amount of reformulation is necessary. The remainder of this paper will be devoted to a consideration of the kind of reformulation which seems to be required by the evidence.

As noted above, Vaillant interchangeably employed the terms "culture," "civilization," "culture complex," and "period" for his concept. Later students added the term "horizon." This terminological variance has led to both ambiguity and confusion. The first two labels seem much too broad to be conceptually useful. The third perhaps has more justification but still appears poorly applicable to the type of data out of which Vaillant erected his construct. The last two describe the concept in terms of a temporal framework; a brief comment will be made on this below.

Analysis reveals that what Vaillant and his followers really have in mind when they employ the term Mixteca-Puebla is, above all, a distinct *style*. Thus when Vaillant speaks of "Aztec civilization" entering the Valley of Mexico at Culhuacan, he actually means that a style of ceramic decoration, out of which evolved the later dominant Valley pottery tradition (Aztec II–IV), seemingly first appears at this site (as Aztec I). Vaillant's other elements, listed above, are not particularly useful criteria, being too widespread temporally and spatially. For example, most, conceivably all, of these traits may have been present, at least to some degree, in both the Classic period Teotihuacan and Monte Alban configurations. Phrased in essentially stylistic terms, however, the Mixteca-Puebla concept can still serve a useful purpose, particularly as a chronologic marker.

What are some of the leading features of the style which lend it distinctiveness? Within the brief compass of this paper, a thorough analysis and definition is impossible, but certain diagnostics can be outlined in a very preliminary way. Perhaps the best touchstone for a definition of the developed style is the Codex Borgia, which, considering its iconographic complexity, esthetic sophistication, and stylistic near-identity to the decorative devices of the local polychrome wares, was very likely painted in Cholula itself. Above all, the style at its best, as in this superb *bilderhandschrift*, is characterized by an almost geometric precision in delineation. Symbols are standardized and rarely so highly conventionalized that their original models cannot be ascertained. Colors are numerous, vivid, and play an important symbolic role in themselves. In general, there is much that is akin to modern caricature and cartooning of the Disney type, with bold exaggeration of prominent features.

These generalities, however, are much less important in distinguishing the style from others in Mesoamerica than certain specific ways of representing various symbols. The presence of even one of these symbols or a characteristic grouping is often enough in itself to define the presence of the style. Among the most highly distinctive individual symbols are: solar and lunar disks, celestial and terrestrial bands, the Venus or bright star symbol, skulls and skeletons (with double-outlined bones), jade or *chalchihuitl*, water, fire and flame, heart, war (*atl-tlachinolli*, shield, arrows, and banner), mountain or place, "downy feather ball," flower (many variants), stylized eyes as stars, stepped fret (*xicalcoliuhqui*), sliced spiral shell (*ehecacozcatl*), and the twenty *tonalpohualli* signs. One of the most frequent and diagnostic symbol groups is the row of alternating skulls and crossed bones (often combined with hearts, severed hands, etc.). Zoomorphic forms are quite distinctive and easily recognizable, particularly serpents (frequently feathered, *quetzalcoatl*, or sectioned, *xiuhcoatl*), jaguars, deer, rabbits, and spiders. The many deities depicted are highly individualized and usually accompanied by special, clearly distinguishable insignia.

The general style can be broken down into a number of regional and temporal variants. The Toltec sub-style is one of the most divergent of these and appears to lack many of the basic elements listed above. Most surviving Toltec relief sculptures and wall paintings (the ceramics rarely display representational or symbolic motifs) seem to deal with predominantly secular themes, although supernaturalistic features are commonly intermixed. If more strictly religious depictions were available, especially pictorial codices, similarities to the general style might well be increased (the rock paintings of Ixtapantongo, State of Mexico (Villagra, 1954), probably provide a fair idea of how a sheet from a Toltec religious manuscript might have appeared). Another notable sub-style is what can be called the Valley of Mexico Aztec style, although its influence extended considerably beyond that range in the wake of the military conquests of the Triple Alliance. It is best typified by the Codex Borbonicus and most of the carved monuments unearthed in Mexico City. Although very close in both spirit and formal detail to the Cholulteca (= Codex Borgia) sub-style, it is marked throughout by greater realism. A third important sub-style is the Mixtec style proper, well-known from the large number of both pre- and post-Conquest codices which have been preserved from this region. It is extremely close to Cholulteca; certain minor but significant differences, however, probably justify its being distinguished. A number of other sub-styles could be delimited, notably that represented by the Codices Fejervary-Mayer and Laud, which perhaps originated in Veracruz (Cuetlaxtlan? The two codices sent by Cortes to Spain?), but space forbids further discussion.

Not only is the Mixteca-Puebla concept best defined in stylistic terms, it is an obvious candidate for one of the most significant recent concepts in New World archeology, the "horizon style." This useful construct, which originated in Peruvian prehistory, was given its first explicit formulation by Kroeber (1944: 108), who defined it as a style ". . . showing definably distinct features some of which extend over a large area, so that its relations with other, more local styles serve to place these in relative time, according as the relations are of priority, consocation, or subsequence." The ideal horizon style is characterized by three principal features: (1) narrow temporal distribution; (2) broad spatial distribution; (3) stylistic complexity and uniqueness. In terms of Willey's "space-time systematics," horizon styles function as ". . . horizontal stringers by which the upright columns of specialized regional development are tied together in the time chart" (Willey, 1945: 55).

Does the Mixteca-Puebla style qualify? Although it falls somewhat short of the ideal, it appears to satisfy the requirements well enough to be conceptually utilized as such. Perhaps its weakest aspect is its rather broad temporal range (in some cases apparently throughout most of the Post-Classic). Stylistically, in spite of numerous temporal and regional variants, it certainly possesses enough complexity and uniqueness to qualify. Its strongest aspect is probably its broad, though quite gappy, spatial distribution.

This latter has yet to be worked out in detail, but some of the most obvious and striking occurrences are worth noting. Apart from its heartland in the areas from which it takes its name and the immediately adjacent regions, especially the Valley of Mexico, it has been located: in almost classic form in the Aztatlan complex of Sinaloa; sporadically elsewhere throughout northwestern and western Mexico; in a distinct regional variant in the Huaxteca (particularly in stone sculpture, shell-work, and wall paintings); throughout the Veracruz littoral in styles often very close to Cholulteca ("Cerro Montoso," Cempoala, Isla de Sacrificios, Cerro de las Mesas Upper I–II, etc.); in Yucatan as the Toltec substyle at Chichen Itza and, in a later variant, as a clearly discernible influence on the wall paintings of Tulum; in the Santa Rita wall paintings, British Honduras (a particularly striking fusion of late Maya and Cholultecoid styles); somewhat weakly and sporadically in the ceramics of Chiapas, Guatemala (where the Cotzumalhuapan or "Pipil" sculptural style also displays certain generalized elements reminiscent of Mixteca-Puebla), and Salvador; and, possibly, as a pale reflection in certain varieties of Nicoya Polychrome in Nicaragua and western Costa Rica. In addition, wherever Plumbate or X Fine Orange is found throughout Mesoamerica, various Mixteca-Puebloid motifs occasionally appear. A thorough check of all Mesoamerican archeological literature would doubtless fill in a number of gaps; further excavation, many more.

The temporal range of the style is bound up with the problem of the time and place of its origin. As of now, Vaillant's hypothesis of earliest appearance in Puebla and/or the Mixteca still seems to be supported by the best evidence;

certainly, as he justifiably stressed, it reached its greatest elaboration there. Ceramically, one of its earliest occurrences is in the "policroma laca" and black-on-orange wares of Cholulteca I–Altar de los Craneos, falling apparently near the base of the Early Post-Classic (coeval with Mazapan, Coyotlatelco, Culhuacan–Aztec I, etc.; Noguera 1937; 1954). The formative stages through which it passed, however, have not yet been clearly revealed, either at Cholula itself or elsewhere. Sculpturally, some of the motifs of the Xochicalcan style definitely foreshadow the developed Mixteca-Puebla style, particularly calendric symbols (I would hesitate to follow Vaillant, however, in classifying it as a Mixteca-Puebla sub-style). It seems likely that Xochicalco, in this as in other respects, may have served as a bridge between the older Teotihuacan–Monte Alban tradition and the newer Mixteca-Puebla stylistic age.

On the basis of present evidence, the following developmental hypothesis can be suggested: it is probable that, as both the Teotihuacan and Monte Alban traditions were sputtering out, a new stylistic synthesis was taking place (in which Xochicalco may have played an important role) somewhere to the east and south of the Valley of Mexico, possibly centered in Cholula. Meanwhile a parallel process of synthesis was developing further to the north, with Tula as a center. The two evolving traditions must have exerted considerable influence upon each other, particularly the southern upon the northern, which became in a sense a sub-style of it, although preserving a strong individuality. The two traditions seem to have met in the Valley of Mexico, where the Chalco region, particularly, displays striking southern ceramic affiliations. The creators of the southern synthesis, the Mixteca-Puebla style *par excellence*, can perhaps be identified, as Jiménez Moreno has suggested (1942: 128–129), with the Olmeca-Xicalanca of the ethno-historic traditions (Historia Tolteca-Chichimeca, Muñoz Camargo, Chimalpahin, Ixtlilxochitl, *et al.*), who may have been the masters of a political empire rivaling and contending with that of Tula. With the break-up of this latter center, an outpouring of migrants, "civilized" Toltecs as well as "barbaric" Chichimeca, evidently overran the southern region. Far from obliterating its stylistic traditions, however, these newcomers appear to have readily accepted them, the Toltec groups probably fusing their own well-developed and similar stylistic canons with those they encountered. The southern tradition, therefore, continued with little basic change, as evolved Cholulteca and Mixtec, eventually strongly influencing the formation of a new Valley of Mexico synthesis, Aztec. All three were flourishing at the time of the Conquest. During both the Toltec and post-Toltec periods, waves of Mixteca-Puebla stylistic influence spread widely throughout Mesoamerica, some echoes perhaps reaching the southeast United States in the "Southern Cult" efflorescence. Although the extensiveness of this diffusion might seem to justify labeling this final Mesoamerican horizon Mixteca-Puebla, the term now coming strongly into use, Post-Classic, is unquestionably preferable, if for no other reason than the fact that the style had such varying influence in different regions, some apparently being affected little if at all.

This tentative reconstruction is only an attempt to modernize somewhat Vaillant's original stimulating hypothesis and, like his, will undoubtedly be significantly modified by further analysis and excavation. Certainly one of the most important tasks for the future is a more refined sequential breakdown of the basic style into successive stages of development. This would probably eventually result in the formulation of at least two major sub-stages; these might be labeled, respectively, Mixteca-Puebla Horizon Style A (= Toltec period) and Horizon Style B (= post-Toltec period; "evolved Cholulteca"). A promising minor lead in this direction, focusing on a single important stylistic element, the ray device of the solar disk, has already been briefly initiated by both Andrews (1943: 75–76) and Caso (1956: 173–174). A careful tracing of both the immediate antecedents of the style and its earliest formational stages is another important desideratum.

In summary: Vaillant's Mixteca-Puebla concept has been subjected to a brief critical analysis, necessitated particularly by the revision of important parts of the overall scheme in conjunction with which it was formulated. It has been suggested that its reformulation in essentially stylistic terms would best preserve its conceptual utility. An attempt was made to define briefly the salient features of the style and to sketch preliminarily its spatial-temporal distribution. Its candidacy as an horizon style was also put forward, and it was felt that it fitted the specifications well enough to qualify in a broad sense. Lastly, further research designed to clarify its sequential development was urged, which, if successful, would greatly increase its value as a chronologic indicator.

University of California,
Los Angeles, California.

References

Andrews, E. Wyllys
   1943. The Archaeology of Southwestern Campeche. Carnegie Institution of Washington: *Contributions to American Anthropology and History*, 8: (40) (Publication 546). Washington.

Caso, Alfonso
   1956. La Cruz de Topiltepec, Teposcolula, Oaxaca. In *Estudios antropológicos publicados en homenaje al doctor Manuel Gamio*. Pp. 171–182. Mexico.

Ekholm, Gordon
   1942. Excavations at Guasave, Sinaloa, Mexico. *Anthropological Papers of the American Museum of Natural History*, 38: (2). New York.

Jimenez Moreno, Wigberto
   1942. El Enigma de los Olmecas. *Cuadernos Americanos*, 5: (5) 113–145. Mexico.

Kroeber, Alfred L.
   1944. *Peruvian Archeology in 1942*. Viking Fund Publications in Anthropology, No. 4. New York.

Mayas y Olmecas
   1942. *Mayas y Olmecas*. Sociedad Mexicana de Antropología, Segunda Reunión de Mesa Redonda sobre Problemas Antropológicos de México y Centro América. Mexico.

Noguera, Eduardo
   1937. *Conclusiones principales obtenidas por el estudio de la cerámica arqueológica de Cholula*. Dirección de Monumentos Prehispanicos (mimeographed). Mexico.
   1954. *La cerámica arqueológica de Cholula*. Mexico.

Vaillant, George C.
   1938. A Correlation of Archaeological and Historical Sequences in the Valley of Mexico. *American Anthropologist*, 40: (4) 535–573. Menasha.
   1940. Patterns in Middle American Archaeology. In *The Maya and Their Neighbors*. Pp. 295–305. New York.
   1941. *Aztecs of Mexico*. New York.

Villagra, Agustin
   1954. *Pinturas Rupestres "Mateo A. Saldaña," Ixtapantongo, Edo. de México*. Mexico.

Willey, Gordon R.
   1945. Horizon Styles and Pottery Traditions in Peruvian Archaeology. *American Antiquity*, 11: (1) 49–56. Menasha.

THE PREHISTORIC TEPEHUAN OF NORTHERN MEXICO[1]

CARROLL L. RILEY AND HOWARD D. WINTERS

THE QUESTION OF CONTACT between the archaeologically known cultures and those of historic peoples is one of considerable magnitude in the north Mexican area. Archaeological evidence indicates a number of relatively high cultures, including Malpaso-Canutillo (Zacatecas), Chalchihuites (Durango), and the Chametla-Aztatlan-Culiacan horizons of the west coast. In addition there was a simple hill or mountain, agricultural, pottery making culture called Loma San Gabriel, known mainly from Durango, but perhaps linked to similar cultures extending along the flanks of the Sierra Madre Occidental from Jalisco to the southwestern United States.

Historic groups in the area include a band of Piman speaking peoples (Upper and Lower Pima, Northern and Southern Tepehuan, and Tepecano) extending from the Gila River of Arizona to northern Jalisco and intersected by a wedge of Taracahitian speaking groups, the best known of these being the Tarahumara, Opata, and various Cáhitan groups of the west coast (Yaqui, Mayo, etc.). Around the peripheries of these two distributions are people speaking dialects, sometimes called Aztecoidan, related to Nahuatl. The present paper, however, is limited to discussion of the Piman-speaking Tepehuan and their relationships to the prehistoric hill culture Loma San Gabriel and the high culture known as Chalchihuites.

Present Tepehuan distribution is fairly complex in nature (see Figure 1). There are three distinct groups, the Northern Tepehuan of the Durango-Chihuahua border area, the Southern Tepehuan of Southern Durango and Nayarit, and the Tepecano of northern Jalisco. In early records no attempt seems to have been made to distinguish among these groups (unless one or the other was included under some other name). Some years ago, however, J. Alden Mason (1952:37) very cogently pointed out that whereas the Tepecano and the Southern Tepehuan are nearest in culture and have mutually intelligible languages, the Northern Tepehuan have a rather different language, involving certain archaic characteristics such as retention of final vowels. In addition, the Northern Tepehuan seem

---

[1] A preliminary draft of this paper was presented by C. L. Riley at the American Anthropological Association meetings at Minneapolis in November, 1960. The archaeological information is mainly derived from the research projects directed by Dr. J. Charles Kelley in the Durango-Zacatecas area—part of the continuing program of Southern Illinois University in that area. The ethnological work was supported by grants (M-3565, C-1 and C-2) from the National Institutes of Health, United States Public Health Service.

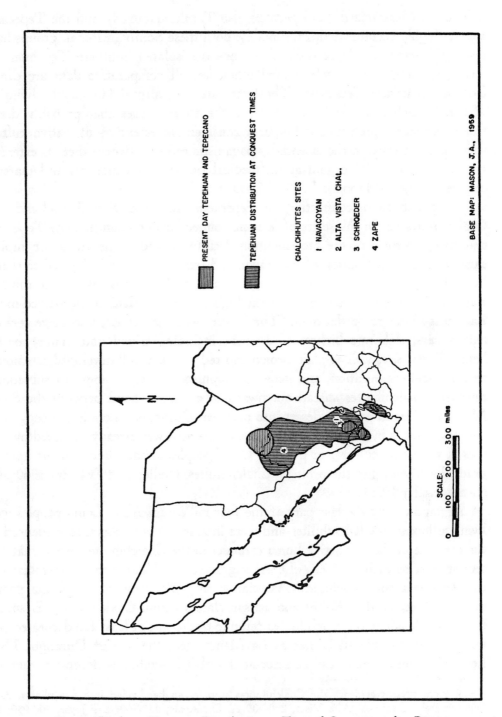

Fig. 1. Tepehuan-Tepecano Distribution at Time of Conquest and at Present.

to be quite Mexicanized (and perhaps also Tarahumaraized) and the Tepecano, too, are highly acculturated. Presumably, both these Southern Piman groups have fewer pre-conquest culture traits than have the isolated Southern Tepehuan. In this paper, unless specifically stated otherwise, all comparative data are drawn from the Southern Tepehuan. The latter are agricultural hill people, living in scattered rancherias with rectangular, adobe stone houses that probably derive from prehistoric prototypes. There is considerable retention of native culture which is manifested in the essentially paganistic religion (where there is extensive syncretism), in social organization, medical practices, technology, and material culture (Riley and Hobgood 1959:355-356).

The possibility of connections of Tepehuan with Loma San Gabriel and with Chalchihuites lies in the series of specific connections between modern Tepehuan materials and those of the aforementioned cultures, and in the known or implied early historical distribution of Tepehuan Indians. First, it might be well to sketch the sequence of events in the Durango area in prehistoric times. In the third or fourth century A.D., the carriers of the high culture, Chalchihuites, arrived in the Zacatecas-Durango border area.[2] The culture was characterized by large ceremonial centers, elaborate bichrome ceramics, including tripod and (later) basket handled vessels, as well as plain brown and red wares, a well-developed ceremonial and political organization, and generally sophisticated technology. In subsequent centuries Chalchihuites spread northward in a narrow band between the Sierra Madre Occidental and the desert into northern Durango. There is one suggestion —though this is by no means certain—that the area was already occupied by peoples of the Loma culture; or possibly Loma peoples already living in the uplands gradually moved into the orbit of Chalchihuites (Kelley and Winters 1960:549; see also Kelley 1956).

At any rate, by the last part of the first millenium A.D., Loma peoples were living adjacent to Chalchihuites and were interacting with them, as evidenced by the presence of the distinctive Loma ceramics in the Chalchihuites ceremonial centers at least as early as 800 A.D. As suggested by Winters in a paper given to the American Anthropological Association in 1959, some of the Loma people may have become the peasant and artisan classes within Chalchihuites. If so, the Loma people adopted Chalchihuites ceramic traditions, at least for decorated pottery, at such "residential" sites as La Manga near the city of Durango. These Loma-like house platforms are associated with Chalchihuites decorated ceramics

---

2 From present evidence the Chalchihuites culture can be divided into five phases, dated approximately as follows: Alta Vista, 250-500 A. D.; Ayala, 450-700; Las Joyas, 700-950; Rio Tunal, 950-1150; and Calera, 1150-1350.

and a utility pottery which in itself suggests a mixture of the Loma and Chalchihuites traditions. Loma pottery consists mostly of plain brown and textured wares or red wares, with occasional crude copies of more elaborate vessel forms and decoration from Chalchihuites (including tripod feet) and red-on-brown pottery suggestive of the late Chalchihuites pottery type, Canatlán Red Band. Of course, it is remotely possible that Chalchihuites plain wares (perhaps used in everyday tasks in contrast to the more elaborate, ceremonial pottery) were indigenous to a Loma-like population overrun by Chalchihuites and so generically related to the specifically Loma ceramics of the hills. While Chalchihuites and Loma ceramics can be distinguished by features of paste and tempering, many vessel forms and methods of surface treatment are shared, and both types of utility pottery belong within a single ceramic tradition, no matter what processes were involved in the development of such similarities in ceramic technology.

The last phase of Chalchihuites, the Calera Phase, represents perhaps a revitalization of Chalchihuites, with previously deserted sites reoccupied. There does not, however, seem to have been the extensive building activity of some earlier periods. Certain elaborations on the basic red ware tradition appeared and one decorated ware, Nayar White-on-Red, represents a segment within a wide distribution of similar decorated pottery along the west side of the Mesoamerican area from Guatemala to the American Southwest (Peithman 1961). The Calera phase (and, thus, the Chalchihuites culture) is supposed to have ended around 1350 A.D., though certain diagnostic pottery, particularly Canatlán Red Band, may have continued till a later date. Of considerable interest is the continuation of generic red wares in the Durango area. Surface collections in sites along the Tunal River, just south of the city of Durango, produce red slipped pottery, in what seems to be a Chalchihuites tradition, but wheel-made and sometimes glazed, therefore post-Spanish.

Archaeologically, then, we have the two separate but more or less inter-digitated cultures, Chalchihuites and Loma San Gabriel. The distribution of Loma sites (plus the probably-related brown ware cultures) suggests the distribution of historic Piman people, while Chalchihuites, as we shall see, seems to have contributed certain specific items to the southernmost Pimans, the Tepehuan.

Though Chalchihuites ended as an entity around or perhaps a little after 1350 A.D., the Loma culture seems to have lasted longer, and there may have been a reemergence of Loma following the disappearance of Chalchihuites. On the Loma frontier, a variant of the Loma tradition appears intrusively as far south and east as the great ruined site of La Quemada (near Zacatecas), where it may possibly be related to the historic Zaceteco Indians.

The Spaniards entered the Durango area in the third and fourth decades of the 16th century. Early accounts indicate that there were warlike Indians in the region though they are not specifically identified. In 1563, the city of Durango was founded in the Guadiana Valley of Southern Durango, only a few miles from the large Schroeder Ruin, one of the main Chalchihuites sites. Though we have little information for the early years, it seems likely that choice of the Guadiana region was due, in part, to the availability of considerable numbers of Tepehuan Indians for labor (Mota y Escobar 1930:166, 177-179). In the latter part of the 16th century, there was an expansion of Spanish settlement up the eastern edge of the Sierra Madres roughly following the line of Chalchihuites settlement a thousand years before.

The first detailed information on the Tepehuan comes in the year 1616 with the sudden violent outbreak of the great Tepehuan rebellion. In the information concerning that rebellion, particularly in a brief account written in the year 1618 and in investigations of subsequent years, a fairly good picture can be gained of the distribution of Indians called Tepehuan. It is, first of all, clear that large concentrations of such Indians inhabited the villages around the city of Durango. Other Tepehuan were found in the Canatlán-Sauceda area to the north; San Juan del Rio in east central Durango; Papasquiaro, Atotonilco, and Santa Catalina in central Durango; Zape, Guanaceví, and Indé in northern Durango. In addition, groups of Tepehuan west of Durango City are mentioned and there is a suggestion that they may also have been on the Zacatecas-Durango border area east of the capital. From the accounts, it also seems fairly clear that the Tepehuan Indians were living in the area directly south of Durango City, where they are found today. From church lists of baptized Indians taken only a decade after the rebellion, it seems that most of these places had permanent populations (Hackett 1926:101-115, 119-147). There is no indication whatsoever as to the exact identification of the Tepehuan in the early centuries. One might hazard a guess that the Tepehuan of the Durango area were Southern Tepehuan but, at present, there is no way of demonstrating this.

In any case, the modern Southern Tepehuan carry certain traditions of Chalchihuites culture. For one thing, Tepehuan plain ware pottery (made in a number of vessels forms) is, in a general way, in the Chalchihuites tradition. Occasionally, red slipped pottery appears among the Tepehuan; and until recently the tripod form was used, and vessel handles, somewhat Chalchihuites-like, are common. Tepehuan ceremonial pottery is sometimes scalloped, a possible carry-over from small unpierced lugs on Ayala phase Chalchihuites vessels. Neckless, globular vessels with sharply flaring rims are also made by Tepehuan potters. This distinctive form occurs in the Chalchihuites culture, where it probably does not appear until Calera phase times. Like Chalchihuites pottery, that of the Tepehuan is non-wheel made. Some of the Tepehuan vessel shapes are reminiscent of those appearing in the Calera phase in the area around Durango with the tripod vessels being identical in concept, although much cruder, unslipped, and undecorated.

Other striking and quite specific similarities exist. A rather elaborate terraced stone incense burner appears in Chalchihuites and an almost identical copy in wood used by modern Tepehuan for burning resin incense (see Figure 2). Even

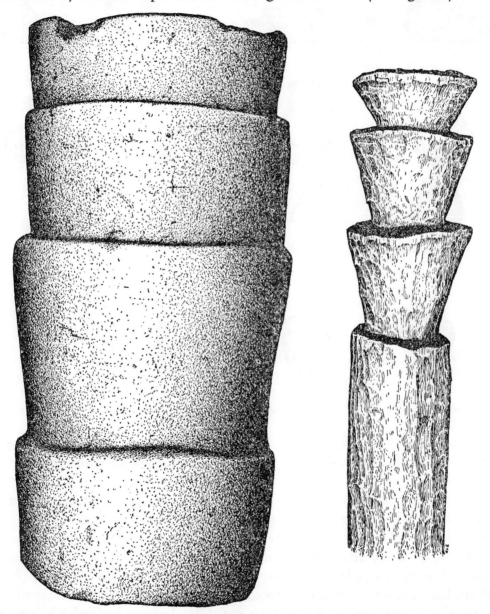

FIG. 2. Incense Burners. Left: Chalchihuites (Tunal or Calera Phase). Right: Modern Tepehuan.

more obvious, perhaps, are Tepehuan clay pipes (see Figure 3). These elaborately incised and polished platform pipes are so similar to Chalchihuites pipes of Calera phase that we originally suspected the Tepehuan of using pipes found in prehistoric ruins. This is, however, not the case; the pipes are made by Tepehuan shamans and are used ceremonially for curing. There remains the possibility that

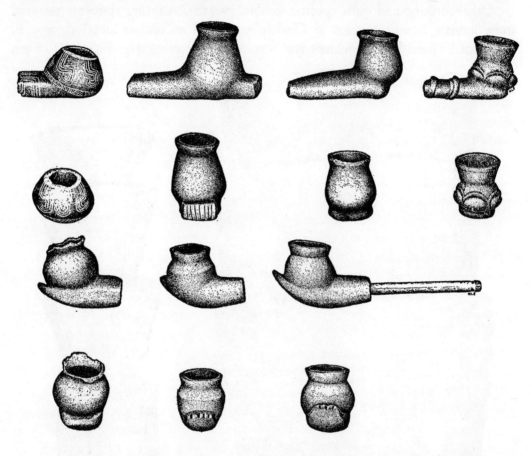

FIG. 3. Pipes. Top: Chalchihuites (Tunal or Calera Phase). Bottom: Modern Tepehuan.

the modern pipes are only copies of ancient models; if so, the copying began some time ago, for the present day shamans consider that their ancestors have always made such pipes.

There are other possible connections—for example, the Tepehuan ceremonial dance wand is suggestive of what seem to be wands carried by human beings pictured on pottery from the Las Joyas phase of Chalchihuites. Quite possibly these wands, if such they are, continued in Chalchihuites culture. Unfortunately, representations of human beings are rare both before and after the Las Joyes phase. Parenthetically, the Tepehuan ceremonial center, the *mitote* ground, is essentially a raised platform similar to such basic structural features in Chalchihuites—although this similarity may be due to certain functional necessities rather than historical derivation.

Surface reconnaissance in several of the areas of early Tepehuan settlement indicates a prevalence of Loma utility pottery, with occasional sherds of Chalchihuites ceramics. The historic patterns of population distribution and the prehistoric distribution of ceramics give ground for advancing a hypothesis that the historic Tepehuan have some relationship with the prehistoric Loma Culture. Indeed, the Tepehuan ceramic tradition might be derived more easily from simple prototypes of the Chalchihuitized phase of the Loma culture than directly from the elaborate and technically sophisticated ceramics of Chalchihuites. In some ways, Tepehuan ceramics resemble more closely the late Chalchihuites pottery itself, though this may simply be due to the fact that Tepehuan and Loma both copy the same tradition.

Specific non-ceramic relationships of Tepehuan to the simple Loma culture are more difficult to define than those with Chalchihuites. But one is probably important: the modern Tepehuan house seems to be essentially the same as the Loma house. It must be stressed here, however, that Chalchihuites houses at sites like La Manga also follow a "Loma" tradition. Certain other minor features suggest Loma: for example, Tepehuan stone spindle whorls strongly resemble Loma disks (unperforated, however) found in the Durango area. In religious features the resemblance of Tepehuan to Loma is negative, for there is a lack of elaborate ceremonial structures, developed priesthood, etc., among all modern Tepehuan and Tepecano Indians.

With the foregoing in mind, a tentative working hypothesis can be suggested to be validated or refuted by further archival, archaeological, and ethnological work. We suggest that the Tepehuan are descendants of a Chalchihuitized Loma group who had been living in the area of eastern and central Durango for many centuries before Columbus. After Spanish entry into Durango, the Tepehuan were first friendly (or over-awed), but later made one major effort to dispel the invaders. With the failure of this attempt, they withdrew into inaccessible parts of the Sierra where, in the south at any rate, they found refuge and managed in part to carry on their old life. The linguistic problem, that of the divergence between modern Northern and Southern Tepehuan, is still unsettled, but possibly the two groups were linked at conquest times by intermediate dialects that have since disappeared; for it now seems that some local Southern Tepehuan dialects may vary in the direction of the Northern Tepehuan. If our suggestions for bridging the hiatus between archaeological and historic peoples in this Durango area should prove correct, we shall have a culture sequence for the Durango area extending into the past almost 2,000 years. Demonstration of connections will not only be valuable for itself, but will also provide another base for attacking the larger problem of Mexican-Southwestern interrelations both in time and space.

BIBLIOGRAPHY

HACKETT, CHARLES W. (ED.)
    1962 *Historical Documents Relating to New Mexico, Nueva Vizcaya and Approaches Thereto to 1773* (collected by Adolph F. A. Bandelier and Fanny R. Bandelier), vol. 2. Washington, D. C.: The Carnegie Institution of Washington.

KELLEY, J. CHARLES
    1956 "Settlement Patterns in North-central Mexico," in *Prehistoric Settlement Patterns in the New World* (ed. by G. R. Willey), pp. 128-139. Viking Fund Publications in Anthropology, no. 23.

KELLEY, J. CHARLES, *and* HOWARD D. WINTERS
    1960 A Revision of the Archaeological Sequence in Sinaloa, Mexico. *American Antiquity* 25:547-561.

MASON, J. ALDEN
    1952 Notes and Observations on the Tepehuan. *América Indígena* 12:33-53.

MOTA Y ESCOBAR, ALONSO DE
    1930 *Descripción Geográfica de los Reynos de Galicia, Viscaya, y León*. México: Bibliofilos Mexicanos.

PEITHMAN, RUSSELL I.
    1961 *Cultural History and Significance of Nayar White-on-Red*. Unpublished M. A. thesis, Southern Illinois University, Carbondale, Illinois.

RILEY, CARROLL L., AND JOHN HOBGOOD
    1959 A Recent Nativistic Movement Among the Southern Tepehuan Indians. *Southwestern Journal of Anthropology* 15:355-360.

SOUTHERN ILLINOIS UNIVERSITY
  CARBONDALE, ILLINOIS

UNIVERSITY OF VIRGINIA
  CHARLOTTESVILLE, VIRGINIA

CIVILIZING THE CHICHIMECS: A CHAPTER IN THE CULTURE HISTORY OF ANCIENT MEXICO

PAUL KIRCHHOFF

Professor, Escuela Nacional de Antropología, Mexico, D.F.

Many early sources, above all those that were written by natives who had learned to write their own language in the European alphabet, deal rather extensively with a series of historical events, ranging over a period of several centuries before the coming of the Spaniards, that relate to the interplay between two strikingly different kinds of peoples—the sedentary, advanced peoples of Mesoamerican culture, and certain nomadic, backward peoples, the so-called Chichimecs, whose culture may be considered part of the simpler layer in what has been called the "Greater Southwest" or "Arid North America." In classical terminology, the former represent civilization, the latter savagery.

Among the richest of these sources are the *Historia Tolteca-Chichimeca;* Alva Ixtlilxochitl; Chimalpahin; the *Anales de Quauhtitlan;* Muñoz Camargo's, *Historia de Tlaxcala;* and the *Relación de Michoacán*. All of these, based on historical traditions that had been handed down from generation to generation, usually in pictographic records, actually make this interplay between "Mesoamericans" and "Chichimecs" the center of their interest. Their writers, as a matter of fact, were descendants of Chichimecs who had become Mesoamericans, or to put it differently, of savages who had become civilized.

The data contained in these sources may be used statically for the purpose of reconstructing the culture of both Mesoamericans and Chichimecs as it was at the time when they first met, but it seems to us that their principal value lies in the light they shed on certain historical *processes*, both indirectly on those which, on either side, paved the way to this interplay between peoples of high and low culture, and directly on those that grew out of their association.

An analysis of these historical processes may be undertaken from the viewpoint of the general problem of what happens when peoples of different cultural levels meet. But it should also be of importance for a deeper understanding and appreciation of Mesoamerican civilization, i.e., of the culture whose bearers succeeded in assimilating one group of Chichimecs after another.

Let us consider briefly what our Mexican data may contribute to the elucidation of both problems.

From the moment that one of the greatest discoveries made by man, the domestication of plants and animals, became the basis for a totally new stage in the history of culture, peoples representing the old and the new way of life must have met again and again. Hundreds and hundreds of peoples who still were mere "takers" of food must have learned how to

---

Reprinted from a paper presented in a lecture series, Some Educational and Anthropological Aspects of Latin America; Univ. of Texas Institute of Latin America Studies, V., 1948. pp. 80-85.

raise crops, not by making this discovery all over again, but by learning its application, first from those who had reached this stage by their own effort, later from their first pupils who by now had themselves become teachers of the new art and all that went with it, and still later, from the pupils of these pupils, and so on in a never-ending chain.

The occurrence of the earlier of these momentous encounters that spread the new way of life from tribe to tribe, we can only postulate; and when we speak here of "earlier" encounters, we refer not only to those that took place in the remote past but to all those cases, even though many of them may be chronologically relatively recent, in which the representatives of the new stage were themselves still rather simple farmers or herders. And as much as we may speculate about the concrete form that those hypothetical encounters between food-takers and the simpler food-raisers may have taken, we shall never be able to say anything very definite about the concrete historical processes that were involved. Above all, we cannot answer the question of whether the new mode of life simply served as an example that was imitated, or whether it was actually taught.

It is only when and where the food-raising peoples (specifically farmers) reach still another, very much more advanced and complex stage which we call civilization, that we can learn something of the actual processes by which the new discovery—by now really no longer new—spreads to peoples who are still without its benefits. One of the many advances achieved by civilization, the art of writing, when applied to the recording of important events, gives us this opportunity.

The historical records of all the earlier civilizations of the Old World seem to contain important data on their relations with less advanced peoples. But it is only exceptionally a question of relations with mere food-taking peoples. The Chinese chronicles, which deal so fully with the relations between the civilized farmers of China and the barbaric herdsmen and farmers to the north, west, and south, are a case in point.

Only in the New World, and here only in ancient Mexico, do we find sources that for a considerable span of time deal with the relations between civilized farmers (less civilized, it is true, than those of China and other Old World civilizations) and savage, roaming food-takers. These sources are, therefore, of unusual importance for the student of the history of culture, and it is surprising to notice how little they have been utilized until now for the study of acculturation processes.

Fortunately the data contained in these sources are full and detailed enough to permit us to answer here the question which had to be left unanswered for those "earlier" cases of relations between food-raising and food-taking peoples of which we spoke above. We are referring to the question of whether the advance of the food-takers to a higher level of culture came about essentially through imitation of what they saw, or whether actual teaching was involved. In the case of ancient Mexico there can be no doubt whatsoever about this point. In most, if not in all cases, the Chichimecs whom we are referring to, were actually *taught* the new ways of life by the civilized Indians of Mesoamerica. But more than that, in many cases the latter seem actually to have gone out to look for more Chichimecs to whom they could teach their own, so much higher way of living—not, of course, because they were so much in love with their own culture that in a missionary spirit they tried to teach it to others, but because in a period of cultural crisis they needed new human elements to help them carry on the multiple and complex cultural activities to which they, as civilized peoples, were accustomed, and whose continuation required the repletion of their decimated ranks.

In their attempt to civilize the Chichimecs, the Indians of Mesoamerica were, on the whole, singularly successful. The overwhelming majority of the tribes of mere food-takers on whom they went to work, changed in a surprisingly short lapse of time from a condition of savagery to that of civilization, so that after but few generations we find the descendants of peoples who, as our sources vividly and dramatically tell us, acted "like drunk" when given their first meal prepared of maize, living a life of civilized people, farmers or city-dwellers, and carrying on the complex activities that characterize a civilization as rich as that of Mesoamerica.

These peoples actually jumped one stage, by going directly from savagery to civilization.

While this rapid conversion goes to show what even very backward peoples are capable of, if only given proper guidance, it also does great credit to the peoples of Mesoamerica, who proved themselves equal to the task of lifting those savages so rapidly to a so much higher level of culture.

It seems to us that the capacity of any given culture to act as a civilizing force in its relations with more backward peoples is one of the most significant traits that we have to consider if we want to arrive at a correct evaluation of the place that a culture occupies in human development. Its civilizing role may be seen, on the one hand, in its geographical spread to, or partial influence upon, regions and peoples beyond its original realm; and, on the other, in the assimilation of immigrating or invading peoples. The spread of Mesoamerican culture to regions and peoples beyond the area where it first developed and held sway, can be reconstructed only by means of the archaeological record and the comparison of the culture of Mesoamerica and of those peoples that seem to have come under its influence. None of the native chronicles refer to it.

All that our sources tell us is the way in which the Indians of Mesoamerica civilized those Chichimecs who settled, or whom they settled, in their midst. While it is true, of course, that these data shed no light on what Mesoamerican civilization did or did not achieve (or attempt) beyond its geographical boundaries, they are, nevertheless, of the very greatest importance for our evaluation of the power behind a culture that could make wild Chichimecs over into civilized Mesoamericans and then utilize these new converts to save their own culture from the crisis in the throes of which it found itself—a crisis, by the way, whose nature and causes are still very imperfectly understood.

What seems to us even more impressive and significant is the fact that their work was so thorough that their proselytes very rapidly turned into missionaries so efficient that from a certain moment forward the main burden of winning new groups of Chichimecs over to Mesoamerican civilization, almost completely fell to them, who from a position of pupils had advanced to that of teachers.

During the last eight or so centuries before the coming of the Spaniards, the history of Mesoamerica, at least in that part of it which lies north of the Isthmus of Tehuantepec, was dominated by one central theme: the relationship between the representatives of Mesoamerican civilization and Chichimec savagery. Our sources, while using the term Chichimecs, do not, of course, use the other term, Mesoamericans, which is a modern, anthropological term. They speak instead of Toltecs. To them, the Toltecs are the representatives of what we call today Mesoamerican civilization, or rather, of a recent phase of that civilization—the only one with which our sources show familiarity.

The stage seems set then, with the Toltecs and the Chichimecs as the principal actors in our drama. But unfortunately the use of these two terms in our sources is very far from being clear or consistent. Let us mention some of these inconsistencies and often flagrant contradictions.

First of all, these two names were used both as designations of particular peoples and of whole classes of peoples. From some sources at least it would appear that the term "Chichimecs," which was principally used to designate a certain class or type of peoples, was also that of a particular people or at least of a particular group of closely related peoples. The term "Toltecs" certainly was used both as the name of an individual people (the Toltecs of Tollan, or Tula) and as that of a whole class of peoples, those who were considered to represent most typically the recent form of Mesoamerican civilization. In this classificatory sense the Olmecs were considered Toltecs, and the Toltecs of Tula Chichimecs!

When used to designate a whole class or type of peoples, the term "Toltecs" always referred to civilized Mesoamericans, but the term Chichimecs was used not only for savage food-takers (who lived in the north) but also for simpler farming peoples (because they also lived in the north[1]), or for two very different classes of civilized Mesoamericans— those whose forefathers had themselves been mere food-takers (and as such had lived in the north), and those who, at some time in their history when they already were civilized Mesoamericans, had migrated to the north, or more accurately, to the northwest, from which region later

---

[1] The Spaniards added another connotation, that of "wild, i.e., hostile" Indians (of the north).

on they had returned, accompanied by Chichimecs in the sense of mere food-gatherers or possibly, in some cases, simpler farming peoples.

What all these different and conflicting meanings of the word Chichimec had in common was the fact that they connected the peoples thus designated with the north. When applied to peoples living in Mesoamerica, the use of this term stressed the fact that they had *arrived* there, but here again we find a significant duplicity of meaning. When used in reference to those few tribes that even after their arrival in Mesoamerica had remained food-gatherers, it had the somewhat contemptuous meaning of "mere Chichimecs." But those who "had arrived," not only in the geographical but also the cultural sense, never tried to hide the fact that they were newcomers, both in Mesoamerica and in the category of civilized peoples; on the contrary they proudly called themselves and others in the same situation "Chichimecs." Both the Toltecs of Tula and the Aztecs of Mexico, to mention only one example each for early and late arrivals, proudly proclaimed themselves Chichimecs. But with equal, if not greater pride, they called themselves Toltecs, or Colhua (an alternative name used by the Toltecs of Tula).

There was, of course, a specific historical reason for the pride with which some of these former food-gatherers, who had become civilized Mesoamericans, insisted on their being "Chichimecs." The reason was that they had become the *politically* dominant element in the northern part of Mesoamerica and even farther south, precisely because they were newcomers who, young, virile, and numerically strong, had been able to take advantage of the difficult and in part truly chaotic situation in which their hosts found themselves.

It goes without saying that no grouping of peoples in which all belong either to one or other of but two classes can possibly avoid confusion and contradictions. Even in the simplest of situations there must be border cases that belong to neither class, or to both. And the situations we are dealing with here are anything but simple. A twofold classification may have been in place at the time Toltec teachers and Chichimec pupils first met. But as soon as the first pupils had themselves become the teachers of new groups of Chichimecs, the question must have arisen: should these erstwhile pupils who had turned into teachers be classed as Chichimecs or as Toltecs? And if they were to be classed as Toltecs, what about their pupils, once they in turn had undergone the same transformation?

In order to designate any one of these peoples who had something of the Chichimec and something of the Toltec, as of one class or other, one of a great number of possible criteria had to be selected to the exclusion of all others. That selection inevitably was ethnocentric, that is, it depended on whether the speakers considered themselves Toltecs or Chichimecs. They could base their characterization of a given people on its present or on its past condition. If they selected the present, and if the people concerned were composed of two or more separate elements, of different language or culture or political history, living together, they could choose any one of these elements among that people as the basis for its characterization, and for any number of reasons: numerical, cultural, or political dominance or preponderance, or, again ethnocentrically, ethnic or political linkage with themselves.

If, on the other hand, they selected as their basis of classification the past of those to be characterized, they might think of their earliest history as they knew it, when they either were still "mere Chichimecs" in the north, or, on the contrary, "Toltecs" in Mesoamerica; or they might think of a somewhat later, intermediate stage, when the former had already ceased to be food-takers, or when the latter had migrated to the north, "the land of the Chichimecs."

Even to speak simply of an ethnocentric characterization and classification of other peoples is not adequate, because in all peoples of heterogeneous composition (which, after all, seems to have been the rule rather than the exception in Mesoamerica), different and conflicting views of who should be considered a Toltec and who a Chichimec, might be held by different sectors of the population.

The detailed study of the reasons why specific peoples were called (or called themselves) Toltecs or Chichimecs or both, is a task for the future. All we have attempted here is to indicate some of the complexities involved in the conflicting classifications of peoples given by various native sources. We have tried to show that these contradictions and this confusion in classification reflect a series of contradictory and confused situations in actual life; and that the way to an understanding of the complexities of the history of Toltec-Chichimec relations, in which civilized Indians proudly called themselves Chichimecs, will be open only if and when we have understood the principles involved in these classifications and the reasons, both generic and specific, for the apparent confusions and contradictions.

The foregoing observations, which we consider as nothing more than an introduction to the study of one of the most fascinating chapters in the culture history of ancient Mexico, we hope may serve to remove some of those stumbling blocks that in the past seem to have deterred the student of acculturation processes from making use of the rich data provided by our Mexican sources.

HUMAN SACRIFICE AND WARFARE AS FACTORS IN THE DEMOGRAPHY OF PRE-COLONIAL MEXICO

BY S. F. COOK

*Division of Physiology, University of California
Berkeley, California*

THE population problems of Latin America are of considerable importance to the student of human sociology and biology for numerous reasons, not the least of which is the fact that in this area has proceeded nearly to completion a fusion of two distinct races to form a new type, the so-called mestizo. The process began with a violent collision between an invading, Caucasian group, and a native, mongoloid stock. In many areas, notably in Central Mexico, the former group was numerically small, the latter large. A long series of readjustments followed, characterized in particular by the formation and rise of the intermediate, hybrid form. To follow this evolution throughout four centuries and understand its implications, it is, however, desirable to appreciate the demographic background, insofar as is concerns the native race, and to expound the forces there at work at the time of the conquest by the Spanish.

In 1519 A.D. the empire of the tripartite alliance which, under Moctezuma II, represented the culmination of the steadily developing civilization of two thousand years, was one of the most remarkable achievements of mankind. Without the knowledge of iron, without the use of any really effective technology, without the support of domestic animals, the Aztecs and their colleagues created a social and material culture that excited the wondering admiration of even their sophisticated conquerors. Two of the most striking external manifestations of this culture were excessive human sacrifice and uninterrupted warfare.

According to the classical concept as set forth by at least the older writers, the focal point of the entire Nahua civilization was a type of religion which in turn centered around human sacrifice. This trend became intensified during the last two hundred years prior to the Spanish conquest to such an extent that the local population could not supply the demand for victims. As a result, wars and forays were undertaken far and wide to satisfy the requirements of the temples. Thus war and religion became inextricably involved with each other on the material level and were simultaneously rationalized into a spiritual unit. Military operations were possible on a scale much greater than elsewhere in primitive America because the Central Mexican plateau and adjacent coasts contained a population of such a remarkably high density as to provide continuous replacement to compensate for losses in battle and by sacrifice.

As an institution, human sacrifice has been known to all primitive peoples at all times in the world's history. In Mexico there is some ground for believing that it was employed by the races inhabiting the country in the Teotihuacan period although the "Toltecs" are generally credited with not embracing the custom. The Aztec and Spanish writers of the sixteenth century generally ascribed its origin to the late Chichimec period, prior to the founding of the Tenochtitlan. The *Codex Boturini* (Radin translation, p. 33) depicts a sacrifice in the time of Aacatl, supposedly somewhere in the eighth or ninth centuries. According to the *Codex Chimalpopocatl*, the great king Quetzalcoatl at Tula did not offer sacrifices although he was strongly tempted by the devil to do so. The *Codex Ramirez* (Radin translation, p. 74) recounts how, when the Aztecs were at Tula, the god Huitzilopochtli became angry because some members of the tribe wished to remain at that locality. One morning these persons were found with their hearts torn out. "In this way it was that they were taught that most cruel of sacrifices . . ." Duran (p. 26) places the first sacrifices just prior to the arrival of the Aztecs at

HUMAN SACRIFICE IN MEXICO

Chapultepec, that is, sometime between 1150 and 1200. Among modern scholars, Mendizabal (p. 621) is convinced that sacrifice was introduced by the nomadic Chichimecs, particularly the Otomi at the end of the "Toltec" era, since the latter people did not possess the institution. Preuss and Mengin (p. 49) similarly state: "It is thus clear that before the invasion of the Naua-Chichimecs some form of human sacrifice already . . . existed, but that its development and specific character was due largely to the Chichimecs, and particularly to the warrior Naua."

Although there is thus general agreement that human sacrifice was known and probably thoroughly incorporated in religious practice before the final settlement of the Aztecs at Tenochtitlan, the institution at that time retained its purely religious significance as an occasional and very solemn act of propitiation to the gods. It was apparently not until the fifteen century that the practice of immolating prisoners of war in masses became common. Torquemada (p. 94) says that in 1330 the Mexicans sacrificed a captured Culhua, with the implication that this was the first case of the sort, but subsequently (p. 126) he mentions 1428 A.D. with the remark that "even at that time they made war to capture victims." Some writers even placed the inception of the custom later. For instance, the *Codex Telleriano-Remensis* (Radin translation) claims: "All the old people say that from the year 1465 . . . the custom of sacrificing prisoners taken in war commenced..." Ixtlilxochitl (*Historia Chichimeca*, p. 250) ascribes the origin of the custom to the famine of 1454: "Thus these wars began, and also the abominable sacrifice to the gods, or (better to say) to the demons . . ." On the whole it is safe to ascribe the beginning of the sacrifice of captives to the very early fifteenth or late fourteenth centuries. The development of the custom to include huge numbers occurred not much prior to the middle of the fifteenth.

It was precisely at this period that the population density of Central Mexico was reaching its maximum and that the margin of subsistence was becoming somewhat precarious. With respect to the demography of the times, there are two issues: first, was the mortality due to sacrifice sufficient to act as a serious check on population increase; second, was this custom a manifestation of a social urge toward such a check.

The second issue is one of extreme difficulty and one which cannot be settled by numerical analysis. Nevertheless the suggestion is worth consideration. It is quite clear at the outset that the religious element cannot be disregarded for it carries great weight. The argument advanced by the sacerdotal class was simply that since human blood was pleasing to the gods, the more blood the greater their pleasure and the greater the benefits to be derived therefrom. But is seems inescapable that this was merely the rationalization of a far deeper tendency or drive. Certainly had it been socially undesirable to perform these acts of sacrifice, very cogent reasons would have been found for not doing so.

The predominant use of war captives is puzzling if the custom is to be regarded as directed toward limiting the population of the tribe itself. However, it should be borne in mind that the entire economic structure and the whole biological complex included all of Central Mexico together with its many linguistic and tribal units. Therefore, whenever the local state, Tenochtitlan or Hueyozingo or Tezcoco or Tlaxcala, immolated its neighbors, it was, in effect, limiting its own population, or at least, balancing the food supply and economic resources upon which it, together with its neighbors, depended. Even the destruction of remoter peoples, such as in Guerrero, or Oaxaca or the Huasteca, achieved the same end by permitting the expansion of the conquering population into new territory and thus restricting not its own total number but its density per unit area. The close association with warfare is obvious. Military operations were inevitable for other purposes, to repel assault, to protect commercial interests, to open new regions for economic exploitation. As a by-product, the population problem could be attacked indirectly by massacre on the spot, or with greater moral justification and religious satisfaction and profit by formal sacrifice.

The sacrifice of slaves was roughly equivalent to that of war prisoners, since both were derived from outside the immediate body politic, and any captive taken in battle automatically assumed the status of slave. On certain occasions, however, it appears to have become necessary to fall back on the method of purchase rather than capture. After one of the wars in Oaxaca, for example, as described by the *Codex Ramirez* (p. 132), victims became so scarce that parties were sent out daily to the public markets at Tlaxcala, Hueyozingo, Cholula, Atlixco and elsewhere so that instead of jewels, sacrificial victims might be purchased. In *Ritos Antiquos* (p. 26) occurs the significant statement in reference to the slave slaughter at the annual festival of the *mercaderes* at Atzcopotzalco, ". . . for the feast they got slaves to be sacrificed, and they were found cheaply, *as the land was well populated.*" Obviously slaves would not be purchased merely to kill them if the supply were not far in excess of the demand in the labor market. However powerful, no purely religious urge can maintain itself successfully for any material period of time counter to fundamental economic resistance.

In the century preceding the conquest, not only war prisoners and slaves but also children were sacrificed. This destruction of infants is especially significant since they were the offspring of the tribe itself. Indeed, child sacrifice seems to have been regarded as so important that no social class was immune for "these were not slaves but sons of the nobles" (*Ritos Antiquos*, p. 25). The numerical as opposed to the ceremonial importance, however, is difficult to assess, for there are few details available. Sahagun's account is the most circumstantial. At the feast of Atlacahualco, he says (vol. 1, p. 72) ". . . . they searched for a great many infants, buying them from their mothers," and killed them at seven places on hilltops and in the Laguna de Mexico. He elsewhere states (p. 54), "According to the reports of some people, they collected the children they sacrificed in the first month, buying them from their mothers, and then killed them at all subsequent festivals until the rainy season came in full force." The payment to the families might be regarded not only as direct compensation for property loss (this alone in the case of slaves) but also as some recognition of an obligation incurred by the state to the individual family through the sacrifice of the child for the public welfare. Sahagun (p. 52.) also mentions that at the feast of Tozotontli "they killed many children."

The *Codex Magliabecchi* mentions several occasions on which children were the victims. At the feast of Xilomaniztli (lamina 17) "they sacrificed children . . . which were drowned in canoes." Drowning seems to have been the standard method for disposing of children. At the feast of Tocoztli (lamina 19) "they sacrificed young children and young girls, and also newborn babies." At the feast of Zazitocoztli (lamina 20) they sacrificed "the children at dawn." At that of Ecaloaliztli (lamina 22) "they offered . . . newborn babies." At that of Michayehuitl (lamina 25) "they sacrificed children" and "on that occasion the feast of the dead children was celebrated . . ."

Both these sources agree substantially that during at least five out of the eighteen annual religious festivals numerous infants and small children were sacrificed to various gods. Just how numerous is uncertain. How many is "many"? If Sahagun is correct in stating that at one feast the ceremonies were held on seven hilltops and at the lake then we might suppose that perhaps one hundred were involved in all. Certainly at each hilltop ceremony the number would be several and judging by other accounts the sacrifice at the lake was on a considerable scale. Then if the three or four other sacrifices were of comparable magnitude, the total annual loss was, say, five hundred.

Similar customs prevailed elsewhere on the plateau. At Tlaxcala (Camargo, p. 199), "The victims who were sacrificed were . . . on several occasions . . . newborn infants." Pomar, in his account of Texcoco, says that at the celebration of Tlaloc ". . . ten or fifteen innocent children up to seven or eight years of age were killed." Some of the Spanish writers are more extravagant in their statements. Torquemada (vol. 1, p. 287) says, referring to Cholula, "Many of our people affirmed when entering the town that they considered as true the report that six thousand creatures of both sexes were sacrificed each year." Oviedo (vol. 3, p. 498) raises the estimate to ten thousand. This author (vol. 3, p. 499) also charges that during the massacre at Cholula by Cortes in 1519, the native allies "carried over twenty thousand creatures, small and large, which were sacrificed"—a manifest absurdity. With respect to the whole country, Torquemada writes (vol. 2, p. 120), "The first bishop . . . Frai Juan de Z .marraga, says in a letter, which he wrote on notable things of this Land, that every year twenty thousand children were sacrificed, according to count." Zumarraga's value, even though "according to count," must be scaled down drastically. Nevertheless, if we remember that these sacrifices were carried on at perhaps one hundred cities, towns and other religious centers, we may conclude that at least 2,000 infants and small children were wiped out annually.

Such a number of deaths, out of a population of surely at least two millions, would increase the mortality rate by no more than a very few tenths of one per cent. This in itself is unimportant but as a symptom of a general tendency it has definite significance, for although child sacrifice as practised could not of and by itself seriously check population increase, it was performed far too extensively to justify on purely ceremonial grounds.

The fact has been mentioned that people were sacrificed not only at Tenochtitlan but also at many other towns. The *Codex Ramirez*

(p. 101) says: "... in this way they sacrificed all prisoners of war ... and the same thing was done by all neighboring nations, imitating the Mexicans in their rites and ceremonies ... This feast of Huitzilopuchtli was general throughout the land ... and so ... there was no province nor village which did not celebrate the feast in the said manner." Regarding this same feast, Duran (vol. III, p. 61) says "... in all the provinces of the Land, the feast was general." Ixtlilxochitl (*Historia Chichimeca*, p. 268) adds "... beside those referred to, they sacrificed many during the kingdom, in the city of Mexico as well as in Tezcuco and Tlacopan and other populous towns and capitals of provinces under the empire ... and in those provinces outside the empire, it was about the same." The early conquerors are quite explicit concerning the wide extent of the custom. Thus states Bernal Diaz (p. 138-140) after describing the condition of certain Totonac towns, "... we found the same thing in every town we afterwards entered," and "... but as many readers will be tired of hearing of the great number of Indian men and women whom we found sacrificed in all the towns and roads we passed, I shall go on with my story without stopping to say any more about them." Among the towns specifically mentioned as conducting such rites are Tezcuco, Tlacopan (Ixtlilxochitl), Cholula (Torquemada), Tlahquiltenango (*Codice Mauricio de la Arena*), Tlaxcala, Hueyozingo, Calpa, Tepeaca, Tecalca, Atotonilca, Quaquechulteca (Duran, vol. III, p. 60), Coatepec (Duran, vol. III, p. 151), Cotaxtla, Cempoala, Xocotlan (Bernal Diaz, pp. 138, 181). It is clear, therefore, in making any numerical estimate that, although Tenochtitlan was the most important single center, the outlying towns and provinces can by no means be neglected.

We have a few direct statements with respect to total numbers annually sacrificed. That of Zumarraga previously quoted, 20,000, although children (*criaturas*) are specifically mentioned, may have referred to all persons. This would correspond to that of Gomara who says (p. 285) "... and there was no year with under twenty thousand persons sacrificed, and over fifty thousand according to other references, in the land conquered by Cortes; but if even ten thousand, it was a great butchery ..." Provisional acceptance of these Spanish estimates would place the number anywhere from 10,000 to 50,000 per year.

More numerous are statements with reference to individual festivals at specific towns. Duran (p. 60) maintains that at the principal fiesta, to Huitzilopochtli, more than 1,000 persons were customarily killed throughout all Central Mexico. At that of Xipe he says (p. 203) at least 6,000 were killed. At the 14th month, according to Motolinia (p. 38) ". . . they sacrificed, according to the size of the village, in some twenty, in others thirty, in others forty, and even fifty and sixty; in Mexico they sacrificed one hundred and over." If there were 100 towns and the average number was 40 then the total for this festival would be 4,000. There were 18 festivals per year—to correspond with the Aztec months—in other words, almost continuous activity in the temples. If the above three cases may be regarded as representative, the average would be about 3,000 per month or 54,000 per year. But most of the fiestas were on a smaller scale. Accordingly the average may be reduced to 1,000, the annual rate to 18,000.

Another item of evidence consists of the famous skull counts made by the Spanish soldiers. There appear to be two of these. The first was by Bernal Diaz who states (p. 181) that at the town of Xocotlan ". . . in the plaza . . . there were piles of human skulls so regularly arranged that one could count them, and I estimated them at more than a hundred thousand. I repeat again that there were more than one hundred thousand of them." The second was by Andres de Tápia who examined, at Cortes' request, the great temple at Tenochtitlan. In his *Relacion* (p. 583), he describes the method of arrangement, then says: ". . . the writer and a certain Gonzalo de Umbria counted the cross sticks which were stretched from pole to pole, as I have described, and multiplying by five skulls per cross piece we found there to be one hundred thirty-six thousand heads, without those of the towers." The towers were two in number, of considerable size, made of "lime and skulls of the dead, without any other stone."

The veracity of these statements, and of the others cited above, has been seriously questioned by modern historians. As much discretion is necessary, however, in rejecting them as in accepting them. The early chroniclers, such as Motolinia, Gomara, and Duran, derived their figures from the statements of others, such as elderly natives and pioneer Spanish. Hence these figures are second-hand, perhaps subject to exaggeration and certainly to inaccuracy in detail, although I doubt if they deliberately distorted what they knew to be facts. Bernal Diaz and Andres de Tápia are in a different category. They were actual participants in the conquest, eyewitnesses of the events they described. Both can be accused of personal bias with reference to the politics of the day, the merits of Cortes and similar matters. But they both state emphatically that they actually counted the skulls in question and as accurately as they were able. They had no motive for falsification and both were reliable, competent soldiers. I can therefore see no reason for not accepting their figures at face value.

With respect to Xocotlan (and Diaz is positive in his identification of the town with no likelihood that he confused it with Mexico) we do not know how long the skulls had been collected. However, it is doubtful whether they antedated the period of Aztec domination, that is to say, the middle of the fifteenth century. If so, seventy years is a fair estimate. Diaz says there were "more than" 100,000, but we may use the flat value. Then the annual increment was approximately 1430.

In Tenochtitlan we have better dating. The temple was built previous to and dedicated in 1487, thirty-two years prior to Tápia's count. This would mean an average of 4,250 sacrifices per year, including the colossal slaughter which accompanied the dedication. Indeed, if we deduct 20,000 for the dedication, the subsequent rate would be 3,630. On the other hand the skulls reported by Tápia as embedded in the towers are not included in this calculation.

Accepting the rates above indicated for Tenochtitlan and Xocotlan, it becomes necessary to extrapolate to the entire region, a process which inevitably involves a large element of assumption. Tezcoco, nearly as large as Tenochtitlan, may be assigned 2,000 sacrifices per year and the remaining lake towns perhaps 500. Hueyozingo and Cholula may have accounted for 1,000 each. At Tlaxcala it is said by Gomara (vol. 2, p. 274) that at the regular 4-year festival 400 were killed at the big temple, 300 in each of the other three *barrios* and in each of the other 28 towns of the province "algunos"—let us say 1,500 in all. Motolinia (p. 57) gives an estimate of 1,200 for the same festival. Counting in the routine monthly festivals, the annual average must have amounted to at least 2,500. Tepeaca, Chalco and vicinity may be allotted 1,000, the Morelos towns, 1,000, the Toluca Valley, 500, and southern Hidalgo and northern Puebla, another 1,000. The total for the Nahua confederacy and its immediate neighbors would then be approximately 15,700. In the outlying regions, Guerrero and the south coast, the Totonacapan, the Huasteca, the Mixteca, the Zapoteca, the Tarascan territory in Michoacan, sacrifices were performed but on a much less extensive scale. If we allow 4,000 to 5,000 for these areas, the general total would amount to 20,000 per year.

A third source of information comes from the reports of war captives sacrificed. These were often reserved for special occasions such as the coronation of kings and dedication of temples. The most sensational single such butchery recorded took place at the dedication of the new temple at Tenochtitlan in 1487, an occasion which may serve as a prototype. The estimates of the slain which appear in the chronicles are almost unbelievable. The *Codex Telleriano-Remensis* (p. 141) says 20,000, Torquemada (vol. 1, p. 186) 72,344, Tezozomoc (p. 268) 80,400, Duran (p. 346) 80,400. The commemoration stone at the National Museum indicates 20,000 (Tezozomoc, p. 519, footnote), a figure accepted by Orozco y Berra (*Ann. Mus. Nac.*, vol. 1, p. 61).

In spite of the many detailed accounts we have no adequate description of how the sacrificial operation was performed. The standard statement is that the victim was thrown back downwards on the stone, being held by five men, his chest "opened" and his heart "snatched out" or "torn out" by the high priest or chief officiator. Immediately the body was thrown down a long flight of steps while the heart was offered to the god with appropriate ritual. Some estimate of the time consumed is possible. To seize the prisoner, already directly in front of the stone, and throw him down would not consume more than a minute, despite his struggles. What happens next depends upon the type of operation employed.

Torquemada (vol. 2, p. 117) after pointing out that the victim was bent nearly double, backward over the stone, states ". . . the supreme priest arrived armed with a knife, and opened him very deftly, and wide open in the chest, and in such a manner that it was scarcely heard or seen . . ." Motolinia (p. 38) says the chest was opened "with great strength" and "rapidly". The Anonymous Conqueror, who had exceptionally good access to information, states (p. 52), "He plunges the knife into the breast, opens it and tears out the heart . . . and this as quickly as one might cross himself." Pomar, in the *Relacion de Tezcoco*, (p. 17) specifies that the chest was opened "from one teat to the other."

It seems evident that the incision was made by a single hard blow with the obsidian knife directly through ribs and sternum such that a wide aperture was formed through which the priest could grasp and tear out the heart. A competent and practised operator should be able to finish within one minute. Another minute should suffice to throw the body down the steps (performed by assistants), stretch the heart toward the shrine, smear the idol with blood and throw the heart in a dish (performed by the priest). Three minutes thus appears a reasonable time during which a single sacrifice could be accomplished, although perhaps under great pressure and by omitting some of the ritual it could be done in two. As an absolute minimum the latter estimate may be accepted.

At the dedication ceremony there were four lines of captives, such that four could be killed simultaneously (Duran, p. 345). The king started but soon tired and was replaced by priests who worked in shifts. Rotating in this manner the process was kept going continuously (Tezozomoc, p. 517) for four days. Now two minutes per victim, four at a time, means 120 per hour. Assuming actual continuous operation for 96 hours (i.e., four days), the total would have been 11,520. Duran states in detail that the four lines extended up the temple steps from (1) the Cuyoacan road "casi una legua," (2) from the Calzada de Señora de Guadalupe, also nearly one league, (3) up the Calle de Tacuba and (4) east to the lakeshore. Calling a Spanish league equal to three English miles, each line was then about two miles long. The captives must have been in single file and if a linear space of three feet standing room is allowed for each the total comes to 1,760 times 2 times 4, or approximately 14,100. These are both considerably smaller than any of the historical estimates but if we include the sacrifices which must have been performed in the adjacent temples and "cues" the figure of 20,000 accepted by Orozco y Berra appears wholly reasonable. The values of 70,000 to 80,000 mentioned by Duran, Ixtlilxochitl and Torquemada seem wholly out of line unless they were referring to the entire Nahua confederacy, in which case such numbers are possible but not probable. It is better, I think, to adhere to the more conservative and better authenticated estimate of 20,000 victims in Tenochtitlan and its immediate environs.

There are a few other cases of wholesale slaughter in the temple for which an actual numerical estimate is offered (most of these by Duran):

1442	War with Chalco	500 persons	(Duran, p. 144)
1447	Huasteca	6,000 "	(Bancroft, *Native Races*, V:418)
1476	Tliliuquitepec	700 "	(Duran, p. 298, p. 301)
1477	Metztitlan	40 "	(Duran, p. 313)
1499	Tehuantepec	17,400 "	(Ixtlilxochitl, *Hist. Chich.*, p. 272)
1503	Icpatepec	5,100 "	(Duran, p. 423)
1506	Tlaxiaco	1,000 "	(Duran, p. 501)
1507	Tututepec (2 campaigns)	3,650 "	(Tezozomoc, p. 631)

The sum of the captives taken for sacrifice in the nine campaigns listed above, plus the holocaust of 1487, is 54,390, an average of nearly 700 per year. But these are only a few outstanding cases. In Appendix I are listed as many campaigns as can be clearly distinguished from the historical records, together with estimated battle casualties. Owing to the highly specialized mode of warfare developed by all the Mexican tribes, the number of captives was fully as large as that of the actual killed and perhaps may have been much larger. The total casualties incurred by both sides in wars in which the Aztecs participated, according to this compilation, was 248,700. Certain adjustments must be made, however, before accepting a final value. The first two wars, those waged at the time of the formation of the tripartite alliance, should be deleted, since the number of captives sacrificed was at that era relatively small. This leaves 192,700, a figure which includes the losses of the Aztecs themselves. Since the latter, however, were the dominant people, and were almost always the victors, their loss was definitely smaller than that of their opponents. A ratio of 2 to 1 in favor of the Aztecs would not be excessive. Hence the enemy losses in battle dead and likewise in captives would approach 130,000. If this figure is spread over the ninety years from 1430 to 1520 the annual average is 1,440. Finally, some account must be taken of the numerous raids and skirmishes which left no historical trace. Including these we may arrive at an annual average of 2,000 war captives sacrificed at Tenochtitlan. This appears a sounder estimate than the 700 mentioned above which was based upon an obviously incomplete record.

The Tápia skull count gives an average of 4,250 sacrifices for Mexico during the last thirty-three years of the empire. But since the number is known to have reached its maximum in the generation preceding the Spanish Conquest, the two estimates are not seriously at variance. Extrapolating the war captive figures to the whole territory in a manner similar to that used with the skull counts, we get an annual average for ninety years of 9,400. To these must be added the children, slaves, and others not taken in warfare, say 2,500, giving a total of approximately 12,000.

To summarize the preceding discussion the values obtained for annual sacrifice rate in Central Mexico are:

- A. Direct estimates by the Spanish, covering last years prior to the conquest.................. 10,000-50,000
- B. Descriptions of individual festivals, covering last years 18,000
- C. Skull counts, covering last 30-40 years........ 20,000
- D. War captive estimate, covering last 90 years... 12,000

Considering the sources of numerical information available, the four methods yield results surprisingly in agreement. Allowing for changes over a century, 10,000 to 20,000 persons were sacrificed per year, with an over-all mean of approximately 15,000.

To secure an exact appreciation of the magnitude of human sacrifice as a demographic factor, the possible birth and death rates should be considered. We have no direct information concerning these variables but it is known that among virile, moderately healthy primitive peoples, uncontaminated by venereal or epidemic disease, the death rate seldom rises over 40 or 50 per thousand persons per year. For purely illustrative purposes let us assume the latter value to have been characteristic of Central Mexican civilization. Furthermore, let us assume that the total population approximated 2,000,000. Then the basic, non-sacrifice death rate would have been 100,000 per year. Therefore a mean annual sacrifice rate of 15,000 would have augmented the death rate by roughly fifteen per cent, a quantity which, over one or two generations, could have been of material significance in aiding to control the population density.

The conclusion appears warranted that the first issue set forth previously, i.e., could human sacrifice have been sufficiently extensive to affect population trends, must be answered in the affirmative on the basis of available numerical data. The second issue, i.e., was human sacrifice the manifestation of an urge toward population control, can be answered by no means categorically. Absolute proof for such an hypothesis is wholly lacking. Yet the possibility cannot be lightly dismissed that a religious institution was unconsciously directed, one might almost say perverted, to a social and biological end during the later phases of Aztec domination.

Our interest in military operations is here confined to the magnitude of battle casualties. For a detailed discussion of other matters reference may be made to the treatise of Bandelier (1877), which has never been surpassed in its scholarly treatment of the subject.

The period which began with the founding of Tenochtitlan in 1325 and coincided roughly with the first century of Aztec autonomy appears to have been remarkably free from armed operations of any kind. There is no recorded war or expedition from 1300 to 1350. Bancroft (*Native Races,* V: 347) states that Tezcoco, during the reign of Techotl (1305-1357) was "almost entirely undisturbed by civil or foreign wars." Meanwhile at Tenochtitlan, according to the *Codex Ramirez* (Radin translation), "they were at peace and increased in numbers, mingling in business and social intercourse with the surrounding peoples;" and "the second king, Huitzilihuitl" (1359-1375) "ruled . . . during a time of great tranquillity and peace."

In 1349 or 1350 occurred the war between Tezcoco and the group of migrating Nahuas known as Teochichimecs. A very bloody battle took place which resulted in the defeat of the invaders. In 1384 there was fighting on the eastern plateau between Tlaxcala and an allied group. In 1395 the Aztecs attacked the town, or province of Xaltocan and crushed the rebellious inhabitants. These three are the only campaigns of sufficient consequence to have been recorded prior to the great struggle for supremacy between the allies and Atzcapotzalco which began about 1415. The inference is plain, and has been commented on by many writers, that during this long era of quiet the Nahua tribes, the Aztecs, Culhuas, and Tepanecs particularly but also doubtless the Chalcans, Hueyozincans and Tlaxcalans were increasing in number and developing their agricultural and economic resources. Beginning at approximately 1415, however, the tripartite alliance launched its career of conquest and from that time wars were incessantly waged. It is, therefore, the final century prior to the arrival of the Spaniards during which warfare may have had a significant bearing on the status of population.

The size of armies as frequently stated by the sixteenth century writers is so huge as to call forth an immediate charge of gross exaggeration. Nevertheless there is some reason to believe that the exaggeration was not as great as might be supposed. Duran (p. 166), commenting on the Aztec power in the middle of the fifteenth century, avers that the central authority could easily field an army of 100,000 men, including those drawn from the home provinces. Now Bandelier (1877) points out that in Anahuac every citizen over the age of 15 years was a warrior and liable for military service. He elsewhere mentions that the city of Tenochtitlan was divided into four *barrios,* each of which was divided into 3 to 4 smaller districts. Each of the latter furnished on the average 300 men. This means a mobile reserve, for the ranks, of 3,600 to 4,800, say 4,000. But to these conscripts must be added the *principales* or nobles whose entire life was devoted to fighting. Their number was large, perhaps equal to that of the citizen soldiers. If so, then Tenochtitlan could put at least 8,000 men into a campaign. Tezcoco could furnish as many, Atzcopotzalco and Tlacopan nearly as many. When the smaller towns of the valley of Mexico are included, 100,000 is by no means an unreasonable estimate.

Some of the values for size of armies which have been mentioned are as follows:

- 1349. Tezcoco and allies against the Teochichimecs. Allied army 100,000 (Veytia, II: 165).
- 1415. Tepanecs and Aztecs against Tezcoco. Allies had 200,000 (Bancroft, *Native Races,* V: 372-379).
- 1428. Mexico, Tezcoco and allies against Tepanecs. In initial operations allies had about 100,000. Chalco and vicinity added another 20,000 (Veytia, III: 93-106). In final campaign allies had 300,000, including 100,000 from Tezcoco and 70,000 from Mexico and Tlatelulco. Tepanecs had 300,000 (Veytia, III: 127). In view of the desperate nature of this conflict, these figures may not be extremely exaggerated. Ixtlilxochitl (*Relaciones historicas,* p. 382, p. 407) cites substantially the same numbers.
- 1430. Mexico and allies against various towns. Allies had 100,000, including 10,000 from Tlaxcala and Hueyozingo (Veytia, III: 157).
- 1458. Mexico against Coixtlahuaca, second campaign. Mexico raised an army of 20,000 (Duran, p. 201).
- 1476. Mexico against Tarascans. Mexican army 32,200, Tarascan 50,000 (Tezozomoc, p. 421), Mexican 24,000, Tarascan 40,000 (Duran, p. 288).
- 1494. Mexico against tribes of Tehuantepec. Aztecs started with an army of 200,000 and were joined by 100,000 allies (Duran, p. 397, p. 400). So many were in the army that not a man could be seen on the streets of the towns in the valley of Mexico (Duran, p. 370).
- 1503. Mexico against Icpatepec and Nopallan. This was a war purely to capture sacrificial victims. Mexican army 60,000 (Duran, p. 423).

1506. Mexico against Hueyozingo. 100,000 combatants on both sides (Duran, p. 451).

1506. Mexico against tribes of the Mixteca. Army of 200,000 (Duran, p. 455).

1515. Mexico against Quetzaltepec and Tototepec. Montezuma set out with all the troops at his command: 400,000 men and boys (Duran, p. 446).

Although some of these figures are excessive, others bear the stamp of quite reasonable accuracy. On the whole, the repetition of values ranging from 100,000 to 200,000, on the part of all contemporary writers, some of whom had known participants in these campaigns, must indicate that the Nahua armies were of the order of magnitude designated. Otherwise we must ascribe to these writers not only an incredible mendacity but also an incredible ignorance.

In the absence of any compelling argument to the contrary we may accept as fact that the Nahua confederacy was accustomed to operate with armies 100,000 strong and if a real emergency arose might levy as many as 300,000 men.

For ordinary wars the mobile field army of approximately 100,000 men could be called into action. This consisted no doubt of the best fighting strength available—all the young men from 18 to 30 years of age plus a certain number of older men from the officer, or noble, class. This age and sex group usually included about ten per cent of the total population. The core of Aztec military power lay in the capital, Tezcoco, the valley of Mexico and adjacent portions of the modern states of Mexico, Hidalgo, Puebla, Guerrero and Morelos. Hence in the latter half of the fifteenth century this central region may have had a population of one million. Another million should be added to account for partially conquered tribes and hostile nations such as the Tlaxcaltecs, Tarascans, Huastecs, Totonacs, Mixtecs, Zapotecs and numerous minor linguistic or ethnic groups, thus indicating a total population for all Central Mexico of at least two million, probably more.

The losses incurred by the Central Mexican peoples during the final century before the Spanish Conquest obviously cannot be determined with rigid and formal precision. On the other hand, there is enough available data to furnish a basis for a rational estimate. Most of the principal campaigns from 1415 to 1519 have been recorded although the memory of numerous minor wars, raids and skirmishes must have been lost. For some of the more important battles, actual numerical statements have been given with respect to casualties; for many others an indication of the severity is apparent from the expressions "many killed," "great slaughter," and the like. A literal acceptance of such figures and statements would be unwarranted and much allowance has to be made for the universal tendency toward overstatement for the sake of emphasis. Nevertheless they frequently provide a basis for a fair guess or estimate.

Another point of difficulty is the confusion as to time and place which characterizes the contemporary or later accounts of these operations. In almost every individual instance sources differ with respect to the exact year and exact locale. To attempt a really thorough examination of all details would be a tedious and perhaps impossible task. Therefore in the compilation of campaigns about to be given, there are undoubtedly repetitions, omissions and flat falsities. Despite these acknowledged shortcomings, however, the list is probably reasonably complete and sufficiently accurate to yield a satisfactory over-all survey. The dates are according to the older authorities where available; otherwise I have followed the chronology of Bancroft. The numerical estimates are based where possible on quantitative statements by the Aztec and Spanish historians. The latter are primarily Tezozomoc, Ixtlilxochitl, Duran, Torquemada and Veytia, and in a few cases the *Codex Ramirez* and *Codex Telleriano-Remensis*. Bancroft's account is also very useful although he also necessarily depends upon the sixteenth century authors. In estimating probable casualties, many contributing factors are considered, such as relative size of armies, intensity of battles, importance of the occasions as gauged by the political issues involved, and success of the resistance offered by the enemy. Finally the estimates include casualties on both sides. (See list in Appendix I).

The total estimated casualties incurred by both sides in the listed wars, raids, and campaigns, including those killed in battle, those who died of wounds and those who, as non-combatants were massacred by victorious troops, amount to 288,700 persons. The list given is, however, by no means complete. The tripartite alliance must have participated in dozens of minor and small-scale conflicts which were too insignificant to merit permanent record in tradition or in written script. Particularly must this have been true during the confused final fifty years of Aztec domination. To account for these as a whole it will therefore be legitimate to increase the estimate by twenty-five per cent, thereby raising it to 360,900. Moreover, during the period while the Aztecs and their allies were extending their power from Guerrero to Tehuantepec, the other peoples of Central Mexico were by no means at perfect peace with each other. The Nahua groups on the eastern plateau, such as the Tlaxcalans and Hueyozincas, were conducting perpetual if intermittent war with each other. Likewise the peripheral tribes such as the Zapotecs, Mixtecs, Tarascans, Totonacs, etc., were raiding and counterraiding. No one knows the full extent of these hostilities but in the aggregate they must have had an intensity at least one-half that characterizing the operations of the triple alliance. If so, the casualties would have amounted to 180,500. The grand total then would have been 541,400, or, in round numbers, 540,000.

At first glance this appears a very large number, perhaps excessive. But the losses were distributed fairly evenly over somewhat more than a century: 104 years from 1415 to 1519. The annual rate of loss, therefore, would have been about 5,200. The mean population throughout this century was probably between 1,500,000 and 2,500,000, say 2,000,000. The direct annual war losses in population, based on these calculations, were then 0.25 per cent. On the assumption that the basic death rate was 50 per thousand and that the population was 2,000,000, the death rate was increased 5 per cent by warfare.

War and human sacrifice together, according to historical evidence, may have accounted for twenty per cent of the mortality in Central Mexico, or, otherwise expressed, may well have increased the normal mortality by about twenty per cent. The final conclusion is consequently justified that these two factors were an important instrumentality in controlling population increase and maintaining a proper balance between the number of inhabitants and their maximum available economic resources.

SUMMARY

In Central Mexico, immediately prior to the Spanish Conquest, the population was reaching the maximum consistent with the means of subsistence. Simultaneously the intensity of warfare rose steadily and the institution of human sacrifice, which depended for victims largely upon war captives, underwent an almost pathological development. An analysis of contemporary documentary sources reveals that the mean annual number of battle casualties reached approximately 5,000 and the corresponding value for sacrificial victims 15,000 during the last half century of Aztec domination. Assuming a probable final population for the area of at least 2,000,000, and a normal death rate of 50 per thousand, the effect of warfare and sacrifice would have been very effective in checking an undue increase in numbers. The suggestion is advanced that these methods may have been developed as a group, or social, response to the need for population limitation.

CITATIONS

BANCROFT, H. H. 1876. The Native Races of the Pacific States of North America. Vol. V., Primitive History. *New York.*

BANDELIER, A. F. 1877. On the Art of War and the Mode of Warfare of the Ancient Mexicans. Harvard University, *Peabody Museum Reports,* II: 95-161.

CAMARGO, DOMINGO MUÑOZ. Historie de la Republique de Tlaxcallan. *In:* Nouvelles Annales de Voyages. 1843. Vol. XCVIII: 129-204, and Vol. XCIX: 129-197.

CODEX BOTURINI. Translation by Paul Radin, 1920. *Univ. Calif. Publ., Amer. Arch. Ethnol.,* Vol. XVII: 33.

CODEX MAGLIABECCHI. *In:* The Book of the Life of the Ancient Mexicans. By Zelia Nuttall. *Berkeley, Calif., 1903.*

CODEX MAURICIO DE LA ARENA. By Manuel Mazari, 1926. *Anales Mus. Nac. Mex.,* Ser. IV, Vol. IV: 273-278.

CODEX RAMIREZ. Translation by Paul Radin, 1920. *Univ. Calif. Publ., Amer. Arch. Ethnol.,* Vol. XVII: 67.

CODEZ TELLERIO-REMENSIS. Translation by Paul Radin, 1920.. *Univ. Calif. Publ., Amer. Arch. Ethnol.,* Vol. XVII: 45.

DIAZ DEL CASTILLO, BERNAL. The Discovery and Conquest of Mexico. Translation by A. P. Maudslay. Edit., E. D. Ross and E. Power. *New York, 1928.*

DURAN, DIEGO. Historia de las Indias de Nueva España y Islas de Tierra Firme. Edit., Jose F. Ramirez. *Mexico, 1867.*

GÓMARA, FRANCISCO LOPEZ DE. Historia de la Conquista de Mexico. Edit., J. R. Cabañas. *Mexico, 1943.*

IXTLILXOCHITL, FERNANDO DE ALVA. Historia Chichimeca and Relaciones Historicas. *Both in:* Kingsborough's Antiquities of Mexico, Vol. IX. *London, 1848.*

MENDIZABAL, M. O. 1933. Los Otomies no Fueron los Primeros Pobladores del Valle de Mexico. *Anales Mus. Nac. Mex.,* Ser. IV, Vol. VIII: 611-629.

MOTOLINIA (BENEVENTE), TORIBIO DE. Historia de los Indios de la Nueva Espana. Edit., D. S. Garcia. *Barcelona, 1914.*

OROZCO Y BERRA, M. Dedicacion del Templo Mayor de Mexico. *Anales Mus. Nac. Mex.,* Ser. I, Vol. 1: 60-74.

Oviedo y Valdes, Gonzalo Fernandez. Historia General de las Indias. Edition of Madrid, 1853.

Pomar, Juan Bautista. Relacion de Tezcoco, 1582. *In*: Nueva Coleccion de Documentos para la Historia de Mexico. By J. Garcia Icazbalceta. Vol. III. *Mexico,* 1891.

Preuss, K. T. and E. Mengin. 1938. Die Mexikanische Bilderhandschrift Historia Tolteca, Chichimeca. Baessler's Archiv: Beiträge zur Völkerkunde, Vol. XXI: 2-66.

Ritos Antiquos, Sacrificios é Idolotrias de los Indios de la Nueva Espana. Written by an anonymous Friar in 1541. *In:* Kingsborough's Antiquities of Mexico, Vol. IX. *London,* 1848.

Sahagun, Bernardino de. Historia General de las Cosas de Nueva Espana. Edition of Pedro Robrero. *Mexico,* 1938.

Tápia, Andres de. Relacion sobre la Conquista de Mexico. *In*: Coleccion de Documentos para la Historia de Mexico. By J. Garcia Icazbalceta. Vol. II. *Mexico,* 1866.

Tezozomoc, Hernando Alvarado. Cronica Mexicana. Edit., J. M. Vigil. *Mexico,* 1878.

Torquemada, Juan de. Monarquia Indiana. Edition of Madrid, 1723.

Veytia, Mariano. Historia Antigua de Mexico. Edit., C. F. Ortega. *Mexico,* 1836.

APPENDIX I

Campaigns and estimated battle casualties

1415–1420	War between the Tepanecs of Atzcapotzalco plus the Aztecs against Tezcoco. Five campaigns............	34 000
1425–1428	War between the allies (Mexico and Tezcoco) and the Tepanecs. Resulted in the formation of the triple alliance	22 000
1430	Allies against Huexotla, Coatlichan and eight other towns	4 000
1432	Aztecs against Coyuhuacan and two other towns......	1 000
1434	Aztecs against Quautitlan and Tultitlan.............	1 000
1434	Aztecs against Xochimilco and Cuitlahuac...........	1 100
1435	Aztecs against Quanhuahuac.......................	1 000
1443	Aztecs against Chalco.............................	2 000
1443	Revolt of Tlatelulco...............................	500
1443	Revolt of Tulancingo..............................	500
1448	Allies against Cohuixco and Mazatlan...............	500
1457–8	Allies against the Mixteca, two invasions............	20 000
1458–9	Aztecs against Cozamoloapan and Quauhtochco......	2 000
1457–9	Allies against the Totonacs........................	3 000
1459	Aztecs against Chalco.............................	5 000
1460	Allies against the Huasteca........................	3 000
1460	Allies against Tepeaca, Quautinchan, Acatzingo......	2 000
1467	Tezcoco against Zumpango.........................	500
1468	Aztecs against Hueyozingo and Atlixco..............	1 000
1469	Allies against Tehuantepec.........................	5 000
1472	Aztecs against Xuchitepec..........................	500
1473	Revolt of Tlatelulco...............................	1 500
1474	Allies against Matlazincas..........................	3 000
1476	Allies against Tarascans............................	25 000
1476	Aztecs against Tliliuquitepec.......................	300
1480	Aztecs against Meztitlan...........................	500
1481	Allies against Cuextlan............................	2 000
1483	Aztecs against Tlaxotepec..........................	300
1483	Tezcoco against Hueyozingo.......................	2 000
1486	Allies against various peoples, including Xiquipilco, the Tzuicoacas and Tocpenecas of Jalisco, the Zapotecs, Nauhtlan and Tlacopan............................	2 000
1488	Aztecs against Chinantla and Cinacantlan...........	1 000
1489	Tlacopan against Cuextlan.........................	500
1489	Allies against four towns on southern coast..........	1 000
1490	Aztecs against Quautla (Cuextlan)..................	500
1490	Allies against Hueyozingo.........................	500

1491	Allies against Huastecs and Totonecs................	2 000
1491	Cholula against Tepeaca.........................	1 000
1491	Aztecs against Oztoman and other towns in Guerrero	10 000
1495	Allies against Mazatecs and Zapotecs (Tehuantepec)	40 000
1498	Aztecs against Atlixco...........................	500
1500	Allies against towns of Cuextlan and the Huesteca....	1 000
1503	Aztecs against Nopallan, Icpatepec and three others...	2 000
1503	Mexico, Hueyozingo and Cholula against Tlaxcala....	10 000
1506	Allies against the Mixteca. Destroyed Yanhuitlan, Tlaxiaco, Zozolan..................................	20 000
1506	Aztecs against Iztitlan............................	1 000
1506	Aztecs against Atlixco and Hueyozingo..............	1 000
1506	Aztecs against Tetutepec and Quetzaltepec...........	1 000
1507	Aztecs against Hueyozingo or Cholula..............	10 000
1509	Aztecs against Amatlan...........................	500
1511	Tezcoco against Tlaxcala.........................	2 000
1512	Aztecs against Tlaxiaco...........................	2 000
1512	Aztecs against Xuchitepec and Icpatepec.............	1 000
1512	Aztecs against Malinaltepec and Izquixchitlan........	1 000
1512	Aztecs against Hueyozingo and Atlixco..............	500
1513	Aztecs against Yopizincas.........................	500
1512–1515	Numerous raids and campaigns. Indistinguishable in detail. Places vary according to account. Places mentioned: Quetzalapan, Quimichintepec, Nopala, Tututepec (Northeast of Mexico), Tutupepec (on the south coast), Itztlaquetaloca, Mictlanzingo, Xaltianquizco, Icpaltepec, Quetzaltepec, Cihuapohualoyan, Cuexcomaxtlahuacan..	25 000
1517	Mexico against northern Culhuas...................	1 000
1517	Aztecs against Tarascans.........................	2 000
1517–1519	Allies against Tlaxcala............................	5 000
1517–1519	Allies against numerous revolting provinces. Matztitecas and Zapotecs mentioned......................	2 000

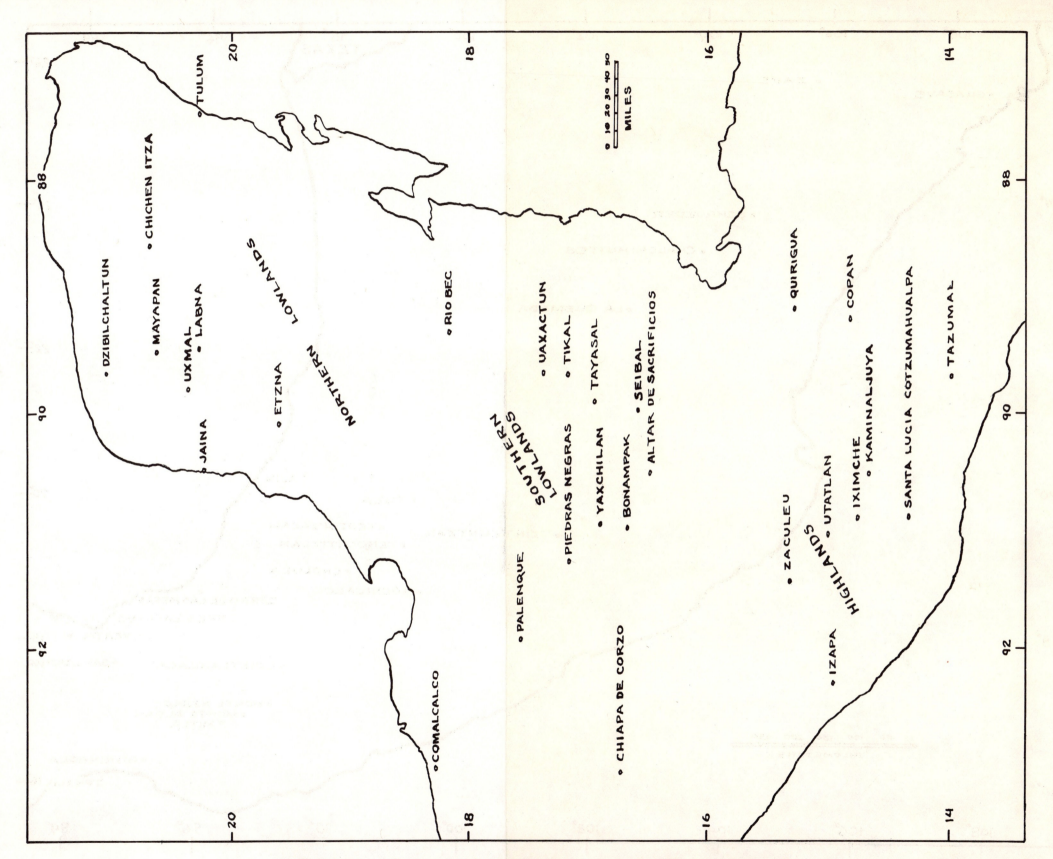

The Maya Country. The three-fold division into Northern Lowlands, Southern Lowlands, and Highlands corresponds respectively to Northern, Central, and Southern areas of some authors.

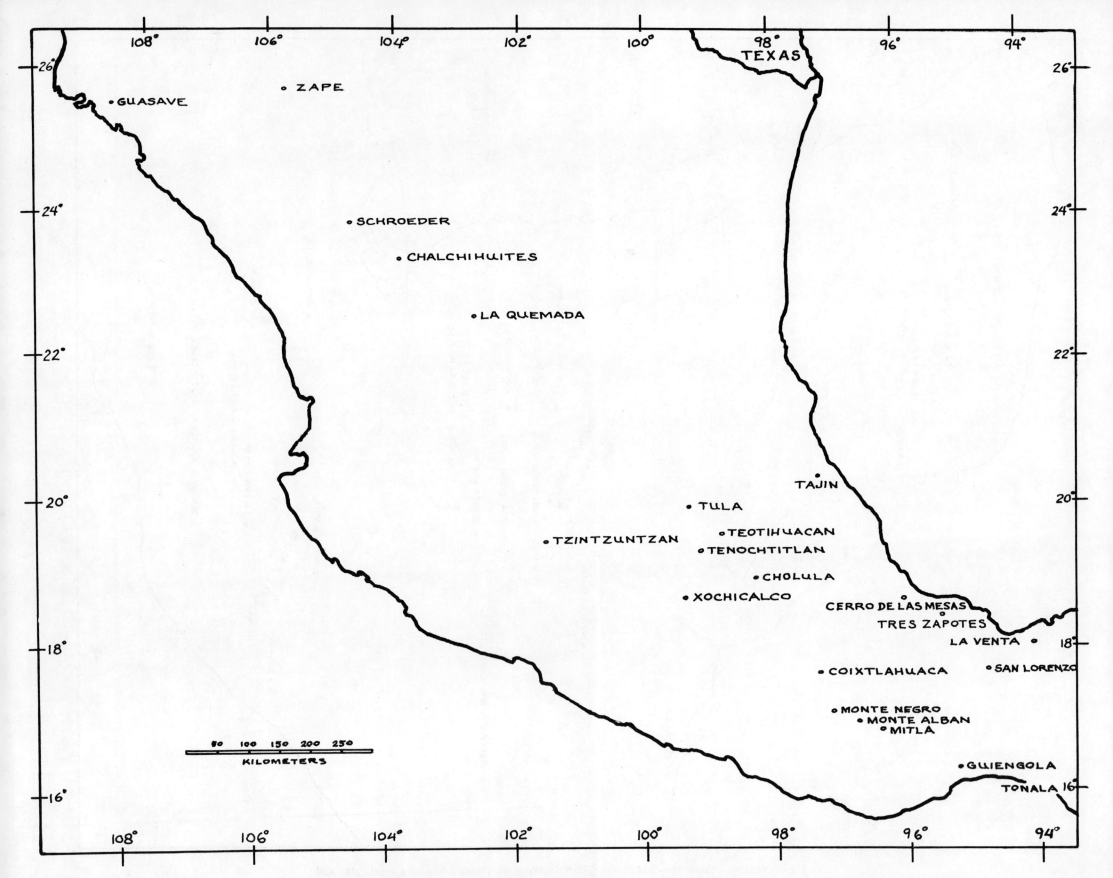

Important archaeological stations of Mesoamerica beyond the Maya country.